The Future of the State

Future Perfect: Images of the Time to Come in Philosophy, Politics and Cultural Studies

Series Editors: Michael Marder, IKERBASQUE Research Professor of Philosophy, University of the Basque Country, Spain

Patricia Vieira, Associate Professor, Spanish and Portuguese, Georgetown University, USA

The *Future Perfect* series stands at the intersection of critical historiography, philosophy, political science, heterodox economic theory, and environmental thought, as well as utopian and cultural studies. It encourages an interdisciplinary reassessment of the idea of futurity that not only holds a promising interpretative potential but may also serve as an effective tool for practical interventions in the fields of human activity that affect entire countries, regions, and the planet as a whole.

Titles in the Series

The Future of Europe: Democracy, Legitimacy and Justice after the Euro Crisis
Edited by Serge Champeau, Carlos Closa, Daniel Innerarity and Miguel Poiares Maduro

Taming an Uncertain Future: Temporality, Sovereignty, and the Politics of Anticipatory Governance
Liam P. D. Stockdale

The Politics of Virtue: Post-Liberalism and the Human Future
John Milbank and Adrian Pabst

The Future of Meat without Animals
Edited by Brianne Donaldson and Christopher Carter

The End of the World: Contemporary Philosophy and Art
Edited by Marcia Sa Cavalcante Schuback and Susanna Lindberg

Manifestos for World Thought
Edited by Lucian Stone and Jason Bahbak Mohaghegh

The Task of Philosophy in the Anthropocene: Axial Echoes in Global Space
Edited by Richard Polt and Jon Wittrock

Futures of Life Death on Earth: Derrida's General Ecology
Philippe Lynes

The Future of Humanity: Revisioning the Human in the Posthuman Age
Edited by Laurie Kruk, Pavlina Radia and Sarah Fiona Winters

The Future of the State: Philosophy and Politics
Edited by Artemy Magun

The Future of the State

Philosophy and Politics

Edited by Artemy Magun

ROWMAN & LITTLEFIELD
Lanham • Boulder • New York • London

Published by Rowman & Littlefield
An imprint of The Rowman & Littlefield Publishing Group, Inc.
4501 Forbes Boulevard, Suite 200, Lanham, Maryland 20706
www.rowman.com

6 Tinworth Street, London SE11 5AL, United Kingdom

Selection and editorial matter © Artemy Magun, 2020

Copyright in individual chapters is held by the respective chapter authors.

All rights reserved. No part of this book may be reproduced in any form or by any electronic or mechanical means, including information storage and retrieval systems, without written permission from the publisher, except by a reviewer who may quote passages in a review.

British Library Cataloguing in Publication Information Available

ISBN: HB 978-1-78661-483-4

Library of Congress Cataloging-in-Publication Data Is Available

ISBN 978-1-78661-483-4 (cloth)
ISBN 978-1-5381-4980-5 (pbk)
ISBN 978-1-78661-484-1 (electronic)

Contents

Acknowledgments ix

Introduction 1

I. THE IDEA OF STATE 23

1. The Categories of the State 25
   Michael Marder

2. The State in the International Legal Order 39
   Alexander Filippov

3. Sovereign State and Democracy in French Constitutional Theory 65
   Olga Bashkina

II. CRITIQUE OF THE STATE AND THE STATE OF THE CRITIQUE 87

4. State Power and Social Transformation 89
   Panagiotis Sotiris

5. Lindsey's "Concealed State" and the Left Strategy 111
   Maria Kochkina

6. Toward a Critical "State Theory" for the Twenty-First Century 123
   Ajay Singh Chaudhary

III. SOCIALIST AND COMMUNIST STATE   **161**

7 Lenin and the Transitional-Revolutionary State   163
Lorenzo Chiesa

8 The March of God or the Žižekian Theory of the State   187
Agon Hamza

9 Democratic Corpses and Communist Specters: Between the Liberal Democratic and Post-Socialist State   205
Christian Sorace

IV. *EX PLURIBUS UNUM*   **233**

10 *Civitas Paradoxa* or a Dialectical Theory of State   235
Artemy Magun

Index   281

Biographies   285

Acknowledgments

The research for this book was generously supported by the grant of the Foundation for Support of Liberal Arts (Russia): "Living together. Questions of diversity and unity in contemporary Russia: historical legacy, modern state, and society." The grant was realized by the Center for Historical Research at the National Research University Higher School of Economics, St. Petersburg, in 2017–2018.

Support for the editorial process came in part from the European University at Saint-Petersburg (Chair in Democratic Theory).

The editor is grateful to the European University at Saint-Petersburg for offering to him a sabbatical leave for the academic year of 2017–2018, and to Bard College, for hosting him during this period, which provided time to work on this volume.

Lia Na'ama ten Brink greatly contributed by having proofread the manuscript.

Besides all the authors of the book, I would like to thank everyone who supported the project, materially, intellectually, or morally, throughout this period: The European University at Saint-Petersburg, Smolny Institute for Liberal Arts and Sciences at St-Petersburg State University, Bard College, The Higher School of Economics (St-Petersburg campus); Jonathan Becker, Lia Na'ama ten Brink, Adel Chereshnya, Carine Clément, Jodi Dean, Mladen Dolar, Andreas Kalyvas, Aleksei Kudrin, Ilya Matveyev, Alexander Pogrebnyak, Danila Raskov, and Alexander Semyonov. I would also like to thank, collectively, the Radical Critical Theory Circle (Nisyros, Greece) where I and other authors delivered and discussed the first drafts of our chapters, and the students of the European University at Saint-Petersburg who followed the developments of this thought during the study seminars. And, of course, special thanks go to the editors at Rowman & Littlefield.

Introduction

1. STATE OF THE STATE

This book takes seriously, philosophically, the concept of the State. It is a collection of chapters by relatively young and mostly left-leaning scholars from across Europe, all of whom seek, in very different, individual ways, to renew the currently accepted neo-Weberian understanding of the state and to explore ways in which it could be transformed in the near future, both practically and intellectually. This means thinking beyond an instrumental or functionalist reduction of the state, against its narrow conception as a late Modern machine of governance, and eschewing an anarchist dismissal of the state as such. There is a relative (4 out of 10) overrepresentation of Russian authors in the volume; this has to do with the specific conditions in which this research project emerged, as well as with a recognition of the need to familiarize readers with the unofficial side of Russian political reflection, in particular as regards the status of the state in contemporary Russia, leaving no illusions as to its high capacity to hold the civil society in check.

The 2020 coronavirus pandemic was in many ways a revealing event. One of its effects was the exposure of the tremendous potential power of state: both the state/governmental power as such and the reality of states qua national sovereigns. Even though states took more or less the same measures, they took them separately and closed mutual borders. While the degree to which the state measures were pertinent, they varied a lot; what was common was the legitimacy of the measures that went against the economic stability and growth and threatened the interests of almost all businesses in the world. In the Marxo-Weberian theory of which we speak later in the book, this would not be likely to happen, as the state would be, in the last instance, an institute subsumed by capitalism or, most generously put, a symbiotic element of state-capitalism. Still, facing an emergency, whose recognition was a sovereign decision of governments in a situation that was by no means univocal (not a war or an invasion of aliens), the state firmly stepped in with its exceptional powers, using the digital infrastructure which, in these circumstances, turned most importantly into a tremendous apparatus of control and propaganda. Thus, these events generally confirmed the expectations about the future of the state that dominate this book (which had been written before them). The state had just been a partly dormant puppeteer behind the apparently decentralizing processes of the neoliberal competition and digital DIY. This said, we do not share the most stereotypical alarmist reaction to the events as to a proof of an upcoming authoritarian despotism. As this book argues, the authoritarian despotism had all been potentially there, but in concealment, so that its exposure is perhaps a good thing. The pandemic proved the global character of threats and policies and thus created a powerful case in favor of a gradual global transformation into a world federative state (or perhaps a new type of polity beyond the state as some authors of the book would prefer to call it). Such new state, with all its governmental capacity and emergency powers, would not necessarily be an authoritarian monster of the kind that exists now in many countries beyond the United States and Europe: these monsters are to a large extent a product of a dialectical opposition with liberal democracies. It is conceivable to have a powerful state/government that would also be *democratic*, in a more comprehensive way than the current half-democracies of the West: this would not happen by itself, but it is important to conceive as an idea and as a desideratum, lacking which, a new order of authority will emerge out of the increasing clashes between humanity and nature by itself, spontaneously and irrationally.

In the philosophical sense, the State is above all the Subject, in the meaning that this notion acquired in post-Heideggerian theory. It is a collective unity that represents itself to itself, controls things qua objects of consideration, but its unity is intensely mediated through abstract symbolic rules and procedures. Taken thus, the State is not a tangible empirical object, so that it becomes all too easy to deny its existence, or to reduce it, if one wants, to a tangible "physical violence." There was a period, starting with the 1960s, that the notion of the subject went out of fashion, deemed too classical and authoritarian. The State, too, was considered (by Foucault and others) through this prism, seen as both repressive and, to an extent, irrelevant to describing more immediate forms of power.

The authors of this volume are for the most part unhappy with the nationalist, bureaucratic, and class-serving structures of power that the state apparatus represents, but they are not ready to give up the very notion of the state as a constitutional system of power, and as a modern, rational type of polity, for the future. The resistance to the state can come from both right and left, but in recent years it has consolidated itself rather as a slogan for the neoliberal right, which so often captures the hearts and minds under its catchier name, the "libertarian." As Ajay Chaudhary argues in his chapter, the project of abandoning or weakening the state historically can even play into the hands of the extreme right. Christian Sorace shows how the weakening of state undermines the legitimacy of Westernizing democracy. The state is first denigrated and reduced to a functional meaning, and then weakened, so as to reinforce nonpublic and nondemocratic structures of power. The Left has insisted, throughout this period, on the importance of the welfare state. But the problem is that there is no strong political theory of the welfare state as a structure of power: it is understood that a top-down distribution must rely on an alienated bureaucracy, and that the bureaucratic welfare system is something the Left defends out of vaguely conservative instincts, but without a particular inspiration. What we lack, and what we, in this volume, start to develop, is not just a critical and sober analysis of what is currently happening with the state but also a left-oriented normative theory, and program, for a State of the Future. This State of the Future is actually the hidden truth of the currently existing state, which tends to conceal itself with a characteristic coquetry. But the fact that the form of just and democratically oriented state is projected into the future should not be seen as a deferral to the future. On the contrary, the creation of new political models is on the urgent agenda, as old institutions cease to be credible, rational, or functional.

2. MARXO-WEBERIAN THEORY AND ITS CHALLENGES

The notion of the state is the most widely used political notion. As such, it means simply the same as "polity" or "nation" and refers to the system of sovereign authority inside this polity, which is impersonal, and which towers above "society," which it oversees: protects, taxes, and supports from its public funds. However, this colloquial usage is wide, equivocal, and therefore distinct from the scholarly usage. The current understanding of state in the English-language social sciences treats it, most commonly, in the sense of the institution, or set of institutions, which, inside a nation (or polity), maintains security ("the monopoly of violence"), the rule of law, welfare for the vulnerable, and assures macroeconomic stability. As such, state is not the same as polity or nation, and is normally opposed to *society* as a set of plural, spontaneous institutions that are not organized from above.

On this understanding, the state is not a perennial fact of human society but a historical phenomenon, which emerges in early modernity when the absolute kings centralize their countries and create a vertical, rational bureaucracy. Thus, traditionally, the state has been understood as sovereign:[1] legally having a final say on every issue, monopolistic of governance—or at least violence—within a given territory. However, the recent decades of globalization have been widely seen as a period of crisis of sovereignty, and thus also of statehood.[2] Too much power is felt to have been ceded to international institutions, as well as to nongovernmental organizations (NGOs) and multinational business corporations outside of the state's material reach and/or jurisdiction. Some have seen this extending to a crisis of state as such, whereas others, while acknowledging this loss of state power, have chosen to redefine the role of state and sovereignty in a new way; states have been deemed powerful, often dominant—but not omnipotent—actors, whose authority is not consistent across all domains (military affairs, economy, international relations, etc.).[3]

While we still observe functional state machines in most developed countries, we certainly witness a crisis in the *legitimacy* of the state. Limited both from without and from within, the state cannot be held fully responsible for the various problems that the electorate expects it to resolve. At the same time, the autonomization of state from society—its recasting as a bureaucratic unit of "experts"—undermines its democratic legitimacy by rendering its claim to representation unconvincing.

There was a period in Anglo-American political science when the state was considered a relatively trivial or derivative object of study.[4] Scholars, disappointed by idealistic legalism, tended to explain political decisions and acts by their social causes and the dispositions of their human actors. There was a wider ideological context to this, in which the excessive role of the state was ascribed to a "totalitarian" Soviet Union, whereas democracies like the United States were seen as pluralist arenas for competition among social groups. By the end of the Cold War, the situation changed, both theoretically and ideologically. Today, the state is once again "in,"[5] yet this is not the old "sovereign" legal state. Rather, it is a dominant institution among others, a social actor, which has its indispensable functions—security, macroeconomic management, welfare—as well as its self-serving "rational" interests. In both cases, much is decided by the state's capacity to pursue its goals.[6] Weak "state capacity" is pernicious for polities—authoritarian and democratic alike—and leads, at its limit, to the "failed state," where instead of pluralism, there emerges corruption, gangsterism, the privatization of state functions, and so forth. The strong state is indispensable to *democracy*, particularly in the period of postrevolutionary transition, at a juncture at which new institutions have to be established and recognized by political actors and their decisions enforced.[7] This new understanding of state still treats it as an outgrowth of society and tends to see it instrumentally, as a political technology meant to *efficiently* fulfill the goals defined by society and by the international community. In part, it describes the contemporary tendency toward the autonomization, instrumentalization, and delegitimization of the state; in part, it ideologically contributes to this very process. The state as described in the accounts of those advocating for the "consolidation of democracy" and "state capacity" is not the exhilarating leadership a populace would readily vote for.

There exists, no doubt, a standard constitutional understanding of the state as a liberal-democratic system, in which officials fulfill the will of the citizens whom they represent, and sovereignty is the statutory personhood under international law that belongs to the people as a specific nation. The tendency of bureaucracy toward autonomization must be corrected by the division of powers. The state towers over the economy and redistributes wealth in favor of the majority. The people occasionally shows itself as an independent constituent power. This was the understanding prevalent among nineteenth- and twentieth-century continental legal theorists.[8] However, it is an idealistic picture, which does not take into account the state as a specific organ in complex interaction with society and its internal struggles and is therefore not a popular one in social science literature on the state. While this book, particularly chapters 2 and 3 written by Alexander Filippov and Olga Bashkina, is generally sympathetic to the normative idealism in relation to the state (as this has been largely abandoned), it is far from subscribing to naïve wishful thinking. There is always a mixture of normative and descriptive logic. Why on earth should we expect and demand from the state a responsiveness to welfare demands, migrants, trade unions, and violent demonstrations, if it is led mostly by members of the upper classes, is set to defend stability and security, and is elected by a nationally circumscribed citizenry?

Theoretically, contemporary literature on the state mostly draws on Weber's classical definition of the state as a "human community that (successfully) claims the monopoly of the legitimate use of physical violence [or more exactly, of "being physically violent," *Gewaltsamkeit*] within a given territory,"[9] and on neo-Marxist theories of "relative autonomy,"[10] which emphasize the dependence of the state on the class-like social forces among which it maneuvers and between whose interests it can adjudicate. These theories modify (Weber) or abandon (Poulantzas) the nineteenth century's continental understanding of the state as a political unity of people in a certain territory that possesses a capacity of coercive power (*power-territory-population*).[11] In so doing, they seem to adopt a skeptical and realist worldview. However—and this is the thrust of this book—they thereby (1) risk losing the right to criticize existing states (they criticize the quality of democracy, which remains a normative concept, yet measured quantitatively, by degree), (2) abandon the normative horizon of the *future* of the state as a positive model for organizing political spaces, and (3) remain blind to the *internal* contradictions of the contemporary state and the need for their eventual resolution through its transformation.

Philosophically, Weber's definition of the state was born from a sociological redefinition of neo-Kantianism. Weber replaced the legal power of the German *Gewalt* (authority backed by force) with a "physical" understanding of power as violence that is implied in the word *Gewaltsamkeit*. Yet he preserved the neo-Kantian dualities between violence and legitimacy, violence and authority, ends and means, and the ethics of conviction and of responsibility. Like most neo-Kantians, he thus rejected Hegelian dialectics as a mode of studying the possible interaction between these poles. Moreover, the neo-Weberians, such as Schumpeter, Tilly, Skocpol, and others, interpret Weber in an even more positivist way than he himself had envisioned.

Nikos Poulantzas, Bob Jessop, and other neo-Marxists proceed from the positivist interpretation of Marx and, in spite of their borrowings from Gramsci and understanding of how the state occasionally acts "back" upon society (which remains prior), lack a dialectical analysis of contradiction or any interest in the state as a normative category. They adopt a critical perspective and identify the state with a special outgrowth of the bourgeois capitalist economy and of class struggle. The question is what exactly *would be done* with the state if one were to come to power, or at least to draft a constitution? Here, the neo-Marxist authors do not go beyond a standard liberal-democratic minimum or a utopian dream of dissolving the state as such. However, much can be envisioned politically on the basis of the democratic principle, even without the full annulment of private property or a universal moral conversion.

The twentieth century's continental philosophical schools, being for the most part anarchistically oriented, left little trace on the theory of the state (Foucault of the 1970s was an exception that proved the rule). The state is relegated to a boring bureaucratic subject, to be studied using boring bureaucratic methods. However, it appears that the need for a philosophy of state is particularly pronounced at the present moment as the current neoliberal system:

1. generates paradoxes (internal contradictions) that require a serious analysis and perhaps a redefinition of the concept of the state.
2. provokes far-ranging resistance, which puts the problem of the desirable state, the State of the Future, on the agenda.

Slavoj Žižek, one of the most famous contemporary political philosophers working in the "continental" tradition, has repeatedly pointed at the need to return to the serious analysis of state as idea and to reevaluate it from within the left-leaning philosophical project as an institution indispensable for any future "communist" society, but this thought never gets developed in his work, and is often accompanied by apologies and disclaimers. Žižek formulated it in his polemic against Alain Badiou, another influential continental philosopher, in whose work "state" became a technical term for a normalizing and a counterrevolutionary structure that would mechanically unite all substructures of the society into a general bureaucratical system. In the mathematical terms that Badiou uses, this "state" is define as a "set of all subsets" for a given set.

Žižek rightly contends that this definition of state depends on the narrow identification of state with what is contemporary institution known under this name. In his opus magnum from 2012, the Slovenian thinker writes:

> Badiou reacted to the "obscure disaster" of the fall of the socialist regimes—and, more generally, to the exhaustion of the revolutionary event of the twentieth century—by taking a step from history to ontology: it is important to note how it was only after this "obscure disaster" that Badiou started to play with the double meaning of the term "state" (état)—the "state of things" and State as the apparatus of social power. The danger of this move is that, by establishing a direct link, a short-circuit, as it were, between a particular historical form of social organization and a basic ontological feature of the universe, it (implicitly, at least) ontologizes or eternalizes the state as a form of political organization: (the political) state becomes something we should resist, subtract ourselves from, act at a distance from, but simultaneously something which can never be abolished (save in utopian dreams). Is not this step from history to ontology, from the State qua political apparatus to the state qua state of things, this short-circuit wherein State = state, an elementary ideological operation? This overblown notion of the State, which effectively tends to overlap with the state (of things) in the broadest sense, is effectively Badiou's symptom.[12]

Here Žižek still stops short of affirming state as a positive value:

> The state (apparatus) does not contaminate (or act as a parasite upon) the "apolitical" spheres of the economy, of private life, of sexuality, etc., rather it constitutes them as apolitical or pre-political—the ultimate task of state apparatuses is to de-politicize these spheres. . . . This is why, in a properly Marxist perspective, the ill-famed "withering away of the State" does not aim at a de-politicization of society, but (in its first step, at least) at its radical and thorough "politicization": one does not "abolish the state" by getting rid of its excess in a transparent-harmonious self-organization of society, but by "abolishing" the specter of apolitical spheres, by demonstrating how "there is nothing which is not political," up to and including people's most intimate dreams.[13]

However, in the 2008 book *In Defense of Lost Causes* Žižek briefly but affirmatively references Chavez's project of "ruthlessly using the state apparatuses."[14] In several recent public talks,[15] Žižek notes (after apologizing for his words) that after a potential communist revolution, pace Engels and Lenin, the state would not need to "wither away" at all but rather has to be captured, "transformed," and controlled by the masses and by the left-wing movements or parties, so that the very division state/society disappears: but not the state itself.

In 2017, a group of Žižek scholars published a volume *Party, State, Revolution*, entirely dedicated to Žižek's political philosophy.[16] Eric Vogt, Geoff Pfeifer, and Agon Hamza attempt to reconstruct a "Žižekian theory of state" out of the sparse comments made by the great Lacanian philosopher on this topic. In the end, however, all three conclude that Žižek's political philosophy, which affirms the state, develops arguments only on the Party, which is needed to lead the state forward, and which is the only institution of "indifference" toward identitarian particularities. "Žižek claims [that] 'the true task should be to make the State itself work in a non-statal mode'. . . . The party's task is to take over the state and state power, and transform it in such a way that the party does not simply remain a party—but effectively becomes the state."[17] We learn nothing, from Žižek or from these secondary readings, of the state itself—no theoretical response to its historical grandeur and mortifying abstraction, no project of how to reorganize it institutionally in the future, and no notion of whether and how to keep it democratic. The Hegelian statism of Žižek goes against his anti-statist Leninism, and this produces both a deadlock and an invocation to square the circle. But he rightly formulates the problem.

Neither Badiou nor Žižek mentions Weber or Poulantzas in this political debate, but Žižek, I think, intuitively goes to the heart of the matter as he contests the very usage of state by Badiou in the sense of the Modern "Weberian" state as an authoritarian meta-institution. In the German and Russian traditions, as well as in the everyday parlance of other European languages, "state" is rather used as a synonym of polity as such. If we restrict ourselves to the more academic and exact, technical meaning of state (as Weber, Poulantzas, Foucault, and Badiou certainly do), then the question is, what happens to the state-qua-polity: its semantic place remains vacant, so to say. This place, in the anti-statist, or anarchist, imagination, is surreptitiously occupied by *society*, which is no more than a complementary notion to "state" in the narrow sense of the word.

All this said, Žižek is too fast in agreeing with Badiou in his plea to reject and overturn the Modern state form itself. The very dual structure "a historically specific political form/the universal political form as such" is embodied in the Modern idea of state, as it emerged, first, in the process of distancing and neutralizing the direct royal and feudal authority and, second, in the process of its democratic contestation. Thus, the Modern state *is* the attempt to rule on behalf of the "universal," which inevitably fails on its promise and has to admit and incorporate many forms of particularistic authority (such as economic power, parental power) by ousting them into the field of "society."

As with any idealist institutions, there are symptoms where the original violence and "natural" submission survive and sustain the abstract framework (the duality that Weber's definition, with its "being physically violent," unconsciously alludes to). But to claim that Modern state, in this duality, is particularistic in itself and has to be distinguished from its own universal—as does Žižek—is to make an ironic turn of the screw which he does not notice.

In the theory of Jacques Lacan, the state-like type of authority is well captured by the notion of "paternal metaphor" as a substitution for the absolute maternal power over a child. Žižek often refers to this construction of Lacan[18] (for instance, Žižek 2012: 775), but never in relation to state or to politics in general. The father, says Lacan (implicitly arguing against Freud, with his myth of "primordial father"), draws his authority in the patriarchal family only secondarily, by derivation, because from the viewpoint of a child, his "symbolic" power comes to limit and replace the apparently absolute power of the mother. Similarly, the state authority, which today often appears to us as a dictatorial monster, is a predominantly symbolic power. Historically, it is the result of a delimiting process with regard to all sorts of "natural" and "material" power. Knowing this does not mean fully legitimizing the state or the father's authority, since in both cases there is a potential for excessive "physical violence," as a compensatory and symptomal excess of the symbolic authority in its fight against the remnants of direct authority. However, the desirable state of affairs would need to overcome the mirage of paternalist and repressive state from within the state itself, through its own logic.

Historically, when "state" takes the position of *the* word for polity, it is already a *negative* modification which testifies to a permanent crisis of political order. Through the notion, this order acquires an abstract, impersonal register associated with the suspicion of direct personal rule, and it soon merges with the idea of liberal democracy. Therefore, typically for the great political concepts, Modernity introduces negativity into the core of polity and state and provides a bad choice between the instrumentalization of state as an already negated, discredited form of power, in liberalism, and the utopia of grassroots, local self-rule, and moral self-control, in anarchism and early Bolshevism. Instead, following Hegel, it makes sense to return to the original, affirmative notion of state as a vertical apparatus of power by reintroducing the democratic negativity and even anarchy back into the framework of state and orchestrating their coexistence.

3. HISTORY OF THE QUESTION

Let us summarize what has historically happened to the state, and why it merits *attention*. The state was instituted and conceptualized in early modernity, mostly for the needs of the emerging absolute monarchs, who needed an impersonal legitimacy—a rational, centralized apparatus—to determine the territory and national identities of their populations. The core of the state's functions used to be *negative*: security and the protection of private property against crime.[19]

Since the nineteenth century, this system has undergone revolutionary changes: states gradually became constitutional republics, so that power became even more impersonal than it used to be, and rulers ceased being called sovereign, even though the state overall still was. Also from the nineteenth century onward, the state, as a system of public recognition, solidarity, and equality, was increasingly contrasted with "civil society" and the "private sphere," with their fragmentations, equalities, and struggles. Since the beginning of its existence—but particularly from the late nineteenth century—the state takes as its charge the protection of the poor and, broadly speaking, the issue of equitable distribution. The security state becomes the *welfare state* and *social state*.[20] Large corporate actors enjoyed special relations with the state as long as they were also responsible for equitable distribution and the public good. Thus, the late modern state is not a pure state: it is rather what I would call *the national-democratic corporatist welfare state*.

Of course, the modern state is unthinkable without *capitalism*. From the start, it protected private property and supported enclosures. The abstract and formal nature of governance was common both to the state and to the new model of economic enterprise.[21] However, it is impossible to equate the state as a body politic with capitalism or even to derive the former from the latter, at least before the "great transformation" of the nineteenth century, as described by Polanyi.[22] Giovanni Arrighi even points to a dialectical alternation between periods of dominance of the sovereignty principle and of the international, decentralized power of financial capital.[23]

We will not understand the current state, with its problems, if we do not take into account the relation between the concept and the phenomenon, as well as national/cultural differences in its formation. The term "state" emerged in Italy and France in the sixteenth century and slowly gained importance as one of the notions describing a centralized bureaucratic polity, in its impersonal, abstract aspect. The "reason of state" was originally the main context in which it was used. However, it was not until the nineteenth century that this word became central for political theory. Most classical authors—Bodin, Hobbes, Spinoza, Locke, Leibniz, Montesquieu, Bossuet—used it rarely, if ever. The main notion for the polity remained the "republic," or "*civitas*." Hobbes and Rousseau only specify the state as the passive aspect of sovereignty: what a sovereign disposes of and what it commands. It is only in the work of Emmerich Vattel, in mid-eighteenth century, that "state" emerges as the term for sovereign polity. This is not to say that the concept had not been developed before—a concept is not the same thing as a term—but it is only from Vattel that we can count its full-fledged hegemony.

After Vattel, it was the Germans (Fichte, Hegel, Humboldt) who gave the word "*Staat*" the broad universal signification of a polity existing under an authority, even though many German authors (Marx, Carl Schmitt) did insist on its historical limitations. German theory and the practice of bureaucracy (what they called "cameralism" and "police") found its new name in "state science," where it obtained stronger overtones of sovereignty and nation. The French used "*état*," but "*nation*" was synonymous and used at least as frequently. English and American theories of state mostly proceeded from those of the Germans. In the nineteenth and early twentieth centuries it was Anglo-American Hegelianism, and at the end of the twentieth century, Anglo-American Marxism and Weberianism, which, as I mentioned, brought the state back "in." Apart from this, British and American authors tended to focus on society and law more than on the sovereign state.

It does not follow from this that the state would have to be understood as a culturally limited phenomenon. We can still use this word universally. However, we cannot univocally speak of a "liberal" or "modern" theory of state, because there never was one: before the neoliberalism and *ordoliberalism* of the twentieth century, liberal authors rarely focused on the state as such. In the German Hegelian and neo-Kantian tradition, "state" was associated not only with the administrative apparatus but also with the philosophical meaning of living in a polity under the rule of law, taken in an idealist form. Britain and the United States did develop the administrative state roughly on the model of continental Europe, even though they did it late. However, its legitimacy was most often understood in a "materialist" way, as a representative and/or federalist "democracy" and as a result of complex social processes ("pluralism").[24] Therefore, the state itself, where relevant, was largely treated in the technical or critical sense, but no neutral word emerged to replace it. The current crisis of state is also a crisis, at least in English, of the *concept* of the state. This book will be trying to square the root of the *democratic* and the *social* state and to revive a philosophical theory of what the modern polity is about.

The state is not just a monopolistic hold on violence, nor an embodied popular will, but it is the very cleavage, or juncture, between the administrative apparatus and the national sovereignty, between a head of state, or nation, and his or her impersonal staff and, inversely, between the specific official taxing you and the abstract impersonal unity on whose behalf he or she acts. In philosophical terms, the word "status" used separately from whose status it is, oscillates between meaning an abstract quality, condition, office, or role (as predicate), and the subject, which this condition eventually becomes. But if this is so, then we do not need to wait until the terminology of state settles, but can project the concept, with its complex dual structure, back onto the past, in search of precedents and solutions.

For the same reasons, we cannot and should not restrict ourselves to liberal theory in the sense of the U.S. university canon. There is no historical data to support the fact that the state was a particularly liberal notion, at least before the German neo-Kantians took care of it. The non-liberal theories of *civitas* that follow in the footsteps of Plato and Aristotle are as well qualified to be applied to today's state as are the contractual theories of Hobbes or Kant.

As mentioned, the late nineteenth century witnessed a certain idealization of the state, particularly in Germany; in Hegel's footsteps but also in the context of welfare expansion and of imperialist colonization. In Germany, Russia, and a number of other countries, the "state" becomes a synonym for any polity (German and Russian translations of Plato and Aristotle use state for *politeia*). This enthusiasm continues into twentieth-century ideas of the "total state," in authors such as Giovanni Gentile and Carl Schmitt. Before the horrors of fascism became defined (by liberals) as "totalitarianism," the idea of the total state had meant that, in the democratic age, it reabsorbed and politicized society, so that state's distinction with society lost its meaning. This model was violently rejected after World War II, but the issue persisted: how can a democratically controlled, nation-based, and extremely resourceful rational state remain artificially limited and preserve the "empty space" of sovereignty?[25]

It is not a secret that the past thirty years were, globally, a time of so-called neoliberal revolution, a movement meant to weaken the preexisting welfare state through deregulation and shift the weight of management and decision-making from top-down (but democratically accountable) policy decisions to decentralized markets and monetary means through privatization. The ideologists of this reform (Hayek, Nozick, and others) were very explicit in their distrust of the state and their will to minimize its functions by reducing them to police oversight. A somewhat different take on the same general tendency was that of German "ordoliberalism," which did not completely abandon the German state-centered culture and combined an insistence on the autonomy of the market with a strong role for the state in the economy.

Parallel to neoliberalization, we witnessed ongoing globalization and regional transnational integration (such as the European Union), which contributed to a shift of power away from the nation-state to unelected business and "expert" structures. The same process contributed to the escalation of migration and the respective erosion of the classical idea of the "people" as nation.

However, the recent period also saw a proliferation of new ethnically defined *nation*-states (fifteen former Soviet republics, five former Yugoslav republics, several states in Africa, such as Eritrea and South Sudan), particularly in the 1980–1990s, and of strong nationalist parties in most developed countries in the 2000–2010s.

Finally, the same period was also characteristic for its explosion of unofficial, non-state, and non-business political actors, such as new social movements, NGOs, and *ad hoc* mass protests organized through social media. The neoliberal revolution did not quash the democratic public but coincided with its upsurge; the public largely protested against various neoliberal budget cuts, but neoliberal governments usually did not mind the new social movements as such; for they were social, not governmental, actors, driven by spontaneous forces within society—the only nuisance being their frequent appeals to the government for more regulation.

Importantly, neoliberal reform was rarely implemented literally. In Western countries, the existing provisions of welfare were largely upheld, albeit with some cuts, adjustments, and the like. The changes were more radical in the newly "democratized" (and neoliberalized) countries—Chile, Russia, the Baltic states, Argentina, and the like. But even there, various chunks of the welfare state remained (partially free education and medicine in Russia, sizeable pensions in the Baltic states, etc.). Yet there was a push, also here, to privatize and monetize public services to the maximum.

The resulting form is *the global national-democratic welfare deregulationist state*. The oxymoron is willed: the neoliberal state remains a state, and a late modern state at that—it does not dismantle the preexisting apparatus of power but builds upon and unbuilds it; it globalizes, all the while preserving its national and nationalist legitimacy, which is the inverse side of electoral democracy.

The irony is that neoliberalism, developed under the banner of fighting excessive state presence, of chasing out "totalitarianism," did not directly lead to the reduction or weakening of the state apparatus. Already David Harvey, in his early and classic book on neoliberalism, notes this paradox; neoliberalism does not mean less state; it restructures the state in favor of unelected institutions such as "expert" units, watchdogs, and courts.[26] He speaks of "the paradox of intense state interventions and government by elites and 'experts' in a world where the state is supposed not to be interventionist."[27] The neoliberal state becomes undemocratic. The very "reduction" of state to police power, as desired by neoliberals, may lead to the expansion of the police-military component within the state, which we observe indeed in general securitization,[28] in the growth of control[29] and surveillance.[30]

The task of fighting against the abuses of state power (corruption, red tape, etc.) requires the creation of additional agencies and units. Moreover, even where state functions may at times be transferred to private or societal actors, this leads to a bureaucratization of society itself. As Beatrice Hibou notes in her seminal research on the neoliberal state, "we are all neoliberal bureaucrats,"[31] which essentially means that in content, if not in form, the neoliberal reduction of the state makes everyone a state servant or (rather) a mini-state.

We see a series of paradoxes that should be resolved dialectically. The crisis of state and the negation of the state to the economic benefit of society results in the universalization of the state in a new form. This is either what Hegel used to call an *Aufhebung*, a sublation, or what Hegel and Marx describe as a passage of quality into quantity: whatever you do to the state results in more state. The emergence of a dialectical logic further testifies to the mechanism of *reflection*: whatever we do to the state and society, it is the state (again) that does this.

Normatively, the contemporary state is supposed to be democratic, which means either that in a long perspective it must perish (this is the position of early Marx and of Lenin—the democratic state is a non-state or a semi-state), or that it has to efficiently represent society and remain under its control. Many post-Marxist theories tend toward anarchism because they address the politics of movements and "subjects" rather than the state, which figure only as an arena—such are the theories of conflict and disagreement in Rancière, Mouffe, Badiou, Butler, among others. As for more conventional theories of democracy, the problem is that in the present context, they fail to address the sociopolitical reality of democracy. Is contemporary democracy (the properly democratic element of liberal democracy) only the rule by the majority through its representatives, with provisions for freedom of speech? Or is it a polity of dissensus where the power of establishment is powerfully *contested*, through emerging political movements, through contentious politics, through the potential of revolutionary upheavals (which are a major catalyst, outside of the West, for the so-called third wave of democratization and its aftermath)? The electoral authoritarian regimes claim that they are democratic because they enjoy popular support and hold relatively honest elections. However, it is the absence of a *real* opposition, which would weaken the consensus of the elite and arguably damage the unity of state policy, that sets authoritarian regimes apart from democracies. Thus, the democratic state is a state that exposes its policy and unity to substantial danger, and this goes beyond what is normally written into liberal democratic constitutions. And indeed, Western polities do allow and promote the values of subversive political participation; they are, to an extent, constituent of forces that use informal means of public politics, such as demonstrations and strikes. Whenever these forces come to power outside of the West, they tend to produce a crisis of statehood and not simply a shift of government, and this is also why they get violently suppressed in the non-Western "authoritarian" countries.

The activity of social movements is in many cases a reaction to neoliberal measures, seen as a class war of the managers against the employees.

This is typical of France with its mass demonstrations, even riots, against changes in legislation—witness the response to the "law of the first contract" or the length of the labor-day—or of Spain, with its massive "Indignados" movement. The defense of these welfare measures is denounced by neoliberal ideologues as "paternalist" and is, indeed, framed as an appeal to the state, the authority of which is thereby recognized by indignant protestors. In this sense, the social movements of the neoliberal era, unlike those of 1968, make the ambiguous gesture of expressing mistrust of an "expert"-driven government while at the same time legitimizing it by their very protests, as the potential donor of welfare. As some 1968 revolutionaries would say, "We fought for free love, and these new movements fight for pensions!" It is in this sense that today's radical left does not have any theory of state worthy of its name, apart from the standard liberal plea for better representation. As Agon Hamza rightly observes, in his defense of Žižek's half-hearted return to the state, "The revolutionary left currently lacks a theory of power which is active and prepositive rather than reactive and merely critical. . . . The notion of the state as such remains highly under theorized, by both Žižek and his critics and followers. However, this is not exclusively a problem of Žižek's work as such. The entire Marxist tradition has largely neglected the theorization of the state."[32] It resorts either to a neo-Marxist reduction of the state to a complex instrument of social domination, an anarchist suspicion of its policing tendencies, or to a plea for equitable distribution by the bureaucrats who should, for some reason, display goodwill.

4. OVERVIEW OF THE CHAPTERS

The book starts on a high philosophical note, with a chapter by Michael Marder, a prolific and influential continental philosopher from Russia, Canada, and Spain, on the "categories of state." Marder approaches the state from an *a priori* Kantian/Aristotelian perspective, looking at the general conditions of possibility which the state sends back to and at the specific trajectories within these categories that the state traces. His take on the categories is not classically Kantian, but rather phenomenological, and dialectical. Marder shows how at the most seemingly abstract level of the categories—such as place, modality and relation, substance, quality and quantity—we discern contradictions and tensions that elucidate actual political problems. Thus, the standing of "state" in space implies not just the rigid and phallic *"stare"* but also the need to take *ad hoc* contextual positions: "politics" can thus be deduced from the "standing" of the state. The modal play of necessity and potentiality leads to revolutionary and critical currents within the state, which are, nonetheless, absorbed into it, as evinced through the category of substance—the carrier of contradictions, according to Aristotle. Finally, the idealistic teleology of the state's quality meets its inevitable quantitative extension, which corresponds, for Marder, with territorial domination and imperialism.

Alexander Filippov, a leading Russian political theorist, approaches the state from both a historical angle and a philosophical perspective of logical analysis. Filippov analyzes the phenomenon of international law, noting its irreducible "substantive" implications (the so-called civilized nations), which explain the neo-imperialist tendencies and moral discussions within contemporary international society. This would seem incompatible with the sovereign state as a "spatial container." Yet Filippov further points to the logical circle, in which substantive international law (a set of universal rules and concepts with a moral meaning) and a state-like authority that draws upon force for its implementation, mutually imply and condition each other. This leads to a sort of dialectical circulation between the international order and the sovereign state.

Olga Bashkina, a young researcher of sovereignty with a background at the European University at Saint-Petersburg and later, the University of Leuven, shares with Marder and Filippov an interest in the idea of the state and its conditions of possibility. Taking an intellectual-historical angle, she focuses on twentieth-century French theories of the state, namely on Raymond Carré de Malberg and Maurice Hauriou. In contrast to fashionable "Left" approaches to the state via the notion of constituent power or other direct engagements of the masses with politics, Malberg and Hauriou take an emphatically idealist point of view of the state, which then becomes a real, materialized abstraction of sorts (to speak Hegelese). This is why, for Carré de Malberg, sovereignty belongs to the "nation" and not to the "people": it is a distilled set of relations, a predicate rather than a realistically conceived subject. This view goes against the identification of the state with any particular social stratum or class but, of course, is commonly challenged by Marxists with arguments such as that made by Panagiotis Sotiris in his chapter for the present volume: the universal idea of the people cannot be realized under capitalist conditions, since it dissimulates the material domination of this or that particular group.

The subsequent section comprises chapters written from Marxist or anarchist perspectives that can be united under Ajay Chaudhary's ambitious slogan of a new "critical theory of state." Chaudhary rightly claims that the existing Marxist theory of the state (Miliband, Poulantzas, Jessop, and others) gradually loses its critical thrust and leaves the space open for a new theory that would be ruthless in its treatment of the existing capitalist state but would still leave space for a state conceived otherwise.

Panagiotis Sotiris, a Greek independent Marxist theorist and activist, comes closest, in this book, to the orthodox Marxist position on the state, as reinforced by Althusser and particularly Poulantzas. He brightly and clearly restates the classical argument of the profound sedimentation of class relations within public legal institutions. So, where most other authors in the book tend to take the lack of an affirmative state theory on the Left as a deficiency—given the practical importance of defending the welfare state against neoliberal pressure—Sotiris, in contrast, warns against such an "idealization of state on the part of many militants on the Left." Nevertheless, he stops short of repeating the vague argument according to which the state would simply "die out." Instead, he tries to answer the question of what the institutions of power would look like after the liberal state is "smashed," or alongside its decay. His answer is "democratic experimentation": the exact alternative to the current state is to be determined in the future, and the masses will be its explorers, active in political laboratories.

Maria Kochkina, a young political theorist from the European University at Saint-Petersburg, gives a detailed critical reading of Jason Lindsey's seminal book, *Concealing the State*. Both claim that the apparent weakening of state in the neoliberal era is an illusion. In fact, the liberal capitalist state only becomes stronger and more insulated from democratic processes. However, Kochkina disagrees with Lindsey when it comes to questions of strategy, specifically in rejecting Lindsey's insistence on the need to demand a "true" democracy, since democracy is an ideal all too deeply inscribed in the liberal state. Instead of democratizing or smashing the state, Kochkina proposes a pragmatic, "cynical" strategy of exposing the state's agency and using the state and its resources for the material purposes of popular movements.

Ajay Singh Chaudhary, an American political theorist and executive director of the unique, independent Brooklyn Institute for Social Research, sketches out, in his chapter, what he calls a "critical state theory." Drawing on the work of the Frankfurt school political theorist Franz Neumann, Chaudhary develops a parallel between the Nazi state—which combined a strong, repressive policy with a dependent, decentralized, and chaotic state apparatus serving the interests of capital—and today's neoliberal state, where, again, a repressive bureaucratic governance coexists with the capture of the state by plural transnational capitalist centers such as "global value chains." In these circumstances, Chaudhary claims that it is necessary to "strengthen popular power" all the while relying on state power to constrain capital and to "decolonize" the states of the North from within by wrestling them away from capitalist interest groups.

The next section deals with the particular kind of political alternative, namely, socialism and communism in their relationship to statehood. This embraces both the past experiments of socialist state-building as well as the visions of our own future.

Lorenzo Chiesa, professor at Newcastle University, one of the English-speaking world's leading specialists on "Italian theory," and a perspicacious theoretical reader of Lacan, contributes to this book with a chapter on Lenin's concept of the state. Chiesa renders Lenin's "State and Revolution" in much detail and reveals the audacity of the concept of State developed therein: a dialectical state that is in the process of dissolving itself is in conflict with itself. Chiesa praises this idea and considers it pertinent for today's projects for the future, but he criticizes Lenin for, nonetheless, placing his dialectical state into a linear sequence, with a mythical, stateless society supposedly emerging in the future. For Chiesa, the self-contradictory socialist state is all there is.

Agon Hamza, an influential Kosovar philosopher and editor of the new journal *Crisis and Critique*, for his part rereads Hegel in light of Slavoj Žižek's scattered remarks on the state. Hamza comes to the conclusion that Hegel described not the liberal nation-state that would be defensively protecting its sovereignty qua monopoly but rather "the condition of historical existence." The true universal is not the state itself, nor an ideal form or transcendental law (as the authors of our first three "idealist" chapters argue), but history, and, nevertheless, the state form remains indispensable as it connects society to its higher mission in its relationships to other political units. This said, Hamza conceives the present historical moment as a revolutionary one, which would transform the liberal state into a paradoxical "non-statal state." This, for him, is a true formula of communism, as opposed to the project of socialist state, which Hamza rejects.

Christian Sorace, a political theorist and a researcher of East Asia from Colorado College, explores the post-socialist state as a particular instance of state transformation in the contemporary world. In a way that recalls Chaudhary and Neumann's discussion of the Nazi state, post-socialist liberal reforms in Mongolia led to a relative weakening of the state and a loss of its autonomy, even though the state did not in fact disappear but just increasingly withdrew from the public gaze. The "successful transition" to liberal democracy in reality led to the impoverishment of the population and loss of control over business, to deindustrialization, and to the evisceration of public services. I must add to this that in the Russia of the 1990s, home to many of the authors of this book, very similar processes led to an abandonment of democracy and its replacement with a version of an authoritarian conservative state with the full support of the majority. Sorace then turns to a theoretical analysis, where he criticizes what he calls the "democratic liturgy" and the widespread tendency to oppose (good) democracy to the (bad) state. In Mongolia, democracy in its liberal shape was actually pernicious for most, while a "traditional" public state would have been potentially beneficial. Drawing on Lenin, Sorace calls for a return to substantive democracy instead of its formal, parliamentary shell.

I, Artemy Magun, am also a contributor of this book (like a playing coach, or even a goalie, in soccer). In concluding it, I offer what I have called a "dialectical theory of state," which is meant precisely to reconcile idealist and materialist, positive and negative, perspectives on the definition of state. For me, there is a logical form of the state, which is prior to the specific arrangements of late Modern bureaucracy. However, the challenge of democratizing the state and freeing it from the hypocrisy typical in widespread versions of liberal idealism requires that we introduce negativity and mass agency into the very form of the state into its project. This was precisely the Hegelian project, even as, at his point in time, Hegel failed to establish a political/methodological project that would be faithful to the dramatic divisions, both ideological and economic, that boil beneath the surface of the "hieroglyph of reason." In the chapter, I try to fill in this gap to the measure of my modest capacities, looking both to the past (the history of proto-dialectical philosophical theories of state) and to the future (the project of an ideal constitution, combining both a strong authority and powerful popular participation).

As may be discerned, this book is interdisciplinary and ideologically pluralist. Although centered on Left theories of the state, it covers a spectrum that ranges from liberal constitutionalism (Filippov and Bashkina), to radical critical theory (Chaudhary, Kochkina, and Sorace), to classical Marxism (Sotiris and Chiesa); from philosophical transcendentalism or idealism (Marder, Filippov, and Bashkina), through to post-Lacanian Hegelianism (Hamza and Chiesa), and to critical materialism (Chaudhary and Sotiris). All of the authors are, nonetheless, united in their critical approach to the prevailing Weberian anti-philosophical instrumentalism in today's thinking on the state, and by a desire to conceive a political alternative for the future, whether on perennial or historically specific grounds.

This book took a long time to prepare and emerged out of the research project "Living together. Questions of diversity and unity in contemporary Russia: historical legacy, modern state, and society," supported by a grant from the Foundation for Support of Liberal Arts issued to the Center for Historical Research at the National Research University Higher School of Economics at St. Petersburg in 2017–2018, which we oversaw together with Professor Alexander Semyonov. As the book's preparation was protracted, two of the chapters, both of which had been written specifically for our volume, Marder's and Chiesa's, have recently been published, respectively in a monograph and in a journal; but this in no way reduces their important place in the composition of our project.

The stormy time when this book is coming out is telling, but our point was not just to forecast the storm or to feel a trend. We wanted to call our readers back to a larger historical panorama, from a myopic focusing on the conjunctures of the narrow present. Today, an open historical crisis calls us to think of the State and to think of what it stands for.

NOTES

1. Helmut Quaritsch, *Souveränität. Entstehung und Entwicklung des Begriffs in Frankreich und Deutschland vom 13. Jahrhundert bis 1806* (Berlin: Duncker & Humblot, 1986).

2. Some examples: Saskia Sassen, *Losing Control? Sovereignty in the Age of Globalization* (New York: Columbia University Press, 1996); Antonio Negri and Michael Hardt, *Empire* (Cambridge, MA: Harvard University Press, 2000); Wendy Brown, *Walled Sovereignties, Waning States* (Cambridge, MA: MIT Press, 2010); Mariano Croce and Andrea Salvatore, *Undoing Ties. Political Philosophy at the Waning of the State* (London; New York: Bloomsbury, 2015).

3. Stephen Krasner, *Sovereignty: Organized Hypocrisy* (Princeton, NJ: Princeton University Press, 1999); Neil Walker, ed., *Sovereignty in Transition* (New York: Bloomsbury 2003).

4. See a detailed history of this in Jens Bartelson, *The Critique of the State* (Cambridge: Cambridge University Press, 2001).

5. Peter Evans, Dietrich Rueschemeyer, and Theda Skocpol, *Bringing the State Back In* (Cambridge: Cambridge University Press, 1985).

6. On state capacity, see Gabriel Almond and G. Bingham Powell, Jr., *Comparative Politics: A Developmental Approach* (Boston, MA: Little, Brown, 1966); Joel Migdal, *Strong Societies and Weak States* (Princeton, NJ: Princeton University Press, 1988); Theda Skocpol, "Bringing the State Back In: Strategies of Analysis in Current Research," in: Peter Evans, Dietrich Rueschemeyer, and Theda Skocpol, *Bringing the State Back In* (Cambridge: Cambridge University Press, 1985), 3–37.

7. On the consolidation of democracy, see Juan L. Linz and Alfred Stepan, *Problems of Democratic Transition and Consolidation: Southern Europe, South America, and Post-Communist Europe* (Baltimore, MD; London: Johns Hopkins University Press, 1996); Larry J. Diamond, *Developing Democracy: Toward Consolidation* (Baltimore, MD; London: Johns Hopkins University Press, 1999); Andreas Schedler, "What Is Democratic Consolidation?" *Journal of Democracy* 9.2 (1998): pp. 91–107.

8. Georg Jellinek, *Allgemeine Staatslehre* (Berlin: Verlag von O. Häring, 1905); Carré de Malberg, *Contribution à la Théorie Genérale de l'État* (Paris: Nabu Press, 2010); Olivier Beaud, *La Puissance de l'État* (Paris: PUF, 1994).

9. Max Weber, "The Profession and Vocation of Politics," in: *Political Writings* (Cambridge: Cambridge University Press, 1994), 309–328, cit. p. 310.

10. Ralph Miliband, *The State in Capitalist Society* (New York: Basic Books, 1969). Nicos Poulantzas, *State, Power, Socialism* (New York; London: Verso, 1978). Bob Jessop, *State Power* (London: Polity, 2007).
11. Georg Jellinek, *Allgemeine Staatslehre*.
12. Slavoj Žižek, *Less than Nothing* (New York; London: Verso, 2012), 842; cf. Geoff Pfeifer, "Political Ontologies of the State. Žižek, Badiou, and the Idea of the Revolution from the Outside," in: Bart van der Steen, Marc de Kesel (ed.), *Party, State, Revolution, Critical Reflections on Zizek's Political Philosophy* (Baden-Baden: Nomos 2017), 93–106.
13. Slavoj Žižek, *Less than Nothing*, 843.
14. "The course on which Chavez embarked from 2006 is the exact opposite of the postmodern Left's mantra . . . far from 'resisting state power', he grabbed power (first by an attempted coup, then democratically), ruthlessly using the state apparatuses and interventions to promote his goals; furthermore, he is militarizing the favelas, organizing the training of armed units. And . . . now that he is feeling the economic effects of the 'resistance' to his rule by capital . . . , he has announced the constitution of his own political party!" Slavoj Žižek, *In Defense of Lost Causes* (New York; London: Verso, 2008), 427. These words read differently today, in 2018, after Chavez's death and the Venezuela's socioeconomic collapse.
15. Slavoj Zizek, "Direct Democracy and the State," talk published July 26, 2016, https://www.youtube.com/watch?v=KVzUomUOuo4. Slavoj Žižek, "A Plea for Bureaucratic Socialism," talk published June 30, 2017, https://www.youtube.com/watch?v=2OYSMWJafAI, last visited January 6, 2019. Slavoj Zizek, "State Power vs. the Ideological Sovereign," talk published May 5, 2017, https://www.youtube.com/watch?v=Ohbhzc8NnzI, last visited January 6, 2019.
16. Bart van der Steen and Marc de Kesel (eds.), *Party, State, Revolution (Staatsverständnisse)* (Baden-Baden: Nomos Verlag, 2017).
17. Agon Hamza, in *Party, State, Revolution (Staatsverständnisse)*, 175.
18. Slavoj Žižek, *Less than Nothing*, 755.
19. Pierre Rosanvallon, *La crise de l'État-Providence* (Paris: Points: 2015 [1981]).
20. Ibid.
21. Weber, *The Profession and Vocation of Politics*.
22. Karl Polanyi, *The Great Transformation. The Political and Economic Origins of Our Time* (New York: Beacon Press, 2001 [1944]).
23. Giovanni Arrighi, *The Long Twentieth Century: Money, Power and the Origins of Our Times* (London: Verso, 2010).
24. Herfried Münkler, "Staat," in: *Historisches Wörterbuch der Philosophie*, hg. Von Joachim Ritter, Bd. 10, Basel 1998, S. 1–30.
25. Claude Lefort, *Democracy and Political Theory* (New York: Polity Press, 1988), p. 225.
26. David Harvey, *A Brief History of Neoliberalism* (Oxford: Oxford University Press: 2005), pp. 64–86.
27. Ibid., 69.
28. Barry Buzan, Ole Wæver, and Jaap de Wilde, *Security: A New Framework for Analysis* (Boulder, CO: Lynne Rienner Publishers, 1998).

29. Gilles Deleuze, *Postscript on the Societies of Control. October*, Vol. 59 (Winter, 1992), pp. 3–7.

30. For instance, see Paul Virilio, *The Vision Machine* (Bloomington: Indiana University Press, 1994 [1988]).

31. Béatrice Hibou, *The Bureaucratization of the World in the Neoliberal Era. An International and Comparative Perspective* (New York; London: Palgrave 2015), p. XVI.

32. Agon Hamza, "The Distance between Party and State. An Outline of a Žižekian Theory of the State," in: *Party, State, Revolution (Staatsverständnisse)* (Baden-Baden: Nomos, 2017), 165–166.

I
THE IDEA OF STATE

Chapter 1

The Categories of the State

Michael Marder

Throughout the history of political philosophy, the state has invariably appeared as a figure for something or someone beyond the institution in question. From Hobbes's *Leviathan*, which presents it in the shape of an "Artificial Animal" or "Artificiall Man" "of greater *stature* and strength than the Naturall,"[1] to Hegel's claim in his *Rechtsphilosophie* that the state is one of spirit's most advanced shapes,[2] this aspect of political reality has been clothed in layer upon layer of mythological meaning, including the mythology of reason itself. Eager to demystify the state and to live up to a self-professed scientific ideal, contemporary political science analyzes it in a rigid institutional framework, buttressed by theories of normativity and rational choice. Unsurprisingly, the upshot of such political disenchantment is similar to the dénouement of a purely analytical thought and (experimental) physical sciences: the object of study is defigured and disfigured, disappearing into a motley of minute structures and microprocesses. In all three instances, knowledge commences at an infra-objective level after the knower has effaced the object's recognizable outlines (the assemblages produced by the Kantian "figurative syntheses" that add up to the "transcendental synthesis of the imagination"), fragmented its cognitive and perceptual unity into component parts, and transcribed them into their numeric equivalents.

My alternative suggestion is to survey the state as a junction for various categories drawn from Aristotle and Kant: positionality, substance, relation, modality, quantity, and quality, among others. The advantage of this political philosophical protocol without concessions to political theory is that it commits to a multifaceted view, which neither figures nor disfigures that to which the categories pertain but outlines the political entity, as much as possible, in accord with its own demarcations, retracing its contours. Rather than an exhaustive theoretical account, mine will be a methodological exercise in "categorial thinking"[3] intrinsically open to revision and further elaboration insofar as it keeps an ear to the ground of the state's givenness in political apperception. The horizon for what I undertake here in broad brushstrokes will thus be a phenomenological, in lieu of an ideological, critique of the state.

1. POSITIONALITY/PLACE

To be in a state or to have a state is to take a stance in a given place, with or against—with-against—others. Derived from the PIE root *stā-, it means "to stand," "to make or be firm." In Persian and Slavic languages, this root gives rise to the word *stan*, which, in addition to signaling where one stands, names the being-country of a country, as in Pakistan, Uzbekistan, or Afghanistan. A position, a posture, a status, the state is the response to an existential question: *How does where one stands itself stand?*

Recalling Aristotle, we will note that positionality (θέσις) is a philosophical category, and standing (στάσις) is a variation on the theme of *thesis* (*Cat.* 6b, 12). Of course, *stasis* embraces the mutually contradictory significations of stability and tumult, stagnation and civil war. The standing position relevant to *stasis*—a precursor of our "state"—is overdetermined, split between a standstill or standing down, on the one hand, and standing up (i.e., to fight), on the other. The position and the state that epitomizes it are divided against themselves. *How* where we stand itself stands is negatively conditioned by a dizzying multiplication of stances: it never stands in one way alone. A subject and an object, it stands over against itself, ever primed for conflict. The position is, as a result, shattered in its standing modality, with figuration both impossible (just try giving a figure to the simultaneity of stability and tumult!) and necessary (after all, only a figured something or someone can assume, or be in, a position).

There are several important ramifications to approaching positionality as a point of departure for thinking the state by means of the categories:

(1) Instead of beginning with place, which is itself the category of *where* in Aristotelian philosophy; instead of setting out from a site, as Heidegger does in his discussion of the matter,[4] and confining politics to a politics of place, this approach calls for a phenomenological interpretation of political formations. When it comes to the *status* of the state, we go directly to emplacement and orientation, to situatedness, coordination, and alignment. Yet because in *stasis* the position is opposed to itself, the nascent phenomenology of the state is exceptionally knotty, its oppositional character externalized in relation to other states and, occasionally, taken inward in a situation of civil war.

(2) The primacy of positionality indicates, in Scholastic terms, that the accidents precede substance as far as the state is concerned. The *how* of the stance is more consequential than *what* or *who* stands. Quite literally, substance is a play on standing: it makes itself firm from below (*sub*) by furnishing a bedrock for beings. Political substance, for its part, is the effect of political subjectivity of the subject position with its unique orientation and style of occupying a place.

(3) Statelessness (the condition increasingly affecting vast populations around the world today) names, above all, not placelessness or the absence of basic rights that go along with citizenship but the denial of a position to the stateless and, especially, of the upright stance, which, in physicobiological, bodily actuality submitted to an ethico-metaphysical interrogation bespeaks something essentially human. Those who are stateless are bereft of the opportunity to have a legal, political, or ontological standing. Their dehumanization and the extreme endangerment of their lives are attributable to the prohibition of assuming a certain position: thou shalt not stand! Neither at a standstill nor in tumultuous movement, they are expelled to the hither side of *stasis*, the empirical deaths of stateless multitudes corroborating their phenomenological and existential erasure.

In its standing position, in its erection which the institution formalizes, the state demands that its citizens stand up for it at the time of war or, in other words, that they be prepared to fight and die for it, to *lay down* their lives. So conceived, its stance is virtually inseparable from a standing army. More suggestively still, expressed in the political state, uprightness is the mark of masculinity—hence, of a part of human sexuality that, in standing up, in getting erect, illegitimately stands in for the whole of humanity. Granted, he does not articulate it in these terms, but that is the subtext of Heidegger's equation of the Greek *polis* with a pole: "*Polis* is the *polos*, the pole, the place around which everything appearing to the Greeks as a being turns in a peculiar way.... The pole, as this place, lets beings appear in their Being and show the totality of their condition."[5] Heidegger forgets two things here: first, that the pole ("the pole, as this place") is *not* the place it marks and orders around itself, adding extra complications to the ellipsis of being as being-in-place-and-in-a-position, and, second, that the static nature of the rock-hard *polos* is but half of the fissured *stasis* phenomenon (erection at a standstill *and* in free fall). Phallogocentric to the *n*th degree, the pole-like shape of the *polis* and *Staat* is, for Heidegger, the perspective from which beings in their totality display themselves. Under-standing (*Verstand*) bows to this hypostasis of the masculinity it converts into a manifestation of iron-clad necessity.

2. MODALITY/RELATION

The "Doctrine of the Elements" in the First *Critique* contains a famous definition of necessity—"nothing other than the existence that is given by possibility itself [*nicht anderes als die Existenz, die durch die Möglichkeit selbst gegeben ist*]"[6]—which articulates the three ingredients of the category of modality (necessity, existence, and possibility). The political necessity *proper* is to take a stance, to assume a position on the fields of positionality dominated by the state. This necessity lurks behind the impossibility of neutrality Schmitt underscores time and again in his works. The state as a stance is the form of existence given by the possibility of the political itself. All oppositions to it, be they of the anarchist or other strains, fall under such necessity by virtue of taking a stance vis-à-vis the standing that is not only *of* the state but also *is* the state.

In current technocracies, we have the ultimate perversion of the oppositional stance, which tries to pass itself for a neutral absence of any stance and to conceal a markedly ideological position behind the façade of a non- or post-ideology, to boot. It is not by chance that a technocratic state is known as "managerial" or "administrative": flaunting the end of the political, it contrives its necessity from an existence given by the possibility, which Lenin reckoned within reach after the Communist revolution,[7] of overcoming politics, in the sense of the partiality of any position in party politics and partisan engagements. At the same time, and contrary to the affirmations peppering the official discourse on the subject, this possibility (of the impossibility of politics) is the highest stage of the political disguised as its other. The perverse technocratic existence, which the possibility of political impossibility yields, belongs to the necessity of the phenomenon it negates, which is why the administrative state is still identified as a state, and justifiably so.

While taking a position on the broad field of political positionality is unavoidable, its exact coordinates admit several degrees of freedom. The state organizes body politic in a standing political formation, at least potentially ready for battle. Other positions are also conceivable: for example, the flat horizontality of certain strands of anarchism, Deleuzian politics, and "grassroots democracy," or a sitting arrangement[8] suspended somewhere between the horizontal and the vertical axes, most notably in sit-ins, the strategies of the Occupy movement, and protests defending native settlement rights, as, most recently, at North Dakota's Standing (!) Rock Indian Reservation. In each case, the position of choice is both literal and figurative; better yet, it is *figurational* or literal-figurative, to the extent that phenomenological description invalidates the distinctions between these two registers of political, ontological, and other types of orientation. Across the board, the possibilities of counter-state positions are nonetheless severely limited due to the stance they adopt *against* the state, and, in this standoff, participate in the dynamics of the state. They confirm Hegel's diagnosis on the political level: an opposition to dialectics is thoroughly dialectical. It may well be that, phenomenally ontically, lying flat or sitting down positions do not befit the state but, modally ontologically, they are altogether absorbed into the state.

An assortment of possible positions boils down to the necessity of being in or assuming a position, the necessity entwined with another category—that of relation. In Aristotle's oeuvre, after all, positions are relational, a *what for* or *what to*, πρός τι (*Cat.* 6b, 12^9). We always take a stance for or against something, and a state is a stance with regard to others, both among those who comprise a polity standing side by side, shoulder to shoulder, and between states, each of them turned toward rivaling political units in a face-to-face alliance or confrontation, whether overt or covert. Further, relations can be of different kinds, as Kant demonstrates in his discussion of the category. Let us consider two of these: community and causality/dependence. The third—substance/accident—will deserve separate treatment, seeing that "substance" is an independent category in Aristotle's philosophy.

Community (*Gemeinschaft*) is the reciprocity of acting and being acted upon, *Wechselwirkung zwischen dem Handelnden und Leidenden* (CPR B106), harkening back to the Aristotelian notion of relation as a correlation of the doing and the done, the sensing and the sensed, and so forth. In a state, the relation of community denotes the correlation of being at a standstill and taking a stand, the outcome of hardening into a vertical position and the act of making firm. (*Stasis* is the perfect specimen of Kantian community, which has internalized the reciprocal movement-rest of *Handeln* and *Leiden*.) Be that as it may, in the so-called "international community," the division of political labor is such that some states monopolize the acting stance, even as others (the majority) are allotted the role of being acted upon. Despite the *de jure* absolute sovereignty of all states, a few of them *de facto* stand out on the international arena and, more vertical than their peers, seem to satisfy to the letter the notion of the state-as-an-upright-stance. Precluding the reciprocity of acting and being acted upon, the international community is not at all a community in accordance with Kant's characterization of this relational mode. And the same unevenness is detectable within states, where the principle of the equality of citizens is disrespected in legal and political practices (cf. access to voting in the United States affected by the voter's race). Only some stand and have a standing, often at the expense of others who don't, fatefully undermining the very possibility of a national community. Where we stand itself stands differently, depending on who this "we" is, unless the state has become communist in the sense of each acting and being acted upon without the inequality of standing. Until then, the being of a state and being in a state evince two entirely different things.

If the relational category of community presupposes reciprocity between its members, then another sort of relation—causality and dependence (cause and effect) [*Kausalität und Dependenz (Ursache und Wirkung)*]" (CPR B106)—implies a hierarchy purged of all reciprocity. The cause is the origin, an autonomous principle, the metaphysical *status principi*, the only thing that stands by itself, irradiating multiple effects. Translated into political terms, the cause-effect relation is that of mastery and vassalage, of total authority and submission, where the cause rules and the effects obey its overwhelming and preexistent power. In its present condition, then, "the international community" is a misnomer; international relations *among* states are, by and large, those of causality and dependence, just as political relations *within* states do not live up to the reciprocity of acting and enduring an action at the heart of the community. Assuming that the state is the cause, the citizens' standing is derivative with respect to how the state itself stands. A totalitarian tendency emerges in the equation of the state with the cause, affording it the supreme standing, relative to which everyone and everything else lies prostrate. Though a fiction, the social contract reversed political cause-effect relations and posited a concert of individual wills at the origin of the state, which, *qua* their effect, could be dissolved whenever the implicit agreement to form it broke down.

3. SUBSTANCE

Colloquially, *state* signifies a condition, a temporarily stabilized being of something. The semantic lever here is the word *temporarily*: the state of things is a transit station on the path of perpetual alteration, as in the changes from the solid to the liquid and gaseous states of matter. On the one hand, the idea of a physical state privileges the static connotations of *stasis* with its relative stability. But, on the other hand, it hints at a series of transformations leading beyond the present state and so accounts for the sense of *stasis* as unrest. The same holds *mutatis mutandis* for the political state, in that its *ousia*—being in the substantive; in Greek: *as-what the thing is present or presents itself*; in Latin: that which stands under, props up and grounds things—may at any moment slide (back or forward) to the verbal sense of being as presencing that does not neatly fit within any of its present shapes.

What does the political state, understood in terms of substance, temporarily stabilize? The answer is unambiguous, and it goes beyond (and below) the thought of early Marx it is reminiscent of: the state is the substantivizing stabilization of conflict and antagonism—not their extinguishing but their channeling, steering, direction, arrangement in standing or standoffish formations, or, in contemporary parlance, their management. In the state, *stasis* acquires its form (in another possible formulation: the state is *stasis* hypostatized) educed from the political things themselves, merely thematizing their standing. The state is the formalization of the condition proper to the *res publica* that hosts the possibility of strife and contention in itself. Keeping to a rigorously phenomenological method, we might say that problems crop up when state form comes unglued from that which it formalizes, is hollowed out, and pretends to lead a life of its own, detached from *res publica* and oblivious to anything but procedural stipulations.[10] It is then that substantive political forms are experienced as impositions and arouse the revolutionary desire to overthrow them. Isn't anarchism the purest expression of this desire still unaware of its deep cause, namely the wish to return from the content-less state form to the status of how the political things themselves stand?

In contrast to the prevalent view of its separateness and independence from what ensues from or in it, Aristotle and Kant agree that substance is a relational category: the former, in his notion of the second ($δεύτερος$) presence that articulates the sense of the first *this* (the first *ousia*) as *that* (*Cat.* 2a, 11–18); the latter, in his inclusion of substance and accident among the three modes of relationality in the table of categories (CPR B106), with the proviso that substance is a *condition of* relations (CPR A187). The category *substance* is, therefore, not an empty form but the formalization of being in its temporal concreteness. It draws out formal similarities from disparate things and discovers connections between the temporally variable conditions of the same thing.

The interpretation of the state as the substantive form of relationality and as the formalization of political being is evident in the republican tradition.[11] Indeed, the previously nonpolitical word *status* is politicized in Latin when it describes the state (or condition) of public things, *status rei publicae*, at the inception of the political state. In Justinian's *Corpus Iuris Civilis*, it is the emperor's duty to reward peace and maintain *status rei publicae*, the state of public things—*pacem decoramus et statum rei publicae sustentamus* (1.17.1pr). And, earlier still, Livy relates in his *History of Rome* the vow that the Great Games of Titus would be held again "if the state of the public thing should remain as it was before [*si eodem statu res publica staret*]" (30.2.8).

It bears mentioning that the substantive form of *status* is affixed not only to the *res publica* it formalizes but also to the condition of the ruler (*status principi*), of the crown (*status coronae*), of the realm (*status regni*), of the empire (*status imperii*), and even of the polity (*status civitatis*).[12] Whatever the *this* it singles out, the *status* is a standing inseparable from that which or the one who stands. There are, then, two paths toward formalization: (1) the premodern experiments in political hylomorphism, where the state is the form equiprimordial with the formalized matters themselves, and (2) the modern work of producing a formal conception of state form, a secondary substance (a *that*) detached from the *this* it was meant to determine. Having lost all ties to figuration, the modern state no longer reveals its substantive whatness or whoness: it no longer responds to the phenomenological-existential question, "Who or what stands?" but presents an abstract form of standing.

The trajectory of the state's increasing abstraction is, admittedly, anticipated in its early formalizations, where regardless of the genitive that follows it— *regni, imperii, rei publicae*—the *status* remains constant and, in its constancy, minimally indifferent to the beings of which it is a condition. The modern state, in turn, merely intensifies this tendency and also, paradoxically, lives up to the primacy of the position, the *how* of the stance that precedes substance. (Formal proceduralism is the case in point of the single-minded focus on the *how* in contemporary juridical and political systems.) Yet an accident is still the accident *of* something, and primacy does not spell out exclusivity. The *how* sundered from a concrete *what* or *who* returns, almost by default, to an abstract whatness in greater need of legitimation, the whatness that in political modernity entails "a form of public power separate from both the ruler and the ruled."[13]

Differently put, the formal conception of state form is a substance that tends to its own desubstantivation. Such a predicament is not easily remedied by the phenomenological program of a return to the things themselves; analogous to the primacy of the accident that evidentially comes to the fore in the historical development of state forms toward their modern formalization, desubstantivation is a feature of (Aristotelian) substance itself that is "numerically one and receptive to contraries [ἕν ἀριθμῷ ὄν τῶν ἐναντίων εἶναι δεκτικόν]" (*Cat.* 4a, 11–12). If the defining feature of substance is its underappreciated metapolitical capacity to receive opposites into itself, then its receptivity to the nonsubstance in the substance is the apex, not a violation, of this logic. That is, finally, what is at stake (it, too—a vertical pole) in the speculative reversals, of which *stasis* is but the tip of an iceberg. The *stā- of a stance or status is equally that of *steering* and *constancy*, *starting* and *destiny*, movement and rest, beginning and end. Substance does not neutralize these "binary" pairings on the common turf it furnishes but undergoes politicization insofar as it welcomes them in itself. No wonder that we have grown accustomed to conflating the state with the political as such: in their substantive aspect, both are incredibly adept at accommodating oppositions, let alone the movements that oppose *them*, and dialectically twisting that which intends to negate them into a refined mode of their own expression.

4. QUALITY/QUANTITY

Qualitative value judgments frequently accompany the *status* in political texts. So, Cicero speaks of the *optimus status civitate*, "the best state of the polity," not only, as we have already seen, in *Letters to His Brother Quintus* but also in *De Republica* (1.33–34, 70–71) and *De Legibus* (1.15, 3.4). In the same year of 1516, Erasmus's *Institutio* (1.75) contrasts the best state of public things (*optimus Reipublicae status*) and the worst (*pessimus Reipublicae status*), and Thomas More's *Utopia* includes in its subtitle the words *de optimo rei publicae statu*. Setting aside for the time being the specific content of these qualities, observe that they address the question of political positionality, namely: How does where one stands itself stand? The two polar options are that public things either stand well or stand poorly. A good standing, a sound *status*, typically betokens spatiotemporal durability, itself a corollary to well-constituted foundations. How it stands, the state of the state, has to do with what it stands upon, even if experientially and conceptually the position comes first, before the substratum that sustains it.

Take, for instance, Erasmus whose *Institutio* is a "must-read" for anyone wishing to grasp the metaphysics of the state's political standing. "The prince's *imperium* over the *populus*," he writes, "is none other than that of the mind over the body [*non alius modi esse imperium principis in populum, quam quale est animi in corpus*]." The "reign of the mind in the body [*animum regnare in corpore*]," is for him, the best (*optimum*) condition and the source of happiness (*felicitas*) (1.80). Consequently, the happiest state (*felicissimus status*) is being led by the best laws under the best prince, who provides for all (6.1). The optimal state for Erasmus is the government of the body by the mind, whose paragon is the prince/principle, or the head of the body politic. His solution to the problem of a sound *status*, shared with the rest of the philosophical lineage he is a part of, becomes blatantly obvious: to stand well, one ought to stand on one's head. The metaphysical inversion of physical positionality shadows the qualitative categorization of the state with remarkable consistency from ancient Greek philosophy through medieval political treatises to Hegel's philosophy of state. It is in a culmination of this long history that the ideology critique Marx levels in *Critique of Hegel's Philosophy of Right* (1843) and *The German Ideology* (1846) sweeps the ground away under the headstand political metaphysics performs, and the best *status* appears as the worst, particular class interests amounting to a false universal.

The axiological qualities of the state are, in any event, contingent upon the physicality of the *status* (most of all, its firmness) which allows it to be vertical. If the state describes how the things themselves stand without abstracting their form from the content, then its hardness is due to its rootedness in hylomorphic political realities. If, however, these ties are loosened, then the state rigidifies into an institution, precisely in order to compensate for the lack of support from what is supposed to predicate its existence. The state that draws the quality of its firmness from the things themselves is the *status* of the republic or of the realm; the one that relies on complex institutional structures and mechanism is an abstract juridical entity in force on a given territory.

Both Aristotle's and Kant's categories can offer invaluable help for philosophical attempts to comprehend the state's territorial boundaries. In Aristotle, the relevant category is quantity, or, more specifically, continuous quantity, το συνεχές ποσό (*Cat.* 4b, 20–21). Whereas discrete quantities refer to numbers, continuous measures are geometrical units. In a state, however, there is no geometry because, there, continuous quantities do not delimit a portion of the earth (*gē*; *terra*) but circumscribe the territory, into which *terra* has mutated. As Heidegger argues, the Roman predilection for the territory is symptomatic of "the basic comportment of the Romans toward beings in general," notably "the rule of the *imperium*." "*Imperium*," he continues, "says *im-parare*, to establish, to make arrangements: *prae-cipere*, to occupy something in advance, and by this occupation to hold command over it, and so to have the occupied as territory. *Imperium* is commandment, command."[14]

The state occupying a given territory is inevitably imperial or imperialistic, whether or not it becomes an actual empire. The territory is that-upon-which . . . of the stance that is the state. But a territorial state does not coincide with the place or places it envelops, nor does it stand, strictly speaking, on earth. The continuous quantities that bring the territory into existence dematerialize the phenomenologico-political *status*, setting it up in its new ideality as subject to occupation, surveillance, control, and measurement, just as the discrete quantities applied to population as a mass, with its own volume and density, pave the way for a governmental state.[15] Be it geometrically or arithmetically, the state serves as a control-and-command center with regard to territories and populations, thanks to the hyperinflation of its quantitative side.

In Kant, the boundary lends itself to understanding in qualitative, rather than a quantitative, categories: limitation (*Einschränkung*) "as reality combined with negation [*als Realität mit Negation verbunden*]" (CPR B111). There is a sense that, in and of itself, "reality" knows no limit and is unaware of its finitude. Limits give the thing its qualities at the price of its drive toward a potentially infinite expansion in a general atmosphere of indeterminacy. *Status rei publicae* is delineated only once the reality of the *res* is mixed with its negation, which, on the positive side of a limit, enables the stance or the standing of the state (*stasis-qua*-standstill) rescued from an indefinite, creeping expansion at the core of the state's imperial ambition (*stasis-qua*-unrest).[16] Conversely, from the standpoint of sovereignty, the negation of the reality of the state is everything that lies outside it. When that negation is on the verge of being realized, the state finds itself embroiled in a war. The political tragedy of world history is that the delimitation of states has swapped self-critique for the threat or actuality of external negation.

It follows that the qualitative category repeats, on a smaller scale, the maneuvers of Kant's entire critical project. Reason is initially not so different from reality[17]: it also knows no boundaries and, by means of critique corresponding to the movement of negation, must encounter its proper limits. Before its self-delimitation, reason still deems itself omnipotent and aspires to extend everywhere indefinitely, which is why it cannot stand on its own. The transcendental function of critique is to dispense to reason its standing, to endow it with qualitative determinations, to combine its reality with negation so as to arrive at its limits. For states, war has satisfied the critical function by providing them with much the same benefits—a concrete standing, determinate qualities, and territorial boundaries stipulated in peace treaties. And critique has silently consented to this contingent historical qualification of political units: reluctant to combine the reality of the state with its negation, "criticism initially kept aloof from the State" up to the point where "criticism became the victim of its ostensible neutrality; it turned into hypocrisy."[18] Over and above such dishonesty, critique (which is perhaps but the adaptation—and, in Kant's body of work, the interiorization—of a bellicose course of action to and in thought) leaves the qualities of the state at the mercy of war, as though it were the *ultima ratio* for refuting or validating every critical conclusion.

One can only imagine how qualitatively different "the reason of the state" (*ratio status*; *raison d'état*) would have been under the guidance of critique. In Kantian terms, it would have been doubly restrained, both as reason and what is essentially "of the state." In political practice, the exact opposite happens: *raison d'état* renounces the critiques of reason and of the state in the name of "national interest," the apotheosis of uncritical argumentation. Accursius's *Digest* dating from the first half of the thirteenth century abstracts *status* from *res publica* and, at the same time, prepares the basis for *ratio status* with the formulation "to preserve the state so that it shall not perish [*ad statum conservandum ne pereat*]" (*D.* 1.1.1.2[19]). The conservation of the *status*, persistence in being, political survival supplies the sole guideline worth adhering to. No sooner does the state lose its original standing as the standing condition of the *res publica* that it oversteps the limits set by (hence, the onto-phenomenological critique emanating from) the political things themselves.[20] The spotlight shifts from qualitative distinctions to the unconditional injunction to perpetuate a vacuous state form.

That said, a renewed emphasis on the category of quality is not the panacea for the dictatorship of quantity Marx hoped it would be. Materially and substantively grounded as it may be, *status rei publicae* is one form encompassing numerous public things. The state is how the many stand in a single position and a unitary formation; it is the archetype of Kant's quantitative allness or totality (*Allheit oder Totalität*), which is "plurality regarded as a unity [*Vielheit als Einheit betrachtet*]" (CPR B111). *Status rei publicae* conveys this more effectively than *status regni* or *status imperii* by articulating the state in a singular with the plural form *rei publicae* and contributing after a fashion to the ancient dialectic of the one and the many. Every *status* dissimulates the overdetermination of *stasis*, which stands divided against itself. But, more than any other, a republican state is a tense assemblage, if not a contradiction in terms, especially when the state form is imposed on public things from the outside. In and of themselves, disparate realities cannot have an identical stance, a homogeneous standing, a unitary position and orientation, no matter the immanence of their *status* or condition. Instead, they are ordered, organized, aligned, and arranged by the state-totality that, faithful to the Kantian category of quantity, espies unity in their plurality. A coherent stance of the state is nothing else than the product of this ordering and alignment that, as a political equivalent to the *a priori* synthesis in the First *Critique*, renders itself absent from that which is ordered or aligned.

NOTES

1. Thomas Hobbes, *Leviathan*, edited by Richard Tuck (Cambridge: Cambridge University Press, 1996), p. 9, emphasis added (the word choice "stature" is far from accidental; it gestures toward the etymology of the state). According to Carl Schmitt, the anthropomorphic version of political thought sees wars as duels between *magni homines* and fantasizes about the state as "a legal subject and a sovereign 'person'" [Carl Schmitt, *The* Nomos *of the Earth in the International Law of* Jus Publicum Europaeum, translated by Gary L. Ulmen (New York: Telos Press, 2003), pp. 142, 145].

2. "The state is the actuality of the ethical Idea. It is ethical spirit [*sittliche Geist*] as the substantial will manifest and revealed to itself" [G. W. F. Hegel, *Philosophy of Right*, translated with noted by T. M. Knox (Oxford and New York: Oxford University Press, 1967), p. 155].

3. I pursue this project in *Political Categories* (New York: Columbia University Press, 2019).

4. "One translates *polis* as state (*Staat*) and city-state (*Stadsstaat*); this does not capture the entire sense. Rather, *polis* is the name for the site (*Stätte*), the Here, within which and as which Being-here is historically. The *polis* is the site of history." Martin Heidegger, *Introduction to Metaphysics*, translated by Gregory Fried and Richard Polt (New Haven, CT, and London: Yale University Press, 2000), p. 162.

5. Martin Heidegger, *Parmenides*, translated by André Schuwer and Richard Rojcewicz (Bloomington and Indianapolis: Indiana University Press, 1998), p. 89.

6. All references to Kant's *Critique of Pure Reason* appear in brackets, containing the pagination of the first (A) or second (B) editions. For the English translation of the work, consult Immanuel Kant, *Critique of Pure Reason (The Cambridge Edition*

of the Works of Immanuel Kant), edited and translated by Paul Guyer and Allen W. Wood (Cambridge: Cambridge University Press, 1999).

7. Cf. Vladimir Lenin, *The State and Revolution*, translated by Robert Service (London and New York: Penguin, 1992), p. 45. Thus, present-day technocrats are Leninists, minus the necessity of the revolution prior to the rise of the administrative state.

8. It is worth noting that, in Russian idiom, "to sit" can mean "to serve a jail term."

9. Here as elsewhere, the reference is to Aristotle's "Categories," in: Aristotle. *Categories. On Interpretation. Prior Analytics*, translated by H. P. Cooke and Hugh Tredennick. Loeb Classical Library 325. (Cambridge, MA: Harvard University Press, 1938).

10. Quentin Skinner [*Foundations of Modern Political Thought*, Vol. II: "The Age of Reformation" (Cambridge: Cambridge University Press, 1978)] outlines these two ways of understanding the state in historical perspective: "Before the sixteenth century, the term *status* was only used by political writers to refer to one of two things: either the state or condition in which a ruler finds himself (the *status principi*); or else the general 'state of the nation' or condition of the realm as a whole (the *status regni*). What was lacking in these usages was the distinctively modern idea of the State as a form of public power separate from both the ruler and the ruled, and constituting the supreme political authority within a certain defined territory" (p. 353).

11. For an excellent account of *res publica* in the republican tradition, see *The Materiality of Res Publica: How to Do Things with Publics*, edited by Dominique Colas and Oleg Kharkhordin (Newcastle upon Tyne: Cambridge Scholars Publishing, 2009).

12. See FN#9. For *status civitatis* refer to Cicero ("*de optimo statu civitatis*": Cic. ad Q. fr. 3.5.1) and Sallust ("*de statu civitatis*": Sal. Cat. 40.2).

13. Skinner, *Foundations II*, p. 353.

14. Heidegger, *Parmenides*, p. 44.

15. Michel Foucault, *Security, Territory, Population: Lectures at the Collège de France, 1977–8*, edited by Michel Senellart (Basingstoke and New York: Palgrave Macmillan, 2009), p. 110.

16. For more on the energy of movement and rest in the political state, consult my *Energy Dreams: Of Actuality* (New York: Columbia University Press, 2017), esp. pp. 130–133.

17. Hegel likewise concedes this point both in his *Phenomenology* and in *The Philosophy of Right*.

18. Reinhart Koselleck, *Critique and Crisis: Enlightenment and the Pathogenesis of Modern Society* (Cambridge, MA: MIT Press, 1988), p. 98.

19. *Corpus Iuris Civilis Iustinianei*, edited with the glossae of Accursius (Lyon: Prost, 1627), https://web.archive.org/web/20110716080918; http://diglit.ub.uni-heidelberg.de/diglit/justinian1627bd1/

20. For a discussion of the critique of *logos* set out by phenomena, see my *Phenomena-Critique-Logos: The Project of Critical Phenomenology* (London: Rowman & Littlefield International, 2014).

Chapter 2

The State in the International Legal Order*

Alexander Filippov

As any other political notion, the modern concept of State is associated with certain primary intuitions. Their primacy is relative. They can vary, depending on the era, the language, the knowledge of geography one received at school, as well as the events from the news media. Something that at some point in time seemed far from obvious starts to appear undeniable: through the process of slow consolidation, it becomes perceived as a discourse product. Therefore, transferring our experience onto the experience of the past eras would be a great mistake. Carl Schmitt characterized the term "State" as "a specified concept, related to a certain historical period."[1] Albeit now this idea seems commonplace, it still needs to be mentioned. Not only theoretically—in political philosophy and legal science—but also practically, such a state as is represented by modern geographical maps and school history textbooks has emerged rather recently and may not last long.[2] Neither theory nor intuition can be relied upon with certainty. Even those who have common intuitions may interpret the theory of the state differently. However, members of the same discursive community may hold opposing intuitions: they may operate with the same concepts, but given that every one of them has an idiosyncratic life experience, the same notion references different background knowledge. Theoretical work would be more productive if in the very least it consisted in casting light on this state of affairs itself. I shall try to show below that in reasoning about the international legal position of a state, it is only in connection with these deeper intuitions that theoretical considerations have been able to be understood correctly until now.

1. STATE AS A TERRITORIAL CONTAINER

Today it seems obvious that every state (with very few exceptions) *is situated somewhere* and has a territory.[3] If we looked at its territory from the outside—which is not an easy task whose complexity is only being masked by our habit of using maps—we would see (let us repeat this) that the state as a country occupying a territory is a spatial form. However, the problem of the modern state is that its borders not only define the territory of a sovereign power but are also permeable to the movement of people, goods, and information flows. Borders are not insuperable barriers; instead, they mark a kind of discontinuity. They can be crossed under certain conditions and according to certain rules. The border is a way of organizing the transition. The intuition of a spatial form can be combined with the intuition of crossing the border, but if *it becomes intuitively clear* that the territory loses significance, then the concept of the state will change in the most radical way. Along with the intuition of a territory, some other categories that presuppose this intuition in one way or another also lose their meaning—in particular, the understanding of the international law, which is based on the recognition of the sovereignty of a state over its territory.

The space of the state belongs to our external experience as a receptacle of things within its borders, as well as the area of communications arranged by it, be it numbered roads, guarded bridges, postal stations, or—let us add more dimensions—the waters of ports and controlled airspace. We observe the form on isolated occasions when crossing protected and clearly marked borders, studying official statistics or referring to the data of *national sample* surveys. One way or another, directly—through the experience of the body—or indirectly—by focusing on what is enclosed within the borders of the state—we confirm the intuition of its spatial form, studied in history and geography classes. This evident notion also serves as a basis for the famous definition of the state given by Max Weber, who emphasizes that the territory of the state is its most prominent feature. Legitimate physical force is legitimate only within the borders of a state.

The self-evidence of the territorial form poses a threat. Brenner et al. rightly see here what they call following Agnew, a "territorial trap":

> First, the state is said to possess sovereign control over its territorial borders. This implies that mutually exclusive, territorially self-enclosed, and unitary state actors constitute the basic units of the global political system. Second, and consequently, the binary opposition between the "domestic" and the "foreign" is regarded as a fixed feature of the modem interstate system. This establishes the national scale as the ontologically necessary foundation for modem political life. And, third, the state is conceived as a static, timeless territorial "container" that encloses economic and political processes.[4]

However, despite criticism of such views, the authors continue to argue: "In its narrow sense state space refers to the spatialities of the state itself, regarded as an ensemble of juridico-political institutions and regulatory capacities grounded in the territorialization of political power. . . . In the modern inter-state system, territoriality operates not merely as a principle of internal geographical enclosure, but also as the foundational organizational principle of the entire system of geopolitical interaction on a global scale."[5] However, especially for those whom Zygmunt Bauman called "the global elite" (they move around the world, work in international organizations and transnational corporations, deal with the information exchange and the circulation of financial flows, etc.), it is equally intuitively clear that the importance of local entities and state borders is diminishing. No great effort is required to describe the general idea: the territorial state alternately recedes into the background and reappears as a force greater than all the agents of globalization.[6]

The fundamental distinction that makes it possible to work with the traditionally understood principle of territoriality is the distinction between the internal and the external. A state in the narrow sense—a container state—can contain something inside because its boundaries separate the inside from what lies outside of it. In this precise, narrow sense, the aspect of space distinguishes the internal and the external. In the everyday view, this distinction is symbolized, for example, by city walls or separation lines drawn on solid ground, boundaries, and wire fences. Recently published in the world media, the photo of a seesaw built on the border between the United States and Mexico clearly demonstrates the merits of the case: children's teeter-totter is arranged by installing wooden boards in between the bars of the border wall. The children are on both sides of the border—they can enjoy a fleeting friendship, which the border should not interfere with. A sociologist could study this friendly or family-like interaction in exact accordance with Ferdinand Tönnies's old concept of community (*Gemeinschaft*) as something organic—based on affection rather than rational calculation or agreement—inseparable, and, at any rate, questioning the state. However, this installation also confirms the exact opposite of its humanistic pathos. In fact, these children physically reside in two different container states—what is considered the internal by one is the external for the other, along with the unity that arose between them despite the bars.[7] The evident notion of a connecting community coexists with the evidence of a divisive state. In its territory, the state has the ability to more firmly connect people together: it divides to connect. The state cannot guarantee solidarity within its territory, but it can divide and distribute the people's bodies according to their attainability.

It is here that I would like to make one important digression. I write these lines in Moscow, in early April 2020, during a global epidemic. It has already become commonplace now and is repeated here by some of my coauthors that the pandemic destroyed the global world and led to a new strengthening of the state. Neither one nor the other seem obvious to me. The epidemic, as we know it now, has only become possible in the global world, albeit it made it strange enough for those accustomed to free circulation of human living bodies. Coronavirus has become so widespread those who cross borders in the usual way, that is, to the elite of globalization, as well as to tourists, to seasonal migrant workers, and to many others, to all those who used previously to be seen as evidences of the simple fact: "borders will disappear." It is not true: the borders matter! But they matter only as much as the old concept of state territory can work under the new conditions. There are no state borders for the animal carriers of the virus, but of course this is not the case for the humans. Because the virus is not visible, the states might not be adequate to deal with it, and be strengthening only in a restricted way, as they can only deal with what is visible. States themselves have become more visible just in those areas in which they can be visible at all: state sovereignty extends primarily to bodies-in-space, since they are visible to state optics. A person as a citizen should be present in the territory of his or her state. This is most often the case: states or sub-state units (districts, cities, and territories) build walls, declare quarantine, take obligations with respect to the bodies of their citizens only while trying to get rid of everyone else. In some ways, citizenship is more pronounced than health or illness. The new plague is characterized by a long incubation period, so that a seemingly healthy person would be seen as potentially dangerous, possibly sick. A decision on his or her being dangerous or safe is a decision of an expert authorized by the state (or another, state-like territorial authority). This is why all that belongs to political space must be studied in detail.

Let us examine the intuition of spatiality more closely. The space of the state is the medium in which the borders are drawn. The internal, the external, and the boundary between them are found in the same medium. More precisely, the internal, having become the internal, becomes radically different from the external, but continues to be dialectically related to it, for otherwise the division between the external and the internal by their common border would not be possible. Not only should the medium allow for a boundary to be drawn, but, once drawn, the boundary should also preserve the medium and allow *to perceive* the distinction between the internal and the external. The medium should be dense, with lasting traces and accessible ways of drawing and preserving the border. What the natural environment does not offer, the humans make up with their efforts.

Beginning his large study on the history of the law of nations, Carl Schmitt wrote: "The solid ground of the earth is delineated by fences, enclosures, boundaries, walls, houses, and other constructs. Then, the orders and orientations of human social life become apparent. Then, obviously, families, clans, tribes, estates, forms of ownership and human proximity, also forms of power and domination, become visible."[8] As for the sea, the situation is quite different: "The sea knows no such apparent unity of space and law, of order and orientation. . . . On the sea, fields cannot be planted and firm lines cannot be engraved. Ships that sail across the sea leave no trace. . . . The sea is free. According to recent international law, the sea is not considered to be state territory, and should be open equally to all for three very different spheres of human activity: fishing, peaceful navigation, and the conduct of war."[9] Schmitt's binding the law to space is connected with the opposition of the two elements: the land with visible boundaries and the sea where the boundaries are not visible, and therefore there are no forms to contemplate. Of course, Schmitt did not overlook the limited applicability of this opposition. In his earlier book *Land and Sea*, he says from the start that the existence of man cannot be called either completely terrestrial or completely marine, "man is not a creature wholly conditioned by his medium."[10] And yet there is that original persuasiveness of an intuition: in the sea, just like in the air, there can be drawn only an imaginary boundary.[11] Certainly, it can be indicated on maps, defined by agreements, and detected by equipment. Despite all the advances in modern technology, the issue of territorial waters or airspace violation is still one of the most complex and controversial ones. The tangible and the imaginary, as well as the undoubted and the conventional are still very different.

Impenetrability, the complete or partial separation of the internal from the external, is metaphorically transferred from territories to other media and affects the logic, in general, and the logic of thinking about the state, in particular.[12] The difference of the media in itself is not critical. On modern maps, states border each other,[13] and even if part of the border is conditionally at sea and is disputed, this does not entail a complete rejection of the intuition of "territory." The firm land—historically, perhaps—is partially where the idea of the container state stems from, and in our time it is merely the optimal way of visualizing it. But the construction of space as the medium most suitable for a stationary container is also a historical fact; it has not always been this way, and nothing confirms this better than the history of frontiers—not lines, but boundary regions.[14]

A few decades before Schmitt, Georg Simmel attempted to create the first project of a sociology of space. In an article written in 1903, he introduced several important concepts. One of them is the "exclusivity of space" (*Ausschließlichkeit des Raumes*). Based on Kant, Simmel wrote that each part of space is unique not because of any special qualities but simply because it is different from all other parts. This uniqueness is transferred onto those objects that are found in the space, so that the more important the spatiality of an object in the practical sense, the more significant its uniqueness.

> This applies especially to land, which is the condition for fulfilling and fructifying the three-dimensional quality of space for our purposes. . . . According to their entire sociological form, certain types of association can only be realized in such a way that there is no room for a second one within the spatial area that one of its formations occupies. In contrast, with others, a certain number all identical sociologically can fulfill the same expanse because, as it were, they are mutually permeable. Since they possess no inner relationship to space they cannot become involved in spatial collisions. The only example that completely coincides with the first type of association is the state.[15]

Simmel often intermingles the philosophical, geographical, and sociological understanding of space, but even here the spatial is transferred onto the social, the solid ground is seen as a space most suitable for "the exclusivity," and the state is a form that embodies this exclusivity of space to the greatest extent. This means, Simmel explains, that two states cannot exist simultaneously in the same territory, whereas other forms of connotations can be interpenetrable because of being connected to the space in a different, nonexclusive way. Simmel tried to balance out the arguments that placed too much emphasis on space with others that emphasized the importance of human activity. He said that if two groups are enclosed and do not interact with each other, being located in different places, the space between them is "practically speaking, nothing." But it can acquire meaning once they start using it for meetings and interactions. Instead of merely transferring its specificity to social forms, space also gains significance from the social perspective.

In order not to fall into the "trap of territoriality," we shall not reason about this relationship too simplistically. The state as a territorial entity occupies *its place exclusively*. This means that in the territory of a state there is no place for another one, even though a territory of one state may have multiple places organized in accordance with different principles. There is no contradiction in stating that there can be several towns in the territory of one state, with several shopping malls located in the territory of a single town, and with several events taking place simultaneously in the territory of a stadium. What we do each time is specify what meaning the term territory conveys and what it means "to be in it." But applied to the state, the concept of territoriality signifies the exclusivity aspect, which coincides with the primary intuition.

2. THE EXTERNALITY OF INTERNATIONAL LAW

For the study of this subject, international law is of particular interest, as it seems to challenge the logic of distinguishing between the internal and the external, the territorial status and sovereignty of the state. On the one hand, the legal norms contain the rules of solidarity, subordination, and procedure; the general distinction between the legal and the nonlegal for those who live within the state, is established by the people, who grant themselves a constitution. On the other hand, these norms cannot be created arbitrarily by the sovereign, whether individual or collective, but are regarded as the expression of the universal in law.[16] As long as law is considered in accordance with the old scheme of *ius naturale—ius gentium—ius civile*, this does not present a problem, as outside the legal regulations of polity there is an indefinite area of the general idea of law that is not thought of as a special space or territory of universal law. *Ius naturale*—the natural law—is not localized, it concerns the whole world, and this is how the cosmic order is referred to in some philosophical interpretations. *Ius gentium*—the law of peoples—stands for the commonality or similarity of the forms of different peoples' social life, who also have their own institutions of civil life—*ius civile*. Serious theoretical problems in this area emerge with the appearance of *ius inter gentes*[17]—that is, international law—arising as a result of agreements between countries that do not recognize any sovereign over them.

If the state is sovereign and if the border of the state is the border of its rule of law, does not this mean that the norms are just as enclosed within the state—contained in it as in a container—like its citizens? It seems quite impossible: the norm is not an object and cannot be located within material boundaries,[18] not to mention that for theoretical philosophy the idea of an empty container space is now unacceptable. But also for practical philosophy, the limitation of space is of key importance. When a person performs an action, they recognize the consequences of these actions in a certain horizon accessible to contemplation. Committing rightful actions, respecting the laws, entering into alliances with other people, the person does it *somewhere*, and the place of committing the right, legitimate actions is determined by the boundaries of communication that are practically available to him. The modern state sets the rules of action in the territory where it can, according to Weber, force obedience to the rules through legitimate violence. The proportion of national and international jurisdiction is precisely what makes it possible to estimate the actual force of law in a certain territory. The relative weakness of international law points to the priority of the state; the relatively greater strength of international law signifies the state's retreating.[19] Constitutions highlight the point of enclosure: the rules lie within the state not as objects but as guidelines for resident citizens. However, in that case, law is not recognized as *the* law—it becomes a temporary, contingent decision, which not only can be radically changed by a new decision of the sovereign will but also does not provide a ground for treaties and mutual understanding with other sovereign nations. As an exclusive legislator, the sovereign knows no other sovereign above himself or herself, and does not recognize any of the other sovereigns' rights but one: no one can establish different rules in their territories without conquering them. International law as external coercion (coercion itself comes from powerful agents, but they act in the name of law) denies the simple logic of sovereignty. The rules of international law do not owe their significance to a sovereign decision—that is, they cannot be superior to it—but they are universal and independent from the sovereign will, which is the characteristic feature of law. International law lives longer than sovereign state law; it is autonomous in relation to each nation that recognizes it and provides grounds for mutual understanding and agreements between different peoples.

This is easily illustrated by historical examples. Vattel, one of the classics of modern international law, reasoned in the following way: "The law of nations is the law of sovereigns. It is principally for them and for their ministers that it ought to be written."[20] It might seem that in this case we are dealing with instructions for sovereigns, but this is contrary to the overall course of reasoning. Vattel explains that "the entire nation, whose common will is but the result of the united wills of the citizens, remains subject to the laws of nature, and is bound to respect them in all her proceedings."[21] But the laws of nature, as we have already seen, are not, in the precise sense of the word, laws that would on their own oblige states *from without* to do anything. By reiterating repeatedly that states are free, sovereign, equal, and *thus* have immutable obligations, he merely outlines the way of connecting the internal and the external, and international and domestic laws in the absence of external political coercion. Nations are *independent* and free, yet they are "bound to observe the laws of that society which nature has established between them; and so far bound, that, when any one of them violates those laws, the others have a right to repress her."[22] It is not that this legally determines the normality and justice of war. In regard to the distinction between the internal and the external, there is a whole array of interesting problems arising at once. Sovereignty and borders are connected with territory, and if no external force can interfere in internal affairs, then, after all, the (in fact, an European) war actually takes place on someone else's territory, while the right of war turns out to be the right of intervention and violation of the border. This, however, does not extend into the area of current state law regulations. A century later, Johann Caspar Bluntschli, when justifying the science of international law, apparently presents a similar argument. On the one hand, all states are sovereign; on the other hand, their sovereignty is limited because otherwise they would behave toward other states as they please. The unity of the human race should not be understood as a denial of sovereignty, and international law should not be concerned with what happens *within* states—in particular, in the area of human rights. In the future, Bluntschli concedes, it may be possible in some cases to intervene in internal affairs if there is a violation of human rights by a state.²³ He sees an important exception to his rule of sovereignty in the prohibition of the slave trade, that is, in the recognition that slavery is contrary to the general sense of justice of mankind.²⁴ Bluntschli's most important concept is the one of "civility." Humanity, states, European countries, and sometimes Asian countries are called civilized (*"civilisirt"*). It is the common opinion and the general attitude of civilized countries that not a single state could resist to. Bluntschli was one of the first in the nineteenth century to overcome the tendency to represent civilized peoples as primarily European, and the international law of civilized peoples as predominantly European.²⁵ Despite the expanding circle of "civilized peoples," it required a lot of time to include *the whole* of humanity. During World War I, Liszt wrote about "the common culture and beliefs," which would over time allow to consider more and more people as civilized (for Liszt, all the participants of the Second Peace Conference in 1907 fell into the category of almost civilized).²⁶ In the standard textbook, which is still used in its modernized form, the term "civilized" becomes purely technical and as such passes into the modern vocabulary.²⁷ It is used today in the Statute of the International Court of Justice.²⁸ With the exception of a few unrecognized states and territories with uncertain status, all contemporary states are members of the United Nations (UN), and all of them are considered "civilized" and sovereign. This is an unprecedented situation in the world history that there is merely nothing outside the system of sovereign states²⁹: the latter is the only external element, in relation to which the states' rules are internal.

Thus, on the one hand, it is recognized that there exist the active agents of international law—states. They are sovereign in two senses: those of supreme power within and of the independence from other states without. States can be civilized, and civility is determined through some universal measure, but it is not a legal or political term. Civility is concerned with humanity and values. Moreover, such considerations always imply the existence of a universal community, which is regarded as something higher and more positive than any political unity.³⁰ This point is complex and controversial. Brierly believed that Vattel's continued influence "has been a disaster for international law. By teaching that the 'natural' state of nations is an independence which does not admit the existence of a social bond between them, he made it impossible to explain or justify their subjection to law; yet their independence is no more 'natural' than their interdependence."³¹ Nevertheless, Brierly acknowledged the relative weakness of the international legal system. He wrote that here the problem is deeper than the mere issue of sanctions for violations; strengthening sanctions cannot make international law more effective. *Within* a state, the imperative character of law is felt so strongly that in *civilized* states obedience to it has become habitual. "If the imperative character of international law were equally strongly felt, the institution of effective sanctions would easily follow. The spiritual cohesion of international society remains weak, and as long as this weakness endures we can expect a weak and primitive system of law."[32] Enumerating those areas in which state is rather free from obligations to other states, he wonders whether international law has failed. No, Brierly says. In the areas in which states have agreed to comply with it, it performs its functions perfectly. Thus, he again comes to the conclusion that *civilized* countries have agreed to respect the law, and their civility is only a meaningful guarantee that agreements can be interpreted not just as arbitrary conventions, which anyone can conclude with varying success, but as conventions in the area of *law*. However, he also provides most alarming ideas of such kind. Citizens cannot switch their legal consciousness automatically to international law. States may enter into agreements that are legally binding on them as parties to treaties, but which may not necessarily be perceived as legal from within states. They will have the force of coercion but not the imperative character of law.

That is why one of the influential international legal concepts proposed at the end of the nineteenth century by Heinrich Triepel retains heuristic value. His most famous work is the book *International Law and National Law*.[33] German lawyers, wrote Triepel a quarter of a century after Bluntschli, are not very inclined to recognize international law—this especially concerns legal practitioners. First, it seems to them that this matter does not concern them at all, and second, the soil of international law is too shaky, so it is better to stay away from it. However, it is impossible to accept this point of view: all law is interrelated; only the internal law is more coherent than external law. And since international law exists, no matter how relatively weak it may be, it is necessary to study its sources and the mechanism. Here, however, we are beset by the difficulties already known. Law is created by will—that is, "the declaration that something must be law."[34] This will is *the source of law*, which in the case of international law cannot be the will of one state. And since there is no superstate that would create a law for all, the only solution that remains is making a *contract* among states. But making a contract is not an easy task. After all, no matter what the contract is, the wills of the parties tend to be opposite to each other. One wants the other to do something—but is that what the other wants? No, and with all the mutual complementarity of the wills of the parties to the contract, a single will does not emerge out of it. Therefore, it is not a contract but an *agreement* (*Vereinbarung*) that should be considered the true source of law.[35] Here, too, many persons declare their will, but the difference is that here the will of each of them is completely identical to the will of the other.[36] Therefore, under a contract, everyone seeks to satisfy *their interests*, whereas, under an agreement, it is common and identical interests that they pursue. But where does the binding force of agreements come from? Anticipating many future discussions, Triepel observes that the grounds for the legal significance of law cannot be purely legal. For those who did not participate in the agreements, no international law is significant. It follows, among other things, first, that Triepel also adheres to the idea of a *community* of nations that agree with each other,[37] and second, that the problem of the ratio between the internal and the external emerges here in the terms that are also topical today. During Triepel's time, the issue of subordinating the national legislation to international law and the automatic adjustment of the national legislation to the external obligations and agreements of a state was not yet present in the form it subsequently took. The issue of complying with the assumed obligations was much more acute. The recognition of the equality of the parties to the treaty and the recognition of the possibility of coercion on the part of some states in relation to others could not be reconciled, especially if it concerned the blame for the outbreak of war or for the acts committed in times of war. Triepel solved the problem strategically. The agreements, according to him, are of a long-term nature; they concern such subjects in which it is possible to achieve the harmonization between the internal and the external so that from within the contract does not seem illegal and unjustly coercive. Already after the end of World War I, it was clear that, for example, from within Germany, the Treaty of Versailles did not seem fair or legally binding. Triepel was therefore among the German lawyers who did not approve of the treaty.

3. PRACTICES, EMPIRES, AND CONSTITUTIONS

Let us now look at the matter from a different angle.

The term "civility" used to speak of the states that are parties to the treaties has been reduced to be merely a technical one precisely because, with hindsight, international law appears to be imperialist. Examining the issue of the post–World War II decolonization in relation to international law, Anthony Anghie observes: "The challenge to universality posed by the new states arose, then, not because of differences in culture, but differences in interest: the difference between the developed and developing states."[38] This is a significant observation. The word "empire" applied to the decolonization processes could be misleading. When Carl Schmitt speaks of the "Res Publica Christiana" as the unity of order and orientation, he does not refer to empires which would later be accused of harboring an ideology of superiority over "uncivilized peoples."[39] It is only for a short time that the Holy Roman Empire could be regarded as a kind of polity. Rather, such empire is a special kind of legal space within which even wars are possible.[40] Speaking of the "imperialism" of this empire is completely meaningless, unlike the later empires, which the sovereign states of Europe evolved into. Nowadays, this point of view is hard to defend. Let us follow Robert Jackson's arguments. He believes that the division of countries into civilized and uncivilized continues the tradition of Christian states' opposing the rest of the world,[41] but at the same time he views Res Publica Christiana in a very different way than Schmitt: it "was the way that religious and secular authorities justified their conduct. It was their mental map and their discourse of authority: the theological-political framework in terms of which they thought of themselves and spoke of their world."[42] There is nothing spatial in this scheme—the principle of territoriality appears later, after the Peace of Westphalia, when "the law of nations became clarified, in part, out of those European imperial endeavors, in response to important issues such as rights of territorial acquisition and freedom of the seas."[43] It is at this time that the idea of territorial sovereignty "arises from the reality that states are earth-bound organizations in the most fundamental sense. They could not exist without bordered territory which is, so to speak, the foundation upon which they rest and the spatial sphere within which they exercise authority."[44] Historical research of this kind is tendentious in one important respect. Since the idea of territorial sovereignty and the international legal regulations that are associated with it *did emerge*, it may just as well disappear or lose its strength or meaning. In fact, this is what Jackson's argument boils down to. If we assume that people are sovereign in their territory, then in the modern world it will be possible to pose the following question: "Who are the self-determining people and where is their sovereign territory?"[45] All the practice of demarcation and drawing borders in the modern world show that territorial borders are of exceptional importance—therefore, they will remain, unless states agree otherwise. However, a mutual external recognition of borders may conflict with the principle of sovereignty, "when people are no longer prepared to underwrite the doctrine that every political community must possess a government that is both superior to all other authorities in the country, and independent of all foreign governments. At some time in the future, probably later rather than sooner, state sovereignty will be abandoned."[46] Prospects of this kind are related to human rights, in favor of which, for instance, humanitarian interventions can be carried out—finding it hard to maintain balance, given that both human rights and states' borders are internationally recognized. Ultimately, this reasoning inevitably leads to concluding that in the era of globalization, other forces, instead of the state, can and should act as a police regulator. In the prospect of global peace and global law, both territoriality and sovereignty are relativized.

Even though arranged differently, other historical accounts aim in the same direction. In her book *A Search for Sovereignty*, Lauren Benton also starts with the description of the spatial environment: only instead of the land, the environment is primarily the sea. It is with the boundlessness of the seas that she relates the history of European "legal practices." "It was even more intriguing that the mariners' perceptions of the sea as a space of interconnected passage ways closely matched ideas about the extension of imperial jurisdiction into ocean space along narrowbands imaginatively marked by the passage of ships."[47] Without limiting herself to the seas, Benton writes that

> Empires did not cover space evenly but composed a fabric that was full of holes, stitched together out of pieces, a tangle of strings. Even in the most paradigmatic cases, an empire's spaces were politically fragmented; legally differentiated; and encased in irregular, porous, and sometimes undefined borders. Although empires did lay claim to vast stretches of territory, the nature of such claims was tempered by control that was exercised mainly over narrow bands, or corridors, and over enclaves and irregular zones around them.[48]

This view allows her to dispose of the historical material differently and, without generally denying the problem of linking territoriality with sovereignty, to revise the usual way of transition from natural law to positive law. She argues that what happened in reality differs from what we are used to imagining after reading the books of political philosophers,[49] historians, and legal theorists—what happened is the movement of people and "legal practices": "Legal cultures traveled with imperial officials, merchants, sailors, soldiers, sojourners, settlers, captives, and even pirates—agents in empire who positioned themselves as subjects and often as representatives of distant sovereigns while interacting with locals and representatives of competing empires."[50] As a result of this transition, "Europeans far from home reenacted legal rituals as they remembered them and imperfectly reconstructed legal practices and arguments."[51]

All of this certainly does not mean that a container state and the territories' borders are not at all in the focus. The only question is how to "merge geographic discourse and law." If we return to the question of the boundary between the internal and the external, which was discussed earlier, we will learn that

> most boundaries are porous and many are contested, and states cannot consistently enforce laws to regulate activities across and within borders. And as we have seen, territory plays tricks. Mere patches of regulated land may appear to signify claims to vast holdings, while integral "sovereign" space may fracture into many odd-shaped pieces. The problem is not just that tumultuous times and distant realms produce unmanageable complexity. Political space everywhere generates irregularities: polities and subpolities secure exemptions from legislation, jurisdictions guard their autonomy, and subjects and citizens seek to expand or protect extraterritorial legal rights.[52]

In this part, Benton's research is directed against Schmitt and Agamben, who in his own way builds on Schmitt's arguments. According to Benton, Schmitt contrasted too sharply the area of European law and the area that, from the point of view of Europeans, at first was completely outside law.

And this implies a too simple idea of the structure of the new global order. "A European preference for describing the global order as an interstate system centered in Europe does not make this formulation either useful as theory or accurate as historical narrative."[53] Thus, the permeability of the borders, the transfer of legal practices, and so forth are not isolated instances in the history. "Subjecthood and citizenship featured as fluid categories permitting the spatially irregular extension of legal authority."[54] This helps to understand better even the modern transfers: "for creating military commissions at Guant´anamo Bay, and the choice of an island garrison, reveal some continuities with the processes examined in this book. The transfer of elements of sovereignty, including negotiations over a status akin to bare sovereignty in such places as Iraq and Afghanistan, points in the same direction."[55]

The simplest solution lies on the surface. The old logic does not work, and neither does the obvious distinction between the internal and the external. Goods, people, ideas, news, cultural objects, and educational standards cross the borders of states in such volumes that could not be envisioned in the previous eras. That is why in the recent decades the end of state has been discussed more often than before.

Perhaps some most recent discussions can add a few additional considerations regarding this topic. Of great importance, in particular, is the discussion of the so-called constitutionalization, the definitions of which are not always clear to non-lawyers. It is apparent that this concerns constitution and its changing role but not solely the state structure. As Günther Teubner writes:

> The current debate is marked by false tabula-rasa assumptions regarding the non- existence of constitutional norms in social sub-areas, not only within the nation state, but also in the transnational sphere. While modern constitutionalism was able to take root in nearly all nation states, it was weakened, so it is said, by the increasing transfer of state responsibilities from the nation state to new transnational organizations, regimes, and networks. At this transnational level, however, a constitutional emptiness is believed to prevail. And it is only against the background of this supposedly constitution- free area of globality that the argument arises as to whether constitutionalism is at an end or is in fact experiencing a renaissance.[56]

In the chapter opening the work of three lawyers, Jan Klabbers writes: "Constitutionalism is the philosophy of striving towards some form of political legitimacy, typified by respect for, well, a constitution. . . . To conclude, then, constitutionalization is, to us, a process, inspired by constitutionalist thought."[57] Constitutionalization, he continues, responds to the modern phenomena of globalization, which entail the emergence of multiple, often unrelated, but at the same time hierarchical orders. It "promises unity and order: it promises to unify the globe by authoritatively imposing hierarchy between vertical regimes and between norms all vying for prominence. Constitutionalism promises to settle the score once and for all, by giving either *jus cogens* priority, or trade, or human rights, or *erga omnes* principles. Here, then, constitutionalization comes in armed with a clear set of normative commitments, which displays that at least in this guise, constitutionalization is an intensely political process."[58] The essential problem is that it is not possible to point to a central body that can be unambiguously qualified as an instrument of constitutionalization. None of the international organizations or the international agreements fully corresponds to this concept. However, the main perspective for considering this is the global one: global society and problems of its constitution. How does this relate to the problem of *state* sovereignty?

Anne Peters explores this issue in the same book. She begins with provisions that are similar to those already discussed in the first part of this chapter:

> From a constitutionalist perspective, the *differentia specifica* of states, their sovereignty, is a legal concept and as such embedded in international law. This view was present in nuce in the infancy of our discipline. Initially, public international law was conceived as natural law, applied to states, which were depicted as being in the state of nature (*jus naturae et gentium*). Because natural law was considered as eternal and immutable, this conception entailed the acceptance of legal boundaries for state action.[59]

With the development of the concept of sovereignty, the external, restrictive property of natural law began to decrease. "Pushed to its extreme, the concept of sovereignty as *auctoritas* or power led to the idea that the sovereign was by definition above the law, and therefore legally unbindable. This view was correlated with the assertion that public international law was not really law, because it lacked sanctions."[60] Later, departing from the understanding that the sovereignty of states, that is, their independence from each other, is possible only within the system of international law, more complex conclusions were made—namely, the assertion of the responsibility of sovereigns. Peters writes this during a period when the issue of whether interventions to prevent humanitarian disasters were needed was widely debated at the UN.

> Constitutionalists welcome the re-characterization of sovereignty as implying a responsibility to protect (R2P), because the concept of R2P takes human needs as the starting point and shifts the focus from states' rights to states' obligations (or responsibilities), which is a typical constitutionalist concern. The sovereign's responsibility exists for somebody (a principal) and for something (the tasks to be performed). These tasks extend in two directions (external and internal duties): the state must externally respect the sovereignty of other states, and must internally protect its inhabitants against avoidable catastrophes, such as famine, mass murder, and mass rape.[61]

This entails obvious problems as the R2P concept, very popular in the early 2000s (which the International Commission on Intervention and State Sovereignty worked with in particular), is both productive and dangerous. It is productive because it implies universal respect for the right to life of individuals, and it is dangerous because humanitarian intervention can become a precedent for the violation of sovereignty. Respect for the sovereignty of others implies noninterference, while protection of own citizens does not encompass the rights to protect foreign citizens. Peters continues by stating that the way out can be found only along the way of the authorization of humanitarian intervention by the UN Security Council on the condition of unanimity of its permanent members. Her argument in this regard is of particular interest:

> The ongoing process of rendering sovereigns responsible is a cornerstone of the current transformation of international law into a constitutionalized system.[62]

We see here a new attempt to establish a complex balance of the external and the internal. Human rights do not come to the state from the outside. They are, so to speak, already inside, and it can only be a question of their scope and the way they are handled, given that "the constitutionalist approach has offered a vocabulary to claim and design improved procedures which move further in the direction of rule-of-law based procedural standards, fair trial guarantees, and review mechanisms,"[63] whereas "the current trend is one of increasing the options for individuals to enforce international law either in international or in domestic forums. Constitutionalists welcome it."[64] This affects not only states themselves but also other international actors, and the rights of the individual in question go even beyond human rights (e.g., the right to consular assistance abroad). In other words, there is a logic of legal reasoning that somehow leads to the idea of unity, including the legal unity of international society and international law, and there is what Teubner clearly writes about, albeit from a different theoretical perspective:

> Yet empirical evidence and theories of world society tell a different story. Within the subsystems of world society—in international politics, in the global economy, in law, and in science—central co-ordination authorities have a feeble presence. The co-ordination between function systems is weaker still. . . . Nor in global law is any hierarchical authority visible that has formulated the 'redemptive narrative' to solve constitutional disputes . . . by destroying the identity of a legal order in favour of the higher principles of another legal order.[65]

In a later work, addressing the problem of fragmentation of international law, Peters writes:

> A legal order is present only when norms refer to each other (ordered norms). But legal order means not only ordered law but also order through law. These two

dimensions are mutually reinforcing: The normative pull of international law is fortified by its stringency and consistency. Understanding this interrelationship means understanding why consistency is particularly important for international law (more than for domestic law): because its normative power is more precarious. . . . What is at stake in fragmentation is unity, harmony, cohesion, order, and—concomitantly—the quality of international law as a truly normative order.[66]

Among other things, this means that sovereign states (or the ones that are gradually losing sovereignty but have not yet parted with it) are opposed, in fact, not by a different and higher order but by something less concrete. Perhaps the new state of international law is exactly the way Benton describes it: not the next, more extensive "container" of norms but a realm of practices, habits, private (individual, not universal) decisions, or even regulatory systems that are generally stronger than states.

4. CONCLUSION

But do the arguments presented earlier mean that the issue of state is indeed solved in a new way and the solution is final? We could assume, coming back to the beginning of this chapter, that the porosity of borders (porosity for the bats, cats, and viruses) and the existence of separate paths and regions that do not fit into the simple logic of the internal and the external do not speak against the basic intuition of the state form but only indicate its relative weakening. We see that the understanding of the "container state" and the space in which it is located is changing from era to era. We see that the spaces of legal regulation are complex and, most importantly, they are arranged differently—at the same time—for different observers and participants. The most difficult here is not to identify and confirm the main trend but to keep in view several trends, some of which could not even be named in the framework of this chapter. New types of regulation emerge constantly, relativizing state borders and rendering meaningless appeals to international law in its usual forms—but only in part. The new concept of law is based on the flexibility and diversity of regions and flows of transition. The old concept is not only concerned with tradition but also implies the willingness to restore borders and to mobilize the population, while still considering the traditional internal space as the main legal and political imperative.[67]

Generally speaking, the fact that states may be assigned additional responsibilities although they may have less rights is not, as we have seen, such an alien idea from the lawyers' point of view. On the contrary, lawyers (not in their entirety but a significant number of them) are in support of the complex of ideas by which a state can be held legally liable under the norms that it did not create, and on the grounds and procedure that it accepts only in a most general form. Lawyers may be delegated by the state to international organizations, but this does not mean that their loyalty to the state and to the interpretation of law that corresponds to the state's interests will always be stronger than their loyalty to the international law corporation which contributes to the generation of new laws and claims authority in the interpretation of old laws. It is obvious, however, that a state can be an efficient vehicle or means of implementing new law only insofar as its existence does not run counter to the rules of solidarity of the civil community. This civil community is the core of the people that constitutes the state's area of responsibility. Its formation goes back to the era of the Modern European political philosophy when the classical concept of sovereignty also emerged. This is the source of the dynamic contradiction that Günther Teubner writes about in detail, drawing on Niklas Luhmann: law and the state need each other as external guarantors. Without law that transcends the state, the state is doomed to consider only its own positive law as law, cannot justify a higher "law of law" and thus risks turning into a permanent, systematic arbitrary rule. It is necessary that the production of law go through *political and legal* procedures:

> Politics transfers to the law the task of constraining unconstrained sovereignty by means of legal procedures—by means of organization as the inner bond and of fundamental rights for constraining arbitrariness towards the outside. This takes the edge off the paradox of politics. . . . But politics' bond with the law only becomes bearable when the law-making machinery in turn guarantees politics a decisive influence on law-making. Only then can the state constitution drive the intricate relation between law and politics so far that a legal secondary codification of politics emerges. The rule of law is extended to cover all political events and thus treat every act of power as an act of law.[68]

Therefore, we return to the beginning. There seem to exist some limits to a further diminishing of state sovereignty, as well as the signs of an ongoing opposite trend. In any case, there are countries that are trying to impose this opposite trend: Trump's United States, Putin's Russia, and Xi Jinping's China to a varying extent do assert their commitment to international law[69] but not a willingness to submit to its creators and interpreters in this sense. The idea of the rule of law calls up the question of power and decision and vice versa. So, for now, the territorial borders literally harden, and the old concept of sovereignty becomes applicable once again. Thus, the new meaning of state consists in reviving its old meaning.

NOTES

* This chapter was translated into English from Russian by Maria Afanasyeva.

1. Cf. Carl Schmitt, "Staat als konkreter, an eine geschichtliche Epoche gebundener Begriff," in: *Schmitt, C. Verfassungsrechtliche Aufsätze aus den Jahren*

1924–1954. Materialien zu einer Verfassungslehre (Berlin: Duncker & Humblot. 1954/58), S. 375–384.

2. In this regard, I would like to indicate from the start that I do not agree with Michael Marder's view on this as stated in his chapter 1 of the present book. He considers state as a "junction for various categories drawn from Aristotle and Kant," and leaving aside the question of compatibility of categories, the question of compatibility of intuitions at once raises doubts. Certainly, general categories should be applicable to different phenomena that are historically distant from each other. However, here we come across a difficulty right away, as there is no reason to suppose that the categories of place and the intuitions associated with them are the same for the Greek poleis and a continental police state. This objection, however, does not alter the fact that we agree on something more important: space is crucial for reasoning about state.

3. I readily repeat what is said above in the Introduction: "The state is not just a monopolistic hold on violence, nor an embodied popular will, but it is the very cleavage, or juncture, between the administrative apparatus and the national sovereignty, between a head of state, or nation, and his or her impersonal staff and, inversely, between the specific official taxing you and the abstract impersonal unity on whose behalf he or she acts"; however, I cannot but emphasize that all of this only has sense if the state *is somewhere*, if it has its place in space.

4. Brenner, Neil, Jessop Bob, Jones Martin, and MacLeod Gordon (eds). *State/Space: A Reader* (New York: Wiley-Blackwell, 2003), p. 2.

5. Ibid., 7.

6. In this regard, see: Ran Hirschl, Ayelet Shachar, "Spatial Statism," *International Journal of Constitutional Law* 17.2 (2019): pp. 387–438. The authors provide a large overview of the concepts *against* the binding of the law to the territory of the state while at the same time showing that "there is little doubt that in some key respects, national sovereignty is diminishing. However . . . in a host of territory-related realms, state control may have transformed, but has definitely not disappeared" (436). This formula *reconciles* what is, in fact, found in a very precarious balance. We can only be partially satisfied with such an interim solution.

7. In her book *Walled States, Waning Sovereignties*, Wendy Brown collected many photographs representing modern walls and barriers. However, her intention is quite different: "What is also striking about these new barriers is that even as they limn or attempt to define nation-state boundaries, they are not built as defenses against potential attacks by other sovereigns, as fortresses against invading armies, or even as shields against weapons launched in interstate wars. Rather, while the particular danger may vary, these walls target nonstate trans-national actors—individuals, groups, movements, organizations, and industries. They react to transnational, rather than international relations and respond to persistent, but often informal or subterranean powers, rather than to military undertakings." Wendy Brown, *Walled States, Waning Sovereignties* (Cambridge, MA: MIT Press, 2010), p. 21.

8. Carl Schmitt, *The Nomos of the Earth in the International Law of the* Jus Publicum Europaeum, trans. G. L. Ulmen (New York: Telos Press, 2003), p. 42.

9. Ibid., 42 f.

10. Carl Schmitt, *Land and Sea*, trans. Simona Draghici (Washington, D.C.: Plutarch Press, 1997), p. 5.

11. After reading Schmitt's book *Land and Sea*, Alexander Kojève wrote to him that *"stratégiquement, « terre et mer » sont « dépassées » (aufgehoben), de manière hégélienne par « l'air » : mais on n'a jamais inventé de toute pièce une guerre [donc guerre = sol] comme quelque chose en l'air, et personne n'a plus envie « d'attaquer»"* (Correspondence 1999: 11). This remark follows the same logic: the solid and the firm are of particular significance for contemplation and action. Deleuze and Guattari's contrast of smooth and striated spaces partially helps to continue with this reasoning. The sea and air, like the steppe, through which nomads move without hindrance, are examples of smooth space [Gilles Deleuze and Felix Guattari. *A Thousand Plateaus: Capitalism and Schizophrenia*, trans. Brian Massumi (London: Athlone, 1987), p. 385]. The concept of "striated space" rather refers to a solid medium preserving traces of development: it has *passages*, it is paved with roads, it has forbidden zones, and the like.

12. "Above all, space seems to be the basic model for the development of logic. One learns about space from logic. Just as it is impossible to build a house where a house already stands, it must also be impossible to conceive of one house with the exact same properties of another. To the degree that logic expands in nonspatial relationships, the degree of freedom and control in fixing contradictions grows." Niklas Luhmann, *Social Systems* (Stanford, CA: Stanford University Press, 1995), p. 404, N 54. Here, Luhmann partly repeats Georg Simmel's argument about the exclusivity of space, to which we shall now turn, while at the same time laying the foundations for the opposite, nonterritorial interpretation of society.

13. We can say that the global space divided into state territories is in fact created by states or, in Henri Lefebvre's words, *produced* by them.

14. "Beside the land frontier there was a sea one too. It may be affirmed that the concept of frontier suits sea waters better than land: as a matter of fact, it is impossible to place boundary stones or metae there to distinguish what belongs to one or the other state; everything mingles and merges; the army corps continually advance or withdraw without finding a safe heaven there." In the vast spaces, there formed what the author calls "society of frontiers": "Sailors, pirates and privateers inhabited this liquid frontier, but these categories very often mingled, even though, at least theoretically, the difference between privateers and pirates was clear, at least within the European world." M. Pia Pedani, *The Ottoman-Venetian Border (15th–18th Centuries)* (Venice: Edizioni Ca' Foscari–Digital Publishing, 2017), pp. 27, 38.

15. Georg Simmel, *On Culture: Selected Writings*, ed. David Frisby and Mike Featherstone (London; New York: Sage, 1997), p. 139.

16. "The particularity of States becomes merely an accident of fact, as is their possible perversity, or their imperfection. For the modern State defines itself in principle as 'the rational and reasonable organization of a community': the only remaining particularity a community has is interior or moral (the spirit of a people), at the same time as the community is funneled by its organization toward the harmony of a universal (absolute spirit). The State gives thought a form of interiority, and thought gives that interiority a form of universality." Gilles Deleuze and Félix Guattari. *A Thousand Plateaus*, 372.

17. We recall that the term "*ius gentium*" existed in Roman law and the term "*ius inter gentes*" was introduced, as is widely believed, by Francisco de Vitoria in the sixteenth century (other sources name Richard Zouch, who lived in the next century, as the initiator of this approach to law). In this interpretation, "*ius gentium*" stands for the legal principles that are peculiar to different peoples; "*ius inter gentes*" refers to the regulations of relations between nations. See: W. G. Grewe, *The Epochs of International Law*, trans. and rev. M. Byers (Berlin, New York: Walter de Gruyter, 2000), p. 25 ff. Already in the next generation after Vitoria, F. Suárez was aware of "the dual meaning of *ius gentium*" and differentiated between *ius gentium inter se* (i.e., the international law itself) and *ius gentium intra se* (similar forms of civil law that can be found in all countries). See also: W. G. Grewe, "Vom europäischen zum universellen Völkerrecht. Zur Frage der Revision des europazentrischen Bildes der. Völkerrechtsgeschichte." *Zeitschrift für ausländisches öffentliches Recht und Völkerrecht* (ZaöRV) Bd. 42 (1982): S. 449–479. However, cf. the argument of Peter Haggermacher: "Vitoria had no intention whatsoever of anticipating Zouche's comprehensive presentation of *ius inter gentes* as a special interstate law." Peter Haggenmacher, "Sources in the Scholastic Legacy: Ius Naturae and Ius Gentium Revisited by Theologians," in: Jean d'Aspremont, Samantha Besson, with the assistance of Sévrine Knuchel (eds), *The Oxford Handbook on the Sources of International Law* (Oxford: Oxford University Press, 2017), Cit. pp. 41–65, 59.

18. Hans Kelsen in the *Pure Theory of Law* failed to provide a satisfactory solution to the problem. He pointed out that the rules of law can have a limited (for some space and time) effect, or it can be unlimited. But this way the borders are deprived of both legal status and significance. See: Hans Kelsen, *Reine Rechtslehre. Einleitung in die rechtswissenschaftliche Problematik*. Studienausgabe der 1. Auflage 1934. Hrsg. u. eingel. v. M. Jestaedt (Tübingen: Mohr (Siebeck), 1934/2008), S. 20–22. In this regard, the priority of international law over national law is not surprising—an idea, which Kelsen never abandoned. But this is not the priority of "a large container" over "a small container."

19. Here, the classic formulations of Hedley Bull can still come in useful: maintaining order in international relations does not always mean observing the rules, including the rules of international law. "We have also to recognise that forms of international order might exist in the future, and have existed in the past, without rules of international law. It is, I believe, one of the defects of our present understanding of world politics that it does not bring together into common focus those rules of order or coexistence that can be derived from international law and those rules that cannot but belong rather to the sphere of international politics." Hedley Bull, *The Anarchical Society: A Study of Order in World Politics*. 3rd ed. (New York: Columbia University Press, 2002), p. xxxiv. Having stated this, he clarifies: "This fundamental or constitutional principle of international order is presupposed in ordinary state conduct. . . . The principle is contained in a number of basic rules of international law. Thus it has been the dominant doctrine that states are the only or the principal bearers of rights and duties in international law; that they alone have the right to use force to uphold it; and that its source lies in the consent of states, expressed in custom or treaty" (Bull, *The Anarchical Society*, 65, 66). In these statements, the spirit of the age, which is

now often regarded as long and irrevocably gone, manifests itself. However, this is the most controversial aspect.

20. Emmerich de Vattel, *The Law of Nations, Or, Principles of the Law of Nature, Applied to the Conduct and Affairs of Nations and Sovereigns*, ed. B. Kapossy and R. Whatmore (Indianapolis, IN: Liberty Fund, 2008), 9.

21. Ibid., 68.

22. Ibid., 77.

23. See: Bluntschli, Johann Caspar. *Das moderne Völkerrecht der civilisirten Staten, als Rechtsbuch dargestellt* (Nördlingen: Beck, 1872), p. 20ff.

24. By that time it had already become a habitual component of political and legal rhetoric. Slaveholding was denounced as the "ultimate petty despotism" [Lauren Benton and Lisa Ford, *Rage for Order: The British Empire and the Origins of International Law, 1800–1850* (Cambridge, MA: Harvard University Press. 2016), p. 8]. Despotism was considered dangerous and contagious to the mother country.

25. See Alexander Orakhelashvili, "The Idea of European International Law." *The European Journal of International Law* 17.2 (2006): pp. 315–347, for more details and eloquent quotations from European jurists and perhaps overly harsh conclusions regarding the ideological nature of European international law. See also Markku Koskenniemi, *The Gentle Civilizer of Nations: The Rise and Fall of International Law 1870–1960* (Cambridge: Cambridge University Press, 2001). Koskenniemi considers the formation of the Institute of International Law in Ghent in 1873 to be the key event in the development of this new law and the community of its supporters—international lawyers. "Among other decisions, the Ghent meeting adopted a Statute for the institute Article 1 of which laid down as the purpose of the institute: '*De favoriser le progrès du droit international, en s'efforçant de devenir l'organe de la conscience juridique du monde civilisé*'." He also argues that the "legal consciousness of the civilized world" formula comes from Bluntschli, who developed the ideas of Carl von Savigny, his professor in the late 1820s of the nineteenth century in Berlin.

26. See: F. Liszt, *Das Völkerrecht. Systematisch dargestellt*. 10, umgearbeitete Aufl (Berlin: Springer. 1915), pp. 2, 8 ff.

27. See: James Leslie Brierly, *The Law of Nations: An Introduction to the International Law of Peace* (Oxford: Clarendon Press, 1928).

28. See http://legal.un.org/avl/pdf/ha/sicj/icj_statute_e.pdf. [Statute of the International Court of Justice (annexed to the UN Charter)], among the sources of international law the following are listed (Art. 38, 1c): "The general principles of law recognized by civilized nations." A standard textbook explains the term simply as follows: "'Civilized' should not be seen as a demeaning term; the Statute is merely referring to states that have reached an advanced state of legal development." Anthony Aust, *Handbook of International Law* (Cambridge: Cambridge University Press, 2005), p. 8, Fn 28.

29. Robert Jackson, *Sovereignty: Evolution of an Idea* (Cambridge: Polity Press, 2007), p. x.

30. This argument is also easily recognized in the famous reasoning of John Rawls, closer to our time, who contrasted "Society of Peoples" with sovereignty in its traditional understanding: "A difference between liberal peoples and states is that

just liberal peoples limit their basic interests as required by the reasonable. In contrast, the content of the interests of states does not allow them to be stable for the right reasons: that is, from firmly accepting and acting upon a just Law of Peoples." John Rawls, *The Law of Peoples: With the Idea of Public Reason Revisited* (Cambridge, MA: Harvard University Press, 1999), p. 29. Jackson rightly identifies "Society of Peoples" as "world society" [Jackson, *Sovereignty*, 158], whose members, ideally, know nothing about their nation, territory, and the like. It is not difficult to see how Rawls develops the concept of civility discussed above, showing its more subtle distinctions—"liberal peoples" and "nonliberal peoples," where the former tolerate that is "recognize these nonliberal societies as equal participating members in good standing of the Society of Peoples, with certain rights and obligations, including the duty of civility requiring that they offer other peoples public reasons appropriate to the Society of Peoples for their actions" (Rawls, *The Law of Peoples*, 59). It would be instructive enough to make a comparison between "world society" and "international society" *from this point of view*.

31. James Leslie Brierly and Andrew Clapham. *Brierly's Law of Nations: an Introduction to the Role of International Law in International Relations* (Oxford: Oxford University Press, 2014), p. 39.

32. Ibid., 81.

33. H. Triepel, *Völkerrecht und Landesrecht* (Leipzig: Hirschfeld, 1899). This book has been reprinted many times in different languages. H. Triepel, *Völkerrecht und Landesrecht. Unveränderter Nachdruck* (Meisenheim/Glan: Verlag Anton Hain, 1958). H. Triepel, *Droit international et droit interne* (Paris: Éditions Panthéon-Assas 1998).

34. Triepel, *Völkerrecht und Landesrecht*, 29.

35. Ibid., 50 ff.

36. Ibid., 52.

37. That is, he is one of those, says the modern researcher Roland Portmann, who considers state to be the only legal entity, while the individual is absorbed by it. "The origins of the basic propositions of the states-only conception of international legal personality, it is argued, rest in the view of the state as ahistorical fact entirely absorbing individuals and in the notion of law as an expression of state will." R. Portmann, *Legal Personality in International Law* (Cambridge: Cambridge University Press, 2010), p. 47.

38. Antony Anghie, *Imperialism, Sovereignty and the Making of International Law* (Cambridge: Cambridge University Press, 2004), p. 201.

39. See Anghie's above quoted book: "My argument . . . is that sovereignty was improvised out of the colonial encounter, and adopted unique forms which differed from and destabilized given notions of European sovereignty. As a consequence, Third World sovereignty is distinctive, and rendered uniquely vulnerable and dependent by international law" (ibid., 6) and on "the basic structures of colonialism . . . are reproduced in all the major schools of international jurisprudence: naturalism, positivism and pragmatism. . . . They all have served to reproduce colonial relations." (ibid., 195).

40. "The encompassing unity of the international law of medieval Europe was called res publica Christiana [Christian republic] and populus Christianus [Christian

people]. It had definite orders and orientations. Its nomos was determined by the following divisions. The soil of non-Christian, heathen peoples was Christian missionary territory; it could be allocated by papal order to a Christian prince for a Christian mission. . . . The soil of Islamic empires was considered to be enemy territory that could be conquered and annexed in crusades. Such wars eo ipso . . . not only had justa causa . . . but, when declared by the pope, were even holy wars. . . . The essential point is that, within the Christian sphere, wars among Christian princes were bracketed wars. They were distinguished from wars against non-Christian princes and peoples. These internal, bracketed wars did not negate the unity of the res publica Christiana" (Carl Schmitt, *The Nomos of the Earth*, 58).

41. See Jackson, *Sovereignty*, 35, 67.
42. Ibid., 34.
43. Ibid., 71.
44. Ibid., 72.
45. Ibid., 100.
46. Ibid., 112–113.
47. Lauren Benton, *A Search for Sovereignty: Law and Geography in European Empires, 1400–1900* (Cambridge: Cambridge University Press, 2014), p. xii.
48. Benton, *A Search for Sovereignty*, 2.
49. See direct criticism toward them: Benton and Ford, *Rage for Order*, 4, 6 ff.
50. Ibid., 3.
51. Ibid., 24.
52. Ibid. 279.
53. Ibid., 283.
54. Ibid., 293.
55. Ibid., 299.
56. Günther Teubner. *Constitutional Fragments: Societal Constitutionalism and Globalization* (Oxford: Oxford University Press. 2014), 7.
57. Jan Klabbers, Peters Anne, and Ulfstein Geir. *The Constitutionalization of International Law. The Constitutionalization of International Law* (Oxford: Oxford University Press, 2010), p. 10.
58. Ibid., 18.
59. Ibid., 183.
60. Ibid., 184.
61. Ibid., 184.
62. Ibid., 190
63. Ibid., 165.
64. Ibid., 166.
65. Teubner, *Constitutional Fragments*, 152.
66. Anne Peters, "The Refinement of International Law: From Fragmentation to Regime Interaction and Politicization." *International Journal of Constitutional Law* 15.3 (2017: pp. 671–704. Cit. 679 ff.
67. In a sense, this is said decisively against the orthodox Marxist views, as represented, for example, in chapter 4 of this volume. From a Marxist point of view, state is nothing more than a repressive apparatus, with all its material and ideological

(i.e., also legal) forces. There is no national community, no core of solidarity among all citizens—however, the significance of the international standards and opportunities for defending human rights must be somehow reconceptualized within this framework.

68. Günther Teubner. *Constitutional Fragments*, 11.

69. That United States should not sacrifice its sovereignty to international law is one of the most ideological messages of Trump's advocates; that Russia will not subordinate its legal order to the international treaties will most probably be one of the changes the Russian Constitution will undergo in the next months.

Chapter 3

Sovereign State and Democracy in French Constitutional Theory

Olga Bashkina

1. THE PARADOX OF DEMOCRACY

Modern democracies are born from and remain trapped in a paradox. Even as they proclaim ideals of collective autonomy and self-government, democratic theories struggle to explain who the self-governing people are and how it is exactly that they maintain their freedom. Are the people free when they govern themselves in a direct manner or does representation play a constitutive role for democratic freedom? Or, in the crisis of representation, do the people turn into a "counter-democratic" critical entity that expresses itself in opposition to a representative regime?[1]

Furthermore, should the people be able to change the laws that govern them at will if they deem them to be oppressive or are there some fundamental principles that cannot be so easily changed? Why can principles established in the past legitimately determine the present? After all, where is the "people" to be found if all we hear are claims made in their name? The difficulties in answering these questions constitute the paradox at the heart of democracy.[2] These questions were traditionally addressed at the level of nation-states. Now they become increasingly complicated as the role of the state itself comes under question. In the age of governmentality, does the state matter in tackling the problems of democracy or not? Two concepts drawn from the history of modern political thought have frequently been used to express the idea of popular self-government and have become essential to our understanding of democratic principles: popular sovereignty and constituent power. What exactly these two concepts express has become increasingly confused as the role of the state remains ill-defined.

The concepts of popular sovereignty and constituent power have undergone renewed scrutiny over the past three decades. Against the backdrop of a collapsing Cold War world order, the continuous emergence of new democratic states, and the formation of new international constellations, popular sovereignty, and constituent power have returned from the dusty shelves of early twentieth-century jurisprudence and come to the fore of political and legal debates. The crisis of state sovereignty associated with globalization and neoliberal reforms has prompted some to shift their hopes to society at large and to direct popular rule in particular, while others fear the disappearance of democracy and with it the sovereign state. This constellation is not all that different from the issues that beset European states in the interwar years of the twentieth century, and hence the relevance of discussions led at that time by public jurists.

Both concepts have undergone reinterpretations in the fields of legal and constitutional theory, deliberative democratic theory, and radical democratic theory. In the intermingling of different traditions and methodologies, as well as of normative and ideological assumptions, the crystallization of their meaning does not immediately settle. While for some popular sovereignty and constituent power constitute the core of modern democracy, for others they appear as obsolete concepts fraught with dictatorial and revolutionary dangers that are ultimately incompatible with the rule of law. Difficulties, again, multiply, as the role of the state remains unclear: on the one hand, the state's influence has diminished, but on the other, the discourse of sovereignty and constituent power continues to be historically and conceptually bound to the state. From within these different theoretical approaches, one can single out several visions of how popular sovereignty and constituent power relate to one other:

1. *No sovereignty and no constituent power.* Both concepts are not so uncontroversial. They are consistently rejected as little more than obsolete residues of modern political theory that are now thoroughly incompatible with the realities of contemporary world. Attacks on sovereignty usually come from two fronts. On the one hand, it is argued that the concept of sovereignty cannot express the complexity of multilevel global governance networks in a post-Westphalian world, in which nation-states do not preserve their independence.[3] On the other hand, it is argued that the concept of sovereignty is more fundamentally incompatible with the core values of constitutionalism, such as the separation of powers, individual liberties, and the rule of law.[4] In this critique, sovereignty is understood as an absolute undivided power. Since within a contemporary state such absolute power does not and cannot exist, sovereignty is deemed inimical to the principle of constitutional policies based upon the rule of law.[5] Similarly, within legal normative thought, constituent power is understood as the extra-legal ultimate source of law. But since normative legal theory

is preoccupied with questions of legality, constituent power thus defined remains outside of its concerns and "the question of constituent power simply does not arise for a liberal account of the rule of law."[6]

2. *Constituent power without sovereignty/sovereignty without constituent power.* Some other approaches, while emphasizing the indisputable value of constitutional regimes and agreeing that we live in a complex international order, do not contend that we can so easily eradicate the concepts of sovereignty and constituent power. Yet this does not mean that the two are equally indispensable. Thus, Andrew Arato argues that the idea of a post-sovereign constituent power should replace the populist unitary idea of a sovereign constituent power.[7] Sovereignty is a perilous concept that expresses an absolute will beyond the law and always runs the risk of turning democratic constitutionalism into a plebiscitary regime.[8] Instead, constituent power proper does not signify any extra-legal power but refers to a democratic participatory method of constitution-making. For Arato, the method used to establish a constitution matters for how democratic the subsequent regime will be, but after the constitution is in place, constituent power recedes and gives way to the rule of law. An inverse position can be found in a recent book by Richard Tuck, *The Sleeping Sovereign*.[9] Within the context of Anglo-American constitutional theory, the book reconstructs a tradition of modern democracy, which, according to the author, has always pivoted on the fundamental distinction between government and sovereignty. Passing through the thought of Bodin, Hobbes, and Rousseau, this tradition today defines the normative core of democracy. It allocates the exercise of all ordinary affairs to representative governments (which for Tuck also includes constitutional interpretation by the judiciary), while the sovereign—the people—remains asleep, but for rare moments when its will is sought by way of a referendum. According to this view, the theory of constituent power as formulated by Sieyès is alien to the norm and practice of modern democracy, since it posits the will of a minority above the law.[10]

3. *Popular sovereignty as constituent power.* Finally, there is a group of approaches which uphold that both popular sovereignty and constituent power should remain in our political lexicon and that they ultimately express the same idea. Notably, Antonio Negri[11] and Andreas Kalyvas[12] define popular sovereignty and constituent power as an extraordinary power that exists prior to all laws and escapes constitutionalization. It bears an "extra-legal, pre-juridical, factual nature"[13] and is tamed by mechanisms of representation. Constituent power, in this radical democratic definition, is expressed as the principle of the people's self-organization.[14] Taking a different approach, Martin Loughlin defines sovereignty as "the name given to express the quality of the political relationship that is formed

between the state and the people, or the sovereign and the subject."[15] For Loughlin, popular sovereignty, constituent power, and political power are synonymous and omnipresent within the constituted order, not outside and independent of it. Yet they are understood in a symbolic fashion: there is no holder of this power; instead it symbolically expresses "open, provisional and dynamic dimensions to constitutional ordering."[16] Yet another approach equating popular sovereignty and constituent power is situated in the growing field of democratic constitutionalism. It chooses to locate popular sovereignty and constituent power neither outside of nor within the legal order but at the moments of its creation and amendment. Those moments of constitutional revisions, it is argued, need to be regular and involve more democratic participation, rather than leaving constitutional revisions to constitutional courts.[17]

Even if we still have faith in the explicatory and normative potential of the concepts of sovereignty and constituent power, from the debate outlined earlier, it nonetheless remains largely unclear what the precise relationship between the two concepts is. Is popular sovereignty expressed through a referendum, does it presuppose a revolutionary rupture of the legal order, or does it fulfill a symbolic function that does not pertain to any particular way of expressing popular will? I maintain that some of the conceptual confusions that arise when it comes to questions of popular sovereignty and constituent power stem from an inadequate attention to and lack of articulation of the relationship between the state and the people. In the continental tradition of political and legal thought, the concept of the people is grasped through what Giorgio Agamben has called "the original split" between the two meanings of the concept.[18] Reflected in the Roman juridically established distinction between *populus* and *plebs* and repeated in Jean Bodin's separation of *peuple menu* and *peuple en corps*, the double meaning of the people includes the people both as the political unity expressed in the state form and the people as the oppressed and the excluded from the exercise of government. It is this idea of the partial people that manifests itself in Abbé Sieyès's famous equation of the Third Estate with the entire nation. But it was Carl Schmitt whose articulation of the double meaning of the people significantly shaped subsequent political thinking of the twentieth century. Schmitt observed that the first meaning of the people is that of a political unity that exists in the state form and endures through time. But this does not exhaust the concept:

> In addition to other meanings, the word "people" has the special sense that it includes a contrast to every state official and magistrate. People are those who do not govern, do not represent, do not exercise organized functions with an official character. . . . It is precisely in a democracy that the people cannot

become the administrative apparatus and a mere "organ." The people is always more than a functioning bureau with the competence for setting official business, and, together with instances of a constitutionally organized activity (popular election and direct popular vote on specific issues), the people in its essence persists as an entity that is unorganized and unformed. In this context, the concept of the people is defined in negative terms, in particular by the contrast with the system of administrators and magistrates organized by position. . . . In a special meaning of the word, the people are everyone who is not honored and distinguished, everyone not privileged, everyone prominent not because of property, social position, or education.[19]

This original split of the concept of the people permeates the history of legal and political thought but seems not to receive sufficient attention with respect to the concepts of popular sovereignty and constituent power. Loughlin, in his recently proposed relational account of constituent power, suggests that the double meaning of the people should be incorporated into a theory of constituent power that expresses the political dynamic of the constitutional state as "the symbolic representation of all with the concerns of the many."[20] At the same time, he attacks radical democratic theories of constituent power, those that employ the Schmittian distinction in the most apparent way. Loughlin labels radical theories of constituent power a materialist fallacy that reduce constituent power to fact.[21] In the same vein, Arato criticizes Negri and conceptions of weak constitutionalism for transcending the limits of democracy by offering an apologia for the overthrow of constitutional democratic regimes by mobilized violent minorities.[22] It, thus, still remains unclear which of the two "peoples"—the people as incorporated in the state or the people as governed—should retain sovereignty and constituent power.

2. POPULAR SOVEREIGNTY AND CONSTITUENT POWER IN FRENCH CONSTITUTIONAL THEORY

Our current debate on the concepts of popular sovereignty and constituent power remains largely informed by discussions in legal theory dating to the beginning of the twentieth century. German legal theory in particular has been highly influential throughout the past century: theorists like Carl Schmitt and Hans Kelsen continue to stir our political and legal imagination and enrich our political vocabularies to the present day. Yet the distinction that Schmitt drew between the people as the state and the people as the governed in fact finds its expression in other legal theories of the time. Less known in the Anglophone literature is the tradition of French jurisprudence preceding and contemporary to the Weimar Republic. In what follows, I present the

French project in counterpart to German theory. I explain how it represents an attempt to give an idealist account of the people and their sovereignty.

In his *Philosophy of Right*, Hegel defined sovereignty in the following way:

> Since sovereignty is the ideality of every particular authority, it is easy to fall into the very common misunderstanding of regarding this ideality as mere power and empty arbitrariness, and of equating sovereignty with despotism. But despotism signifies the condition of lawlessness in general, in which the particular will as such, whether of a monarch or of the people (ochlocracy), counts as law (or rather replaces law), whereas sovereignty is to be found specifically under lawful and constitutional conditions as the moment of ideality of the particular spheres and functions within the state.[23]

Hegel's emphasis on sovereignty's "ideality," rather than its association with a factual power or particular will, articulates how sovereignty can express not only a despotic power of command but also the ideal unity of various state powers, thus laying at the foundation of the idea of the constitutional state. Hegel himself observed that sovereignty as ideality is only possible if it is grounded in subjectivity, which in Hegel's case means the concrete individual subjectivity of the monarch.[24] This, he argued, is necessary in order to give legitimation and concrete representation to a complex system of separated powers and forces. Subsequent German theories of state, for example, that of Georg Jellinek, turned this into the idea of the legal personality of the state, where the state itself would be deemed a person ruling the people. This forms a dualist system with two principles—the state and the people—where the state is understood as the instance of command and the people can be either a separate organ of the state or a resistant force directed against the state. This mode of thinking was further developed in Max Weber's reduction of state to "physical violence" and "legitimacy," the latter often deemed to be personalistic but never democratic. This, in turn, powerfully marked the American tradition of thinking about the state. In contrast, the French project can be understood as an attempt to theorize the state and sovereignty as pure ideality in Hegel's terms, that is, grounding it neither in a concrete subjectivity nor in a dualist system that divides the state and the people. Thus, it represents an attempt to offer an idealist theory that could account for the people, the state, and the sovereignty, while removing the connotations of command and domination engrained in these concepts. In what follows, I explain how this project is developed and which insights it can offer about the state, sovereignty, and constituent power.

The conceptual distinction explicated in this tradition, I suggest, helps both to grasp the relationship between "the two peoples" in a more distinct manner and to clarify whether popular sovereignty and constituent power amount to one and the same thing, as well as what exactly the exercise of popular sovereignty and constituent power pertains to. This conceptual distinction is that between popular and national sovereignty.

A commonplace explanation of this distinction ascribes the concept of popular sovereignty to the tradition of "direct democracy" epitomized by Rousseau and that of national sovereignty to the tradition of representative government portrayed by Sieyès. In constitutional law, both conceptions are understood to have several practical implications. Thus, popular sovereignty presupposes universal suffrage, a republican regime, and the extensive use of direct mechanisms for the expression of popular will, that is, referenda. National sovereignty, on the other hand, is regarded as compatible with limited suffrage, the strong rejection of imperative mandate and the dismissal of direct democratic procedures in favor of representative deliberation.[25] The distinction between popular and national sovereignty understood in this way was consolidated in the French public law tradition and also influenced the constitutional theory and practice of other countries, that is Belgium, where it was used to make an argument in favor of the national sovereignty model and to rule out the use of referenda as unconstitutional.[26] In France, the distinction was used to describe different constitutional arrangements in French postrevolutionary history. Thus, the Constitution of 1791 is held to represent the national sovereignty model, as Articles 1 and 2 of Title III proclaim that "sovereignty is one, and cannot be divided, alienated or extinguished. It belongs to the Nation, and no section of the people, nor any individual, may claim its exercise" and that "the Nation, from which all powers stem, may only exercise them by delegation." Meanwhile, the popular sovereignty model is expressed in the Constitution of 1793, which postulates that "sovereignty rests with the people . . . no part of the people may exercise the power of the entire people; but each section of the sovereign assembled shall enjoy the right to express its will with absolute freedom."[27]

This distinction—which in its textbook formulation comes down to the difference between direct and representative democracies—presents a more intricate set of problems in its original articulation. It is elaborated most thoroughly in the works of two constitutional theorists, Raymond Carré de Malberg (1861–1935) and Maurice Hauriou (1856–1929). Carré de Malberg and Hauriou form the canon of French constitutional theory together with Adhémar Esmein (1848–1913) and Léon Duguit (1859–1928). While Esmein developed the idea of national sovereignty but did not operate with the separation of popular and national sovereignty, Duguit proposed getting rid of the concept of sovereignty altogether, deeming it to be incompatible with the precept of the rule of law—a solution similar to that offered by some contemporary critics of sovereignty.[28] It was Carré de Malberg and Hauriou who, from different methodological perspectives, significantly contributed to the crystallization of the conceptual distinction. Both drew the foundations of their theories from French revolutionary discourse, including to a large degree the work of Abbé Sieyès. It is due to the latter's influence that Carré de Malberg and Hauriou grappled with the concept of constituent power and its relation to both popular and national sovereignty in their legal theories. What does the distinction pertain to and how does it help us to clarify the concept of the people?

Jurists of the Third Republic, Carré de Malberg and Hauriou—although they lived under the France's most long-lasting regime—bore witness to a host of external and internal turbulences. Born out of the collapse of the Second French Empire during the Franco-Prussian War of 1870, the Third Republic saw the loss of Alsace and Lorraine regions, the establishment of the Paris Commune, the rise of the French syndicalist movement, the polarization of party politics, and World War I, among other events, until its demise before Nazi Germany and the formation of the Vichy Government. It was against this tumultuous background that the canon of French constitutional thought took shape. It was formed as an exercise in systematizing over a century's worth of political experience precipitated by the French Revolution and represented an attempt to establish a theory of the constitutional state and a modern theory of sovereignty. As a bulwark against a series of changing revolutionary and plebiscitary regimes, French constitutionalists aimed at theorizing a regime, which, they believed, would truly correspond to the ideals of the French Revolution. The Revolution aimed to put an end to the rule of tradition, religion, and the arbitrary power of men, establishing in their stead the foundation for the true liberty of a self-governing people protected by the law. This modern idea located the source of authority in society itself, while rendering no one a *legibus solutus*. Precepts of constitutionalism thus required the formulation of a new theory of sovereignty not as absolute personal power but as the rule of the free people.

A theory of the sovereignty of the people, which pervaded the minds of those behind the French Revolution, was certainly that of Jean-Jacques Rousseau. Rousseau's theory sought to argue for a just and legitimate political order governed by laws made by society itself. It opposed free society to despotism, or personal rule, and defined sovereignty as "nothing but the exercise of the general will that can never be alienated" and that "is nothing but a collective being which can only be represented by itself."[29] Yet it was precisely Rousseau's popular sovereignty that French constitutionalists like Carré de Malberg and Hauriou found incompatible with the constitutional regime. They both criticized the social contract theory for its assumption that the agreement between individuals can produce a collective; in other words, that by putting together parts one can generate the whole.

More fundamentally, their critique of Rousseau's popular sovereignty emphasized the constitutive role of representation that Rousseau allegedly failed to recognize. In order to guarantee a regime that is truly free, in which nobody can usurp and hold power, they argued, representation needed to become the foundational principle; nobody has the entitlement to govern unless they govern in the name of the people, and no one can claim to be the people directly. They argued, moreover, that representation is always operational in creating the collective—the people—that it claims to represent. In their assessment of the role of representation, which extends much beyond the electoral delegation of representatives, Carré de Malberg and Hauriou align with some contemporary reevaluations of representative politics.[30] A theory of sovereignty that Carré de Malberg and Hauriou deemed compatible with the idea of constitutional state would posit representation at its basis, and they developed it as a theory of national sovereignty. Yet the two authors had different takes on what the relationship between national sovereignty and popular sovereignty can be.

A native of Strasbourg, Carré de Malberg to a large extent incorporated his national allegiance into his theory. The Franco-Prussian war, "a great trauma"[31] of Carré de Malberg's childhood, left the mark of rivalry and competition on his reception of German legal thought and on his conception of the unique character of the French constitutional state. Carré de Malberg developed his political and legal views against the backdrop of the discussion of the destiny of the Alsace-Lorraine region.[32] From his earlier articles, devoted to the status of Alsace-Lorraine under the German Empire and to the legal basis of the reparation payments, through to his later programmatic work on the state, he depicted Germany as an imperialist aggressor enforcing domination and stirring unrest on the continent. Thus, while he was significantly influenced by German public lawyers, such as Georg Jellinek, he counterposed the French tradition—built upon the principles of representation and constitutionalism—to the German tradition, which posited the power of the state as *Herrschaftsgewalt*. For Carré de Malberg, as for most French theorists of the time, the German doctrine took the state as a *Herrscher*, a dominating instance, and theorized the state as positioned above the people, who remain subjects of sheer state power. The goal of French thought, as Carré de Malberg saw it, was to establish a theory of the people and their sovereignty that would allow us to think the people not as dominated and governed but as self-governing.[33]

The idea of sovereignty itself bears the mark of domination. As absolute undivided power, in its Bodinian and Hobbesian versions, sovereignty is epitomized in the figure of the ruler that governs over its subjects. The nineteenth-century demand for constitutional limitations to personal rule brings forth the German version of the sovereignty of the impersonal state. The state self-imposes the constitution onto itself in order to limit its various powers (the doctrine of auto-limitation)[34] but remains in domination over the people and in this capacity is sovereign.³⁵ Carré de Malberg's project in his magnum opus *Contribution à La Théorie Générale de l'Etat* (1920) is to disassociate sovereignty from domination and to reflect upon how the people can rule instead of being ruled. The sovereignty of the people as suggested by Rousseau, Carré de Malberg contends, did not work for several reasons. First, Rousseau erroneously assumed that a combination of the dispersed wills of an unorganized multitude could produce a general collective will. Second, a direct expression of sovereignty would not allow for the founding of a durable state, since institutions would be at the behest of the ever-changing will of the people. Finally, a direct unconstrained will risks compromising individual liberties and is likely to bring about an oppressive majority.³⁶

Thus, debunking Rousseau's doctrine, Carré de Malberg observed that the French Revolution posited the principle of representation at the foundation of the newly emerged republic. When the Constitution of 1791 proclaimed that "*tous les pouvoirs émanent de la nation*," it transferred the eradicated sovereignty of the monarch not to the French people but to the French nation. This transference was enacted in the first act of representation, whereby representatives of the Third Estate announced themselves as the National Assembly. Carré de Malberg makes this point to distinguish between the nation and the people as two subjects of sovereignty. "The people" refers to an immanent principle of organization that Carré de Malberg denies. Popular sovereignty always remains an impossible idea, as the people are a multitude, unable to organize and cooperate. "The nation," on the contrary, is an entity that manifests itself solely through representation, as expressed by Sieyès, who trumpeted that "the people cannot act, cannot speak, other than by means of their representatives."³⁷ "The nation" points to the inescapable transcendence of the people, who can never be fully presented to themselves. It also reveals, as Carré de Malberg underscores, that only by reference to something that by definition can never be fully expressed can those claiming to represent it be granted with temporary power.

For Carré de Malberg, a way to escape the dualism of state and people engrained in German theory is to think of the state and the people (the nation) as co-original. The state should not be thought as something separate from those it governs and upon whom it imposes norms as commands. Rather, the people and the state appear at the same time as organized by the founding document, the Constitution. Thus, the state is not framed as a subject above the law that creates the norm at will and is somehow separate from the people that compose it. Instead, it is by virtue of the founding norm that the nation (as organized people) and the state emerge as one and the same thing:

> The state is the result of a certain organization of the national collectivity. . . .
> If one now wonders where the holders of power, whoever they are, rulers or

assembly of the citizens, draw their quality of organs of the State, and by virtue of which right they have been able to acquire this quality, it is necessary to answer, from the legal point of view, that they hold this title and that they have received their vocation from the legal order established in this respect in each state. This legal order is contained in the Constitution. They derive their vocation from the Constitution, and it is by virtue of this Constitution that they exercise their competence.[38]

Positing a founding norm as the factual basis of the legal order, Carré de Malberg attempts to remove the element of force from the original moment of foundation and substitute it with a transcendent principle. We cannot locate any one at the moment of foundation who has imposed his or her will upon others, as the governing and the governed emerge simultaneously. Yet in postulating this transcendental principle, Carré de Malberg distinguishes himself from another brand of legal positivism and transcendental theory—that of Hans Kelsen. In his *Confrontation de la Théorie de la Formation du Droit par Degrés avec les Idées et les Institutions Consacrées par le Droit Positif Français Relativement à sa Formation* (1933), Carré de Malberg scrutinizes the legal theory of the Viennese school. He contends that the *Stufentheorie* developed by Kelsen and Adolf Merkl is mistaken as to the original source of the norm, or that, at the very least, such a theory does not cohere with French practice.

For Kelsen, the validity of a norm does not derive from force (might does not make right). Kelsen argues that every norm is valid only insofar as it is established according to another higher norm, which leads him to hypostasize a basic norm (*Grundnorm*) that is the transcendent foundation to any normative order.[39] For Carré de Malberg, this conclusion is misguided, since norms are man-made and Kelsen's infinite regress of norms bars any grounding of their legitimacy. Instead, the original norm has a concrete source; it is made by a constituent representative assembly. What distinguishes, however, the act of this assembly from an act of the enforcement of law is that the assembly does not impose its own will but makes a claim to speak in the name of something other than itself—the nation.[40] This original act of representation is what founds the legitimacy of subsequent legal ordering.

Carré de Malberg's insistence on the representation of the people, rather than the people's internal cause as the foundation of sovereignty, resonates with Jacques Derrida's claim about the American Declaration of Independence: "'The people' do not exist as an entity, the entity does not exist before this declaration, not as such. If it gives birth to itself, as free and independent subject, as possible signer, this can hold only in the act of the signature. The signature invents the signer."[41] The primary act of representation, as a reference to something that cannot be expressed, reveals that the very concept of representation encompasses more than the appointment of delegates. In fact, Carré de Malberg rejects a delegation model, as it assumes the preexisting organization of the people who entrust their power to representatives. This would be the American model of popular sovereignty.[42] The foundational act of representation, on the contrary, reveals that no one exercising power or speaking in the people's name does so on the grounds that they have received this power directly from the people; they thus ostensibly withdraw any claim to an absolute power. The represented nation remains entirely transcendent and only in this capacity can it be the foundation of legitimacy and of sovereignty.

Carré de Malberg's formulation of national sovereignty thereby jettisons popular sovereignty entirely. It is opposed to national sovereignty as immanence is opposed to transcendence. The principle of popular sovereignty (immanent causation, unorganized multitude) excludes the principle of national sovereignty (the people as political unity, organized and represented by the Constitution). It was Sieyès whom Carré de Malberg held to be the founder of the specifically French theory of representation and national sovereignty.[43] And yet precisely Sieyes's conception of constituent power is deemed by Carré de Malberg to be inconsistent with the representative nature of national sovereignty, as well as with the rest of Sieyès's own doctrine, since it continues to be formulated in terms of delegation.[44] Attempting to avoid the immanence of the people at any cost, Carré de Malberg thus draws a clear conceptual distinction between national sovereignty, on the one hand, and popular sovereignty and constituent power, on the other.

Maurice Hauriou (1856–1929), Carré de Malberg's colleague from Toulouse, was wary of such a sharp incongruity of transcendence and immanence, of national and popular sovereignty. He sought to conceive of a model that could explain the dynamic between the two principles. His attempt to get out of Carré de Malberg's "positivist straitjacket" anticipates Hannah Arendt's later reflections on authority.[45] Like Léon Duguit, Hauriou was influenced by Émile Durkheim's sociological method and conceded that society exists as a separate reality with its own inherent principles. Those principles, both held, should be reflected in the fundamental law of the state. In this sense, they followed the tradition of Jellinek, with his twofold state/society structure of the law, yet made an effort to bridge the divide he had suggested. Duguit, however, believed that the concept of sovereignty does not help to explain the relationship between state and society and should be abandoned as a "metaphysical mystery."[46] For Hauriou, like for Carré de Malberg, the concept of sovereignty remained crucial for signifying the project of collective self-government. Without the fiction of sovereignty, it would be impossible to think of a society that freely governs itself: the stark reality in which there is always one who governs and one who remains governed would be exposed.[47] While for Carré de Malberg this collective fiction is guaranteed by a representation of the transcendent, Hauriou locates the realization of collective self-government in history and conceives of national sovereignty as a process rather than as a fact.

Hauriou, like Carré de Malberg, thinks of the foundation as an original representation. National sovereignty is similarly understood as guaranteed by a constitutional regime and built around the representational principle.[48] Popular sovereignty is understood as a principle expressed as the extra-representational existence of the people, which Hauriou denies; yet he admits the independent existence of society that needs to be accounted for in a theory of sovereignty.[49] Further, Hauriou acknowledges that the original foundational representation cannot be assumed to be complete. In his earlier writing, *Leçons sur le movement social* (1898), he discusses the relationship of representation to society. Against the "German" view of the state, which submits that the state issues commands as its own will, Hauriou argues that society has its own principle of organization and its own norms. Society is larger than law.[50] Yet while he recognizes the immanent principle in society itself, he also assigns the central role to representation:

> The social organism, like all other organisms, in spite of its superiority vis-a-vis representation, is in this singular situation of being intelligible to us only through the intermediary of representation. Indeed, we conceive it only through the intermediary of the concepts presented to us. We are therefore obliged, practically, to establish ourselves in representation. It is as if, conversing via an interpreter with a person who speaks a language unknown to us, we can only get hold of the version of the interpreter.[51]

By introducing an understanding of representation as interpretation, Hauriou points to the disparity between the claim to represent "the people" (the nation) and the actual people whose condition is, however, inaccessible for them directly. Precisely because every representation is incomplete, the foundational act is situated in history and requires ongoing interpretation. In this sense, those who originally claim to speak in the name of the transcendent nation in fact express their own take on what the national will is, yet apply it as the general will. Partial original representation, on the one hand, constitutes the whole in whose name it speaks ("the people," the nation) but simultaneously points to its radical unrepresentability (the people as multitude). Hauriou shares Aristotle's view that in a democracy, governors and governed are identical.[52] This identity can only be fulfilled in a constitutional regime of representative national sovereignty, wherein no one exercises personal power but acts only as a representative of the nation.

The concept of sovereignty here remains crucial not because it signifies personal power but because it conveys a shared collective enterprise: unlike for Carré de Malberg, who conceived of a collective self as an atemporal transcendence, Hauriou thought that a sovereign self unfolds in time, wherein sovereignty (complete autonomy) serves both as a signifier of legal ordering but also as a normative ideal. The identity between the governors and the governed is not already realized at the moment of foundation, as Carré de Malberg had hoped. Rather, Hauriou conceives it as a "directing" or "leading idea" ("*idées directrices*").[53] This intuition is similar to Jürgen Habermas's Kantian claim that constitutional development is animated by the regulative ideal of facts and norms that merge together at some point in the future.[54] Attempting to bridge the gap between the two supposedly incompatible principles of constitutionalism and democracy, Habermas introduced the formula of the co-originality of human rights and democratic will-formation, or of private and public autonomy. In this view, democratic self-legislation is only possible when everyone is free both collectively and individually; only then is the ideal of reasonable will-formation fulfilled. But equally, it can never be seen to be an accomplished fact; rather "this internal connection between will and reason can develop only in the dimension of time, as a self-correcting historical process":[55]

> The allegedly paradoxical relation between democracy and the rule of law resolves itself in the dimension of historical time, provided one conceives of the constitution as a project that makes the founding act into an ongoing process of constitution-making that continues across generations.[56]

Similarly to Habermas, Hauriou conceives of the historical process in a teleological way. What starts off as the enforcement of the will of the governors on the governed will eventually turns into a regime of total representation, wherein the (temporary) governors and the (temporary) governed coincide as representatives of the nation. Hauriou's position on the relationship between the principle of constitutionalism (expressed as national sovereignty) and the principle of democracy (expressed as popular sovereignty) lies somewhere between Schmitt's decisionism and Carré de Malberg's positivism. While for Schmitt sovereignty is expressed as a concrete decision and for Carré de Malberg sovereignty stands for transcendence, Hauriou accounts for how decisions can be seen not only as a particular will but as representations of the universal. For Schmitt, the political reveals itself outside of the legal order. What is within the strictly legal realm is a matter of administration rather than political contestation. Conversely, the political is a matter of decision in a space unregulated by law. Hauriou's vision of the historical process instead invites the distinction between original constituent representation and its subsequent reinterpretations.

Hauriou's immanent idealism is an attempt to see representation as the driver of history and the locus of creativity. His theorizing of national sovereignty runs counter to Carré de Malberg's positing of an ahistorical transcendence as the foundation of representation. Yet both privilege representation in order to insist that popular sovereignty and constituent power express a materialist principle and cannot be given ontological primacy. While for Carré de Malberg, national sovereignty and popular sovereignty are wholly incompatible, Hauriou presents history as a certain augmentation of national sovereignty as the representative principle. Popular sovereignty, while it comes to stand for immanent social organization, does not play a historical role because of its association with the passivity of matter. This is supposed to rescue the people from its complete immobility and to prevent the postulation of a materialist principle that would invoke a dialectical materialist movement deemed too determinist. Such as vision also illuminates how constituent power is rooted in an immanent materialist logic and is thus opposed to the rationale of representation.

For Hauriou, the telos of the historical movement is justice, which can be approached through the realization of what he calls the "anthropomorphism" of the state: the triumph of the sovereign mind. It implies the organization of governing institutions according to the principles of rationality, so that the operation of the state is as intelligible for the people as possible:

> The harmonization of liberties, which is the objective of justice, is realized in the last analysis by the subjective considerations of individual minds; to have a sense of justice is the property of the mind of man. But, in social groups, collective forces are unleashed that are so brutal that they escape the control of the minds of individuals, even of governors, unless by a prodigious effort of organization the collective forces are themselves arranged after the fashion of a mind. This arrangement will make them more manageable and will subject their exercise to such reasonable procedures that it will be easy for individual minds to act upon them in the perspective of justice. There you have the whole secret of the personification of social institutions: it is an application of the maxim similia similibus. You will protest that this is anthropomorphism, but the result is good since it is to humanize social institutions, which are for men.[57]

3. THE TWO SOVEREIGNS?

The distinction drawn between national and popular sovereignty within French constitutional thought offers us greater conceptual precision than does current theory. It allows us to see that the people of "popular sovereignty" is a complex category. When we speak of popular sovereignty and constituent power, we should be more specific as to who the bearer of this power is.

Distinguishing between the nation as the abstract entity that only manifests itself through representation and the people who remain an unorganized multitude outside of the constituted order helps us to delineate the dynamics of the constitutional state. It also illuminates that "the original split" between the two peoples, or the two sovereigns, is not overcome by a simple increase in participatory mechanisms.

In its traditional formulation, the distinction between national and popular sovereignty pertains to the difference between representative and direct government. The distinction sounds straightforward and appears to be a question of who exercises the functions of governance—whether it be delegated representatives or the citizens directly. Understood in this way, the two principles can potentially be combined by introducing a mixture of both representative and direct mechanisms of decision-making. Yet the distinction proves to be more profound and approaches the core of the paradox of constitutionalism. Surpassing merely functional concerns, the relationship between national and popular sovereignty points to a particular ontology of collective selfhood. The question of national sovereignty points to the constitutive role that representation plays in the appearance of a people who can govern themselves without arbitrary power.

If the idea of the primacy of representation is acknowledged, it introduces the potential for voicing doubt as to each particular mode of representation and manifestation of power. Instead of justifying representative institutions per se, Carré de Malberg and Hauriou defend a more fundamental significance of the representative principle that organizes society. Equally, the question of popular sovereignty is not exhausted by the issue of participation. Popular sovereignty, in the exposition of the French constitutionalists, stands for the principle of immanence. Increasing democratic participation is one way to institutionalize it. But the ultimate conclusion to be drawn from their theory is that popular sovereignty and constituent power are based upon a different ontological assumption: a materialist rather than idealist immanence.

A further conclusion to be drawn from the French idealist framework in theorizing sovereignty and the state is that sovereignty can express the idea of collective subjectivity and cooperation and not a dominating commanding power of the state. Remaining a Hegelian "ideality," perhaps even a fiction, "sovereignty" can serve as a concept that expresses a shared project that unites people, rather than being construed as a struggle between forces of domination and resistance. Today, similar ideas can be found in approaches to sovereignty inspired by Claude Lefort's acclaimed theory of the people as the empty place of power, a late expression of the French liberal philosophy of representation. Lefort's idea of symbolic representation, reliant on the psychoanalytic categories of the Symbolic and the Real, in a way surpasses the divide between idealism and materialism by taking a stance from within a particular society. In this reading, a concept such as "sovereignty" can serve as a category of self-description that allows a society in its real plurality to think of itself as one. This in turn allows to think of a plurality that expresses itself in the political conflict that transpires within the state and does not aim to destroy it.

As an illustration of a Lefortian approach, Martin Loughlin's recent "relational" account of constituent power[58] endeavors to understand it as the power that irritates and interrupts the constituted order. In the terms of the French constitutionalists, as discussed earlier, the answer depends on the choice revealed in the distinction between a national sovereignty that attributes creativity to representation and the popular sovereignty that attributes this creativity to society. Surpassing this divide, Loughlin claims that the constituent power of the people "resides neither in 'the people' nor in the constituted authorities; it exists in the relation established between constitutional imagination and governmental action."[59] For him, this means that constituent power cannot be equated with the will of the ruler or of the multitude, for this would constitute materialist and decisionist misinterpretations of the concept. Nor can it be equated with the founding norm, as it would then fall into a normativist misinterpretation, eliminating the role of the political domain. From this it follows that the middle ground, or the relationship between these two principles, can only unfold in time, where constituent power epitomizes the symbol of change. For Loughlin, theories of constituent power such as Negri's present a "materialist fallacy."[60]

While this Lefortian relational account potentially allows us to square the representative principle of unity with the social principle of plurality, it only does so at the state level. On the transnational level, a mismatch constantly occurs between expressions of social pluralism manifesting themselves in global resistance movements and in legal or political representations that lack democratic accountability predicated upon the nation-state. On the transnational level, the solution to thinking popular sovereignty and constituent power appears to fork two ways. First, to think of popular sovereignty and constituent power in a materialist way, as a self-organizing global civil society. Or, following Hauriou's take on the state, to attempt to rationalize transnational regimes from above by anthropomorphizing their structure and organizing them in a state-like fashion.

All in all, the French perspective on sovereignty is instructive as it allows us to think of sovereignty as a concept that combines features of unity and plurality, cooperation and conflict. Centralized sovereignty, then, does not have to repress disagreement (radical disagreement being a form of constituent power) but can integrate it. The condition for this is the preservation, following Lefort, of a stage wherein different positions obtain representation and conflict is rendered visible. The problem of foreseeing the shape of transnational integration and the global state, in this analysis, is that of imagining how the international staging of this conflict could appear.

NOTES

1. Pierre Rosanvallon, *Counter-Democracy: Politics in an Age of Distrust*, John Robert Seeley Lectures 7 (Cambridge, UK: Cambridge University Press, 2008).
2. Martin Loughlin and Neil Walker, *The Paradox of Constitutionalism: Constituent Power and Constitutional Form* (Oxford, UK: Oxford University Press, 2007); Bonnie Honig, *Emergency Politics—Paradox, Law, Democracy* (Princeton, NJ: Princeton University Press, 2011); Chantal Mouffe, *The Democratic Paradox* (London; New York: Verso, 2000).
3. For a summary of these positions, see Martin Loughlin, "Ten Tenets of Sovereignty," in: Neil Walker (ed.), *Sovereignty in Transition* (Oxford, UK: Hart Publishing, 2003), 55–86.
4. For a summary of these positions see Raf Geenens, "Sovereignty as Autonomy." *Law and Philosophy* 36 (2017): pp. 495–524.
5. Pavlos Eleftheriadis, "Law and Sovereignty." *Law and Philosophy* 29.5 (2010): pp. 535–569.
6. David Dyzenhaus, "The Politics of the Question of Constituent Power," in: Neil Walker and Martin Loughlin (eds), *Paradox of Constitutionalism: Constituent Power and Constitutional Form* (Oxford, UK: Oxford University Press, 2007), 129–147.
7. Andrew Arato, *Post Sovereign Constitution Making: Learning and Legitimacy* (Oxford, UK: Oxford University Press, 2016); Andrew Arato, *The Adventures of the Constituent Power beyond Revolutions?* (Cambridge, UK: Cambridge University Press, 2017).
8. Arato, *Post Sovereign Constitution Making*.
9. Richard Tuck, *The Sleeping Sovereign: The Invention of Modern Democracy* (Cambridge, UK: Cambridge University Press, 2016).
10. Ibid., 180.
11. Antonio Negri, *Insurgencies: Constituent Power and the Modern State* (Minneapolis: University of Minnesota Press, 2009).
12. Andreas Kalyvas, "Popular Sovereignty, Democracy, and the Constituent Power." *Constellations* 12.2 (June 1, 2005): pp. 223–244.
13. Ibid., 230–231.
14. In the same vein, Giorgio Agamben recently even suggested that we should talk of destituent rather than constituent power. Constituent power is necessarily bound up with the constituted order and "a power that was only just overthrown by violence will rise again in another form, in the incessant, inevitable dialectic between constituent power and constituted power. Instead, only a negative concept of destituent power is capable of capturing the spirit of permanent resistance." Giorgio Agamben, "What Is Destituent Power?" *Environment and Planning D: Society and Space* 32 (2014): p. 70.

15. Loughlin, "Ten Tenets of Sovereignty," 55–86.
16. Martin Loughlin, "The Concept of Constituent Power." *European Journal of Political Theory* 13.2 (2013): pp. 218–237.
17. Joel Colon-Rios, *Weak Constitutionalism: Democratic Legitimacy and the Question of Constituent Power* (Abingdon, UK: Routledge, 2012).
18. Giorgio Agamben, "What Is a People," in: *Means without End: Notes on Politics* (Minneapolis: University of Minnesota Press, 2000), 32.
19. Carl Schmitt, *Constitutional Theory* (Durham, NC: Duke University Press, 2008), pp. 270–271.
20. Loughlin, "The Concept of Constituent Power," 218–237.
21. Ibid.
22. Arato, *Post Sovereign Constitution Making*.
23. G. W. F. Hegel, *Elements of the Philosophy of Right* (Cambridge, UK: Cambridge University Press, 1991), pp. 315–316.
24. Ibid., 317.
25. Jacques Ziller, "Sovereignty in France: Getting Rid of the *Mal de Bodin*," in: Neil Walker (ed.), *Sovereignty in Transition* (Oxford, UK: Hart Publishing, 2003), pp. 264–266.
26. Raf Geenens and Stefan Sottiaux, "Sovereignty and Direct Democracy: Lessons from Constant and the Belgian Constitution," *European Constitutional Law Review* 11.2 (2015): pp. 293–320.
27. Ziller, "Sovereignty in France," 264–266.
28. Léon Duguit, *Traité de Droit Constitutionnel* (Paris: E. de Boccard, 1921).
29. CS, II, 1.
30. For example, F. R. Ankersmit, *Political Representation (Cultural Memory in the Present)* (Stanford, CA: Stanford University Press, 2002); Mónica Brito Vieira and David Runciman, *Representation*, *(Key Concepts)* (Cambridge, UK: Polity Press, 2008); Nadia Urbinati, *Representative Democracy. Principles and Genealogy* (Chicago, IL: University of Chicago Press, 2006).
31. O. Beaud, "Carré de Malberg, Juriste Alsacien. La Biographie Comme Élément d'explication d'une Doctrine Constitutionnelle," in: O. Beaud and P. Wachsmann (eds), *La Science Juridique Française et La Science Juridique Allemande de 1870 à 1918* (Strasbourg: Presses universitaires de Strasbourg, 1997), 222.
32. Ibid., 232–233.
33. Raymond Carré de Malberg, *Contribution à La Théorie Générale de l'Etat* (Paris: Dalloz, 2003), p. XIX.
34. Georg Jellinek, *Gezetz Und Verordnung. Staatrechtliche Untersuchungen Auf Rechtgeschichtlicher Und Rechtsvergleichender Grundlage* (Freiburg: Akademische Verlagsbuchhandlung von J. C. B. Mohr, 1887), p. 197.
35. For a discussion of Jellinek and the doctrine of auto-limitation in light of the dialectical theory of state, see chapter 10 in this volume by Artemy Magun.
36. Carré de Malberg, *Contribution à La Théorie Générale de l'Etat*, 155–157.
37. Emmanuel Joseph Sieyès, *Dire de l'abbé Sieyès, Sur La Question Du Veto Royal, à La Séance Du 7 Septembre 1789* (Versailles: Baudouin, 1789): "*Le peuple, je le répète, dans un pays qui n'est pas une démocratie (et la France ne saurait l'être), le peuple ne peut parler, ne peut agir que par ses représentants.*"

38. Carré de Malberg, *Contribution à La Théorie Générale de l'Etat*, II, 144: "*L'État résulte d'une certaine organisation de la collectivité nationale. . . . Si maintenant l'on se demande d'où les détenteurs du pouvoir, quels qu'ils soient, gouvernants ou assemblée des citoyens, tirent leur qualité d'organes de l'État, et en vertu de quel droit ils ont pu acquérir cette qualité, il faut répondre, au point de vue juridique, qu'ils tiennent ce titre et qu'ils ont reçu leur vocation de l'ordre juridique établi à cet égard dans chaque État. Or, cet ordre juridique se trouve contenu dans la Constitution. Ils tirent donc leur vocation de la Constitution, et c'est en vertu de celle-ci qu'ils exercent leur compétence.*"

39. Hans Kelsen, *Pure Theory of Law* (Clark, NJ: Lawbook Exchange, 2005).

40. Raymond Carré De Malberg, *Confrontation de la théorie de la formation du droit par degrés: avec les idées et les institutions consacrées par le droit positif français relativement à sa formation* (Paris: Dalloz, 2008). "La souveraineté ne se crée pas par voie de prescription juridique, pas plus qu'elle n'est susceptible d'être transférée par aucune règle de droit; elle est un fait, et non le produit consécutif d'une règle de celte sorte. En posant en principe que le Parlement exprime législativenient la volonté nationale, et en traitant ainsi le Corps législatif comme l'égal du souverain, la Constitution de 1791 ne prétendait pas non plus lui conférer sa souveraineté: elle se bornait à la reconnaître, non point comme la conséquence d'une délégation constitutionnelle, mais comme une réalité antérieure à elle-même et fondée sur tes rapports spéciaux qui, selon la conception révolutionnaire, unissent entre elles, au point de les identifier l'une avec l'autre, l'assemblée élective des députés et l'universalité des citoyens composant la nation souveraine," 64.

41. Jacques Derrida, "Declarations of Independence." *New Political Science* 7.1 (1986): pp. 7–15.

42. Carré de Malberg, *Contribution à La Théorie Générale de l'Etat*, II, 169.

43. Carré de Malberg, *Contribution à La Théorie Générale de l'Etat*, II, 257, Carré de Malberg claims that Sieyès "defined the representative government, at the beginning of the new era of public law, with an accuracy and precision that has not been exceeded since then."

44. Carré de Malberg, *Contribution à La Théorie Générale de l'Etat*, II, 487–488.

45. Arato, *Post Sovereign Constitution Making*, 37.

46. Duguit, *Traité de Droit Constitutionnel*, 53

47. Which what Duguit was ready to concede to.

48. Maurice Hauriou, *Principes de Droit Public*, Repr. de lòuvrage . . . 1910 aux éd. Sirey, Bibliothèque Dalloz (Paris: Dalloz, 2010), p. 247.

49. Ibid.

50. Maurice Hauriou, *Leçon Sur Le Mouvement Social Données a Toulouse En 1898* (Paris: Librairie de la Société du Receuil Général des Lois et des Arrets, 1899), p. 135: "*L'objet auquel s'applique la loi est plus que la loi, la sociète est plus que le Droit.*"

51. Ibid., 136: "*L'organisme social, comme tous les autres organismes, malgre sa superiorite vis-a-vis du represnetatif, est dans cette situation singuliere de n'etre intelligible pour nous que par l'intermediaire du 'representatif'. En effet, nous ne le concevons que par l'intermediaire des concepts qui se presentent a nous. Nous*

sommes donc bien obliges, pratiquement, de nous etablir dans le representatif. C'est ainsi que, conversant par interprete avec un personnage qui parle une langue a nous inconnue, nous ne pouvons faire etat que de la version de l'interprete."

52. Hauriou, *Principes de Droit Public*, 460.

53. Maurice Hauriou, *Précis de Droit Constitutionnel* (Paris: Sirey, 1929), pp. 73–74.

54. Although not directly related, Hauriou's project and Bruce Ackerman's theory resonate here as well. Arato notes the striking similarity between Hauriou and Ackerman as regards the importance of inherited institutions in revolutionary moments: every revolutionary moment inevitably relies on preexisting governmental institutions and thus establishes a form of continuity with a debunked regime. Arato, *The Adventures of the Constituent Power beyond Revolutions?* 54.

55. Jürgen Habermas, "Constitutional Democracy. A Paradoxical Union of Contradictory Principles?" *Political Theory* 29.6 (2001): p. 768.

56. Ibid., 768.

57. Albert Broderick, ed., *The French Institutionalists: Maurice Hauriou, Georges Renard, Joseph T. Delos* (Cambridge, MA: Harvard University Press, 1970), p. 60, http://catalog.hathitrust.org/api/volumes/oclc/1194855.html.

58. Or popular sovereignty, which is, for Loughlin, synonymous.

59. Loughlin, "The Concept of Constituent Power," 231.

60. Ibid.

II

CRITIQUE OF THE STATE AND THE STATE OF THE CRITIQUE

Chapter 4

State Power and Social Transformation

Panagiotis Sotiris

1. INTRODUCTION

The question of political power has returned to the fore of political and theoretical discussion. This is not a coincidence. The acute economic crisis, its serious social consequences, the open political crisis in certain social formations, and the very sight of the overthrow of governments and regimes under the force of political mobilization—despite, in the case of the Arab Spring, the tragic end of such processes—all these mean that such questions are once again urgent.

In a similar manner, the recent Greek experience—with which this writer is more directly familiar—made two important points obvious. First, that it is impossible to achieve radical social change simply be engaging in collective struggles and exercising pressure upon the state and that actually fighting for power becomes a necessary condition for social change. This was evident in Greece, where despite the advent of one of the most impressive sequences of struggles—of an almost insurrectionary character—and despite the deep political crisis that had been precipitated, there was no change in policy during the first phase (2010–2014) of the austerity packages imposed by the EU-IMF-ECB "Troika."[1] Second, the experience of SYRIZA in government, its quick capitulation to Greece's creditors, and its subsequent implementation of austerity policies, demonstrated that simply rising to the position of government does not mean really gaining political power.[2]

Such experiences bring the question of political power and the state to the forefront not only of theoretical discussion but also of strategic thinking. This development comes after a long period of retreat, during which it was more than obvious that the forces of capital had the initiative and were hegemonic. This notwithstanding the fact that the hegemonic practice of the bourgeoisies tended toward a neoliberal form of a "passive revolution,"[3] aimed at fragmenting, disaggregating, and discouraging the subaltern classes, rather than gaining their active consent, combined with what has been described, especially in the context of European integration, as a form of "bureaucratic caesarism."[4] During this period, from the late 1970s until the end of the 2000s, social movements and the radical Left refrained from confronting the question of political power. It was as if the political limit of radical or emancipatory politics was a politics "at a distance from the State,"[5] namely a politics of movements from below, of putting pressure on the state, of resisting capitalist reconstruction, of opening cracks, of giving face and voice to the excluded, but not of aspiring to achieve hegemony, seize political power, and initiate processes of social transformation. In a certain way, this was exemplified in the whole conception of "changing the world without taking power."[6] However, the very materiality of political power is still with us and presents an unavoidable terrain of social antagonism and at the same time an unavoidable question for any thinking of radical politics.

The very evolution of contemporary forms of protest and contestation—and the fact that, in most cases, despite dynamics from below, political developments from above have remained within the contours of a preexisting political configuration and, in most cases, have taken an even more reactionary turn—means that the question of political and state power remains a nodal point.

In this sense, the question that unavoidably emerges is the following: is it possible to achieve/set in motion a process of social transformation that could move beyond the limitations imposed by capitalist social relations and forms, without dealing with the question of which social classes retain political—and state—power? This, however, brings forth another important question: What is today the relation between social and political power, between social and political relations, forms and antagonisms, and how are what we tend to define as class rule or class power established, secured, and reproduced? And finally, this brings us to another set of questions: What about the state as apparatus, practice, and material configuration? Would the process of social transformation be accomplished by means of existing state apparatuses? Would it entail a transformation of the state, or would it lead to some kind of stateless, anarchic, and informal cooperation? And what would a democratically transformed state look like? To all these questions, I will attempt to offer some tentative answers.

2. A MATERIALIST CONCEPTION OF SOCIAL AND POLITICAL POWER

Let's now see where we stand as far as our understanding of social and political power is concerned. In contrast to a traditional view of the economy as a socially neutral "technical" production process, whose exploitative class character is determined primarily by legal relations of ownership guaranteed by political relations of force, there is a Marxist tradition that offers a more complex apprehension of the importance of social relations of production; as complex and overdetermined social, political, and ideological power relations within production, and, at the same time, as social and political matrices for capitalist social forms, including forms of ideological miscognition.

In this sense, we now have a much more complex conception of the grounding of political power in social relations and forms. This has been the main point of most radical currents within Marxism from the 1960s onward that insist upon the primacy of the relations of production and the centrality of class antagonism, from the work of Althusser[7] to the seminal research of Bettelheim on the class nature of the USSR,[8] through Italian *operaismo*[9] and other Marxist currents,[10] including those that link the prevalence of the value-form to the dominance of capitalist social relations of production.[11] All this gives new relevance to Karl Marx's original emphasis on the centrality of relations of production as the material ground for political relations of domination:

> The specific economic form, in which unpaid surplus labour is pumped out of direct producers, determines the relationship of rulers and ruled, as it grows directly out of production itself and, in turn, reacts upon it as a determining element. Upon this, however, is founded the entire formation of the economic community which grows up out of the production relations themselves, thereby simultaneously its specific political form. It is always the direct relationship of the owners of the conditions of production to the direct producers—a relation always naturally corresponding to a definite stage in the development of the methods of labor and thereby its social productivity—which reveals the innermost secret, the hidden basis of the entire social structure, and with it the political form of the relation of sovereignty and dependence, in short, the corresponding specific form of the state.[12]

Moreover, in contrast to a negative conception of political power as coercion and repression, Foucault's work has helped us to recognize the "productive" aspects of the disciplinary or biopolitical functions of the modern capitalist state; it offers us important insights into the social and historical processes that subsume populations under the norms of capitalist production to create "productive" subjects, presenting a more dialectical approach to the relationship between social and political power. Social relations, along with the social norms and forms of subjectivity that support them, are produced and reproduced both on the terrain of economic production and exchange and through the constant intervention of the state.[13]

At the same time, ever since revolutionary movements in the wake of the October Revolution were confronted with the complexity of power and hegemony in the advanced capitalist social formations (in Western Europe), we know that we can treat neither politics (and political apparatuses and institutions) nor ideology (and ideological apparatuses) as mere epiphenomena of the economy nor as simple instruments in the hands of the ruling class. Gramsci's theory of hegemony and of the integral state offers us a framework for apprehending the expansive forms of the capitalist state and the complex interplay of hegemonic apparatuses.[14] In opposition to an instrumentalist theory of the state, Gramsci proposes a highly relational definition of the state that is not limited to manifest state apparatuses, but also incorporates the apparently "private" institutions of civil society: "The State is the entire complex of practical and theoretical activities with which the ruling class not only justifies and maintains its dominance, but manages to win the active consent of those over whom it rules."[15] To a certain extent, this relational and social praxis-oriented definition of the state—which combines coercion, consent, direction, and leadership—is further developed in Althusser's notion of "Ideological State Apparatuses,"[16] but also within Nicos Poulantzas's conceptualization of the state as the material condensation of a social relation:

> The state is not an "entity" which an intrinsic instrumental essence, but it is itself a relation, more precisely the condensation of a class relation. This implies that:
> (a) the various functions (economic, political, ideological) that the state apparatuses fulfil in the reproduction of social relations are not "neutral" functions *sui generis,* initially existing as such and later being simply "diverted" or "misappropriated" by the ruling classes; these functions depend on the state power inscribed *in* the very structure of its apparatuses, in other words on the classes and class fractions which occupy the terrain of political domination;
> (b) this political domination is itself bound up with the existence and functioning of the state apparatuses.
> It follows that a radical transformation of social relations cannot be limited to a change in state power, but has to "revolutionize" the state apparatuses themselves. In the process of socialist revolution, the working class cannot confine itself to taking the place of the bourgeoisie at the level of state power, but it has also radically to transform (to "smash") the apparatuses of the bourgeois state and replace them by proletarian state apparatuses.[17]

At the same time, we live in a period of expansion of state repressive apparatuses, new technologies of surveillance and suppression. In this sense, contemporary state violence is both a determining and overdetermining factor in social and political antagonism(s), exemplified in the various forms of excessive preemptive and asymmetrical violence deployed by dominant forces. We live in a period marked by an increasing awareness of those aspects of the state that do not have to do simply with violence, and, at the same time by confrontation with the extreme violence of contemporary capitalist states. All this also has to do with the increasingly authoritarian dimension of contemporary neoliberalism that is exemplified in its particular "disciplinary character," both as an extension of repressive practices and as a constant undermining of democracy.[18]

3. THE "SMASHING THE STATE" THESIS, REVISITED

In this sense, it is interesting to return to the classical definition of "smashing the state" in the Marxist tradition. We should remember that it was not an easy conception to formulate. On the one hand, it referred to the actual need to capture political and state power and to use state coercion in order to expropriate the capitalists of their ownership of the means of production, to impose measures of social equality and the public provision of services, and to initiate a process of social transformation. This is evident in the following extract from the *Communist Manifesto*:

> Of course, in the beginning, this cannot be effected except by means of despotic inroads on the rights of property, and on the conditions of bourgeois production; by means of measures, therefore, which appear economically insufficient and untenable, but which, in the course of the movement, outstrip themselves, necessitate further inroads upon the old social order, and are unavoidable as a means of entirely revolutionizing the mode of production.[19]

At the same time, this use of state coercion on the part of the proletariat was meant to be just the beginning of a broader process of social transformation that would lead to a society of full equality, without any forms of exploitation and coercion—a stateless and classless society. This is the main point of not only the *Communist Manifesto* but also most of Marx's interventions:

> When, in the course of development, class distinctions have disappeared, and all production has been concentrated in the hands of a vast association of the whole nation, the public power will lose its political character. Political power, properly so called, is merely the organized power of one class for oppressing another. If the proletariat during its contest with the bourgeoisie is compelled, by the force of circumstances, to organize itself as a class, if, by means of a revolution, it makes itself the ruling class, and, as such, sweeps away by force the old conditions of production, then it will, along with these conditions, have swept away the conditions for the existence of class antagonisms and of classes generally, and will thereby have abolished its own supremacy as a class.

In place of the old bourgeois society, with its classes and class antagonisms, we shall have an association, in which the free development of each is the condition for the free development of all.[20]

As such, this represents a decisive break with a *locus communis* of the political philosophy of modernity—namely, that the guarantor of the just and free society is the state. In contrast, in Marx's intervention we have the insistence that the state is the problem and that social emancipation and the advent of a rational and just society also implies a rupture with the very logic of the state. And yet this also represents an aporia. Marx seems to oppose the state—in its narrow sense as governmental apparatus and repressive apparatuses—to a form of free association. However, in its evolution, the capitalist state also included many aspects and functions that answered some of the demands of the subaltern classes—from public education and health services to labor legislation and nationalizations. Some of the demands that Marx posed as necessary were in fact accomplished through the state. On the other hand, the form of this association remains ambiguous as regards its political form and whether or not it would include some form of public authority. In this sense, one might say that what Marx points to is not a complete negation of any political form, but to an insistence on the need for a constant process of transforming and revolutionizing the state by means of a continuous intervention by the subaltern classes and their autonomous forms of social and political intervention.

Marx and Engels attempted to strike a delicate balance between three conflicting positions: the utopian insistence on an exodus from the state, exemplified in the projects of building socialist communities "outside" existing social and political institutions; the anarchist insistence on an "instantaneous" abolition of property, exploitation, and any form of state organization; and also the "reformist," statist view of the state as an instrument of social rationalization and as enhancer of justice, exemplified in the context of nineteenth-century Germany in the personality of Lassalle. This balance was not easy to achieve, and Balibar has commented on Marx and Engels not being able to write an *Anti-Bakunin* or *Anti-Lassalle* as evidence of the very difficulty of drawing such lines of demarcation:

> In my opinion, one does not wonder enough about the fact that such indefatigable polemicists such as Marx and his faithful assistant Engels turned out to be incapable of writing an "Anti-Lassalle" or an "Anti-Bakunin" which would have been practically much more important than an Anti-Dühring or even than the reissue of an Anti-Proudhon. . . . What is Marx's response when Bakunin systematically associates the totality of Marx's "scientific socialism" with Lassalle's "state socialism?" He has no other recourse than to reaffirm the meaning of the *Manifesto*'s democratic program, which, as a matter of fact,

had allowed Lassalle to proclaim himself in its favor. Conversely, Marx also proclaimed himself, as against Bakunin, in favor of "real anarchism," which he supposedly discovered and defended "long before him." The high point of this "response" consists in the affirmation that Marxism and Bakunin's anarchism are the opposite of each other, which ends up admitting an enormous concession that they are constituted from the same terms.[21]

Moreover, again as Balibar has stressed, after the experience of the Paris Commune, Marx felt compelled to "rectify" the *Communist Manifesto* by insisting that the state apparatus could not be used as it was after the revolution. As Marx and Engels emphasize in their preface to the 1872 German edition of the *Communist Manifesto*, repeating a point they also make in the *Civil War in France*: "One thing especially was proved by the Commune, viz., that 'the working class cannot simply lay hold of the ready-made state machinery, and wield it for its own purposes.'"[22] This implies that the process of transformation, of revolutionizing, of "withering away" the state starts from the ground up; there can be no simple "use" of actually existing apparatuses, since the dominant social relations are inscribed in the very materiality of the state apparatus under capitalism. Balibar summarizes this point in the following manner:

> The *fact* that is revealed here we can express in the following way: *the exploiting classes and the exploited class* that, for the first time in history and because of its place within production, is in position to take power for itself, *cannot exercise their power* (and even their absolute power: their "dictatorship") *with the same means and thus in the same form*. They cannot exercise it with the same means and in the same form, not because of a moral impossibility, but because of a material impossibility: the machine of the state *does not function* "on behalf" of the working class; either it does not function at all, or it functions but on behalf of someone else, that can be no other than the class adversary. It is impossible for the proletariat to conquer, then keep and use political power by using an instrument analogous at that which served the dominant classes, or it will *lose* it necessarily, under one form or the other, "violent" of "peaceful."[23]

The question of the materiality of the state and its efficacy came to prominence after the first wave of revolutionary struggles in two crucial ways. First, the very complexity of the state in "western" social formations expressed in a tragic manner what came to be known as the "defeat of the revolution in the West"; namely, the defeat of the revolutionary upsurges that followed the October revolution in Germany, Italy, Hungary, and the advance of fascism. This was the painful apprehension of the difficulty (or even impossibility) of "repeating" an insurrectionary sequence similar to that of October 1917, which led to the elaboration of the United Front strategy,[24] to interventions such as Lukács's "Blum Theses,"[25] and above all to Gramsci's *Prison*

Notebooks.²⁶ In particular, Gramsci attempted in prison a profound rethinking of the complex interplay of hegemonic apparatuses within the "integral state" as the crucial aspect marking the difference between "East" and "West":

> Ilitch, however, did not have time to expand his formula-though it should be borne in mind that he could only have expanded it theoretically, whereas the fundamental task was a national one; that is to say it required a reconnaissance of the terrain and identification of the elements of trench and fortress represented by the elements of civil society, etc. In Russia the State was everything, civil society was primordial and gelatinous; in the West, there was a proper relation between State and civil society, and when the State trembled, a sturdy structure of civil society was at once revealed. The State was only an outer ditch, behind which there stood a powerful system of fortresses and earthworks: more or less numerous from one State to the next, it goes without saying-but this precisely necessitated an accurate reconnaissance of each individual country.²⁷

The other aspect of course was the evolution of the Soviet Union, where, in the name of socialist construction, not only did the state continue to expand but ultimately an impressive coercive apparatus was also deployed, along with a top-down version of a "social welfare state." Moreover, the trademark of communist reformism, but also of post–World War II social democracy, was to view the state as a neutral and even positive apparatus that not only represented the possibility for redistributive politics, but could also be considered—along with the "progressive" development of productive forces—an antechamber of socialism.²⁸ Such a conception tended to create a conviction that the state was somehow opposed to the capitalist economy, even though the expansion of state functions was in fact enabling the reproduction of capitalist relations of production.

In a curious twist of history, it was the neoliberal counterrevolution with its anti-state rhetoric that led to another wave of the "idealization" of the state on the part of many militants of the Left. I am not denying, of course, that the defense of welfare, public services, and the redistributive intervention of the state is positive nor do I deny the urgency of these tasks. What I am trying to highlight is how all these have led to certain retreat from the critique of the state as an integral part of left-wing or communist politics. Moreover, discussion of such questions remains pertinent today in light of recent discussions of "democratic socialism," a tendency toward a more positive appreciation of a potentially more radical social democracy,²⁹ and the new, positive appraisals that have emerged of figures belonging to the reformist tradition, like Karl Kautsky.³⁰

In this sense, we need a new critique of the state and a full apprehension of the extent of its workings. To this end, as we have already stressed, both Antonio Gramsci's conception of the "integral state" and his elaboration of the mechanisms of hegemony, and Michel Foucault's analysis of biopolitics, can be of use. They can help us to recognize the strategic, relational, and in no sense neutral character of the state.

But what about those "positive" aspects of the state that are now under attack by neoliberal fundamentalists? Here a more Poulantzian approach is necessary: if the state represents the material condensation of a balance of class forces, then the positive aspects of the capitalist state cease to be expressions of some inherent political and social rationality that the working classes could simply take up and instead appear as what they are: the uneven and ever-threatened expressions of the presence of working class and popular struggles and demands within the state and their tendential ability to impose restrictions upon capitalist violence.

However, at the same time we must stress that this does not mean that we can have a process of self-transformation of the state "from within," based only upon the efficacy of popular struggles. There is always going to be an aspect "in dominance," and this is the role of the state in the reproduction of the prevailing social relations of exploitation and class domination and in enhancing capitalist strategies of accumulation. Moreover, even maintaining its positive aspects (such as the public provision of basic goods and services) is far from certain if we take into consideration the widespread use of management techniques derived from the private sector and industry, and the constant pressure of privatization. In this sense, Louis Althusser's warning against any reformist reading of the "relational" conception of the state remains valid. The state represents a materialization of the class relation of forces, one that is characterized by an excess of force on the part of the dominant classes:

> The relatively stable resultant (reproduced in its stability by the state) of this *confrontation* of forces (*balance* of forces is an accountant's notion, because it is static) is that *what counts is the dynamic excess of force* maintained by the dominant class in the class struggle. It is this *excess of conflictual force, real or potential, which constitutes energy A*, which is subsequently transformed into power by the state-machine: *transformed into right, laws and norms.*
>
> Just as Marx said that 'the tailor disappears in the costume' (the tailor and all the energy that he expended cutting and sewing), so the whole hinterworld of the confrontation of forces and violence, *the worst forms of violence of class struggle, disappear in their one and only resultant: the Force of the dominant class, which does not even appear as what it is—the excess of its own force over the force of the dominated classes- but as Force tout court.* And it is this Force or Violence which is subsequently transformed into power by the state-machine.[31]

I think that this point by Althusser is very important and a necessary addition or even corrective to Poulantzas's conception of the state as the condensation of a class relation of forces. It points toward this relation being structurally uneven, since the excess of force of the capitalist class is materialized in state apparatuses and practices, whereas the efficacy of class struggles, despite being always present, reaches certain limits. Consequently, the only way to counter this uneven relation of forces is by an excess of popular power or counterpower "from below," in the form of radical social movements with expansive anticapitalist practices and forms of self-organization that defy exactly these limits. It is here that the notion of dual power acquires a broader significance than in its original conception by Lenin.[32] It is no longer just a question of a period of organic crisis and catastrophic equilibrium, during which there is an antagonistic coexistence of two competing state forms. Dual power refers to the emergence of new social and political forms, as part of the elevation of struggle and the fight for power and hegemony on the part of an alliance of the subaltern classes. It is not a political "stand-off": it is a process of intense struggle, but also of learning and experimentation. Moreover, dual power is in fact the best way to describe the actual social and political balance of forces after the seizure of power, especially if we are talking about a potentially "democratic" process. In such a case, we will encounter new forms of popular power, self-management, worker's control, attempts to institutionalize new social and political arrangements and the continuous resistance of important parts of the state apparatus—along with the attempt from part of the forces of capital to resist attacks against capitalist property and capitalist relations of production. Forms of dual power will be the way to actually influence the balance of forces. We can see not only the potential but also the difficulty of such an endeavor in the attempts to organize forms of popular power from below in Venezuela, and we can see not only their dynamics but also their limits and the obstacles they have faced.[33]

4. SOCIAL TRANSFORMATION AND THE STATE

This gives a new urgency to the reminder that the existing state apparatuses cannot be used "as they are" in any process of social transformation. This has to do with the constitutional and legal protection of capitalist social relations of production, with the role played by repressive apparatuses, and with the active role of ideological apparatuses in regard to social reproduction, notwithstanding their "positive" contribution to crucial aspects of social life.

Therefore, what is needed is not just to struggle so that hospitals and schools remain a responsibility of the state but also to struggle to transform them. How can we make them accountable to actual human needs and not the targets set by the government? What forms of democracy *within* the workplace should be introduced? What forms of democracy that would not limit themselves only to employees in a particular branch but also extend to the "users" of these services, in an attempt to implement self-management and actual collective decision processes? These are important and urgent questions of a directly political nature, which cannot be answered not only in theoretical terms but also through actual experimentation within particular historical and political contexts.

At the same time, the problem of the repressive apparatuses of the state remains important. They are the last line of defense against any potential process of social transformation, and we must expect them to act to this end. Drastically reducing the size of the repressive apparatuses of the state (such as the police), smashing all parallel "security" and "intelligence" structures (doing away both with the chain of command and their immense material means), and imposing forms of democratic social control at all levels can be steps in this direction.

All these are not just theoretical questions. One of the most interesting aspects of contemporary developments and the conjuncture of an economic and political crisis is that the question of governmental power once again presents a possibility as a limit case, in the "weak links of the imperialist chain," to use the old metaphor of the Third International. At the same time, the Greek case made it evident that a failure to proceed with the necessary ruptures, along with a capitulation to the demands of capital and of institutions of capitalist and imperialist integration (such as the European Union [EU]), can lead only to the defeat and demoralization of the subaltern classes and the return—with a vengeance—of the neoliberal Right to power.[34]

Consequently, whether the Left's attainment of governmental power can indeed form part of a revolutionary sequence depends, to a great extent, upon how it deals with the question of the state. For unless there is a process of actual transformation—and, in this sense, a process of revolutionizing the state in ways that enable workers' control and democratic planning in an anticapitalist direction—ultimately the political and economic strategies already inscribed in the state will prevail. This has to do not only with the mentalities of civil servants but also with the material processes inscribed within state apparatuses, their degree of transparency but also mystification, and the knowledge processes implied therein. Constitutional arrangements, legal frameworks, institutional "memories," "specialization," and "compartmentalization"—along with habit and "received wisdom"—represent exactly the materializations of class relations and the means of their reproduction and pose potentially absolute limits to any process of social transformation that would challenge the hegemony of the forces of capital. Of particular importance is the evolution of what Poulantzas foresaw in the late 1970s as "authoritarian statism"[35]—namely, the tendency of actual decision processes to be displaced toward apparatuses and networks insulated against any intervention by the subaltern classes. This is particularly evident in processes of capitalist-imperialist integration like the EU that involve the imposition of reduced sovereignty for member states, as exemplified in the monetary and institutional architecture of the Eurozone, one based upon a system of central banks that are immune to any exercise of popular sovereignty or even political control.[36] It is in this sense that it is impossible to proceed with any process of transformation without also seeking a rupture with such processes of integration.

But what does it mean today to smash the state? Does it mean the abolition "by decree" of state bureaucracy, specialized coercive apparatuses, the judiciary? And what will they be replaced by? Revolutionary militias, people's courts, and ad hoc collective decisions? In a strange dialectic, the answer is both yes and no. On the one hand, one could imagine that for a whole period some form of public authority will remain in place but that it will be "of a completely different type." This will also include institutions guaranteeing full political rights and a protection against arbitrary decisions. At the same time, forms of a "people in arms" should be put in place in order to implement de facto democratic social control of coercive apparatuses, and the same goes for the combination of progressive legal reform, greater emphasis on participation in the execution of justice, and a new conception of legality based not only upon abstract and universal rules but also upon the concrete analysis of each case in its peculiarities (a practice common to all forms of popular justice associated with major popular movements—the role of jurors being to attempt to first reconcile, to find solutions, and to take into consideration the specificity of each case, rather than simply to impose punishment).

Here another point must be made. It remains an open question whether in advanced capitalist societies, with their extended economic, political, and ideological state apparatuses (or "hegemonic apparatuses" of the "integral state"), a "classical" insurrectionary opening of a revolutionary sequence—in the form of an "organic crisis" and subsequent collapse of the state—is possible; or whether, by contrast, a "democratic road" is possible, in the form of a hegemonic crisis that leads to sharp changes/shifts in electoral representation and the Left's accession to governmental power, as the experience of Bolivia, Venezuela, or the electoral dynamics in Greece in the mid-2010s appeared to suggest.

However, this would be an underestimation of the potential of bourgeois counterattack, of segments of the state apparatus that defend the previous social "status quo," and of course, of the imperialist forces that might wish to undermine, sabotage, or even openly to oppose any process of social transformation. In this sense, even though the beginning of the process can possibly be "democratic," its evolution will not necessarily be "peaceful," and this must be an aspect that no one interested in communist politics should underestimate. In this sense, the question of popular violence—as a democratic, political, nonidealized, noninstrumental, form of violence—remains an integral aspect of revolutionary politics. It is exactly the challenge of what Georges Labica described as the impossibility of nonviolence.[37] And it is here that it is important for any potential revolutionary political organization to actually have a political position as regard violence, to actually think through such questions and try to draw the line between emancipatory popular violence and the instrumental violence of oppression.

This requires a deepening of and experimentation with extended democratic practices. This is in sharp contrast to the suspicion of open democratic practices that plagued the historical communist movement. Democracy means contradictions, differences, struggles, conflicts—not just a "voicing of opinions." This is not only unavoidable but also positive; it is the only way to deploy an actual "dialectic in action," to experiment with a different configuration, and to make good use of struggles and demands even during "socialist construction." It is also the only way to actually wage class struggle against all forms of the reemergence of capitalist social forms, practices, norms, and relations, which in most cases take the form of "the most obvious solution." One might even say that only in the context of socialism, of communist politics, can democracy find its real nature. In a certain sense, capitalism is innately undemocratic, since the democratic impulse—not as the sanitized "deliberation" proscribed by liberalism but as collective will or social transformation—is an expression of subaltern demands and aspirations. In a way, the syntagma "liberal democracy" is a contradiction in terms, representing both the history of struggles for democratic rights on the part of the subaltern classes and the attempt of the bourgeoisie to establish its hegemony through parliamentary procedures.

5. SOCIAL TRANSFORMATION AS SOCIAL EXPERIMENTATION AND THE QUESTION OF ORGANIZATION

Moreover, we have to think of this process as a process of experimentation. This goes for both its political and social forms. This conception of social transformation as social experimentation can be traced back to Marx in the *Critique of the Gotha Program*, where he insisted that such questions can only be answered "scientifically"—that is, by means of extended experimentation:

> The question then arises: what transformation will the state undergo in communist society? In other words, what social functions will remain in existence there that are analogous to present state functions? This question can only be

answered scientifically, and one does not get a flea-hop nearer to the problem by a thousand fold combination of the word people with the word state.

Between capitalist and communist society lies the period of the revolutionary transformation of the one into the other. Corresponding to this is also a political transition period in which the state can be nothing but *the revolutionary dictatorship of the proletariat.*[38]

In this sense, emergent forms of popular self-organization, of networking, of equal voicing, of open and democratic decision-making, and in general all forms of the contemporary "democracy of struggle" should not be seen instrumentally as merely ways to organize struggle more efficiently. Occupations of open spaces, with their egalitarian and democratic organizations—from syntagma to Zuccotti Part and Gezi Park; mass assemblies, mass coordinations of broader movements; horizontal networks of struggle and contention, like those employed during the *Gilets Jaunes* movement in France, which entailed horizontal coordination at the national level, with forms of local assemblies: these are also emergent forms of popular power from below, of experimentation with new forms of democracy, and can be considered to be emerging contemporary potential forms of dual power. In a similar way, contemporary forms of solidarity, self-management, alternative noncommercial networks of distribution, open access to services are not only ways to deal with urgent social problems. They are also experimental test sites for new social configurations, for new non-capitalist social relations and collective practices, drawing on the "traces of communism" within contemporary social resistances and collective demands and aspirations. Revolutionary politics is also a learning experience, a process of learning through the experience of struggles. In this sense, "smashing the state" is a process of collective experimentation with new political and social configurations, based upon the experiences of struggle and self-organization, which emerge long before the nominal seize of power. It is therefore important to revisit the experiences of such forms of self-organization, as well as the centrality of the notion of the "council," along with historical experiences such as the soviets. Anweiler offers important insights, even if one could disagree with his harsh criticism of the Bolsheviks.[39]

In the long run, this experimentation needs to evolve to deal head on with the social relations and forms that act as terrains of reproduction for capitalist relations of production. One side has to do with the attempt to overcome the compulsion(s) of the market. The market is not just a mechanism of exchange. It is also a form or socialization of private labors and an expression of the reproduction of capitalist forms. Moreover, it is also a powerful ideological mechanism, which constantly compels us to treat capitalist social forms as "natural." The experimentation with non-market-led forms for coordinating economic practices is therefore an important aspect of any move toward socialist transformation. Another side has to do with the social division of labor. An important aspect of the Marxist tradition has been that the transition to communism also entails the abolition of the division of manual and intellectual labor. Moreover, the very experience of class struggles in the USSR and other social formations of "actually existing socialism" has shown that the reproduction of the capitalist division of labor and workplace hierarchy lead, in the end, to the reproduction of state-capitalist forms of exploitation, even under a condition of the abolition of private property. This was also the main thrust of the critique of the Chinese Cultural Revolution.[40] Therefore, the attempt to socialize knowledge and technical expertise, to offer full access to scientific study and training in all sectors, and to implement forms of democratic decision at all levels in the workplace still remain among the most important exigencies of any process of social transformation.

Moreover, only such an attempt at achieving extensive democratic participation at all levels of social life, including the supposedly closed terrain of the economy, can take the necessary steps toward an overcoming bourgeois separation of the economic and the political. The division between economic agent and citizen, so fundamental for bourgeois politics, must be superseded in any process of social transformation through a necessary repoliticization of the economy along with a resocialization of politics. This is exactly the meaning of a new form of politics, a new political practice, based upon an extended democracy in the workplace, new extended forms of participative democracy, forms of representation drawn from the workplace (an important element in the early projects of socialist voting systems), and the institution of limits against the creation of a professional political class.

These aspects are important exactly for an endeavor to actually smash the state, to decrease the need to resort to state coercion, establish democratic decision-making and self-organization (the very meaning of "free association") at all levels, and to actually create a much more equal and free society. This will be the result not only of struggles but also of experiments.

To take a Gramscian perspective, when we broach the question of revolutionary strategy in contemporary terms, we are in fact always faced with a combination of a war of position and a war of maneuver. Moreover, a war of position—namely an attempt at constructing hegemony—remains necessary both before and after the seizure of power. This should not be read as a reference to "cultural" hegemony or "preparation," as in the reformist reading of the 1970s. Rather it refers to the continuous process of struggles, collective experimentation, the creation of new forms of popular power and workers' control. "Smashing the state," therefore, is not opposed to the attempt to build hegemony; rather, the two are part and parcel of the same dialectic of social transformation. Hegemony on the part of the subaltern class refers to a deepening of politicization and political participation at all levels of society, a process of "socializing" politics, together with a cultural transformation (or cultural revolution)—all these represent exactly those elements that capture the essence of any process of "smashing the state."

This dialectic of hegemony and the need for a process of cultural revolution can also be seen as the only means through which to create the ideological and cultural conditions for the necessary politicization of everyday life and the socialization of the political process that "smashing the state"—and even more so, the "withering away of the state"—entails. This requires that people think and act beyond the compulsion of the market but also move beyond their reliance on an impersonal and benevolent—"paternalistic"— state apparatus. A revolutionary process also requires a new collective ethos of participation and collective responsibility in order to avoid the danger of the retrenchment of an alienated relation to social and political processes—one that can easily lead to the reproduction of capitalist social forms and norms.

This also means that the question of the political program is important. What is needed is a set of demands that not only bridge the gap between immediate demands and socialist transformation but actually articulate a narrative of transition and point to the necessary ruptures that can set a revolutionary process in motion. Such a program cannot remain limited to demands for "redistribution"; it must also point to an alternative economic and productive paradigm, include demands for a rupture from processes of the internationalization of capital, such as the euro, for mass nationalizations of banks and strategic enterprises, for self-management and alternative distribution networks. It must suggest a new orientation, away from "export-oriented growth" and consumerism and toward a new hierarchy of economic priorities, based upon actual social needs and environmental sustainability— something that is now particularly urgent, faced as we are with the imminent danger of ecological disaster. Moreover, such a program should also point to the radical transformation of social reproduction[41] as part of the struggle against sexism and patriarchy—especially as the reproduction of patriarchy and heteronormativity has been an important aspect of the reproduction of capitalism and forms part of a broader oppressive condition that facilitates exploitation and capitalist rule. For despite neoliberals' insistence that they oppose sexual discrimination, the reality of most capitalist states manifests the enduring linkage between capitalism, patriarchy, and heteronormativity.

"Smashing the state," then, entails a return to all the major questions of revolutionary strategy and an actual attempt to initiate a process of social transformation; it should be seen as a highly original and open process of social transformation.

And this brings us to the question of political organization. Against the organized force of the state and its collective organizational and intellectual capacities, the question of organization remains central, in the sense of it being the only way to counter the radical unevenness of class struggles. What kind of political organizations do we need in order to be able to attempt such a revolutionary process? This is the sense that the "party question" takes today. The traditional model that viewed, in a schematic and mechanical way, confrontations with the question of power in terms of a military logic, placing all the emphasis on discipline, is of course inherently inadequate, and moreover runs the risk of imitating the model of the bourgeois state. It is necessary to think that in the struggle for a different society, based upon principles and practices that would be antagonistic to a bourgeois/capitalist logic, we would need organizations that reflect emerging new social forms. In contrast to the traditional view—according to which the exigencies of the struggle and the need for a disciplined commitment to the revolutionary process justify placing limits upon intraparty democracy, the suppression of free discussion, and adhering to a rigid hierarchy—we want political organizations that are at once laboratories for the collective elaboration of new projects—new mass forms of critical political intellectuality—and experimental sites for new social and political relations. In this sense, they have to be more democratic, more egalitarian, and more open than the society around them. Gramsci was among the first to stress this conception of the political organization as laboratory:

> One should stress the importance and significance, which, in the modern world, political parties have in the elaboration and diffusion of conceptions of the world, because essentially what they do is work out the ethics and the politics corresponding to these conceptions and act as, as it were, their historical "laboratory." . . . The relation between theory and practice becomes even closer the more the conception is vitally and radically innovative and opposed to old ways of thinking. For this reason one can say that the parties are the elaborators of new integral and all-encompassing intellectualities and the crucibles where the unification of theory and practice understood as real historical process takes place.[42]

However, this should not be grasped as an abstract exigency, but as an urgent task—one that also implies an entire process of reconstructing and reinventing political organizations and includes a revisiting of theoretical debates on organization.[43] Contemporary radical political organizations do not only reflect the dynamics of the conjuncture and present struggles, but they are also the result of a lengthy period of crisis and the retreat of the communist and revolutionary socialist movement. This is also evident today in the limitations of the main organizational forms that are proposed or imaginable: a "horizontal coordination" of movements, which is indispensable in order to create alliances and open spaces of struggle, yet at the same time does not help in the necessary elaboration of political programs and usually does not permit any discussion of questions of political power and hegemony; a left-wing "electoral front" that largely remains founded on a minimal program of immediate anti-neoliberal reforms, which can easily take on the cast of a reformist agenda for progressive social democratic governance; a classical model of the revolutionary group or sect (along with their attendant international currents) that tends to reproduce fragmentation, sectarianism, and a parochial authoritarian version of an "imaginary Leninism," including, in some cases, the reproduction of sexist and patriarchal hierarchies. In contrast to all these, "repeating Lenin" today means thinking with maximum originality, seeking to not merely reproduce a given model but to create laboratories for new political projects. This can be accomplished neither through simple electoral coalitions nor through the antagonism between groups for "hegemony" on the radical Left. We need democratic political fronts, based upon anticapitalist programs that can also act as processes that bring together different currents and experiences within the movement, and political sensitivities that can actually act as laboratories for new and antagonistic political projects. In this sense—precisely as Gramsci defined the integral state as the "entire complex of practical and theoretical activities" that ensure the hegemony of the bourgeoisie—the Modern Prince can only be understood as the entire complex of the theoretical and practical activities that emerge out of the subaltern classes in their struggle for integral autonomy and hegemony.

A more strategic approach, an attempt to ground our politics in the "traces of communism" present within today's resistances (however minor or small-scale they might seem), a new emphasis on the articulation of alternative narratives and not merely "demands," an attempt to create fronts and networks that draw together different experiences and currents—all these are today indispensable aspects of any attempt to reinvent the Left as a force of radical change.

Rethinking revolutionary strategy is no longer a political and theoretical "luxury." We are going through one of the most important transition periods in the history of capitalism. We see great new divides and inter-imperialist rivalries. We have witnessed a new historical cycle of movements, of an almost insurrectionary character, and—at the same time and in a dialectical relation of mutual determination—of a deep political and, in certain cases, hegemonic crisis (expressed also in the rise of the far Right). We have absorbed the bitter lessons of defeat and failure. It is now urgent to once again begin to think in terms of strategy if we do not want to miss the opportunities at hand. After all, we must never forget that history has more imagination than we do.

NOTES

1. Spyros Sakellaropoulos and Panagiotis Sotiris, "Postcards from the Future: The Greek Debt Crisis, the Struggle against the EU-IMF Austerity Package and the Open Questions for Left Strategy." *Constellations* 21.2 (2014): pp. 262–273.
2. Stathis Kouvelakis, "SYRIZA's Rise and Fall." *New Left Review* II.97 (2016): pp. 45–70.
3. Antonio Gramsci, *Selections from Prison Writings*, edited and translated by Q. Hoare and G. Nowell Smith (London: Lawrence and Wishart 1971); Peter Thomas, *The Gramscian Moment. Philosophy, Hegemony and Marxism* (Leiden; and Boston, MA: Brill, 2009).
4. Cedric Durand and Razmig Keucheyan, "Un Césarisme Bureaucratique," in: Cedric Durand (ed.), *En finir avec l'Europe* (Paris: La Fabrique, 2013).
5. Alain Badiou, *Metapolitics*, translated by Jason Barker (London: Verso, 2005).
6. John Holloway, *Change the World without Taking Power. The Meaning of Revolution Today* (London: Pluto, 2002).
7. Louis Althusser, *For Marx* (London: Allen Lane, the Penguin Press, 1969); Louis Althusser et al., *Reading Capital*, translated by Ben Brewster (London: Verso, 2016).
8. Charles Bettelheim, *Class Struggles in the USSR*, 2 Vols., translated by Brian Pearce (New York: Monthly Review Press, 1976–1978).
9. Mario Tronti, *Operai e capital* (Roma: Derive Approdi, 2006); Toni Negri, *Revolution Retrieved. Writings on Marx, Keynes, Capitalist Crisis and New Social Subjects (1967–83)* (London: Red Notes, 1988).
10. Harry Braverman, *Labor and Monopoly Capital. The Degradation of Work in the Twentieth Century* (New York: Monthly Review Press, 1974); Benjamin Coriat, *Science, technique et capital* (Paris: Seuil, 1976).
11. Michael Heinrich, *Die Wissenschaft vom Wert. Die Marxsche Kritik der politischen Ökonomie zwischen wissenschaftlicher Revolution und klassischer Tradition* (Münster: Westfälisches Dampfboot, 2006).
12. Karl Marx, *Capital* Vol. 3, in *MECW*, vol. 37 (London: Lawrence and Wishart, 1975–2004), 777–778.
13. Michel Foucault, *Discipline and Punish*, translated by Alan Sheridan (New York: Pantheon Books, 1977); Michel Foucault, *Society Must Be Defended. Lectures at the Collège de France 1975–1976*, translated by David Macey (London: Picador, 2003); Michel Foucault, *Security, Territory, Population. Lectures at the Collège de France 1977–1978*, translated by Graham Burchell (London: Palgrave/Macmillan, 2007); Michel Foucault, *The Birth of Biopolitics. Lectures at the Collège de France 1977–1978*, translated by Graham Burchell (London: Palgrave/Macmillan, 2008); Michel Foucault, *The Punitive Society. Lectures at the Collège de France 1972–1973*, translated by Graham Burchell (London: Palgrave/Macmillan, 2015); Pierre Macherey, "Le sujet productif," http://philolarge.hypotheses.org/1245, 2012.
14. Christine Buci-Glucksmann, *Gramsci and the State*, translated by David Fernbach (London: Lawrence and Wishart, 1980); Peter Thomas. *The Gramscian Moment: Philosophy, Hegemony and Marxism* (Leiden; and Boston, MA: Brill, 2009).

15. Gramsci, *Selections*, 244.
16. Louis Althusser, *On the Reproduction of Capitalism*, translated by G. M. Goshgarian (London: Verso, 2014).
17. Nicos Poulantzas, *Classes in Contemporary Capitalism*, translated by David Fernbach (London: NLB, 1975), 26.
18. Cemal Burak Tansel (ed.), *States of Discipline. Authoritarian Neoliberalism and the Contested Reproduction of Capitalist Order* (New York: Rowman & Littlefield, 2017).
19. *MECW*, vol. 6, 504.
20. *MECW*, vol. 6, 505–506.
21. Étienne Balibar, *Masses, Classes, Ideas. Studies on Politics and Philosophy before and after Marx*, translated by James Swenson (London and New York: Routledge, 1994), 134.
22. *MECW*, vol. 23, 175.
23. Étienne Balibar, *Cinque études du matérialisme historique* (Paris: Maspero, 1974), 95–96.
24. John Riddell (ed.), *To the Masses: Proceedings of the Fourth Congress of the Communist International, 1922* (Leiden: Brill, 2012).
25. Georg Lukács, "Blum Theses," in: Michael McColgan (trans.), *Tactics and Ethics 1919–1929. The Question of Parliamentarism and Other Essays* (London: Verso, 2014).
26. Antonio Gramsci, *Quaderni di carcere*, edited by V. Gerratana (Torino: Einaudi, 1975).
27. Gramsci, *Selections*, 238.
28. Christine Buci-Glucksmann and Göran Therborn, *Le défi social-democrate* (Paris: La Découverte, 1981).
29. Bhaskar Shunkara, *The Socialist Manifesto. A Case for Radical Politics in an Era of Extreme Inequality* (New York: Basic Books, 2019).
30. Eric Blanc, "Why Kautsky Was Right (and Why You Should Care)," https://www.jacobinmag.com/2019/04/karl-kautsky-democratic-socialism-elections-rupture, 2019.
31. Louis Althusser, *Philosophy of the Encounter. Later Writings 1978–1987*, translated by G.M. Goshgarian (London: Verso, 2006), 109.
32. Vladimir Ilyich Lenin, "The Dual Power," in *Collected Works*, vol. 24 (Moscow: Progress Publishers, 1964).
33. George Ciccariello-Maher, "Dual Power in the Venezuelan Revolution," in *Monthly Review* 59, No. 4, https://monthlyreview.org/2007/09/01/dual-power-in-the-venezuelan-revolution/, 2007; George Ciccariello-Maher, *We Created Chávez. A People's History of the Venezuelan Revolution* (Durham, NC: Duke University Press, 2013); George Ciccariello-Maher, *Building the Commune. Radical Democracy in Venezuela* (London: Verso, 2016).
34. Stathis Kouvelakis, "SYRIZA's Rise and Fall." *New Left Review* II.97 (2016): pp. 45–70; Stathis Kouvelakis, "Borderland. Greece and the EU's Southern Question." *New Left Review* II.110 (2018): pp. 5–33; Panagiotis Sotiris, "Defeat and Recomposition. Thoughts on the Greek Election," 2019, http://www.historicalmaterialism.org/blog/defeat-and-recomposition-thoughts-greek-election.

35. Nicos Poulantzas, *State, Power, Socialism*, translated by P. Camiller (London: Verso, 2000).

36. Costas Lapavitsas, *The Left Case against the EU* (London: Polity, 2019).

37. Georges Labica, *Théorie de la Violence* (Naples/Paris: La Citta del sole & Vrin, 2008).

38. *MECW*, vol. 24, 95.

39. Oscar Anweiler, *The Soviets: The Russian Workers, Peasants, and Soldiers Councils, 1905–1921*, translated by Ruth Hein (New York: Pantheon Books, 1974).

40. Charles Bettelheim, *Cultural Revolution and Industrial Revolution in China. Changes in Management and the Division of Labor*, translated by Alfred Ehrenfeld (New York: Monthly Review Press, 1974).

41. Tithy Bhattacharya (ed.), *Social Reproduction Theory. Remapping Class, Recentering Oppression* (London: Pluto, 2017).

42. Gramsci, *Selections*, 335, translation modified.

43. Peter Thomas, "The Communist Hypothesis and the Question of Organization." *Theory & Event* 16.4 (2013).

Chapter 5

Lindsey's "Concealed State" and the Left Strategy

Maria Kochkina

It seems that 2019 was the year we finally started to realize the catastrophic conditions we live in. In September, 6 million people around the world joined strikes and demonstrations to demand immediate action on the ecological emergency. On September 23, a sixteen-year-old activist Greta Thunberg delivered an impassioned speech at the UN's Climate Action Summit, which got quoted across the media and instantly became historic. In the speech, Thunberg excoriated world leaders for their failure to address the climate crisis. Thunberg's tone was full of bitter disappointment. The governments had not proposed any effective measures to tackle the problem or had even chosen to ignore the issue (e.g., Trump had vowed to pull the United States out of the Paris agreement and China had declined to make any new commitments).

It is obvious that global problems like climate change require a united action by all the governments to regulate emissions, pollution, and fossil fuel extraction—as Greta said, it simply cannot be solved by what most world leaders propose: "business as usual and technologies that barely exist." But we also live in a reality of nation-states with their own sociopolitical conditions, economic interests, and the limited leverage people have over the decision-making process. Even if we assume that it is possible to address the state there are still two questions complicating the contemporary situation:

1. Does the state have power in the age of globalized capital?
2. If the state has its own current agenda, how does a political movement relate to it?

In this chapter, I discuss the ideological strategies the state uses to promote the image of the necessity of the current state of affairs and the impossibility of change. I argue that what we need to do in order to be able to demand the changes needed to solve global issues is to unravel the state's agency and to use all of its capacities to make a change. This means adopting an attitude of "cynicism" toward the state when we take everything we can from it without putting any trust in it.

1. DOES THE STATE STILL HAVE POWER?

There is a tendency in contemporary political thought to maintain that the conceptualization of the state becomes the more irrelevant, the more the effects of globalization and the expansion of the capital grow apparent and undermine the sovereignty of nation-states. The condensation of capital by transnational corporations, the expanding influence of supranational organizations (such as the International Monetary Fund and World Bank), the development of information technologies, and the increasing migration are the signs of the change that is taking place. This idea of the weakening of the state is especially prominent in Michael Hardt and Antonio Negri's influential book *Empire*.[1] In their view, today's sovereignty is dispersed and there are no territorial centers of power. This happens due to the transformation in dominant productive processes, in which industrial factory labor gives way to "communicative, cooperative and affective labor."

Even if we do not accept this idea of the shift toward the immaterial production, advocated by postoperaist thinkers, such as aforementioned Hardt and Negri, Paolo Virno, Maurizzio Lazzarato, and others, it is hard not to admit that computerization has changed the way production is organized. As Nick Dyer Witherford shows in his thorough study of this process, although digital capitalism is usually headquartered in the United States, Europe, and East Asia (Japan), "it has nevertheless spread out from the center of the capitalist world-system on a runaway trajectory transforming the relation of its core and peripheral regions."[2] In his view, the greatest impact of digitalization is not in what commodities are produced, that is mobile phones, portable computers, applications, search engines, and so on, but how all commodities are produced, that is, in the fact that it became possible to split production into different locations via electronically coordinated supply chains or global value chains.[3] What this means is that the corporations can exist and pursue their interests in the territories of many countries at the same time, threading their way between governments' regulations, for example, H&M, the second-largest clothing retailer in the world, headquarters in Stockholm where it follows strict regulations regarding workers' rights, taxation, and environmental impact. However, the company's factories are located in countries where the state cannot guarantee the same control. It was reported that H&M paid only US$75 in taxes to Bangladesh in 2008.[4] It becomes clear that imposing control on the operations of a transnational corporation is challenging as it can always transfer its production to a different country, so that, from a global perspective, this does not change much in how it exercises its power.

On the other hand, it seems that the state's power is weakening not only because corporations operate beyond the limits of one state but also because of the withdrawal from many spheres of society's life through adopting neoliberal politics. The state becomes increasingly biased:

> In the event of conflict, a typical neoliberal state will tend to side with a good business climate as opposed to collective rights (and quality of life) of labour or the capacity of the environment to regenerate itself. The second arena of bias arises because, in the event of conflict, neoliberal states typically favour the integrity of financial system and the solvency of financial institutions over the well-being of the population or environmental quality.[5]

However, some contemporary thinkers do not agree that globalization weakens state power. Jason Royce Lindsey is one of the most prominent authors who oppose this point of view. As he writes, the private sector is highly dependent on the state for three reasons.

First, because "much of the research investment underlying impressive new technologies, medical treatments, and the continued development of the fine arts is dependent upon the state financial support."[6] Mariana Mazzucato, in her book *The Entrepreneurial State*,[7] examines the role of the state in stimulating long-run innovation which leads to economic growth. Mazzucato demonstrates on the example of the United States that many innovative industries (like digital technology, biotechnology, and green energy) are propelled through the state sponsorship. In the fields where private companies do not take risks that cannot guarantee the benefit, the state does take the high-risk investments. On many occasions, the state does not get credit, and private corporations appropriate the products of such investments ("Apple" is one such example).

Second, business relies on the state because "the legal framework for corporations and the initial guarantee underpinning most transaction agreements originate with the state's sovereignty."[8]

Third, states are important consumers. As statistics cited by Lindsey show, governments account for around one-fifth of all economic activities (for OECD countries in 2007). Moreover, the state outsources many of its functions to private companies (e.g., in the United States there are firms specialized in garbage collection, public education, and prisons).

According to Lindsey, the image of its weakening is promoted by the state itself. It is highly beneficial to the state because it is meant to conceal its real power. Lindsey calls this condition of the state "hiding" its agency the "concealment of the state."

2. HOW DOES THE STATE CONCEAL ITS AGENCY?

Lindsey further explains that the concealment of the state is a strategy to deal with an ambiguous position of the state in globalization. On the one hand, the weight of a state's voice in the international arena and the capacity of pursuing its interest heavily depend on the economic health of the country and its relationships with the powerful market players. On the other hand, globalization creates problems which citizens urge the state to mitigate (like migration, job insecurity, currency fluctuation, price instability, and environmental threat). The concealment of its agency allows the state to balance between these two forces:

> The state can retreat behind the screen of the "free" market to answer both camps in contemporary society. For the winners of globalization, the state appears to get out of the way of market innovation and productivity. For the citizenry alarmed at globalization's outcomes, the state claims to be powerless against the inevitable.[9]

The result of this strategy of concealment is that the bigger part of the state's functioning and decision-making transitions to the so-called deep state. Of course, secrecy as a tool of the state comes as no surprise: in the Modern times, these secrets were called "arcana imperii." The dependency on secrets intensified during the Cold War but has been maintained after the major Communist threat was neutralized.[10] However, according to Lindsey, the contemporary shift is characterized by the fact that the furtiveness is spreading from the areas where it has traditionally existed (like defense and intelligence) into mundane policy-making:

> Examples include budget recommendations, environmental regulations, consumer and workplace safety, scientific investment, transportation planning, and educational policies.[11]

Maïa Pal studied the conditions in which the establishment of the largest free-trade zone agreements in the world (The Transatlantic Trade and Investment Partnership, Trans-Pacific Partnership Agreement, and Comprehensive Economic and Trade Agreement) was accepted. She notes that the exceptional secrecy of the negotiations ensures that "what communities are being excluded from is, in a sense, the regulation of regulation."[12] It means that the people who are being regulated do not even know that they are being regulated.

The significant decisions being made "behind closed doors," the range of questions remaining to the public shallows down. The focus of politics increasingly shifts to "national identity, cultural controversy, consumer frustrations, and symbolic acts of solidarity with constituents."[13] However, I would argue that despite the intensification of the secrecy measures, sometimes it is not necessarily the surreptitiousness that is responsible for the public consent to the regulations. It is enough that a highly important and contentious policy-making is lost in an array of ordinary procedures or masked as a necessary operation for the people not to acknowledge that they are being regulated or that something significant is being taken from them. For example, the current administration of Canada with the highly popular Prime Minister Justin Trudeau is enjoying the image of a headliner in its efforts to combat climate change. At the same time, the extent of oil extraction (Canada being the largest exporter of petroleum to the United States) in Alberta's tar sands and other Canadian plants, which is extremely detrimental to the environment, is not widely addressed.[14] Also a state can have high ecological standards and achieve great progress inside the country but export unsustainable practices elsewhere in the world, which from a global point of view does not make it much of a game changer. This is the case with Norway where the government heavily incentivizes ownership of electric cars (31.2 percent of all car sales in 2018).[15] However, the state funds these initiatives through its sovereign wealth fund, which is almost entirely consisted of profits from Norway's oil and fossil fuel exports. What this shows is that rather than using secrecy, the state can rely on ideology (like the image of a green country). Lindsey identifies "free market" as an ideological technology of concealment, but I also believe that "democracy" can similarly serve as one.

As mentioned, Lindsey argues that the idea of the weakening of the state is a tool used by the state itself to conceal its agency and to narrow down the space for awareness and involvement of the public in its activities. The concealment is achieved through the proliferation of an ideological scheme according to which nowadays most social and political processes are determined by the economy:

> The state claims that its creation, the market has become even more autonomous than in the past and stands as an alternate entity to the state.[16]

Although the state still functions as a guarantor, an initiator of or actor in affairs as it "provides the regulatory infrastructure the market relies upon and the sovereign guarantee necessary to underpin all other agreements,"[17] its role becomes obscure and actions unaccountable. If we think that key processes occur because of economic necessity, we do not only stop viewing the state as the subject of these changes, but we also stop looking for the cause at all.

The reason for this is that the mechanics of the market are viewed in a way similar to natural phenomena. This was already emphasized by Marx in *The Poverty of Philosophy* (1847):

> When the economists say that present-day relations the relations of bourgeois production—are natural, they imply that these are the relations in which wealth is created and productive forces developed in conformity with the laws of nature. These relations therefore are themselves natural laws independent of the influence of time. They are eternal laws which must always govern society.[18]

This means that the market excludes a figure of the subject as well. The "free market" is an anonymous space. Nobody there exercises power or acts on his or her own accord; one only follows the market rules and fluctuations. The "invisible hand" is the only real sovereign. This invisibility of the sovereign position is reminiscent of the characteristic trait of *democracy*, which can also function as a concealment strategy. Claude Lefort argues that the unprecedented feature of democracy is that "the locus of power becomes an empty place."[19] The exercise of power is a subject of procedural accuracy and is restrained by the rule of law. In a way, it is supposed to be a mechanical system to guarantee that there is "a gap between the place of power and whoever occupies it."[20] Political representation implies that those who are in the position of power are an instrument of law and are busy with the implementation of the will of the citizens. In this way, they are unaccountable for the collective decisions that are being made through proper democratic procedures.

As a result of this desubjectivization, the state appears as possessing only the executive functions. In many cases, this is used as a *carte blanche* for the state's actions. Jodi Dean observes this phenomenon by studying the case of George Bush administration's decision to intervene militarily in the Middle East:

> When Bush speaks he does not fully occupy the place of power. His word is not law. Rather, it is law that speaks and Bush carries it out. . . . Thus, he carries out the will and desires of others, not his own, in accordance with law. To do so, he too has to presuppose that he knows these desires. Here, we might think of Bush's frequent invocations of the Iraqi people and their desires for freedom and democracy. He too acts in behalf of them, to realize their desire for liberty. In helping them do so, he, like America itself, is a tool in the hands of nature and history.[21]

To rely heavily on the assumed desire of the people is a very widely used ideological tool for the politicians in the contemporary democratic states. The assumed desire is the basis to pursue the type of democracy that the state seeks. I would call it "the required democracy." This means that while the state conceals its agency, it uses democratic procedures, the idea of legality and the figure of the majority to achieve the desired effect it wants from the citizens. For example, you might have a right to vote, but you are obliged to vote a certain way. Kristin Ross studies this phenomenon using the case of the Irish referendum on the European Constitution in 2008. The Irish rejected the document, and the European press reacted with "a mounting suspicion toward the vote," viewing it as "a potential occasion for irrational and destructive behavior on the part of the public."[22] French foreign minister stated that "it would be very annoying for the right-thinking people if we couldn't count on the Irish" (as quoted by Ross–Interview, RTL, June 9, 2008). Thus, media divided the population of Europe into two groups: those who consent to the adoption of the document and those who decided that there was a different option. The case was not only about the content of the treaty but its form as well:

> It was purposefully drafted to communicate to voters through its very form that it was best to leave such complex matters of governance up to the experts, the technocracy.[23]

The European Union (EU) officials demanded a revote to achieve the desired result. This example can function as one more instance of the concealment, which does not necessarily require secrecy measures but appeals to ideology. The answer "no" was considered to be not only a stance against the particular treaty but "against democracy itself,"[24] since the document allegedly was to achieve "greater political effectiveness, greater clarity, and transparency in decision-making in the EU."[25]

The democracy that is implied here is the rule of the "silent majority" on behalf of which the politicians speak. The people who are showing discontent are always the troublesome minority who do not respect the proper democratic "rules."

3. HOW DO WE ADDRESS THE STATE?

The first problem that arises in the condition of the concealment is accountability. Accountability and transparency are the pillars of democratic values, yet in "democratic" societies with increasingly complex state structures, it becomes difficult for ordinary citizens to tell who is responsible for what. The issue of accountability has two sides. The first is the more "physical" one—the mere exclusion from the affairs that takes place in the deep state. The second issue is more of a cultural, or ideological, one: the invisibility of the state's actions and, more generally speaking, of its agenda, which is covered up by the screen of the popular discussions and tropes. As it has been said earlier, it is impossible to demand accountability, when you are blind to the policy that affects you. This condition is ambiguous. If the state is concealed, we lose sight of its capacities—not only ones that negatively affect us but also the ones that might affect us positively. With the impact of globalization becoming more apparent, it is clear that some issues like climate change need to be addressed by the state. If we think that the state is powerless, we start seeking solutions elsewhere: for example, in the market possibilities (waiting for the time when the sustainability technologies become beneficial to capitalist enterprises or for conscientious social businesses to take lead) or in the changes in individual lifestyle which are either highly unlikely or barely make any difference.

Another effect of the concealment strategies, the state losing its subjectivity, and the shallowing of political problems ("turning politics into lifestyle, consumer, and de facto entertainment questions"[26]) is the lack of political participation. If the state is just accommodating to the demands of the market and the economy is an objective force, then it is logical that all the responsibility for the mishaps of life falls on individuals who are supposed to be autonomous actors in this free game. In this ideological framework, it is hard to find an incentive for collective action that would address the state.

Jeffrey Edward Green argues that the idea of participation within democracy should be revised. The citizen in contemporary states becomes more of a spectator rather than a participant in the political processes.[27] The role of the citizen is now to observe critically the deliberations of those who are in power. Although Green's observations are accurate and reflect what has been said earlier, his conclusions and apologetic attitude toward the status quo deserve a repudiation. The fact that we can observe this trend means that the institutions should be challenged and the status quo needs to be thoroughly critiqued.

There is another side to this condition. When the state and economic actors are out of the picture, while somebody still has to be accountable for the state of affairs, the geopolitical and migration discourse comes into place. Nowadays, in different countries of Europe and the United States, we can observe the growing popularity of the far-right sentiment. If the state just exercises its executive role, and the business owners just look for profit according to the laws of the market, then there must be some other force to be responsible for the changes in the life of the people. It might as well be a foreign force that would be taking advantage of the citizens of the country.

4. WHAT IS TO BE DONE?

Taking this into consideration, it seems that to challenge the contemporary condition, the political movements need to re-subjectivize the state and to subjectivize themselves as political actors. This means integrating two seemingly contradictory strategies: addressing the state and dismissing it. The first step is revealing the state's agency and the activities, which implies a systematic and thorough investigation into the affairs of the state and acknowledging its capacities. The second is using the channels of the state to the advantage of the people.

It might seem that the thing that has to be done is to draw attention to the fact that the claimed "democracy" of the state is not a real democracy. The state is biased, and if it is not democratic enough we should claim more democracy. However, I would argue against this approach. To appeal to the state for more democracy, to beg it "to listen to the people," is asking for something that it cannot give, but, at the same time, is asking for something that it can provide in relying on the "silent majority." To the state, any discontent (or a "no" to the "required democracy") is an uncomfortable appeal from a minority that it cannot satisfy. By invoking democracy, protesters put themselves into the same domain. Jodi Dean shows it using the mentioned case with George Bush and his opposition:

> We realize that protesters invoke a democracy imagined as resistance. They appeal to practices of constitutionally protected questioning and critique. . . . Like the protesters, Bush, too, is following and invoking a democratic script, carrying out his mandate. He is executing a decision which, while necessarily in excess of the complex string of reasons and knowledge bearing upon it, takes place nonetheless within a space of power opened up and guaranteed by democratic procedures.[28]

The problem is that the democratic discourse "presents ideals and aspirations as an always already present possibility," where "potential problems are solved in advance, through democratic channels."[29] So the claim for more democracy—more transparency, more participation, more deliberations—is a quantitative claim. It is important to step away from this loop, to form demands and concerns outside of the democratic emblem. By invoking democracy those who oppose the state's policy conceal their agency in a similar way to the state:

> The appeal to democracy seems disingenuous, a way of avoiding the true, partisan, position of the protestors, of masking the fact that their appeal is actually ruptured by a certain excess of power or desire that they can't fully acknowledge. The organizers of the screening don't really seek an inclusive conversation. They want organized political resistance, but they don't state this directly. Instead, they appeal to democracy, shielding themselves from taking responsibility for the divisiveness of politics.[30]

Thus, in order to channel this negativity, there has to be a (collective) subject contesting the "democratic" state. The question is how this contestation can be achieved. Lindsey suggests that "our politics needs to highlight the ability to organize and to get things done *without* the state. Such activities undermine the ideology of concealing the state because they teach us that our current dependency on the state is not a dead end."[31] What this basically means is the creation of organizations that resist cooptation of both the state and the market.

I would suggest something different. I believe we should neither appeal to the state's understanding of the situation and to the true will of the people nor strive to create autonomous organizations that dismiss the state at all. The state is using us, and the only way to gain an advantage of it is to use it as well. As the state exercises its power by denying its agency, we need to return subjectivity back into politics by subjectivizing the state itself and the people resisting the state. To maneuver around the resources that state can give us and take from us, we might need to adopt what I call a "cynical" attitude toward the state. This means that a political movement needs to be "in" the state (utilize it, protest it, address it) but deny its authority. What I understand by the "cynicism" is very similar to the attitude Stefano Harney and Fred Moten described in relation to a position of an intellectual in the modern university:

> It cannot be denied that the university is a place of refuge, and it cannot be accepted that the university is a place of enlightenment. In the face of these conditions one can only sneak into the university and steal what one can. To abuse its hospitality, to spite its mission, to join its refugee colony, its gypsy encampment, to be in but not of.[32]

In other words, we need to use the enormous capacities of the state against the global capital and its own "economic interests" to the advantage of the people, disregarding how "democratic," "green," or "progressive" a particular country might seem. By revealing the subjectivity of the state, we reach a horizon where change indeed might take place and where we can see ourselves as subjects of this change. It seems that in her speech Greta appealed to the world leaders because, as she said, she believed that they didn't truly understand the urgency and scope of the global threat because if they had understood it and still had failed to act, they would have been evil. To adopt a "cynical" attitude means that we need to stop believing the state and always assume that it won't do anything for us unless it does not have another choice.

NOTES

1. Michael Hardt and Antonio Negri, *Empire* (Cambridge, MA: Harvard University Press, 2000).

2. Nick Dyer-Witherford, *Cyber-proletariat. Global Labor in the Digital Vortex* (London: Pluto Press, 2015), 33.

3. See more on this in chapter 6 of Ajay Chaudhary in this volume.

4. "H&M Criticized for Tax Planning," *Radio Sweden*, June 22, 2010, https://sverigesradio.se/sida/artikel.aspx?programid=2054&artikel=3802445.

5. David Harvey, *A Brief History of Neoliberalism* (Oxford, New York: Oxford University Press, 2007), pp. 70–71.

6. Jason Royce Lindsey, *The Concealment of the Sate* (New York: Bloomsbury Publishing, 2013), p. 1.

7. Mariana Mazzucato, *The Entrepreneurial State: Debunking Public vs. Private Sector Myths* (London: Anthem Press, 2013).

8. Lindsey, *The Concealment of the State*, 2.

9. Ibid., 4.

10. Daniel Nemenyi, "Submarine State: on Secrets and Leaks." *Radical Philosophy* 193 (2015): pp. 2–8.

11. Lindsey, *The Concealment of the State*, 6.

12. Maia Pal, "Old Alliances, New struggles. The Transatlantic Trade and Investment Partnership." *Radical Philosophy* 190 (2015): p. 12.

13. Lindsey, *The Concealment of the State*, 5–6.

14. Troy Vettese, "Black Snake in the Grass. The Business Case for the New Pipeline is Terrible." *Alternatives Journal* 43.1 (2017): pp. 58–62.

15. "Norway's Electric Cars Zip to New Record: Almost a Third of All Sales," *Reuters*, January 2, 2019, https://www.reuters.com/article/us-norway-autos/norways-electric-cars-zip-to-new-record-almost-a-third-of-all-sales-idUSKCN1OW0YP.

16. Lindsey, *The Concealment of the State*, 4.

17. Ibid.

18. Karl Marx, "The Poverty of Philosophy," in: David McLellan (ed.), *Selected Writings* (Oxford, New York: Oxford University Press, 2000), 227.

19. Claude Lefort, *Democracy and Political Theory* (Cambridge: Polity Press, 1991), p. 27.

20. Jodi Dean, *Democracy and Other Neoliberal Fantasies: Communicative Capitalism and Left Politics* (Durham, NC: Duke University Press, 2009), p. 85.

21. Ibid.

22. Kristin Ross, "Democracy for Sale," in: Amy Allen (ed.), *Democracy in What State?* (New York: Columbia University Press, 2011), 82–99, cit. p. 83.

23. Ibid., 84.

24. Ibid., 85.

25. Ibid.

26. Lindsey, *The Concealment of the State*, 138.

27. Jeffrey Edward Green, *The Eyes of the People: Democracy in an Age of Spectatorship* (Oxford: Oxford University Press, 2009).

28. Dean, *Democracy and Other Neoliberal Fantasies*, 81.

29. Ibid., 78.

30. Ibid., 84.

31. Lindsey, *The Concealment of the State*, 49.

32. Stefano Harney and Fred Moten, *The Undercommons: Fugitive Planning and Black Study* (Wivenhoe, NY: Minor Compositions, 2013), p. 26.

Chapter 6

Toward a Critical "State Theory" for the Twenty-First Century

Ajay Singh Chaudhary

There has never really been a fully developed critical theory of "the state" in the same way that other features of the Marxian "superstructure" have come to be understood as radically more complex than initial dialectical and structural approaches would suggest. Few would speak of race, gender, nation, or even religion in the kind of arbitrary, unmoored, deterministic, static, or transcendental mode in which many thinkers approach—from multiple directions—"the state" and "the class character of the state" today.

In this chapter, I intend to sketch the lineaments of a "critical state theory." Such a theory, I argue, gives us a much better understanding of the multiplicity of political forms in the contemporary world and a framework through which to understand actually existing states. I begin with a relatively quick review of some debates in state theory and then proceed through a long interpretation of the unfinished work of Franz Neumann who took a rather unique approach to these questions and whose work has particular salience for the current historical juncture, particularly given the multiplicity of state and non-state forms and the changing nature of the global economy. Finally, in reviewing the structure of twenty-first-century global capitalism and state forms within it, we can see what a full critical state theory might look like and portend.

1. STATE THEORIES

Liberal political theory has far from *nothing* to offer a critical theory of "the state." Indeed, even the most orthodox attempts to construct a "Marxist theory of the state" have (if somewhat covertly and while often accusing interlocutors of internalizing or aping "bourgeois" social science and categories) borrowed quite liberally (no pun intended) from liberal theories of the state. In what is still regarded in some circles as the most pivotal recent debate concerning a "Marxist theory of the state," both principal participants, Ralph Miliband and Nikos Poulantzas, utilized categories, concepts, and analyses from Anglo-American, non-Marxian social science.[1] Of course, they had to. Historically, there *is* no Marxist theory of "the state." Marx intended to write a fifth volume of *Capital* that would have addressed the state but never made it even as far as completing the copious notes for Volumes II and III that Engels eventually compiled and published.

Beyond the fact of this historically unfinished project lies the method of what I have called elsewhere "reverent exegesis," or a Marxological approach—looking for answers to empirical and historical questions by studiously poring over the works of the Master.[2] This method, predicated more on philology than on materialist analysis, is a rather bizarre way to conduct Marxian analysis. In the aforementioned debate between Miliband and Poulantzas, the latter seems to be, following in the tradition of his mentor, Louis Althusser, the far more hermeneutically focused of the two. However, both did tie their positions not to what one might deem a Marxian, critical theoretical, or historical materialist method but rather to a few paradigmatic insights extrapolated from key texts by Marx himself and by a small subset of early, influential European Marxist thinkers (typically Lenin, Luxemburg, Trotsky, and Gramsci). Running these against historical evidence or placing within such "frameworks" theoretical principles borrowed from elsewhere, they produced what has passed for a "Marxist theory" of "the state."

It goes far beyond the scope of this chapter to fully recapitulate the whole of this debate, and it is worthwhile to note that even those most interested and invested in it find that the debate ends with no resolution and little possibility for synthesis. Even so, both research programs *do* yield a range of fruitful results, from Miliband's differentiation between states and governments—understanding the different characteristics and personal and overall motivations of individuals across various state institutions—to Poulantzas's observation that, far from operating as a united, single whole, the capitalist class is composed of "class fractions" with sometimes diverging interests and demands. Without appearing overly tendentious, one might observe that these two positions are perfectly compatible if still rather incomplete. What the Miliband-Poulantzas debate represents for my purposes here is the Marxist left in the Global North's rather deleterious proclivity for endlessly replicating a short series of foundational theoretical dilemmas in the history of European Marxism, in this case, for example, casting Miliband as a quasi-Lenin (with an "instrumental" view of "the state") and Poulantzas as a quasi-Luxemburg (with a "structural" view of "the state").[3] This despite both thinkers being rather explicitly nonrevolutionary oriented in either the Leninist or Luxemburgian sense and the *radically* different historical-material conditions separating the 1970s from the beginning of the twentieth century (and equally from today). Like almost all "state theory," these debates treat historically specific phenomenon as transhistorical and transgeographical truths. At bare minimum, we must do more to account for the changing natures of states and capitalism itself. There is no eternal "State."

A critical theory of "the state" must, thus, begin from the Marxian precept that institutions arise from the material activity of human beings procuring their wants, needs, and desires (the most limited possible expression of historical materialism and of the conceptual category of a "mode of production"). But the story of such institutions is hardly the simplistic base-superstructure relationship, which few even Marxists truly hew to. We must ask—as many liberals do too—to what degree are institutions autonomous? How do various—not only class—conflicts play out in states (but, as many Marxists would surely agree, not only in states)? What is the relationship between states and capital? How have such relations and categories and conditions changed over time and through different arrangements of economic and political power? What does the political *ecological* context for human social life tell us about the interrelationship of natural and social systems? About the pivotal role of energy?

Some fruitful attempts have been made in answering these questions. Although many mentioned here draw on the work of Gramsci, whose theory on understanding states and politics—albeit incomplete and of course attuned to a different historical moment—probably remains one of the best.[4] It is not the case of simply applying Gramscian answers or analyses to the present day. As Stuart Hall once said, "We can't pluck up this 'Sardinian' from his specific and unique political formation, beam him down" to our own era.[5] Gramsci's work is not even fully consistent. What he does allow—and what we will want to be looking at broadly in our sketch—is a view of *states* as a field of political action, with some of its own rules and procedures which cannot be simply derived from conflict in the social world (i.e., class conflict) as well as a broad (but not total as is the case with some Marxist thinkers) category. Against the widespread exclusively society-centered reading, for Gramsci, some "trenches" in political conflict are in civil society, some are in states proper. State power works alongside economic *and* ideological power; hegemony *is* state power but also of course, as with Weber and others, state legitimacy, cultural "common sense" (i.e., ideology).[6] Michelle Williams, in studying democratic socialist politics across the Global South (in South Africa and Kerala, India, in particular), has employed a neo-Gramscian framework to see how such unlikely formations as the Communist Party of India (Marxist) in Kerala, a top-down *and* participatory democratic party, and an array of social movements are able to take and manage a form of attenuated state power in the context of a larger Indian Republic whose dominant powers have been either mildly (as with liberalization) or *intensely* antagonistic to it (as with the rise of Hindutva neo-Fascism).[7] This again is reflective of the more creative and open approaches taken by both political actors and theorists in the Global South.

However, even as this work does gesture at new theoretical horizons, they do not establish a critical theory of states, as I outline later. Similarly, the question of the relationship of capital and states—at least within nominally liberal democratic ones—has received a number of fruitful economic treatments from Michael Kalecki, Adam Prezworski, Michael Wallerstein, Paul Sweezy, Samir Amin, and many others. These range from arguments about the ultimate power that capital would have over states—the power to withdraw, or even threaten to withdraw investment of social surplus (i.e., profit)—to models of which and how that might occur (or might not), to accounts of different positions of states within an evolving world system. But as with the work of Williams et al. on *politics*, this work on *economics* is always of a limited temporal range, largely abstract models, and even within the more globally minded thinkers, a remarkable limitation on difference of state form and historical challenges.

In constructing a critical theory of states, we must account for the following:

(a) The multiple forms of states and non-states in the contemporary world. Any reader by now will have noticed my annoying proclivity for putting "the State" in scare quotes. This is because historically and theoretically—and, importantly, especially in the current moment—there are a variety of states and non-states at any given period in modern capitalism. There is not one State.
(b) The changing relationship between capital and states. This is a dynamic relationship over time with institutions and overall state forms and transnational organization changing dramatically.
(c) The changing nature of capitalism itself.
(d) The political economy of states:

   a. in the neoliberal period, and
   b. in the twenty-first century.

(e) What this means for politics today.

Here, I'd like to start with an account of the existing, if incomplete, critical theory of state and law by Franz Neumann because his account is one of the only ones to take truly seriously that there are in any given moment multiple state *and* non-state forms. As we will see, Neumann's attempts to account not merely for what determines a state's "class character" but also for who is "sovereign" and how in a modern state provide a key stepping stone toward understanding actually existing states today. Put into conversation with other thinkers, what begins to develop is a critical state theory in which the sovereignty of many state forms is put into question. In addition to many of the sources already mentioned here, we should pay close attention not only to insights from the broadly conceived left (or even of liberals) but to the history, motion, and practices of *the right*, as well as economic and legal history, political economy and ecology.

But I am also interested in Neumann's theory because it is a "critical theory" in the formal sense.[8] It is a description—aiming for empirical and historical accuracy—that also holds at its core the possibility for social transformation. Much as Gramsci read a thinker like Machiavelli as providing a kind of instruction guide for a new power establishing a new state, Neumann reads Spinoza's early and radical commitment to democracy "as a theory of an opposition that feels its strength and that hopes soon to transform its social power into political power."[9] Neumann's interest is in how one "social power"—popular democratic power—might overcome another, far more entrenched one, the power of capital. "The truth of political theory is political freedom. . . . Since no political system can realize freedom fully, political theory must by necessity be critical."[10]

2. THE BEGINNING OF THE SKETCH: NEUMANN, THE NON-STATE, AND THE CHANGING FORMS OF CAPITALISM

> The liberal state has always been as strong as the political and social situation demanded. It has conducted warfare and crushed strikes; with the help of strong navies, it has protected its investments, with the help of strong armies it has defended and extended its boundaries, with the help of the police it has restored "peace and order."[11]

Even if we confine ourselves to Europe at the beginning of capitalism, we are faced with a multiplicity of states. States—in the modern sense of the word—are far from eternal but neither are they simply a reflection of the development of the capitalist mode of production. But the principle in this quotation expresses a specific quality across these differing states—say England, France, and Germany—namely, that the "strength" and even institutions of a state would match what "the political and social situation demanded." It is always important to note when reading Neumann that he uses "social" in the sense of civil society, such that economic concerns are "social concerns" just as popular concerns could be "social concerns." In both early periods of what Neumann dubbed "autocratic capitalism," and "competitive capitalism," capitalists needed states, as classical political economy would have it, to mint standardized money, to enforce contracts, to establish uniform weights and measures, and to establish the legal parameters in which the "free market" might function. The shift to "competitive capitalism" was largely a political, not an economic, shift. It came with the increasing participation of the bourgeoisie (through incorporation, representation, or outright revolution) in states.

Taking for example the English case, "'the night-watchman state', —to use Lassalle's well-known and very dangerous expression—proved itself capable of preserving the internal security of England, of dealing with the Chartists and the labor movement, and of establishing an immense colonial empire."[12] Thus, we see political liberalism as *largely* an early fiction[13] and conclude, as Neumann notes, that economic liberalism (capitalism) is theoretically and historically compatible with nearly every form of state—whether an absolutist state or a liberal state does not matter much in this regard. And thinking ahead, of course, authoritarian states are also perfectly compatible. The liberal state is, despite protestations of its negative or minimal character, capable of the vast coercive work capital needs and is not necessarily better (for capitalist development) than an absolutist one. The primary difference, in this period, is between whether states are acting on behalf of a political-economic class who are essentially united by both a pre- and nascent-capitalist accumulation (as the case in pre-Revolutionary absolutist France) or directly benefit from the development of productive forces (as was the case in Britain).[14]

Neumann sees his understanding as perfectly Marxist even if he has a central criticism:

> Marxist theory suffers from a misunderstanding: the confusion of sociological analysis with the theory of political action. The Marxist thesis of the class character of the state has been correctly understood as a theory of society; it has been misunderstood as a theory of action. In Marx's sociological theory politics appears as a function of economic class structure: the state is seen as a class state which serves the preservation of the class structure; the classes in turn are based on the production economy but does it follow that according to Marx the action of the proletariat must be predominantly economic and not political?[15]

Although Neumann, like Miliband and Poulantzas, wraps this in a vague Marxological wrapping—largely drawn from the analyses found in texts like the *18th Brumaire*—he supplies an answer that is certainly not easily or transparently apparent in Marx: No. As with Gramsci, economic antagonisms play out in a broadly construed political realm, including in states. Even in the condition of "competitive capitalism," it is *possible* (if not tremendously likely) for political action to supersede private interest. Sociologically "the state" is a "class state," but the question is why?

As with Weber's theory of capitalism and Protestant Christianity, in Neumann, the early modern state and capitalism meet with an elective affinity that becomes an intense bond. New bourgeois relations increase revenue, of which some goes to state coffers, so that states—even if their ruling class is not economically bourgeois in this period—have a tremendous interest in both the formal and the repressive action that nascent capital needs since it boosts revenue and state power. However, Neumann is not adopting the Weberian theory wholesale. Weber—following classical political economy—views the relation of capital and state as dependent: capital needs the liberal state's predictable rule of law to be able to conduct the everyday functioning of commercial life. However, as we've already seen, Neumann observes that non-liberal states can (1) have a predictable rule of law and (2) have a similar relationship to capital. But far more importantly, Neumann sees what Weber describes as a general principle as being specifically historically bounded to the conditions of "competitive capitalism." And even then, one can already observe a far more complex interplay of social forces than the elegant Weberian formula captures.

In discussing the Chartists in England, Neumann observes that, in the light of early nineteenth-century struggles (following Marx's observations on the struggle over the working day in *Capital Vol. I*[16]), "political democracy appeared to the English people as the instrument designed to bring social liberation," although it was "decisively beaten."[17] This failure in some ways goes beyond the inquiry of this chapter into an equally significant question of how, when, and why mass politics can function, but for our purposes here two items suffice.

First, the Chartists underestimated how "political power can be used consciously in shaping the economy."[18] Some read Marx's arguments on labor reform as state intervention on behalf of the reproduction of Capital (extending Capital's life by ameliorating some of its most self-destructive excesses). Others, as a successful multifaceted struggle through both civil society and political action (including the use of unlikely coalitional politics) in which the working class was able to achieve a significant reform at the very heart of capitalist social relations—the production of surplus value. Whichever preferred interpretation or among many positions which combine these two, it was clear that political power could—against the will of capital writ large, exert some economic power in this period of "competitive capitalism." Second, "how dangerous pure interest groups which concern themselves *only* with the improvement of the economic situation, can be in politics."[19] The irony which prompts this position from Neumann is the pivotal role that trade unions had played in breaking the Chartist movement by making a case that "the economic situation of the worker could be improved in the long run without political power." But this hardly amounts to Weber's belief in the ultimate rational nature (and authority) of "the state" or in the kind of proto-pluralism he ascribes to parliamentary democracy. In these arguments, Neumann is not simply engaging in a theoretical dispute with Weber or Marx. He is preparing a grand critique of his fellow social democrats on the grounds of misunderstanding political struggle, politics, and state.

Neumann observes that as early as the 1848 Revolution in France, when the entrance of mass political agents both into general economic and political life and into state politics in particular is taking place, we can see how quickly basic features of "liberal states" can evaporate and how limited "victory" in *government* can be versus taking state power. Neumann here pairs two incredibly unlikely figures: Louis Blanc, entering state with full faith in the mode of socialist reforms, and Auguste Blanqui, instead leading committed, insurrectionist revolutionary cells directly against the state. Blanc proceeded with a reformist agenda of the "shortening of working time, social insurance, unemployment relief, national workshops."[20] Eerily echoing many contemporary theories separating a "good" state power from a "bad," Blanc's opponents, "let him alone; but while he drafted social reform bills they turned to the capture of political power. They took over the army, created a reliable militia, controlled the administration of Paris, invaded the administration of finance."[21] With this power Blanc and his movement were stymied, ejected from power, and what reforms they had achieved, including what was supposed to be the pivotal economic form—the new "national workshops"—were dismantled and repressed. For Neumann, Blanc is a cautionary foreshadowing of the German moment in 1918 when "Social Democracy refused to employ the political power it possessed for the strengthening of its power," instead focusing merely on "social policy and social reform."[22] Neumann's critique of early twentieth-century social democrats here contains not only the echoes of Gramsci's "war-of-position," which occurs *both* in formal politics and in "culture,"[23] but also of Miliband's arguments about the differences between merely being in government and fully grasping state power,[24] about the different power centers in states, but also of Poulantzas' contention—not dissimilar from Gramsci's—that the state constitutes an uneven terrain of struggle.

Neumann's critique of Blanqui is *more* damning. Again, eerily echoing current fixations on spontaneism and the unmediated agency of dominated classes, Blanqui here hopes to seize on the flash of a moment in which "the spontaneity of the oppressed makes possible the activity of such small groups of conspirators."[25] Not only has he no plan for *political* action, but he also has no program nor institution(s) by which to extend such brief moments. This is also the position that Gramsci takes up in his *Prison Notebooks*, noting that immediate grievance, or spontaneous social uprising, is fleeting and lacks power unless attached to or expressed as or through a more formal (although Gramsci is open to a number of forms far beyond the traditional political party) organizational structure, capable of working over the *longue durée* not only of taking power but of establishing hegemony.[26] Blanc and Blanqui are both, then, in a way, "anti-political."

What is important to glean from these brief discussions of Neumann's critique of various movements and political theories is that he observes states changing (just as he catalogues changing forms of capitalism). This is all during the conditions or form of capitalism that can be roughly characterized, as Neumann does, as "competitive capitalism." In this form, capital *is* dependent on states even as the social power of capital grows. However, capital simultaneously remains the "locus of power."[27] Many Marxist theorists propose stages of capitalism or perhaps "forms of capitalism"—"monopoly capitalism," which is a key interest of Neumann's, imperialism as the "final" stage of capitalism, and so on. Imperialism and colonialism, which we will turn to shortly, are both *intrinsic* to capitalism and enrich an understanding of the variety of states. But by bracketing (which is a massive bracket) the question of "immense colonial empire," already present since the inception of capitalism within Neumann's own account, Neumann sees a dialectical transformation of both capitalism and states even within core capitalist states. There is a highly contingent—as with Gramsci—play of social forces within states at any given conjuncture. Not only might Blanc have succeeded but, far closer to Neumann's direct interest, the German Social Democrats could have actually taken *political* power in 1918.

Liberalism as a political movement is as equally self-deceived if it should be taken seriously at all. "Pure liberalism is just as much an illusion as social reformist Social Democracy. What social reform is to Social Democracy, education is to liberalism."[28] In both these cases, Neumann sees an almost comical faith in "the law" versus actual power, both economic and political. "The dissolution of politics into law is supposed to remove risk from politics. One wants to achieve everything, but risk nothing."[29] As with his Institute for Social Research colleagues, Neumann sees this illusion grounded in an uncritical absorption of a theory of mechanistic progress whether in a kind of Hegelian rationalism for liberals or an overly economistic vision for some Marxists of his era. They fail to account for the actually existing social forces—not least popular mass power, in addition to those bound up in capital and states. "They all express the unpolitical character of the masses; they deny or do not want to know that the struggle for political power—that is, the struggle for the control of the coercive organizations, for police, justice, army, bureaucracy, and foreign policy—is the agent of historical progress."[30]

This is particularly damning for the Social Democrats of 1918 who refused political power on theoretical, economistic grounds even as it was literally being thrust upon them.

In contrast, "the significance of political power was always clear to reactionaries, even when they appropriated liberal political and economic theory; indeed the non-intervention of the state was accepted by reactionaries only when the state began to become democratic."[31] This is one of the key observations that we will want to return to in looking at the extraordinary attention the *Right* has given to securing and defining state power. Democracy and capitalism (or economic liberalism, or even simply private ownership as in pre-capitalist societies) are fundamentally in either extreme tension or open contradiction.[32] With increasing democratization come twin demands: the expansion of the realm of democratic principle beyond formal legal equalities and more importantly the limitation, abrogation, or democratization of private property. Under the historical conditions of "competitive capitalism," the institutions for the expression of democratic *sovereignty*—for Neumann representative bodies like parliament or the executive, for "neutral" adjudication (in particular the judiciary) and for coercive enforcement, are all conducted within what appear to be wholly illusory liberal formulas which can momentarily become real because various interests from among the bourgeoisie and remaining aristocratic formations largely coalesce. It is not that these institutions are immutable. In fact, Neumann would like us to pay far closer attention to how, when, and why institutions change. Like many Marxists, Neumann argues that it is capital that is this ultimate "locus of power" and that fully modern states are the product of an historical "mode of production"—that is to say, capitalism fashions states according to its needs. But capitalism involves the increasing participation and movement of the masses, whether through coercion—enclosure, forced adherence to wage-labor, and so on—or through consensus. Thus, the very principles that political liberalism and especially democracy expound—in combination with an increasingly large state apparatus capable of maintaining and facilitating the needs of an ever-changing capitalism—are a kind of utopian kernel contained within the mere formality of liberal law.

Even if we agree with Marx that "capital produces its own gravediggers," Marx has failed to notice (or at least consistently argue) that capitalism has created an imperfect medium—as with *most* capitalist technologies—through which a "social power" might come to "political power" as a real new locus of power. The "rule-of-law" may be a complete fiction—"the law cannot rule, only men can exercise power over other men"[33]—but it contains possibilities in its own unrealized formulations of freedom, equality, and security for people on a universal basis. And it contains real power necessarily invested in it: the coercive powers of the state.

As Neumann writes, "If it were correct that the process of capitalist production must necessarily lead to the collapse of this production, this still would not mean a political collapse would have to follow on the economic collapse."[34] Neumann argues that we have seen a host of such political formations in reaction to specific historical conjunctures. Although the point is relatively straightforward, its implications have gone underexplored. Whether social democracy in the sense of an expansive class compromise welfare state, or fascism, or authoritarianism, or, indeed, neoliberalism, are—correctly—viewed as modes of the political preservation of capitalism, in most analyses, states essentially fall away in a kind of functionalism. Adam Przeworski, viewing both Miliband's supposed-instrumentalism and Poulantzas's supposed-structuralism as functionalist theories, helpfully summarizes:

> In fact, ultimately even the state as institution disappears from this functionalist analysis. Since, by assumption, the state invariably responds to the functional requirements of capitalist reproduction and since its policies have, by assumption, the function of fulfilling these requirements, one can proceed from requirements to reproduction without bothering with the state at all. The very concept of the state is based on a reification. The state is ready-to-wear; it is tailored before class conflicts, as if in anticipation of those conflicts, appearing fully clothed whenever these conflicts threaten the reproduction of capitalist relations. The state is always given, already in its functional garb, before any conflicts occur, before any problems call for resolution.[35]

The question remains, for Przeworski, "why conflicts among specific groups under concrete historical circumstances would regularly result in the state performing its functions."[36] For Neumann, the answer is that they do not. Neither "the state," "the class character of the state," nor the "class-state" is a given. As we will examine in a moment, even as modern states developed in tandem with the changing forms of capitalism, they are not therein reducible to just that development. Similarly, the liberal individual for Neumann should be simultaneously conceived as a partial invention of capitalism (as well as of other sources, in particular Christianity) and yet is not by dint of this genealogy, or by virtue of empty legal formalism, reducible to a mere fiction.

Neumann lacks a fully elaborated structural theory of the power of capital over antagonistic state formations, at least as understood in largely economic terms. The obvious and fundamental contradiction between *democracy* and capitalism does not account for a "class character of the state." At points, Neumann seems to favor the view that had already appeared in Gramsci, that states are part of a mode of production but not wholly determined by economic conditions. Or the one that would later be expanded in Miliband—that it is the actual interests of individuals and even of institutions within states and their identity or connection to members of the capitalist class that, at least in part, make a state a "class-state." Capitalism rules through hegemony—a combination of coercive power and popular consensus. Capital is the true "locus of power" in a general sense, but in coming to rely on states as semi-, partly-, or -quasi autonomous entities to engender sufficient popular support, "the political"—in addition to having its own logics as Gramsci too notes—threatens that power. To see the structural limitations, in economic terms, of class compromise states, we will have to turn to other sources. But Neumann has a structural *political* argument to make.

It is here that we see the intersection and influence of Marxian and Weberian analysis with the other major influence on Neumann's political thought, Carl Schmitt. "Who is to interfere and on whose behalf becomes the most important question for modern society."[37] This is a question of *sovereignty*. In Schmitt's famous formulation "sovereign is he who decides the exception."[38] In the case of war—and particularly civil war, as we'll observe momentarily—the need for exception might seem obvious even within liberal thought. For someone like Neumann, the answer as to "who is to interfere" is obvious. While some Marxist visions see a devolution of power as a continual democratization of all aspects of state and society, Neumann, viewing the extraordinary existing power of capital and the capacities of the state, instead wanted to see a state power capable of suppressing and subordinating the power of capital, strengthening popular power through movements necessarily organized outside the state (labor and social movements) but also using the tremendous coercive apparatus of a strong centralized state power which was a *sine qua non* for the suppression of capital. In contrast, although Schmitt wanted "the political" to have a primacy, he thought that economic life should be wholly separate. While Schmitt insists that the sovereign power be a person, Neumann sees no reason why it could not or should not be a popular sovereignty.

Schmitt's fear about the subordination of "the political" to economics proved to be well founded. When Schmitt was writing, Marxists were still largely formulating their ideas of internationalism in terms of nation-state units: the solidarity of one state unit's proletariat with another, as Marx himself had put it, in the struggle against each particular state's bourgeoisie. This included an analysis of imperialism that, while increasingly understanding global functions of capital, still saw the millennium in the competition between capitalist-imperialist states. Meanwhile, Schmitt was already anticipating an economic order in which states would themselves be "governed" under an international economic order, a "world-embracing economic and technical organization" for the facilitation of commerce.[39] As we will see when we turn to economic history, Schmitt's vision was both prescient and his later writings on the subject remain some of the clearest about the international order that developed over the course of the twentieth century and its trajectories. Schmitt posed but also partially dismissed this idea in his early work, writing that "to demand seriously of human beings that they kill others and be prepared to die themselves so that trade and industry may flourish for the survivors or that the purchasing power of grandchildren may grow is sinister and crazy."[40] This of course proved to be historically short-sighted. However, Schmitt leaves the question of a world technical economic order open, asking, without answering, "upon whom will fall the frightening power?"[41] In his later work, particularly *The Nomos of the Earth*, Schmitt would explore this far more closely. But, when writing his key early works on states, this possibility was far from his mind. Instead, he viewed national communities and the "sovereign dictator" as the solution to the indecisive, contradiction-riddled Weimar state. Neumann's magnum opus is, thus, the most thorough account of, as he quite accurately puts it, "the Structure and Functioning of National Socialism," but also, more quietly an answer to why Schmitt's theory failed on Schmitt's own grounds because of the ways in which his critique in some sense *needed* Marxism. Simultaneously, it was also a further departure from traditional Marxist state theory.

Up to now in my presentation, it may seem like Neumann was a largely theoretical thinker. But in his work, and especially *Behemoth: The Structure and Practice of National Socialism,* Neumann's method is historical and empirical (and his contribution to a critical state theory is in part this methodology). Finding existing theories (Nazism as *simply* a *stage* of capitalist development, or Nazism or Fascism as particular to the "national characters" of some peoples, purely psychological, or great man theories of history arguments, and so on) sorely lacking, Neumann begins by reconstructing the trajectory of state and capitalism from the end of "competitive capitalism" to "monopoly capitalism." This is an observation he shares with many other Marxist thinkers of that period and far later. However, Neumann's argument focuses on the unique ways in which monopoly capitalism radically altered laws, institutions, and states. As capital consolidates into monopolies, the hitherto private power of capital becomes "quasi-legislative" and technically "public." Firms now take on activities previously proscribed to states.[42] Looking at legal changes, bank records, party documents, movement histories, employment statistics, commercial accounts, where, when, and how profits were made, where, when, and how decisions were made, what institutional changes took place, Neumann noticed a remarkable facet of this changing society. Whereas once capital had needed the state to enforce general conditions for the basic functioning of capitalism, this was no longer the case. For example, contracts which firms had once needed to hold both labor and each other to account under state authority, no longer marked the passage between a nominal realm of public freedom and private tyranny as they do in Marx's *Capital*. Rather, firms, reflecting their massively increased power, preferred to view contracts on an ad hoc basis open to interpretation. Since monopoly power (which in many contemporary cases is also monopsony power[43]) commanded the labor market, formally binding contracts, instead of binding one worker to one firm or another, now mostly served as potential restrictions on firms' activities. State enforcement would be getting in the way, instead of reproducing capitalism. Similarly, whereas states, particularly any form of liberal state, had previously used general laws as a basic principle of legality, now any possibly effective law had to be particular, since whole sectors of the economy, whole swaths of social life, were essentially "governed" by particular firms.

Some Marxists—particularly in the Social-Democratic Party of Germany viewed this as a positive development; under the openly mixed constitution of the Weimar Republic, this would provide the medium through which bourgeois legal formalism could give way to a form of "concrete" social law in which the needs of the working class could be posed outside of the falsely universal frames of liberalism. Since Social Democrats had essentially refused the reins of state as discussed earlier, capital (firms) viewed this as also a positive development as it shifted the locus of power to the judiciary, the state institution invested with the most power and that is furthest from popular accountability. This is just one of the many such changes that begin to occur.[44]

Meanwhile, the "social base" for liberalism had become vanishingly small even where whole social conditions had sharply deteriorated. In common versions of a Marxist story, capital turned to far-right nationalists with their petit-bourgeois base, as a mass base to preserve capitalism against communism and socialism. Only such a mass movement was capable of providing precisely the kind of democratic legitimacy needed. Traditional conservatives and some liberals, viewing the greater threat in the left broadly conceived, support the new government. Neumann largely shares this view. However, most Marxist accounts here turn to analyses which bring "the state" in "ready-to-wear" as Prezworksi writes in the earlier quote. Liberal accounts are usually replete with a combination of psychologism and antidemocratic prejudice wherein Nazism is the cautionary tale of the tyranny of the majority (never mind that the Nazis *never* won a majority election before they broke up all the other parties). In the background throughout stands "the state" curiously monolithic; Nazism is an extreme break from liberalism. It is the tyranny of total government.

It is here that things break down though and Neumann's method and critical theoretical approach give him insight (even as set against the views of his own colleagues) that eludes others. Neumann's view does not give the same ideological depth as Adorno's analyses of antisemitism, or Benjamin's ideas about war mysticism, the aestheticization of politics. He does not comment on the economic function of war as a kind of sponge for surplus production that does not threaten private property, or on the more formal arguments like Kalecki's about Fascism's ability to carry out policies—such as full employment—which capital objects to in other circumstances. What Neumann was instead able to discern was how and why this seemingly disparate set of interests worked together.

To begin with, Neumann finds the concept of "state capitalism" to be an absurdity both in terms of the empirical record and as a theoretical concept. It is perhaps most appropriately applied to a state like the Soviet Union after the end of the NEP and even then, as Neumann notes, unless one is going to call any mode of accumulation "capitalism." This is not a ringing endorsement; perhaps such systems he says should be called "slave states" or "managerial dictatorship" or "bureaucratic collectivism."[45] But the Nazi economy looks *nothing* like the economy of the Soviet Union or the New Deal United States—all supposedly forms of "state capitalism." The reverse argument, that Nazism is a genuine form of socialism albeit not Marxist and on a national level only, is even more absurd. As Neumann argued, and I have demonstrated elsewhere, there was no place, particularly before the war started, that was more thoroughly capitalist than Nazi Germany.[46] Even during the war—when essentially all the Western powers adopted forms of war planning economies, Nazi Germany was still producing not only to the needs of the war effort but also to ensure a high profit rate to German firms. There would not be a more profit-oriented regime in Europe until well into the neoliberal period. I will not rehearse the entirety of Neumann's case here.[47] But he accurately finds the profit motive fully intact—private investment still functioning. Although terror was possible throughout the Third Reich, it was primarily targeted at either shared opponents (communists, socialists, trade unionists) or "racial enemies," the area of the Nazi Party's greatest interest. Aryanization of Jewish property—which was acceptable to the German capitalists who backed the Nazi party—was probably the most intense, specifically Nazi intervention into the economy. Personnel overlapped, there was a state sector, and the party also reaped massive dividends, but there was a clear distinction between the sphere of economic life and the Party. The political demand of monopoly capital was the suppression of substantive democracy. This the party provided eagerly through its own para-state bodies and its direct takeover of the police. The economic needs of the Party were the industrial capacity to wage their desired war for *Lebensraum* and to achieve full employment and a stabilization from the interwar years. Capital was freed from worry about how such policies might result politically (since the Nazis promised and delivered a dissolution of opposition and formal democracy itself) and now able to reap the tremendous profits that consumption stimulation of this kind for both individuals and the war economy would produce without an effect on price or wage.

Although one of the principal objectives of the Party was martial, here too we find that the Nazis—far from the all-powerful totalitarian portrait—largely left the armed forces, their command structures, except where Jewish or otherwise "undesirable"—little changed. In fact, as Neumann underlines, even when Himmler tried to gain jurisdiction over the army he failed. The army's interests seemed to lie in maintaining their extraordinary pride of place in the country and in seeing that Germany not lose the coming war. The Party oversaw the programs for racial control, the police, and its own paramilitaries. But these did not threaten the huge portions of the bureaucracy which were continuous with Weimar. The rump or remaining bureaucracy, inhabited by actors who were mostly concerned with professional or technical affairs, advancement, and the prestige of the institutions they work in, continued to carry out their work, with neither strong pro- nor anti-Nazi proclivities.

Propagandistically, the Nazis claimed themselves to be a "total state" or "totalitarian" and Hitler the indisputable *Fuhrer*. But in reality:

> Under National Socialism, however, the whole of the society is organized in four solid, centralized groups, each operating under the leadership principle, each with a legislative, administrative, and judicial power of its own. Neither universal law nor a rationally operating bureaucracy is necessary for integration. Compromises among the four authoritarian bodies need not be expressed in a legal document nor must they be institutionalized (like the "gentlemen's agreements" between monopolistic industries). It is quite sufficient that the leadership of the four wings agree informally on a certain policy. The four totalitarian bodies will then enforce it with the machinery at their disposal. There is no need for a state standing above all groups; the state may even be a hindrance to the compromises and to domination over the ruled classes. The decisions of the Leader are merely the result of the compromises among the four leaderships.[48]

Or as put by William Scheuerman (hardly an uncritical reader of Neumann): "A profoundly confused set of conflicting and overlapping power blocs without a central coercive authority, Nazi Germany lacks even a state apparatus in any defensible modern sense of the term."[49] As the title implies, Nazi Germany was *not* some kind of perfected Leviathan. It was Hobbes's land-monster, Behemoth. It was "anarchy," "chaos": a "non-state" (*Unstaat*).

Neumann of course has his critics. Liberals accuse him of being too much of an orthodox Marxist, while Marxists accuse him of misunderstanding that "the state" *must* have been in there, somewhere. There are places where Neumann overstates or understates the case, has committed an error, needs updating or flat-out (as with his theory of antisemitism) has just basically tried to oversimplify an issue. However, few quibble—beyond some pedants, particularly who refuse to see capital playing any role whatsoever—with the empirical and even descriptive case that Neumann makes. But what interests us here falls out of these arguments entirely.

First is that the non-state is possible and its "chaos" can be horrifyingly orderly. It is about states as opposed to "the State" we should be theorizing. It is possible not only as some kind of marker of a "failed state" in the periphery, but rather in the capitalist core—in a highly developed and largely functional society. Neumann is not making the case that this jumble is bound to fail (he finishes writing the book before the war is over and even then is deeply insistent that it is not). It's actually remarkably capable, even efficient, at least in several of its functions: racial genocide and profit generation. Neumann is perfectly aware that *capitalism* continues to exist. But recall, Nazism as a political movement and as a form of non-state (of which there can be multiple kinds) is produced by capital in multiple ways. Not only is the actual party's eventual success backed by a choice of capital but the conditions which lead to the rise of Nazis are specifically predicated on changing capitalism and changing states. Although we will look at more economic theories of structural dependence in a moment, one could even make the case that the non-state has a "class character"—capitalist.[50] However, monopoly capitalism is not just a tendency in the market; it does not just change relations between capitalist firms; it is a change in the composition of capital, the relationship of capital and society and, in particular, that between capital and states. Neumann is saying not only that there are political solutions to crises but that there is a much wider range of them than we initially imagine. Capital, in the form of monopoly capitalism, has the power to unwind the same strong state apparatuses that it both helped to create and (in some cases) that preexisted capitalism *within* the territory—and here we are still in a historical mode—in which that "national" capital resides. But even short of that, it can, through its concentrated private power, reshape state structures, bring certain institutions—like the judiciary—to the fore, force a restructuring of not only the content of laws but of the legal form *not* through any of the mechanisms usually discussed but through the sheer fact of its concentrated social power. It may very well be that states—at least forms of modern class-compromise states—need capital, but capital *may not need states*, at least not in a recognizable form.

In an otherwise glowing review of *Behemoth*, Paul Sweezy, while noting that he understands the political theoretical argument in principle, writes that he cannot fathom why Neumann would choose to conclude with the argument about the "non-state."[51] The review, written very early in his career, may have been written before Sweezy turned his attention to imperialism but it is in thinking about colonialism that we see why what seems such a trivial technicality to Sweezy has the clearest parallels in thinking of forms of capitalist rule without state sovereignty. In fact, there is hardly one type of colonial possession or state but they all exhibit features of the non-state Neumann is describing. They are not *exactly* the same; why would they be? As Rosa Luxemburg famously argued, imperialism carries out what Marx called "primitive accumulation" but at an always present and increasing rate through the new means of "modern colonial policy."[52] In such conditions, capital rules more directly, "here, violence, fraud, oppression and plunder are displayed quite openly and without any attempt to disguise them."[53] Law might be a fiction for Luxemburg, but here it seems to be one that matters. Luxemburg describes in such places the "direct rule of capital." She is not particularly interested in substantiating a Marxian theory of law and state but she, perhaps without realizing it in precisely that form, has observed, in the same way as Sweezy wrote in his reading of Neumann, "that this apparatus does not operate according to 'law' in the special sense of rational and predictable norms of conduct."[54] She observes precisely this form of "law" in no lesser hands than John Stuart Mill and other luminaries of British Empire. As Schmitt would write after the war, "they were called 'states,' but the word 'sovereign' was avoided."[55]

As with other Frankfurt School theorists (pace Martin Jay's ungrounded assertions that Neumann, Kirchheimer, and Grunberg should be considered ancillary figures who share little to no elements with the more well-known thinkers),[56] Neumann sees fascism not as an aberration but as a dialectical continuation or an intensification, of liberalism. But even more centrally, he sees, far more happening in fascism than the mere reflection or even mere reproduction of capitalism in "superstructure." Neumann is perhaps closer to Benjamin than Horkheimer. All agree that activities in the "superstructure" are real production, integral, not ancillary, to the overall process of late capitalism. But Neumann sees the possibility of a dialectical recuperation of *some* of "the formal emancipatory claims of liberal thought."[57] Adorno views the idea of autonomy as a bourgeois fantasy but at the same time autonomy—however impossible under capital—can, for him, be recovered as a principle of epistemological resistance in cultural form. For Neumann, as with most Marxist accounts, "the guarantees of liberty and equality in capitalist democracy ... are merely negative formulations of property rights."[58] But this does not make them empty. Neumann sees a *positive* capacity within the recuperation of some liberal political principles, just as Benjamin saw in the possibilities of mass culture, however, disfigured by capital.

The liberal individual is then simultaneously an ideological fiction—utilizing universality as a cover for the particularity of the protection of private property, the ground for some minimum capacity (which Neumann explicitly, till his latest works, distinguishes from private property) for negative freedom from sovereign coercion, *and* also a utopian ground of the free flourishing of human beings to their fullest capacity. The rule of law is, as we already explored for Neumann, simultaneously an absolute liberal farce, covering the fact of domination by capital, that "men rule other men." But it contains within it the possibility of rule by more rational norms and the utopian grounds of a truly rational law, in which case, one could surmise, "the state," would truly wither. Finally, while some commentators (Scheuerman in particular) stop with attenuated notions of these first two conceptions it is actually the third that is most vital to grasp: sovereignty. As we have already seen as set against liberals like Kelsen, the "law" cannot be sovereign; this is merely a reversion to a notion of the sovereign rule of law as fiction for the general rule of capital. But both with and against Schmitt, "Sovereign is he who decides the exception." Only in this case there is only one (or, if one prefers, one set) exception to be decided upon—capitalism (or put more accurately, if less elegantly, heteropatriarchal racial capitalism). Sovereignty, of course, contains within it the possibility of popular sovereignty—the rule of the people and genuine democracy.

Sovereignty is the degree to which a state can express a form of popular will as against capital. It is predicated on *some* degree of a rule of law, some degree of rational juridical norm for the *possibility* of that sovereignty. Does this mean that, Neumann is arguing, like Chantal Mouffe with her "Left-Schmittianism," for simply a recognition or restoration of pluralist liberal democracy?

Not at all. As we will see, there is still much we need to add and augment to Neumann's contribution, but Neumann has no sympathy for the political pluralism of the kind associated with liberal pluralism today, even with Mouffe's rebalanced liberal democracy.[59] It may be the case that the Nazi "non-state" is "colonized by particularistic interests to a greater extent than was even the case under parliamentary democracy,"[60] but as we have already seen Neumann views the development of Nazism as a somewhat organic—if far from deterministic—outgrowth of preexisting conditions in Weimar and in 1920s and 1930s liberal capitalist states more broadly. His argument about the inability of social democrats to grasp the necessity of state power in its *coercive* sense is one his sharpest critiques.

In his younger years, Neumann thought there might be something to attempt to integrate new social bodies—in a neo-corporate manner—into existing liberal democratic states. But with *Behemoth* and his later writings, Neumann viewed measures of this—quite presciently—as ultimately destructive to the capacity for developing and maintaining the radical social movements necessary in society to organize for political change and as institutionalizing and neutralizing class conflict instead of playing it out as political conflict.

It would create layers of mediation, splinters in social solidarity, particularly within labor.[61] This is particularly the case within democracies:

> Democracy is not to be defined as a constitutionalist state but as a state which involves the subordination of social power to political power, and which makes political power responsible . . . political power is to be rationally employed, not only to negatively keep down private social power, but positively to shape a decent existence. This is often ignored. Thus it is claimed that democracy is nothing more than a system of liberties which rest on natural law. Today such theories are almost uniformly anti-democratic theories.[62]

It is this form of political power—"the imposition of binding political norms on the economic order"[63]—which we find in a now historicized and materialized conception of sovereignty. Social democracy—or really democracy of any kind

> *begins* with the establishment of material equality and the detachment of human life and liberty from the defense of property. Democracy, however, does not have its end and purpose in the technical securing of a social balance. Neumann's theory of social democracy therefore has a strongly dialectical character. The social component of democracy (equality) is not possible without its political component (liberty). But the social aspect of social democracy serves, lastly, to facilitate real *political* democracy, in which freedom can be positively structured.[64]

What are the institutions, what are the formations of power, which potentially threaten capital? It may very well be *risky* to strengthen these but in a sense it is even riskier not to do this. States do not drown in seas of democracy; they dissolve or are diminished by private power.

Neumann argues that the *only* value in the separation of powers is to be found in an independent judiciary which has a minimal mandate of basic (read noneconomic) individual rights. Beyond this, Neumann, although generally in favor of institutions such as legislatures which could in principle express popular sovereignty, does not actually hold much to the separation of powers: "While the independent judiciary can be considered the irreducible minimum of the doctrine of separate powers, the separation of administrative and legislative functions not only does not guarantee freedom, but hampers the utilization of the state's power for desired social ends."[65] He derides "constitutional fetishists" who try to place more emphasis on particular constitutional structures than on the concrete social, political, and economic conditions. Of course, he *is* deeply interested in institutions, just not in the same way. He does not think a particular arrangement, parliament versus plurality, federal versus central power, and so on has much meaning. But he is interested in those institutions which can potentially express popular power, in the aspects and structures of states that can turn such social power into "political power," and what limiting conditions are necessary to preserve this possibility for when—in a far from deterministic way—socioeconomic conditions are right. The Bolsheviks may have become a "totalitarian dictatorship" but for Neumann that was only after it became clear that the peasantry was not going to be a consistent social base for Communism without significant coercion. At least—like reactionaries—and unlike Neumann's own Social Democrats in 1918, they had *decided* that the historical opportunity was worth trying and saw the necessity of taking hold of the coercive apparatus of state.

What we have then in this bundle is not a "liberal" or "pluralist" democracy— nor indeed a democracy only. What we have is the beginning of *a critical state theory* which seriously calls into question not only the transcendental State of so many liberal, Marxist, and anarchist imaginations but also the ubiquity of states. Instead, we notice their relatively brief historical existence and the paucity of their actual number. States are not *wholly, genealogically* the product of capitalism: they become intertwined with its changing modes.

To a degree, one might argue that this version of sovereignty is contained within the incredibly broad category of Gramsci's formulation of hegemony. Neumann would in that sense be describing those parts of hegemony that are located more centrally in the state as a true, coercive power. Andreas Kalyvas has demonstrated that a synthesis of Schmitt and Gramsci in a conception of "hegemonic sovereignty" can successfully expand the overly juridical confines of Schmitt's arguments about democracy and sovereignty into the full range cultural, social, and ideological considerations of Gramsci's hegemony, while avoiding Gramsci's tendency—against his own express positions—to fall back into purely economic modes.[66] However, Neumann achieves everything that Schmitt does, without Schmitt's irrationalist baggage, while at the same time regrounding conceptions both of state and capitalism in actual history. Neumann directs our gaze not only toward different state (and non-state) formations but also toward the way in which the form of capitalism helps to shape states. A Neumann-Gramsci synthesis directs us to be attentive to trenches across states and civil societies without ignoring "trenches" within states. But this leads more to questions of political strategy than to a critical state theory.

3. NEOLIBERALISM AND BEYOND

It is as we approach the current moment that the importance of this "bundle" of historically bounded state qualities becomes clearer. In response to endemic crises, capital turns to a host of political solutions for fundamental systemic preservation. Some of these (as with imperialism and colonialism) build upon pre-capitalist foundations but fundamentally alter them for the needs of capital (cf. Luxemburg, Bukharin, Sweezy, Baran, Amin, and the like), while already creating a multiplicity of state forms, here generally predicated on the distinction between imperial periphery and core center. As already discussed, this condition is far from deterministic. Williams, Sargar, Heller, and many others demonstrate how mild and radical forms of social democracy can take form in the Global South. But, as a general principle, it underwrites *some* political choices in the Global North. For a more empirical portrait of this relation, we can look to Amin's concept of "imperialism rent" or Milanovic's "citizenship premium."[67] Under the general conditions of a tendency of capital to *stagnate*, such sources of value not only serve an economic function but also provide capital with greater room for maneuver.[68] These can result in a range of Nationalist class-compromise forms. The "non-state" would seem to be one extreme and remarkably isolated case even if we are able to generalize it as a theory of fascism and not merely Nazism.[69] Financialization is, among many other things, such a strategy of *forestalling* political conflict.[70] Historically, capital's structural power is this greater freedom to maneuver and convert potential intrastate conflicts (inherent within the contradictions of capitalism and democracy) into win-win situations. Although Neumann, to a certain degree, shares with his Frankfurt School colleagues a kind of all-roads-lead-to-Auschwitz perspective, fascism is only *one* possible outcome and possibly not even the most desirable. Neoliberalism, a far harder and larger political project, is in many ways far more attractive. As China Miéville quipped, "We live in a utopia, it is just not ours."[71]

What we see in miniature and *limited* in Neumann needs to be put into a global perspective. Nazism may have been to the extraordinary great advantage of capital, it may have been fundamentally capitalist, we may even stipulate that even as a "non-state" it retained a capitalist "class character," but it was a particular choice, under particular conditions, at a particular conjuncture. The Nazi Party wanted total mobilization for its racial and military projects. While this promised an end of popular democracy's threat against capital, it still contained the disturbing (for capital) logic of democratic legitimacy. Various class compromise versions of liberal and social democracy still represent a real *compromise*. The chief contribution of economic empirical analyses into structural limitations of social democracies vis-à-vis capital is to demonstrate that capital managed—and not always with great ease or as a foregone conclusion—to stay on top. But only barely and not within the ever-present and acute threats to profitability experienced across the Global North in the 1970s. Neoliberalism provides a rather more attractive option; it is, following Miéville, capital's utopia.

It goes far beyond the limits of this chapter to provide a full definition of neoliberalism. Inspired by Philip Mirowski, one can conceive of neoliberalism as a nested doll. Mirowski uses this metaphor to explain the peculiar institutional structure of the intellectual movement of neoliberalism. But I think it fits well as an overall characterization of the system. The outermost doll in such a view would be neoliberalism as a system of global governance and institutions. Nestled inside that would be neoliberalism as a set of national political projects, commonly associated with figures like Ronald Reagan and Bill Clinton in the United States or Margaret Thatcher and Tony Blair in the United Kingdom. Nestled inside that one would be neoliberalism as set of economic principles (market efficiency, and the like) and economic practices (financialization, privatization, and the like) And our innermost doll, neoliberalism as a system of cultural logic and as the extension of market principles into all aspects of social and individual life. If we view the postwar period as one of Keynesian class compromise—however stable or unstable—neoliberalism—despite speaking so frequently in economic terms—is the political (and legal) response to the crises of the 1970s.[72]

Depending on one's point of view, any of these dolls might be the most crucial. I cannot address all of these aspects here but will focus on the "outermost" dolls for the purposes of understanding a critical state theory today. How to understand neoliberalism as a different form of capitalism (or *if* to) is an often-heated debate particularly on the left. Some wish to see it only as an extension of the already existing logics of monopoly capitalism, others as just more capitalism tout court, and still others, as a total eclipse of the entirety of the previous capitalist systems into a total world "Empire." As regards states, some view them as increasingly superfluous (Hardt and Negri) while others (Varoufakis) see the imperial system largely in place if in a state of flux.[73] What the full theorization of the "non-state" and its relation to other states gives us are a host of ways to understand specific forms of states and of a truly different global system of governance and form of capitalism. The argument is not that "the State" has become "weak"; rather that *some* states have remained "strong" while not sovereign.[74] We need to be able to explain the "anti-state state" that Ruth Wilson Gilmore so extensively documents in her work *Golden Gulag*.[75] We need to be able to understand how, as Mirowski argues, "a primary ambition of the neoliberal project is to redefine the shape and functions of the state, not to destroy it."[76]

What I have been calling "a critical state theory" beginning with my extended reading of Neumann gives a far clearer theoretical picture of what the material realities reflect. This needs to be approached from two angles: that of the struggle for political power and that of how a different form of capitalism itself shapes states and "the political" themselves. Of course, the two interact once in power.

As Neumann observed, "The significance of political power was always clear to reactionaries." It is clear (1) that a new form of global governance was already nascent in the early 1980s; (2) that one of the principal changes it spurred is an increase in the mobility of capital; and (3) that changes in the form of Capital (and not only capital) has engaged in explicitly political struggle to determine the political outcome of economic and social crises, to delimit political options, and discipline states and political actors. As recently documented by Quinn Slobidian, neoliberalism as a set of doctrines about global governance traces its origins to the end of World War I (and then with increasing consistency and effect, after World War II).[77] Looking at the demise of multinational empires and the rise of democratic socialism in places like Vienna ("Red Vienna") neoliberals actively posed the question of how the market could be *protected* from decolonization and democracy.

Slobidian documents the intellectual history of neoliberal thought but also how such thought was integrated with business associations, nascent international institutions (often formed for quite different purposes), and political parties. As against its rhetoric, neoliberalism was not simply a call for a return to "laissez-faire." Nor did it want to do away with political power; it wanted political power to promote and protect the "free market" not only at the level of state policies but also in a kind of global "economic constitution." As Slobidian notes, at this level at least, these ideas are all adapted from Schmitt. But neoliberals viewed Schmitt's hell as heaven. Schmitt looked with horror as international treaties increasingly included clauses bound seemingly to one principle, "progress toward a single market":

> In short: over, under, and beside the state-political borders of what appeared to be a purely political international law between states spread a free, i.e. a non-state sphere of economy pertaining everything: a *global* economy.[78]

Or as Hayek openly called it in *Law, Legislation, and Society*: the dethronement of the political.[79] What neoliberal thinkers could see was the possibility of a global governance without sovereignty, which, looking largely *like* law, in fact had no general norms. What they could envision was a global economic *Unstaat* that, nevertheless, was binding on state actors. At its center would lie what Slobidian calls "the human right to capital flight," the absolute unrestricted mobility of capital and goods. What mechanisms could make it binding? Here is where simplistic stories about the vanishing of states fail so spectacularly. Schmitt viewed such an order as the end of Eurocentric empire. Neither Marxists theorists of imperialism (Amin) nor neoliberals saw it this way. It would require the coercive power of states, concentrated in imperial centers, to create such an order. It would require a different set of mechanisms to maintain it.

I am not the first person to see the roots of neoliberalism through Neumann-inflected lens: "What freewheeling bankers wanted in the postwar were not the capital controls and financial repression of the 1950s, but the market free-for-all created in the largely unregulated, off-shore Eurodollar market hosted by the City of London. There they revealed themselves, just as Neumann would suggest, as subversive agents of disorder already in the 1950s."[80] At a more global level, they were only ever partially implemented and adhered to even beyond business resistance. While neoliberalism was certainly a class project in the sense of "representing" the interests of capitalist classes, this does not go all the way to explaining its particular qualities. One can retroactively see neoliberalism as capital's "utopia" but while many capitalists bristled at the different degrees of state restriction, Keynesianism remained, in some sense, hegemonic as a capitalist political economy.

For the purpose of understanding a critical state theory, what we observe first here is that capital—in a new *bloc*—engaged in political struggle at the state level. In the Global South, the imposition of experimental neoliberal projects, *politically* differed little from neocolonialism in any form. But in the Global North, capital had to put to use every aspect of what I have been calling its structural "preponderance" in motion.[81] In the United States and the United Kingdom, this meant the successful election of Reagan and Thatcher, the successful political struggle of movements embodied in them, who could begin to implement neoliberal policies at the state level and break opposition (labor, social movements), that is, continue the political struggle.

Of course, the opposite happened in France with the election of Mitterrand in 1981 on a strong left mandate backed with a coalition of communists and socialists. In a case seemingly tailor-made for the limitations of social democracy and the "structural dependence" of states on capital, facing a massive wave of capital flight, Mitterrand famously backed off his initial plans and embraced liberalization. But, the story may be not quite that simple. Prezworski and M. Wallerstein, as part of their larger argument that the strategic issues of social democratic parties should not, at least in formal modeling, be treated as the actual essential definitional qualities of states, say that Mitterrand simply balked too soon.[82] Others, crucially, point to specific, shifting international contexts.[83] Even in the French case, "structural dependence" looks far less deterministic.[84]

Neoliberal responses had already started in some institutions in the United States and the United Kingdom before the period of the Reagan and Thatcher "revolutions." These included financial deregulations (although the bulk would be implemented over the 1980s and 1990s) as well as the infamous Volker Shock of 1980—the highest interest rate hike in the history of the Fed.[85] Both factors support a trend that had already begun since the crises—the increasing financialization of firms. What we see in the U.S. case in particular is the ascendant rise of a *political form* struggling to take power. Its struggle is proportionate to state power. However, what we see in the French case suggests something quite different. If we follow the third line of reasoning, we see (1) that a new form of global governance was already nascent in the early 1980s; (2) that one of the principal changes it spurred is an increase in the mobility of capital; and (3) that changes in the form of capitalism, even nascent, can begin to shape the form that states might take.

Recall Neumann's argument about monopoly capital and general law. Monopoly capital had by its very nature (beyond political influence) made general law in certain areas essentially impossible. Particular and *ad hoc* law in turn was favorable to monopoly capital. But this was true under the Weimar Republic as well as Nazi Germany. Socioeconomic conditions underwrite or structure state and legal forms, but state and legal forms are not reducible to those conditions. Capitalism plays a greater role in states than liberal institutionalists and pluralists would have you believe but less deterministic than orthodox Marxists suggests. Capitalists had to forge a bloc with Nazis, traditional conservatives, army officers, and bureaucratic professionals to achieve through political struggle *overcoming* state barriers to monopoly capital altogether.

The case here is slightly different on several accounts. First, it is indeterminate not only because of the generally greater contingency in politics than acknowledged in many theories but also because the conditions of the new economic form are, at best, nascent. Second, there is a vast difference between the Nazi project (for which economic concerns were not even remotely central despite their performance as hyper-capitalists) and the neoliberal project (whose express purpose—at least at the outer two nesting doll levels that I am addressing here—is to set up a transnational system of governance for the protection and absolute freedom of capital). Third, Neumann is still working within what Hyun Song Shin would call an island model of national economies. Even in a strong reading of this possibility that Mitterrand faced a greater threat to capital flight, this would be in the context of, again, a nascent form of neoliberalism, fundamentally transnational. The closer analogue would not be to any internal political transformation but rather to *colonialism*. What is even stranger in such a reading—although absolutely of a piece with capitalism in the twenty-first century—is that France would remain an *imperial* power collecting "imperialism rent" or " citizenship premiums" quite directly from many of its former colonies, as it does to this day, even as it transitioned away from qualifying as "sovereign state" in the minimal bundle definition.

Here we see, far beyond Neumann's initial scope, and even where our initial syntheses lie, a vital contemporary transnational extension of Neumann's theory and a key component of an overall critical state theory. On the one hand, to repeat, achieving political power is not automatic for "capital" or "fractions of capital"; it is achieved through political struggle (in which capital has distinct advantages). But on the other hand, capital can also shape states (and quasi-states and non-states) by the literal material structures of production, circulation, and consumption. Again, this is obvious in the case of imperialism and colonialism. But how so for developed states of the Global North, even potentially the core imperial centers? To answer this, we must jump ahead to the global financial crisis in which a radically, qualitatively different form of capital exists than in previous phases. For the sake of simplicity, I will call this global capital.

4. STATES AND GLOBAL CAPITAL IN THE TWENTY-FIRST-CENTURY GLOBAL ECONOMY

To begin with, although layers of states and state-like structures are still present, they have not been "overcome" or "dissolved," global capital no longer can be principally measured or understood in terms of "national economies" but rather "multinational corporations coordinating far-flung "value chains."[86] This is how Adam Tooze starts to describe the twenty-first-century global economy. What does this mean?

In most accounts, liberal, Marxian, or otherwise, of international trade, for example, theoretical frameworks use nation-states as the principle measure. To this day, this is a fairly common way of discussing trade and international economy. One state has a trade surplus or a trade deficit with another. Similarly, supply chains seem a relatively trivial thing which, as some would point out, much as others do about globalization itself, has existed in some form for centuries. Put at its most simple a "global value chain" or GVC

> describes the full range of activities that firms and workers perform to bring a product from its conception to end use and beyond. This includes activities such as research and development (R&D), design, production, marketing, distribution, and support to the final consumer.[87]

The key distinction is in recent transformations facilitated by the new mobility of capital coupled with the quasi-legal international free trade regime. It cannot be stressed enough that there has never been a time in which capital has had less friction in moving transnationally and within state boundaries as well. In this way GVCs become "unbundled" in a specific manner. Not only are these activities separated but they are able to be fairly far-flung geographically, searching as far as possible for comparative advantage. Although "lead firms" are largely concentrated in the imperial centers of the Global North, the United States, Europe, and Japan, this is both decreasing empirically and needs proper framing.[88] G7 share of world gross domestic product (GDP) peaked at 67 percent in 1988 and, although this is still quite disproportionate to population size, as of 2010, less than 50 percent. (Interestingly, this correlates with Milanovic's calculation that the "citizenship premium" seems to have peaked approximately ten years ago.[89]) More crucially nearly 80 percent of global trade flows through a GVC. Of that, 60 percent are in intermediate goods and services. In other words, most trade is happening *firm to firm* and/or within a cross-border GVC.[90] This is unmediated—often not even possible to account—at the state level.

Even within the technical, noncritical literature, the extent to which the form and function of GVCs is acknowledged to be fundamentally at odds with principles of self-determination, democracy, and sovereignty is shocking. The simplest and most familiar form—"my factories for your reform"—is openly stated.[91] Even for states like the United States, this form of the organization of capital stymies such basic state functions like taxation and facilitates similar incentive structures as within "Special Economic Zones." The pay-off for being the global "home" of a transnational corporation (TNC) governing a GVC is largely indirect, promoting precisely the kind of profit-payout structure in which "profits are, above all, salaries, bonuses, commissions for special services, over-valued patents, licenses, connections, and good will."[92] Beyond the *recorded* tax avoidance which is a feature[93] of such formations (for an easy example think of how global quasi-legal environments and mobility of capital allow a TNC like Apple to openly create subsidiaries in low- or no-tax arrangements, in that case, in Ireland, in which profits from elsewhere can be moved), some 40 percent of TNC profits now go completely unaccounted for.[94]

The power of capital as expressed through patrimony and patronage is radically expanded in such a situation. In the case of the United States, it should be noted that goods and capital continue to flow back, due to the centrality of the U.S. dollar as the global reserve currency backed by the *power*—vis-à-vis other states—of the U.S. state. But these flows, as we will see when we turn to finance, are too qualitatively different than in previous forms of capital, are no longer distributed via the previous structures the underwrote the logic of postwar class-compromise, and are overall decreasing.[95]

This is just the tip of the iceberg of the *suprasovereign* nature of GVCs and of global capital. Proponents and critics essentially agree that GVCs are ungovernable. GVCs are structured to mitigate risk at all levels away from the TNC, not only risk in the economic sense but also in terms of law or politics. These are often, *at best*, tallied as part of the cost of doing business and there is little de facto binding power. Sympathetic analysts openly discuss the replacement of public with private governance or novel forms of self-regulation.[96] Instead of the familiar national story about withholding investment, the structure of GVCs in the context of rapid mobility of capital places puts both "host" and "headquarter" geographies in a subordinate position, promoting a race to the bottom for optimal labor, regulatory, and tax environments which can boomerang back to "headquarter" geographies with actual divestment or promises of "reshoring."[97]

State actors—even in the Global North, with decreasing capacity to collect taxes—are highly incentivized to seek this direct investment. This is to the great advantage of TNCs which coordinate—in their own words, "govern"—GVCs, as such chains are highly dependent on specific geographical features, resources, infrastructural, and labor capacities spread unevenly across the world. Although ideas of global capital can often seem disconnected from the material, floating in some kind of ether, GVCs are predicated on precise access to specific material substrata. As one economist of GVCs puts it, one of the only real challenges that he sees ahead is "a price of oil that raises the cost of unbundling."[98] Ultimately, and echoing Neumann's argument almost perfectly,

> Globalization's 2nd unbundling and the global supply chains it spawned have produced and continue to produce changes that alter all aspects of international relations—economic, political and even military. The spearhead of these changes has been the extraordinary economic growth accompanying emerging markets' integration into global markets at an unprecedented speed and scale—an accomplishment that is largely due to the development of global supply chains and heightened international mobility of capital.[99]

Although the question of the special role of the United States—central and only subordinate in certain capacities—is beyond the scope of this chapter, what we see is that indeed TNCs are the "prime movers and shakers" of the global economy.[100]

As Adam Tooze recounts, "The same is true for the global business of money."[101] He is actually understating the case. Financial services are the most prominent GVCs; financial services account for a larger share of profit for most TNCs than goods and other services, even those who are primarily engaged in the production of a nonfinancial commodity.[102] Although things like "company scrip" or market concentration have existed in plenty of periods of capitalism, it must be underlined how these levels of concentration, with this level of power (money produced through repo and "shadow banking") have vastly exceeded the amount of actual state-produced asset backed money at all times in the past decade and a half except during the acute moments of the financial crisis.[103] The current transnational system is fundamentally and radically unlike previous periods of capitalism.

> As Hyun Song Shin, chief economist at the Bank for International Settlements and one of the foremost thinkers of the new breed of "microfinance," has put

it, we need to analyze the global economy not in terms of an "island model" of international economic interaction—national economy to national economy—but through the 'interlocking matrix' of corporate balance sheets—bank-to-bank ... [in previous eras] Good economic policy was what was good for GDP growth. Questions of distribution—the politics of "who whom?"—could be weighed up against the general interest in "growing the size of the cake." By contrast, the new macrofinancial economics, with its relentless focus on the "interlocking matrix" of corporate balance sheets, where the real action in the financial system is. This is hugely illuminating. . . . But it exposes something that is deeply indigestible in political terms. The financial system, does not, in fact, consist of "national monetary flows." Nor is it made up of tiny, anonymous, microscopic firms—the ideal of "perfect competition" and the economic analogue to the individual citizen. The overwhelming majority of private credit creation is done by a tight-knit corporate oligarchy—the key cell in Shin's interlocking matrix. At a global level twenty to thirty banks matter. Allowing for nationally significant banks, the number worldwide is perhaps a hundred big financial firms.[104]

Governance and regulation in such a system largely escape the purview of states, except in the form of mild local restriction and taxation which is often either ignored or accounted as a simple cost in financial and commodity flows over which states—and even the World Trade Organization—have little control.[105] Governance as such is largely *ad hoc* and determined in predominantly private systems. The only nonmarket-based limitation on GVCs, as noted by one economist, is "the price of oil."[106] This is illuminating as the next step in a critical state theory would be to examine (as suggested in Tim Mitchell's *Carbon Democracy*) the political *ecology* of states. From Deleuze on down there can be a tendency when looking at such systems, to think that "states" vanish altogether. But rather, particular geographies begin to matter even more. The value chain can be flung as far as technology, communication, and energy needs allow and only as needed for profitability. But it does not make all places "equal." Local conditions—the presence of rare-earth metals or fossil fuels—are vital. Even financial transaction, conducted from nearly anywhere on Earth, far from being completely "deterritorialized," can be highly dependent on dense, technological infrastructures. Physical distance even over fiber-optic networks affects the outcomes of the dizzying array of digital transactions that occur in the macrofinancial world.

Furthermore, preexisting hierarchies of empire remain *largely* intact. However, neoliberal depoliticization has rendered this potential fulcrum inert (even if we might look to local examples of reversal).[107] Instead, what we saw in the 2008 crisis was swift and decisive action by a concert of these same actors in global finance, business, law, and also especially American government, we saw "emergency" action on behalf of transnational capital. When we look at such a portrait in terms of the challenges faced by post-growth capitalism and ecological limits, it is no wonder that a set of legitimation crises spring up across GVCs (and not only in developed Global North societies). But states are definitely still acting. "The ferocity of the financial crisis in 2008 was met with a mobilization of state action without precedent in the history of capitalism."[108] It was unquestionably a class project but in what nature were states—particularly the United States—acting? Thus, far from needing to be "reterritorialized" by "the State," we see capital here *shaping* political forms precisely as anticipated by neoliberal theorists.

Capital had reshaped the state and was now operating primarily through elite actors. The form of capital had effectively *instrumentalized* states. To take this further would be to move into questions of political strategy but neoliberalism is, simply put, no longer a hegemonic project. Such brute force transformation of even global imperial centers into functional hierarchies of developmentalist states all the way down poses profound possibilities for political struggle in the twenty-first century. Global capital needs states for policing, for access to resources, but in the face of widespread legitimation crises there are horizons of private rule—neofeudalism—that even exceed the instrumentalization of neoliberalism. Or, there is a threat of a return to fascism and other forms of hyper-nationalism. Direct force can make power, following Arendt, more brittle. The "bourgeois state" may have been the "perfect shell" for capitalism but *not* because of an intrinsic "class character of the state." The structure of a particular matrix of states in and with capital allowed for the brief efflorescence of this. The question is forced under the more strained economic and ecological conditions of the twenty-first century.

However, in terms of a critical state theory, I am far from the first to hear echoes of Neumann in this form of capital. Scheuerman—whose reception of Neumann is always dampened by his critique of Neumann's anticapitalism—can't help but notice that the current form and speed of capital presuppose Neumann's original arguments about monopoly but at a transnational scale. In the function of the global economy at the point of the 2008 crisis, Tooze notes: "One could hardly ask for a more direct expression of Neumann's basic diagnosis: the survival of oligopolistic capitalism requires adhocracy. When the going gets rough, as it inevitably does, order goes out the window."[109] But what even these analyses miss is that we already have a Behemoth-like structure at the global international level. The swift action in response to the global financial crisis might seem like decisive "sovereignty," but it is precisely *not* sovereign and non-state-like in the ways we have been exploring here. Capital's utopia is global Behemoth.

Critical state theory is an approach to understanding actually existing states: how sovereign is the United States today? How do global supply chains and energy needs shape not only a unique political entity like Saudi Arabia but necessary ideological and informal offshoots? How do states that retain an intense focus on the qualities Neumann identifies (like China) retain a different relationship while still operating within the framework of global capital? How can we understand the continuing subordination of postcolonial states in Africa? The disintegration of states in the Middle East? To answer these questions would require a more complete account of the material substratum—of the ecological substratum—of twenty-first-century capitalism, states, and society.

States might seem as a pure fiction or a pure function to those who benefit from them. But as Frantz Fanon (as much as Franz Neumann) argued, it is a difference that matters intensely. The *political* horizon therein does not, however, simply point toward nationalist and sovereigntist fantasies. But rather toward the creation of a global order through the necessary political medium of states—more open to assault as that initial "trench" than at any recent time in history. The war-of-position cannot simply leap into the transnational[110]— there are trenches to be occupied across states and societies as well as new opportunities—in understanding the form of global capital and the changing nature of states—for seeing the breaking points previously unimagined. These trenches are local, they are transnationally institutional, and they may involve class fractions and changing personnel. But they are also in and through actually existing states.

What a critical state theory suggests today is that nearly a century of theoretical investigation and movement common sense about states and the Left are outdated. Capital's room for maneuver is tight and its need for coercion great. While, as outlined here, a turn to an exclusively state-based politics would be foolish, it cannot be ignored that, even in the Global North, states have been instrumentalized. They more closely resemble the quasi-sovereign political entities found in the colonized world, tools of a power above, vested with a vastly increased coercive capacity but with weak legitimacy, porous to capture from below. In other words, the beginning of a critical state theory for the twenty-first century suggests a *politics* and a set of strategies more commonly associated with the Global South—literal decolonization.

NOTES

1. Ralph Miliband, *State in Capitalist Society* (London: The Merlin Press, 2009); Nicos Poulantzas, *Political Power and Social Classes* (New York; London: Verso, 1975). For the argument similar to mine, see Stanley Aronowitz and Peter Bratsis, "State Power, Global Power," in: Stanley Aronowitz and Peter Bratsis (eds.), *Paradigm Lost: State Theory Reconsidered* (Minneapolis: University of Minnesota

Press, 2002), 7–8. Examples of liberal references include everything from classic works of social and political theory like those of Max Weber to more contemporary liberal thought from Robert Dahl to Talcott Parsons and far beyond.

2. Ajay Singh Chaudhary, "The Climate of Socialism." *Socialist Forum* (Winter 2019), https://socialistforum.dsausa.org/issues/winter-2019/the-climate-of-socialism/.

3. Aronowitz and Bratsis, "State Power, Global Power," xiii.

4. Ajay Singh Chaudhary, "The Amazon Drama," *The Baffler*, March 15, 2019, https://thebaffler.com/latest/the-amazon-drama-chaudhary.

5. Stuart Hall, "Gramsci and Us," in: *The Hard Road to Renewal: Thatcherism and the Crisis of the Left* (London: Verso, 1988), 161/1.

6. Chaudhary, "The Amazon Drama."

7. Michelle Williams, *The Roots of Participatory Democracy: Democratic Communists in South Africa and Kerala, India* (New York: Palgrave Macmillan, 2008).

8. Max Horkheimer, "Traditional and Critical Theory," in: *Critical Theory: Selected Essays* (New York: Continuum, 1975).

9. Franz Neumann, "Change in the Function of Law in Modern Society," in: Herbert Marcuse (ed.) and Peter Gay (trans.), *The Democratic and the Authoritarian State* (New York: The Free Press, 1964), 104.

10. Neumann, "The Concept of Political Freedom," in: Herbert Marcuse (ed.) and Peter Gay (trans.), *The Democratic and the Authoritarian State* (New York: The Free Press, 1964), 162.

11. Neumann, "Change in the Function of Law in Modern Society," 101.

12. Neumann, "Economics and Politics in the Twentieth Century," in: Herbert Marcuse (ed.) and Peter Gay (trans.), *The Democratic and the Authoritarian State* (New York: The Free Press, 1964), 259.

13. See chapters 5 and 10 of this volume on the "concealment" involved in a liberal state.

14. Ellen Meiksins Wood, *The Pristine Culture of Capitalism: A Historical Essay on Old Regimes and Modern States* (New York: Verso, 2015), pp. 22–23.

15. Neumann, "Economics and Politics in the Twentieth Century," 259.

16. Karl Marx, "Chapter 10: The Working Day," in: *Capital: Volume One* (New York: Penguin Classics, 1990).

17. Neumann, "Economics and Politics in the Twentieth Century," 261.

18. Ibid.

19. Ibid; emphasis added.

20. Ibid.

21. Ibid., 262.

22. Ibid.

23. Chaudhary, "Amazon Drama."

24. Cf. Ralph Miliband, *State in Capitalist Society* (London: The Merlin Press, 2009).

25. Neumann, "Economics and Politics in the Twentieth Century," 262

26. Antonio Gramsci, *Selections from the Prison Notebooks* (New York: International Publishers, 2014), pp. 147–149; 177–178.

27. Neumann, "The Concept of Political Freedom."

28. Neumann, "Economics and Politics in the Twentieth Century," 264.
29. Ibid., 266.
30. Ibid., 264.
31. Ibid., 264.
32. This is both intuitive and not a particularly original observation as I've argued elsewhere with my colleague Raphaële Chappe. Ajay Chaudhary and Raphaële Chappe, "The Supermanagerial Reich," *Los Angeles Review of Books*, November 7, 2016, https://lareviewofbooks.org/article/the-supermanagerial-reich.
33. Neumann, "The Concept of Political Freedom," 168.
34. Neumann, "Economics and Politics in the Twentieth Century," 268.
35. Adam Przeworski, *Capitalism and Social Democracy* (Cambridge: Cambridge University Press, 2008), p. 201; Peter Bratsis makes a similar claim to Prezworski here and where I began the analysis in this chapter, there is a "tendency" for "Marxist theories to take the state as a given." Aronowitz and Bratsis, *Paradigm Lost*, 248.
36. Przeworski, *Capitalism and Social Democracy*, 201.
37. Franz Neumann, *Behemoth: the structure and practice of National Socialism, 1933–1944* (New York: Harper Torchbooks, 1966), p. 260.
38. Carl Schmitt, *Political Theology* (Chicago, IL: University of Chicago Press, 2006).
39. Carl Schmitt, *Concept of the Political*, trans. George Schwab (Chicago, IL: University of Chicago Press, 2007), p. 57; as is a common view, I agree that empirically the period up to World War I appears to play along the exact lines of these analyses. The multiplicity of arguments that appeared in Marxism in the twentieth century—particularly Western Marxism and Soviet Marxism—turns on why this was *not* the case.
40. Schmitt *Concept of the Political*, 48.
41. Ibid., 57.
42. This too is not entirely unique in history; recall Neumann's own brief aside to British colonialism. The East India Company was a private monopoly interest which did precisely this, although outside the boundaries of Britain proper (India was not British territory until much later than the company's long presence in the subcontinent) and its monopoly position was granted by the Crown. But while the colonial comparison is apt, there are weaknesses and strengths in discussing today's world.
43. Monopsony power is when a single market has essentially only one employer, that is, exerting a monopoly over the labor market as opposed to a commodity market–A.C.
44. I have given a fuller account of political economy and law in Nazi Germany and Neumann's reading of it in "The Supermanagerial Reich," co-authored with Raphaële Chappe. Chaudhary and Chappe, "The Supermanagerial Reich."
45. Neumann, *Behemoth*, 224.
46. Chaudhary and Chappe, "The Supermanagerial Reich."
47. I have done so elsewhere with Raphaële Chappe in "The Supermanagerial Reich" alongside significant data and historical analysis as well as a comparison with where Nazism does and does not overlap with fascism, since the two are often conflated.

48. Neumann, *Behemoth*, 468–469.
49. William E. Scheuerman, *Between the Norm and the Exception* (Cambridge, MA: MIT Press, 1997), p. 133.
50. In viewing the "representative of monopoly capital" not as just some bundle of completely individual interests nor as a simple capitalist bloc, Neumann is able to give us a better account *and* a better theory. We learn a *method*—how the capital is structured in a given juncture, what are its (various) political options, how it is not only facilitated but also delimited by certain of the *available* political options. These are not determined by capital. Capital might be the *most* powerful, but it is not *all powerful*.
51. Paul M. Sweezy, "Behemoth: The Structure and Practice of National Socialism, by Franz Neumann (Book Review)." *Science and Society* 6 (January 1, 1942): p. 281.
52. Rosa Luxemburg, "The Accumulation of Capital: A Contribution to the Economic Theory of Imperialism," in: *The complete works of Rosa Luxemburg. Volume II, Economic writings, Volume II* (New York: Verso, 2016), chapter 27.
53. Ibid.
54. Sweezy, "Behemoth."
55. Carl Schmitt, *Nomos of the Earth*, trans. G. L. Ulmen (Candor: Telos Press Publishing, 2006), p. 233.
56. Martin Jay, "Introduction," in: *The Dialectical Imagination: A History of the Frankfurt School and the Institute of Social Research, 1923–1950* (Berkeley: University of California Press, 1996).
57. Chris Thornhill, *Political Theory in Modern Germany: An Introduction* (Cambridge: Polity Press, 2000), p. 95.
58. Ibid., 95.
59. Cf. Chantal Mouffe, *For a Left Populism* (New York, Verso, 2019).
60. Scheuerman, *Between the Norm and the Exception*, 140.
61. See Oliver Nachtwey's recent *Germany's Hidden Crisis*, for an analysis of the fall out of such measures in contemporary Germany. Oliver Nachtwey, *Germany's Hidden Crisis: Social Decline in the Heart of Europe* (New York: Verso, 2018).
62. Neumann, "Economics and Politics in the Twentieth Century," 269.
63. Thornhill, *Political Theory in Modern Germany*, 113; Thornhill on this page misunderstands Neumann's case about the "primacy of politics." Neumann views it as a historical fact and not, as with Schmitt, a kind of idealist "dignity."
64. Neumann "Montesquieu," in: Herbert Marcuse (ed.) and Peter Gay (trans.), *The Democratic and the Authoritarian State* (New York: The Free Press, 1964), p. 142.
65. Neumann "Montesqieu," 142.
66. Andreas Kalyvas, "Hegemonic Sovereignty: Carl Schmitt, Antonio Gramsci and the Constituent Prince." *Journal of Political Ideologies* 5.3 (2000): pp. 343–376, DOI: 10.1080/713682944.
67. Samir Amin, *Modern Imperialism, Monopoly Finance Capital, and Marx's Law of Value* (New York: Monthly Review, 2018); Branko Milanovic, *Global Inequality: A New Approach for the Age of Globalization* (Cambridge, MA: Harvard University Press, 2018).

68. In more empirical accounts of the "structural dependence" of "the state" on capital, this turns out to be precisely the case. Outside of a significant if historically bounded debate about structural limits to social democratic strategy—best outlined in Prezworski's *Capitalism and Social Democracy*—it does appear that even in this condition, from a purely economic point of view, capital's political power is not deterministic but rather preponderant and—following Gramsci—at least partially ideological.

69. Chaudhary and Chappe, "The Supermanagerial Reich."

70. Greta R. Krippner, "Conclusion," in: *Capitalizing on Crisis: The Political Origins of the Rise of Finance* (Cambridge, MA: Harvard University Press, 2012).

71. China Miéville, "Introduction," in: Thomas More, *Utopia* (New York: Verso, 2016).

72. For just one study among many, please see Philip Mirowski, *Never Let a Serious Crisis Go to Waste: How Neoliberalism Survived the Financial Meltdown* (New York: Verso, 2014).

73. Cf. Michael Hardt and Antonio Negri, *Empire* (Cambridge, MA: Harvard University Press, 2001) and Yanis Varoufakis, *The Global Minotaur* (London: Zed Books, 2015).

74. Cf. Mirowksi, "Shock Block Doctrine," in: *Never Let a Serious Crisis Go to Waste: How Neoliberalism Survived the Financial Meltdown* (New York: Verso, 2014).

75. Ruth Wilson Gilmore, *Golden Gulag* (Berkeley: University of California Press, 2007), p. 245.

76. Cf. Mirowski, "Shock Block Doctrine."

77. Quinn Slobidian, *Globalists: The End of Empire and the Birth of Neoliberalism* (Cambridge, MA: Harvard University Press, 2018).

78. Schmitt, *Nomos of the Earth*, 235.

79. F. A. Hayek, "The Containment of Power and the Dethronement of Politics," in: *Law Legislation and Liberty* (Chicago, IL: University of Chicago Press, 1978).

80. Adam Tooze, "Framing Crashed (10): 'A New Bretton Woods' and the Problem of 'Economic Order'"—also a reply to Adler and Varoufakis, personal blog, February 9, 2019, https://adamtooze.com/2019/02/09/framing-crashed-10-a-new-bretton-woods-and-the-problem-of-economic-order-also-a-reply-to-adler-and-varoufakis/#_ftn9; see also Adam Tooze, *Crashed: How a Decade of Financial Crisis Changed the World* (New York: Penguin, 2019), p. 80.

81. Such a "structural preponderance" is achieved by adding the most significant factor of capital's power—the private control over investment—with all other theories of influence previously explored, including ideological work, and the more prosaic forms one might find in liberal literatures: campaign finance, access, misinformation, patronage, shared interests, and the like.

82. Adam Przeworski and Michael Wallerstein, "Structural Dependence of the State on Capital." *American Political Science Review* 82.1 (1988): pp. 11–29.

83. Matt Bishop and Tony Payne, "The Political Economies of Different Globalisations–Part 3: 'Deglobalisation from the Left,'" *Sheffield Political Economy Research Institute Blog*, March 21, 2019, http://speri.dept.shef.ac.uk/2019/03/21/the-political-economies-of-different-globalisations-part-3-deglobalisation-from-the-left/.

84. Jeffrey Sachs and Charles Wyplosz, "The Economic Consequences of President Mitterrand," *Economic Policy* 1.2 (April 1, 1986): pp. 261–306, https://doi.org/10.2307/1344559.

85. Krippner, *Capitalizing on Crisis*.

86. Tooze, *Crashed*, 8.

87. Gary Gereffi, *Global Value Chains and Development: Redefining the Contours of 21st Century Capitalism* (Cambridge: Cambridge University Press, 2018), p. 306.

88. Richard Baldwin, "Global Supply Chains: Why They Emerged, Why They Matter, and Where They Are Going," CEPR Discussion Papers 9103, C.E.P.R. Discussion Papers, 2012.

89. Branko Malinovic, *Global Inequality: A New Approach for the Age of Globalization* (Cambridge, MA: Harvard University Press, 2016).

90. United Nations Conference on Trade and Development (UNCTAD), "Global Value Chains and Development: Investment and Value Added Trade in the Global Economy," (United Nations, 2013), https://unctad.org/en/PublicationsLibrary/diae2013d1_en.pdf.

91. Baldwin, "Global Supply Chains."

92. Neumann, *Behemoth*, 355.

93. UNCTAD, "Global Value Chains and Development."

94. Thomas R. Tørsløv, Ludvig S. Wier, and Gabriel Zucman, "The Missing Profits of Nations," *National Burero of Economic Research Working Paper No. 24701*, issued June 2018, Revised August 2018 (DOI): 10.3386/w24701.

95. Varoufakis, *The Global Minotaur*, 226.

96. Gereffi, *Global Value Chains and Development*.

97. UNCTAD, "Global Value Chains and Development."

98. Baldwin, "Global Supply Chains."

99. Ibid.

100. Gereffi, *Global Value Chains and Development*.

101. Tooze, *Crashed*, 9.

102. Gereffi, *Global Value Chains and Development*, 145.

103. Tooze, *Crashed*, 147; see also Mark Blyth in *Austerity* about the fundamentally private nature of the twenty-first-century financial system. Mark Blyth, *Austerity: The History of an Idea* (Oxford: Oxford University Press, 2013).

104. Tooze, *Crashed*, 11–13.

105. Cf. multiple authors in Gereffi.

106. Baldwin, "Global Supply Chains."

107. Chaudhary, "Amazon Drama."

108. Tooze, *Crashed*, 166.

109. Tooze, "Framing Crashed (10)."

110. This is also why this form of critical state theory is so helpful at broadening a transnationalized neo-Gramscian framework (cf. Michele Williams and Vishwas Satgar (eds.), *Marxisms in the 21st Century: Crisis, Critique, and Struggle* (Johannesburg: Wits University Press, 2013), p. 77.

III

SOCIALIST AND COMMUNIST STATE

Chapter 7

Lenin and the Transitional-Revolutionary State

Lorenzo Chiesa

There is not only a struggle *against* the state; the state itself is exposed as a *weapon of class struggle* . . . a proletarian weapon in the struggle for socialism and for the suppression of the bourgeoisie. (Lukács, *Lenin: A Study on the Unity of His Thought*)

Genuine revolutionaries have most often broken their necks when they began to write "revolution" with a capital R, to elevate "revolution" to something almost divine. (Lenin, "The Importance of Gold")[1]

1. INTRODUCTION

A detailed and unbiased reading of Lenin's *The State and Revolution* leads us to an unequivocal conclusion: the proletarian revolution that almost instantaneously dissolves the bourgeois state—but not the bourgeoisie as a class—is accompanied by the establishment of a *transitional* socialist state that paves the way for communism. The socialist state is closely associated with the so-called dictatorship of the proletariat as a gradual—and on close inspection perhaps asymptotic—*withering away* of the State as such. The socialist state dialectically undoes itself precisely through its consolidation. However, it also seems always to survive in some residual and thoroughly reconfigured form. Contrary to the allegations of contemporary communist thinkers such as Alain Badiou,[2] for Lenin, "communism" and "state" are far from being incompatible concepts. Their juxtaposition is instead a necessary presupposition for the construction of communism.

This chapter aims at analyzing the theory of the socialist-communist transitional state as envisioned by Lenin, and at introducing an assessment of the political, economic, and anthropological temporality of this transition. I will mostly focus on *The State and Revolution*, which predates the revolution of October 1917 by a few months, stressing its general consonance with Marx's ideas as exposed especially in *The Critique of the Gotha Programme* (1875). In the near future, I also intend to scrutinize from the same perspective Lenin's writings and speeches subsequent to the October Revolution, which most often concern pressing military, economic, and administrative matters. Building on the present chapter, it will be a matter of showing how, in spite of a number of complications, "zigzags," "retreats," and counter-retreats[3]—as well as some sheer contradictions—mostly due to the capitalist reaction to the Bolshevik's seizure of power, they overall consistently adhere to the theory of the state advanced in *The State and Revolution*. Contrary to a wide consensus prevalent even among sympathetic readers—ranging from Edward Hallett Carr to Fredric Jameson and Slavoj Žižek[4]—my working hypothesis is therefore that this however ambitious manifesto cannot simply be labeled as "utopian," in the sense that it would promptly be refuted by Lenin's subsequent course of action.

2. THE STATE *AS* REVOLUTION

As made sufficiently clear by its subtitle, "The Marxist Doctrine of the State and the Tasks of the Proletariat in the Revolution," *The State and Revolution* does not simply oppose "state" and "revolution" as antithetical terms, whereby the latter would be deemed to constructively replace the former as a mere negative reference. "State" and "revolution" need to be articulated dialectically. Against Badiou's insistent claims ("Marx has never imagined a Marxist state"; the phrase "State of Communism" is a terroristic and disastrous oxymoron invented by Stalin[5]), for Lenin, there most definitely is a Marxist—and Marxian—doctrine of the state. In Lenin's own words, "Our first task is to *restore* the true doctrine of Marx on the state."[6]

In approaching *The State and Revolution*, the first methodological tenet to bear in mind is thus that this text primarily and intentionally amounts to a close reading of Marx and Engels. Lenin is here returning to the revolutionary kernel of their teachings in order to counter the reactionary readings of the "opportunists" and "former Marxists," as he calls them (in short, Kautsky and the Second International, on the one hand, and the Mensheviks, on the other—who were at the time in power in Russia).

Theoretically, the crucial point is that, for Lenin, the violent "destruction" or "smashing" of the *bourgeois* state,[7] which he unrepentantly advocates against the revisionists, goes together with the emergence of a *socialist* state—roughly corresponding to the dictatorship of the proletariat as the *first* stage of communism—with which the "withering away" of the State in general only *commences*. To the extent that the State cannot simply be regarded as a bourgeois institution, since it is more deeply rooted in class difference, Lenin *does* positively theorize it in an innovative way precisely insofar as he privileges its gradual withering away over its direct destruction (which is simply an impossible anarchic and "left-communist" dream).

Or better, the *real* destruction of the State can be achieved only by means of a state that increasingly withers away *thanks to* its strengthening. Consequently, the immediate revolutionary destruction of the bourgeois state accomplished in October 1917 ultimately stands for nothing more than the preliminary, or at best initial, stage of a long-term process. In other words, only a new socialist state can *perpetuate* the revolution against the State. Only a new socialist state can rightly assess the dialectical *state of the revolution* and direct it against itself and the State as such. As Lenin puts it in a text of November 1918, which he pertinently introduces as an addendum to what he already formulated in *State and Revolution* (itself published as a pamphlet only in 1918), "Revolution is a continuous desperate struggle."[8] Revolution begins to take place as a—at first sight rather modest and uninspiring—passage from one kind of state to another: "The transitional stage between the state as an organ of the rule of the capitalist class and the state as an organ of the rule of the proletariat is *revolution*."[9]

Let us analyze *The State and Revolution*'s key arguments more closely. For Lenin, the state is clearly *not* a necessary political formation. It is rather the product of the "irreconcilability of class antagonisms."[10] The conciliation of classes—and hence the elimination of antagonistic class violence—would eliminate the state. More to the point, the state is an organ of the ruling class (currently, the bourgeoisie), that is, a dictatorial instrument of the exploitation of the oppressed class (currently, the proletariat), that "stands above" society. Marxism, thus, aims at the destruction of the bourgeois state, which can only be achieved, following the concluding passages of *The Poverty of Philosophy* and *The Communist Manifesto*, by means of a violent revolution ("the substitution of the proletarian state for the bourgeois state is impossible without a violent revolution"[11]). In other words, there is a basic irreconcilability between Marxism and Western parliamentarian democracy.[12]

But if this is the case—if the *dictatorship* of the bourgeoisie as a state apparatus can be dealt with violently once and for all—how should we then understand Engels's claim that "the state is not 'abolished', *it withers away*?"[13] Certainly not in the way in which the "opportunists" understand it, that is, by claiming that the state will gradually disappear once the socialist parties seize power through parliamentarian elections—that is, without a violent revolution. For Lenin—and this is an extremely important citation—"Engels speaks here of the 'abolition' of the *bourgeois* state by the proletarian revolution, while the words about its withering away refer to the remnants of the *proletarian* state *after* the socialist revolution."[14]

The State and Revolution entirely revolves around Lenin's dialectical explanation of the way in which the violent (as insurrectional) abolition of the bourgeois state establishes a proletarian state that as such, that is, as a *state*, commences its own withering away (in this sense, it is always already a "remnant") and that of the State in general. First, in violently seizing power and control over the means of production, as well as in eliminating the structural violence of the army and the police as instruments of state power, the self-acting armed organization of the population destroys the preexisting state. Second, the proletariat, nevertheless, needs state power and violence to crush the resistance of the bourgeois exploiters; this is the preeminent function of the dictatorship of the proletariat as a, in Lenin's words, "repressive force."[15] But, third, this very state power and violence, which cannot simply hold to the ready-made bourgeois state, "immediately" begins to wither away.[16] The "essence of Marx's doctrine of the state"[17] is therefore, for Lenin, the dictatorship of the proletariat as a transition to a stateless society that will no longer know violence. Peaceful statelessness can be achieved only in "*complete* communism."[18] But consequently, for the time being, "a Marxist is one who *extends* the acceptance of the class struggle to the acceptance of the *dictatorship of the proletariat*. This is where the profound difference lies between a Marxist and an ordinary petty (and even big) bourgeois."[19]

Lenin then asks the question: What is more concretely the proletarian state that replaces the bourgeois state? What does it mean to supersede the smashed state machine with a "new state machine"—as overall identifiable with the dictatorship of the proletariat, in spite of the fact that, in the course of the transition, the latter will include "an abundance of political forms?"[20] Lenin believes that Marx himself developed a cogent answer following the Paris Commune, which he saw as a gigantic historic experiment. In addition to the already mentioned substitution of the standing army with the armed people, in *The Civil War in France*, Marx—and Lenin agrees with him—singles out as crucial the maintenance of political representation, which should, however, be made easily revocable (on the one hand, "the way out of parliamentarianism is not the abolition of the representative institutions," but their conversion from "'talking shops' into working bodies"; on the other hand, "all officials [must] be elected and subject to recall"[21]). Marx and Lenin also stress the importance of the imposition of workmen's wages for all public servants. In this way, what Lenin can explicitly describe as "the socialist reconstruction of the state" dialectically amounts at the same time to "something which is no longer really a state."[22] To put it simply, the new state machine no longer merely stands "above" society as something "special."[23]

Lenin initially spells this out with regard to the armed people: "It is still necessary to suppress the bourgeoisie and crush its resistance . . . but the organ of suppression is now the majority of the population, and not the minority, as was always the case under slavery, serfdom, and wage-slavery. And since the majority of the people *itself* suppresses its oppressors, a 'special force' for suppression is *no longer necessary*. In this sense the state *begins to wither away*."[24] In short, some form of the state as an organ of the class rule of the proletariat is still needed, yet, at the same time and with the same movement, for the majority of the people (including not only the proletariat but also the mass of toilers it leads), the state is no longer alienated from society, and in this sense, it is no longer really a state.

3. OF SOCIALIST MANAGERS, STRICTEST CONTROL, EQUAL INEQUALITY, AND THE STATE OF DEMOCRACY

In the rest of *The State and Revolution*, Lenin proceeds to provide a quite detailed discussion of both the socialist "reconstruction of the state" and its concomitant withering away. We can summarize here some of his main arguments and see how the same dialectic holds for different aspects of socialist society—as the first phase of communism—under the banner that socialism "simplifies" the state as an "inherited evil":[25]

1. *Administration*. The socialist revolution does not give way to the dispensation of what Lenin calls "managers."[26] That is a vain "anarchist dream."[27] But the function of "accounting" will be performed in the socialist state "by each in turn" and, as such, will increasingly die out as "the *special* functions of a special stratum of the population" along with its associated grandeur.[28] This generalization of management is made possible by capitalism itself, which has greatly simplified administrative tasks, thanks to technological innovations (Lenin speaks of the railways, the postal services, and the telephone); administration can already be reduced to "such simple operation of registration, filing, and checking," and in this way it can be carried out by "every literate person" for a workman's wage.[29] Lenin can thus speak, without contradiction, of the socialist state as one in which "the whole of society will have become a single office," yet, at the same time, in such a state no one is a bureaucrat, because of the "equality of work and equality of pay."[30] To put it simply, transitional universal bureaucracy is the only way out of bureaucracy. If the "essence of bureaucracy" lies in the fact that "privileged persons [are] divorced from the masses and *superior to* the masses," then for the withering away of the

state to take place "*all* shall become 'bureaucrats' for a time . . . so that, therefore, *no one* can become a 'bureaucrat'."[31]

2. *The economy*. The socialist revolution expropriates the capitalists and thus assumes control of production and distribution. In this sense, the economy belongs to the whole of the working people; bourgeois exploitation is terminated. Lenin claims that, after the proletarian insurrection, it is "quite possible" to bring about such a process "immediately, overnight."[32] But, again, it would be a great mistake to think that this will also entail an overnight abolishment of the function of the state in the economy. This is where communism profoundly differs from anarchism. To begin with, in the socialist state as the first phase of communism, "*all* citizens are transformed into the salaried employees of the state, which consists of the armed workers."[33] In economic matters, the dictatorship of the proletariat as the state of the armed workers is also reflexively exercised over the same workers as employees of the state—surprisingly, here Lenin does not evoke any vanguard or party as separate from them.[34] As already outlined by Marx and Engels in *The Communist Manifesto*, the most urgent task for the defense of the revolution and the establishment of a truly classless society is indeed a rapid increase in the productive forces, which is certainly possible but can be achieved only by, in Marx and Engels's words, "centraliz[ing] all instruments of production in the hands of the state."[35] So, for Lenin, the fact that the working people immediately become collective owners should be matched in the transition to the abolition of the state by "the strictest control, by society and by the state, of the amount of labor and the amount of consumption."[36]

3. *Political representation and the question of democracy*. As shown by the historical example of the Commune, the proletarian revolution entails a certain "reversion" to—and renewal of—"primitive," or direct, democracy.[37] However, the latter does not involve an anarchic abolition of political representation, but its conversion into what Marx called "working bodies," through which, as Lenin specifies, parliamentarians are "directly responsible to their constituents."[38] Here we should talk of "democracy without parliamentarianism," in the sense that parliamentarianism is smashed as a "special system"[39] (especially because the representatives are easily recalled). Yet—and this is crucial—democracy, including proletarian democracy, is still for Lenin undoubtedly a *state*, that is, as seen, a violent organ of class rule. As he spells out, "Democracy is *not* identical with the subordination of the minority to the majority. Democracy is a *state* which recognizes the subordination of the minority to the majority, *i.e.*, an organization for the systematic use of *violence* by one class against another."[40] If democracy—including

proletarian democracy—is necessarily a state, then it is in itself intrinsically violent. So much so that the proletarian democratic state (i.e., the dictatorship of the proletariat as supported by a non-parliamentarian form of political representation) is one in which an "immense expansion of democracy" involving for the first time "the poor"—whereby the state begins in this sense to wither away—simultaneously imposes a "series of restrictions" on the former capitalist exploiters aimed at crushing their resistance against the revolution.[41] Lenin recalls and endorses Engels's claim that "a revolution is the most authoritarian thing there is" and that "the victorious party, if it does not wish to have fought in vain, must maintain its rule by means of the terror which its arms inspire in the reactionaries."[42]

It is here important to stress how Lenin counters the "opportunists'" accusation that, on the basis of what we have just explained, the dictatorship of the proletariat would contradict democracy[43] (in spite of its expansion) and turns it against them. *Both* the dictatorship of the proletariat and *democracy* are nothing but an expression of the remnants of the state. With the withering away of the state, which is started precisely by the establishment of the democratic dictatorship of the proletariat, *both* the dictatorship of the proletariat and democracy wither away.[44] What also withers away with them is, more generally, *politics* as such, at least as it has been conceived so far—and this in accordance with Marx's view in *The Poverty of Philosophy* that "there will be no more political power properly so-called" in the classless society.[45]

The other vital, and usually underestimated, aspect we should emphasize in Lenin's argument is that the democratic dictatorship of the proletariat as an inevitable transition to a classless society is not only a violent—and even terroristic, if needed—limitation of the freedom of the minority (i.e., the former exploiters) but also the last remaining obstacle to the equality of the *non-bourgeois majority* itself. In short, the first—socialist—phase of communism as the end of bourgeois exploitation and the establishment of "equal right" still presupposes *inequality*. Lenin draws here from Marx's *Critique of the Gotha Program* and expands on it. Why would equal right equate with inequality? Because "every right is an application of the *same* measure to *different* people who, in fact, are not the same and are not equal to one another."[46] Consequently, the socialist realization of "an equal amount of labor for an equal quantity of products" is quite bluntly, as Lenin concedes, "not yet communism."[47] As Marx has it, to achieve complete communism, "right, instead of being equal, would have to be unequal."[48] In other words— and this is important—right as such is at bottom "bourgeois right."[49] From a legal perspective, socialism is then simply bourgeois right without the bourgeoisie—or, we may add, equal inequality. Lenin does not speak here of a violence of the democratic dictatorship of the proletariat toward the proletariat itself, yet he describes this states of affairs as a "violation"[50] that basically entails injustice. To conclude, the first phase of communism—that is, socialism—is thus necessarily violent toward the former exploiters and necessarily unjust toward the proletariat who, as armed people, limit the freedom of the former exploiters.

At this stage the inevitable question to be asked is: How does the *second* phase of communism ("complete communism") differ from its socialist, and far from ideal, state-phase and its lingering violence and injustice? When can it be achieved? In terms of right and justice, which are as such inextricable from economic considerations, Lenin's answer is straightforward: we need to move from "formal" to "real" equality.[51] Following once again Marx closely, this can more practically be grasped under the banner of "from each according to his ability, to each according to his needs."[52] For this higher phase of communism to be reached, two basic interrelated preconditions must be satisfied: first, the overcoming of the division of labor, primarily in terms of the antithesis between mental and manual labor (which cannot immediately be solved by the socialist state) and, second, on a more anthropological-ontological level, the realization that, at the level of the life of our species, labor is not merely a means to live but a "primary necessity of life" (this is a realization that by "developing" the "individual" would also at the same time enhance the productive forces).[53]

Lenin is convinced that socialism, as well as its remaining violence against the former oppressors and concomitant injustice toward the former oppressed, will eventually give way to complete communism. He is also adamant that, in communism, "the need for violence against people in general," including the proletarian subjection of the minority to the majority, will "vanish."[54] However, to achieve complete communism—and the dissolution of the *socialist* state—people will have to "*become accustomed* to observing the elementary conditions of social life *without force* and *without subordination*."[55] In the end, what is at stake is an "element of habit"—whose acquisition may require "severe punishment."[56] Lenin remains somewhat hesitant and vague with regard to the duration of this demanding process. On the one hand, he insists that complete communism is no utopia—precisely insofar as it is born out of the concrete historical existence of capitalism and the critique of it. Following Engels, he suggests that a "new generation" will suffice.[57] On the other hand, he nevertheless speaks of a "rather lengthy," or elsewhere "protracted," transition.[58] We can be certain about the "gradual and spontaneous" socialist withering away of the state—for it is possible to anticipate it from within capitalism—but we are in no position to define "the exact moment" of the overcoming of socialism itself—for "no material is [yet] available."[59]

4. MARX'S "LITTLE WORD" AND THE WITHERING AWAY OF THE STATE

In *The Proletarian Revolution and the Renegade Kautsky* (1918), Lenin is understandably outraged by Kautsky's accusation that his theory of the state, as exposed in *The State and Revolution*, "rests upon a single word of Marx"—a passage from the *Critique of the Gotha Programme* in which he maintains that "between capitalist and communist society" lies "a political transition period in which the state can be nothing but the *revolutionary dictatorship of the proletariat*."[60] Lenin retorts that Marx and Engels "*repeatedly* spoke about the dictatorship of the proletariat, both before and after the Paris Commune"—they spoke about it "*for forty years*" between 1852 and 1891."[61]

While polemical statements like these are undoubtedly correct at face value, we should also be wary of the fact that Stalinism later used them to untenably justify an alleged seamless and "scientific" continuity between the *Critique of the Gotha Programme*, *The State and Revolution*, and the implementation of the Five-Year Plans—to which Lenin himself would have objected. As the editors of the 1932 English edition of the *Critique of the Gotha Programme* write in their introduction, "It was precisely on the basis of the *Critique of the Gotha Programme* that Lenin, in ... *The State and Revolution* ... developed that brilliant picture—based on real scientific insight—of the transition through Socialism to Communism, which the Seventeenth Conference of the Communist Party of the Soviet Union laid down as the basis for ... the building of a Socialist society in the Second Five-Year Plan."[62]

Here I think it is vital to endorse an important specification Lukács made as early as 1924. On the one hand, Lenin not only "revived" Marx's theory of the state, but he was alone in regaining the latter's "theoretical heights,"[63] precisely insofar as he understood that the proletarian revolutionary attitude toward the state should *not* be confined to a "left-wing" struggle *against* the State (or, worse, a revisionist acceptance of and connivance with the bourgeois state). Yet, on the other hand, this revival did not primarily amount to "a philological rediscovery of the original teaching, nor a philosophical systematization of its genuine principle"[64]—however pressing these also were in Lenin's declared intention ("our first task is to *restore* the true doctrine of Marx on the state" against renegades, opportunists, and anarcho-syndicalists).

According to Lukács, first and foremost, Lenin realized that, given the historical situation of Russia and the imperialist development of capitalism since Marx's death, the question of Marx's *theory* of the state—as the dictatorship of the proletariat—had to be extended to "its concretisation in everyday *practice*."[65] More specifically, acknowledging the real actuality of the revolution (and this was his major contribution to Marxism; "the actuality of the proletarian revolution is no longer only a world historical horizon arching above the self-liberating working class, but . . . *revolution is already on its agenda*"[66]), Lenin also grasped the actuality of the problem of the *state* of the proletariat as an *immediate task*. Again, state and revolution are dialectically inextricable; the former is not simply replaced by the latter; and this awareness honestly, intelligently, and in part successfully is translated into Lenin's practical directives after the seizure of power in October 1917 (one somehow always tends to forget that, shortly after writing *The State and Revolution*, he became a serving head of state).

Going beyond Lukács, we should add that what Kautsky contemptuously regards as Marx's isolated "little word"[67] on the state already emphasizes such an indissoluble link between revolution and the state. According to Marx, the transition period in which the state can be nothing but the dictatorship of the proletariat "*corresponds*" to the "period of the *revolutionary* transformation" of capitalist into communist society. However, it is also fair to admit that Marx did not systematize his insight—neither in the *Critique of the Gotha Programme* nor elsewhere. Lenin can thus rightly claim that Marx spoke of the dictatorship of the proletariat for forty years, but as proved by the very references he uses in *The State and Revolution*, Marx's remarks remain indeed scattered across a long period of time and may consistently and convincingly be interpreted together only with hindsight—that is, moving from the timely assumption that revolution is now really on the agenda—as well as by integrating them with Engels's (not always fully compatible) individual pronouncements.

If we submit these references to a close textual reading, it is adamant that Lenin mostly derives the key idea of the gradual "withering away" of the socialist state, as distinct from yet dialectically correlated with the immediate abolition of the bourgeois state, from Engels. Yet Engels seems to be putting forward a different and frankly far more utopian argument. In *The Origin of Family, Private Property and State* (1884) he first contends that, in its contemporary and parliamentarian ("representative") form, the state duly amounts to an "instrument of exploitation of wage-labour by capital."[68] He then adds that the State "has not existed from all eternity,"[69] whether as the dictatorship of the "democratic" bourgeoisie or as some other previous form of exploitative class rule. As we have seen, Lenin fully adopts these two points without modifying them.

But Engels also argues that, in bourgeois society, we are "rapidly approaching" a stage at which, due precisely to the contradictions internal to the development of capitalist production (in short, the growing centrality of the proletariat in it), the State as an expression of class rule will as such "inevitably fall."[70] More to the point, as further specified in *Anti-Dühring* (1878) in what Lenin himself deems to be a crucial passage, Engels clearly *equates* the proletarian seizure of "state power" (i.e., the transformation of the means of production into "state property") with the "*end* [of] all class differences and class antagonisms" (whereby, significantly, the proletariat also "puts an end to itself").[71] Lenin's reasoning—implicitly but decidedly—always disputes this. For him, the proletarian seizure of the state only *intensifies* class differences and antagonisms; the bourgeoisie's resistance is organized *after* the overthrow of its dictatorship; and the most immediate task of the dictatorship of the proletariat as state power is therefore repressing the resistance of the former repressors.

Let me spell this out from a slightly different perspective, since it is vital to understand Lenin's subtle, understated, and yet fundamental departure from Engels. For Engels, the proletarian state as the withering away of the state begins not only with the immediate abolition of the bourgeois state (which Lenin endorses in contrast to the revisionist stance), but also with the instantaneous abolition of *classes*. The beginning of the *proletarian* state thus amounts to its very end. Engels could not be more explicit: the "first act" of the proletarian state (i.e., "the taking possession of the means of production in the name of society") is concomitantly "its last independent act as a state."[72] Although—as we will later discuss—this claim can be problematized, if not contradicted, by other passages from his work, strictly speaking, for Engels there is here no transitional *state* that, in Lenin's words, somehow still "stands above society."[73] There is just the withering away, since, in overcoming class differences overnight, revolution also eliminates the basic presupposition for the State as such. The question to ask Engels would then be: *what* is it precisely that withers away in a supposedly already classless society?

Contrary to this stance, for Lenin, the first act of the proletarian state as the last act of the state as we have known it so far should *at the same time* be understood as the *first* act of a new *socialist state, within which* alone the *withering away* of the State can take place. According to Lenin, the first act of the socialist state (in his opinion, seizing political power) is to be followed by a series of other specific acts. These are indeed meant to be self-refuting in retrospect, since they are ultimately aimed at the abolition of classes, or statelessness, but the latter can be achieved only dialectically, that is, by *also* preserving the "independence" of the state as an agent. The expansion of democracy leading to its transformation into real equality requires the violent suppression of democratic parliamentarianism; the overcoming of bureaucracy demands the relentless imposition of universal accounting; mass control over the means of production necessitates the strictest organizational supervision.

We would be mistaken—that is non-dialectical—if we regarded Lenin's withering away of the state as a simple step-by-step process of *weakening* of the state after revolution (let us tentatively call this naïve option "revolutionary-progressive socialism"). The withering away of the state instead *concentrates* power in the new state's hands, and consequently somehow also strengthens it. This is the case not simply in the sense that the dictatorship of the proletariat promptly needs state power to counter the always more circumscribed, desperate, and thus more resilient resistance of the former bourgeois oppressors (in the fields of politics, administration, and the economy alike), but also because, in parallel, the dictatorship of the proletariat as a state must be able to effectively turn its power *against itself*—and the party in particular. It is the socialist state that now stands above society.

As becomes always more evident in Lenin's later writings, in the socialist state, the protracted war against internal and external imperialists goes together with the purging of bureaucratic (i.e., basically inefficient, if not corrupt) party officials as sheer *state* directives. Yet at the same time, and without solution of continuity, these very actions dialectically enable the state to wither *itself* away. Eloquently, protecting "our state" means nothing other than "protecting the workers from their own state."[74] And it is no coincidence if in the very period of so-called war communism (involving the hypercentralized fight against the whites as well as at least seven capitalist countries) and shortly before the first purges against "the Communists who *imagine* that they are administrators"[75] (of which he was the main initiator), Lenin pays an incredible amount of attention to the emergence of the *subbotnik* phenomenon.

The *subbotniks* are events in which vanguard volunteers work for free on Saturdays in the name of the "general good."[76] Lenin reproaches those who abuse the word "communist," since the expropriation of capitalists and the ensuing building up of socialism (as the withering away of the state) presents "nothing communistic yet."[77] Only in the case of the *subbotniks* can we already appropriately speak of a "communism in fact."[78] That is, they practically demonstrate that communism, as the "complete triumph" of socialism,[79] and the final *dissolution* of the State that accompanies it are indeed possible. Lenin also significantly specifies that the unpaid work during the *subbotniks* should nonetheless still dialectically be regarded as satisfying the "needs of the *state*"—since the universalization of the remolding of entrenched antisocial behaviors is a "work of decades."[80]

We may thus conclude that the *state* that withers *itself* away after the political revolution carried out by the proletariat all in all amounts to a—in Lenin's own words—"*cultural* revolution"[81] that anthropologically manages to change the capitalist, and more generally class-related, "habits" acquired by our species.

5. A COMMUNIST FUTURE STATE?

In light of these considerations, Lenin has a strong point when, in his notebook of January–February 1917 titled *Marxism on the State* (then largely incorporated in *The State and Revolution*), going against the grain of what has by now become an almost indisputable assumption, he notices that in the *Critique of the Gotha Programme* "Marx looks much more 'statesmanlike'—if it is permissible to use this insipid expression of our enemies—than Engels."[82]

In *The State and Revolution* Lenin tends to approach Marx's theory of the state chronologically and aims at showing how it more and more calls for the dictatorship of the *proletariat* as a separate *class* (whose rule leads to the abolition of classes). Assessing and temporally complicating Lenin's interpretation, which is very plausible but presented in a too linear fashion that runs the risk of glossing over some Marxian oscillations, we may say that it revolves around four main issues.

First, Lenin treats what seems to him—and should be—uncontroversial: from *The Poverty of Philosophy* (1847) and *The Communist Manifesto* (1848) to the *Critique of the Gotha Programme* (1875), passing through *The Eighteenth Brumaire of Louis Napoleon* (1852), *The Civil War in France* (1871), and his 1871 letter to Kugelmann, Marx always advocated the inevitability of a violent revolution as a—in his words—"forcible overthrow"[83] of the bourgeois state.

Second, Lenin brings into play what, in opposition to his narrative, we should frankly regard as a tension in Marx's pronouncements concerning the aftermaths of the proletarian revolution. On the one hand, as argued in *The Poverty of Philosophy* (1847), in the place of the bourgeois state, the working class will install "an association which will exclude classes and their antagonism."[84] The proletarian revolution engenders a classless society; "political power" as an "expression of antagonism" is in turn superseded;[85] and if this is the case, there is for good reason no mention of any state. Yet, on the other hand, in the contemporary *The Communist Manifesto* (1848), Marx also unequivocally speaks of a "state, i.e., ... the proletariat organised as the ruling class."[86] Here the proletariat retains "political supremacy" and uses it "to centralise all instruments of production in the hands of the state."[87]

I think we need to conclude that these two sets of statements remain irreconcilable, unless, of course, one tacitly identifies—as Lenin appears to be doing—the "association" that *will* exclude classes with the proletarian state in the course of its withering away. But such a reading seems forced and unsubstantiated by the sources under consideration. To say the least, why would then Marx adopt two distinct terms—"association" and "state"—instead of proposing a dialectical mediation between them, such as "state that is no longer really a state?" In my opinion, these relatively early texts present alternative options that can be merged only in retrospect when one articulates together the *different* stages of communism in the light of the actuality of the revolution.

Third, Lenin does however concede that in *The Eighteenth Brumaire of Louis Napoleon* (1852), after learning the practical lesson imparted by the failed Revolution of 1848–1851, Marx is trying to elaborate some new form of proletarian *state* that replaces the bourgeois state. We should thus infer, against Lenin, that the optimistic option ventilated in *The Poverty of Philosophy*—in short, direct classless communism—was left aside. But, for Lenin himself, Marx now also realizes that this replacement is far more complicated, and drastic, than expected. In *The Eighteenth Brumaire*, Marx would manage to come up with the "how" but not yet the "what" of the new state.[88]

With regard to the concrete "how," beyond the "extremely abstract" argument made in the first edition of the *Communist Manifesto*,[89] the question in *The Eighteenth Brumaire* is no longer simply the forcible overthrow of the bourgeois state, but—in Marx's words—its definitive "smashing."[90] In Lenin's view, this smashing is most conclusively, and not coincidently, expressed in Marx's last preface to *The Communist Manifesto* (1872), which, following the Paris Commune, he thought should make his view on the matter absolutely clear and easily accessible: "*The working class cannot simply lay hold of the ready-made state machinery and wield it for its own purposes.*"[91] In other words, the elimination of the bourgeois state is *final*, and there is no possibility for the proletariat to appropriate its apparatus in order to modify it.

Most importantly, Lenin takes notice of the fact that, in *The Eighteenth Brumaire*, the destruction of the state is to be *continued* after the seizure of power in a way that is, however, *far from straightforwardly negative*. According to Marx, Louis Bonaparte's reactionary *coup d'état* already "*perfected the parliamentary power, in order to be able to overthrow it*"[92]—to the benefit of the *bourgeoisie*'s power, which was eventually reinforced. What the proletariat revolution must do is take one unprecedented step further, namely, "perfect the *executive power*, reduce it to its purest expression, isolate it, set it up against itself as the sole target, in order to *concentrate all its* [revolution's] *forces of destruction against it* [executive power]."[93] Lenin is unsurprisingly excited by this passage. Although Marx does not seem to grasp that the executive power to be perfected so that it can be destroyed is, at this stage, nothing other than the *revolutionary* executive power (revolution *as* the new state) that destroys *itself*, here state and revolution are already dialectical concepts. "Perfecting the executive power" (Marx) coincides by now with the irreversible renunciation of "perfecting the state machine" (Lenin).

Fourth, Lenin finally singles out those passages in which Marx indeed opens the question of the proletarian state as, more specifically, the dictatorship of the proletariat's *transition* to a classless society—which is in Lenin's opinion the "what" of the new state. He gives great prominence to a letter to Weydemeyer (1852) and to *The Civil War in France* (1871). The former concisely formulates for Lenin "the essence of Marx's doctrine of state"; in Marx's words, "the class struggle necessarily leads to the dictatorship of the proletariat" and "this dictatorship itself only constitutes the transition to the abolition of all classes and to a classless society."[94] The latter describes in detail the new transitional state along the specific lines we already treated; moving from the concrete experience of the Paris Commune, the dictatorship of the proletariat should basically involve the replacement of the standing army with the armed people, the equal remuneration of public service at workmen's wages, and the revocable election of public servants.

For Lenin, there is no doubt that Marx always remained a "centralist," and that his postrevolutionary agenda does not in the least contradict his promotion of "national unity"—against anarchic federalism.[95] What Marx was still not able to convey is rather the "political *forms*" of the dictatorship of the proletariat as a transitional state that is "bound to disappear."[96] We may thus conclude that, according to Lenin, in Marx's work we move from the question of the "how" of the proletarian state (the violent *smashing* of the bourgeois state already in part conceived as a dialectic between revolution and the state) to that of the "what" (the proletarian state's *transition* to a classless and stateless society), *and* that the Bolsheviks' primary task is giving "political form" to the "what" at stake (this form cannot but be the *party* as a self-dissolving vanguard of the proletariat—although, in line with the marginalization of the party in *The State and Revolution*, Lenin does not mention it explicitly).

Discussing the "what" of the proletarian state in Marx, Lenin also returns to Engels. In spite of his initial doubts in *Marxism on the State*, Lenin's efforts are here aimed at demonstrating that, in the end, Marx and Engels held "identical" views on the matter.[97] I think we should contest this—even by just dwelling on the passages from their works cited by Lenin. In line with Marx, Engels does indeed speak of "the dictatorship of the proletariat as the *transitional* stage to the abolition of classes and, with them, of the state" (in *The Housing Question* of 1872); of "the state as a *transitional* institution . . . with which the proletariat holds down adversaries" (in the letter to Bebel of 1875) and of the proletariat's need for the state "*after* its victorious struggle for class supremacy" (in the introduction to *The Civil War in France* of 1891).[98] But Lenin does not acknowledge that these statements blatantly challenge the very passage from *Anti-Dühring* (1878) that introduces the—for him crucial—theme of the withering away. While, as seen, in the *Anti-Dühring*, Engels problematically identifies the proletarian seizure of power with the elimination of class struggle and differences, these other passages unquestionably presuppose their continuation and intensification—the abolition of classes first requires a transition; the *proletariat* has to hold down adversaries; the revolution only installs proletarian *class supremacy*.

Lenin senses a contradiction in Engels's argument but, instead of unraveling it, prefers to launch into a rather misleading tirade against "hair splitting criticism."[99] He shows that the there is no contradiction between the abolition of the state *advocated* in *The Housing Question* and its *overnight* abolition *opposed* in *Anti-Dühring*. One could not be more in agreement with Lenin on this point, but he misses the fact that the real deadlock in Engels's outline concerns the abolition of classes, and not that of the state. In short, Lenin does not appreciate that it is as if in the late Engels there still persists the same tension we flagged up with regard to *The Poverty of Philosophy* and *The Communist Manifesto*: can *classes* be abolished overnight by the revolution? If so, why would do we still need the *proletariat* organized as a ruling class?

The second and related issue to be problematized in the conclusion of *The State and Revolution* pertains to Lenin's reading of *The Critique of the Gotha Programme*—which he rightly considers as Marx's definitive text on the question of the proletarian state. As already discussed, beyond all his previous texts (including *The Civil War in France* and *The Eighteenth Brumaire*), in *The Critique of the Gotha Programme*, Marx fully assumes the dialectical character of the state and revolution; again, the "revolutionary transformation" leading from capitalism to communism exactly "corresponds" to a "transition" during which "the *state* can be nothing else than the *revolutionary* dictatorship of the proletariat."

This prompts Marx to explicitly speak here of two phases of communism, the first of which he calls "socialism" and vehemently disassociates from any kind of "free state."[100] Not only, as also spelled out by Lenin, does Marx's socialist state impose equal right as the right of *inequality* (for Marx, this is "unavoidable in the first phase of communist society"), but, perhaps even less idealistically, its concomitant task is distributing *poverty* "equally over the whole surface of society."[101] Most importantly, although the socialist state is already no longer really an "entity" standing above society—and the ultimate objective of communism "consists in converting the state from an organ controlling society to one completely controlled by it"—this very society nonetheless amounts to nothing other than the "foundation of *the future state*."[102] Marx also adds that the latter "applies to *any* future society."[103] Hence we have to assume that it will still apply to the society that "completely controls" the state. If this were not enough, he then bluntly asks: "What change will the form of the state undergo in *communist* society?"[104]

Lenin does not overlook this question. It gives him a serious headache. In *Marxism on the State*, he observes: "Is there not a contradiction in this?"[105]

On the one hand, "it is clear" that the dictatorship of the proletariat, "the State of this period," is a "transition from the State to no State"; on the other hand, "further on Marx speaks of 'the future State of Communist society'!! Thus, even in '*Communist* society' the State will exist!!"[106]

In spite of such a proliferation of question and exclamation marks, Lenin concludes that there is ultimately no contradiction in Marx. He proposes a linear threefold sequence that would allegedly solve the apparent contrast, which is then repeated much more quickly in *The State and Revolution*—where he also speaks in passing of Marx's apparent recognition of "the need for a state even under communism," yet "such a view would be fundamentally wrong."[107] According to Lenin, what Marx really means is that we have, first, in capitalist society, a "State in the proper sense of the word"; second, during the transition—that is, the dictatorship of the proletariat—a "State of the transitional type (not a State in the proper sense of the word)"; finally, in communist society, "the *withering away* of the State."[108]

I think this schema does not work at all. Lenin is here compromising his otherwise extremely persuasive understanding of the passage from capitalism to communism in terms of revolution and the state as *dialectical* notions. With some hermeneutic forcing, but not unfairly, given the succinctness of Marx's remarks, one could read his communist "future state" as the *socialist* state—since, after all, Marx is speaking from the standpoint of capitalist society, and, as Lenin reminds us, "the word 'communism' is also applicable to [socialism], providing we do not forget that it is *not* complete communism."[109] But Lenin is not proposing this hypothesis—which would still have to account for the fact that the "foundation of the future state" applies to "*any* future society." As made clear in *The State and Revolution*, for Lenin, Marx's "future state in communist society" is instead "completely identical" to Engels's *withering away* of the state as, however, referring here to a *post*-socialist phase—or at any rate one that is *subsequent* to the dictatorship of the proletariat.[110]

In other words, the main problem with Lenin's attempt at systematizing Marx's—inspiring yet frankly enigmatic—remarks is that, against all his other efforts, he is here compelled to neatly *distinguish the transitional state from the withering away of the state* (which evidently transpires from the threefold sequence reported earlier). And this leaves him exposed to a—by all means serious—political objection; a proletarian state of the "transitional type" that does not immediately begin to wither itself away actually still remains a state "in the proper sense of the word"—that is, identical, at least in form, to the capitalist state.

Paradoxically—yet, unbeknownst to him, also dialectically—the more Lenin tries to mitigate Marx's "statesmanlike" indications for the sake of a supposedly perfect consistency with Engels's much weaker (and, as seen, already as such puzzling) notion of the state, the more he *isolates* a second dictatorial phase from a yet to come third phase in which "the State is not necessary." Obviously, the unintended consequence of such a highly abstract mistake is paving the way to a highly pragmatic Stalinist appropriation of these debates, which is distant from Lenin's intentions yet—one should also admit—not devoid of textual corroboration.[111]

I also believe Marx remains ambiguous. But he may well not be contradicting himself—although not in the way exposed by Lenin. In the sentence that immediately follows his most lucid formulation of the dialectic between the state and revolution we have repeatedly quoted, Marx adds that the Gotha program (which Lenin correctly identifies with an anticipation of Kautsky's renegade revisionism) "has nothing to say" about the revolutionary dictatorship of the proletariat "*nor* yet about the future forms of the state in communist society."[112] This seems to me a quite robust—albeit fragmentary—hint at the fact that the state as an "organ" is to be preserved in some thoroughly reconfigured yet never fully disposable form even when society has "complete control over it." Arguably, Marx is here referring to a "higher phase" of (post-socialist) communism in which, among other things, the distinction between manual and intellectual labor has disappeared, thanks to a "all round development of the individual" that changes his basic habits.[113]

Marx does not say anything else on the matter. In *The State and Revolution*, Lenin limits himself to fleetingly pointing at the fact that, although complete "communism makes the state absolutely unnecessary," one should not deny "the possibility and inevitability of excesses on the part of *individual persons*, or the need to repress such *excesses*."[114] Beyond this shareable pessimism, I think the "future *state* of Communist society" will increasingly become for him a most pressing issue after the seizure of power of October 1917 and not merely for its residual repressive function. After all, the statesman Lenin has a profound awareness of how protecting the *state* amounts to protecting the *people* from their own state. This certainly applies for him to the dictatorship of the proletariat, but—against any remaining utopianism—it might well be extended to a classless society that, however tangibly glimpsed already on the day after the revolution, also continues to remain an asymptotic achievement. As Lukács conclusively puts it, Lenin's revolution is a "revolutionary *Realpolitik*"; "in Lenin's writings and speeches—as, incidentally, also in Marx—there is little about *socialism as a completed condition*. There is all the more, however, about the *steps* which can lead to its establishment."[115]

NOTES

1. V. I. Lenin, "The Importance of Gold", in: *Selected Works* (London: Lawrence and Wishart, 1937), vol. 9, 295–302. Translator uncredited.

2. See for instance A. Badiou, *Of An Obscure Disaster* (Maastricht and Zagreb: Jan van Eyck Academie and Arkzin, 2009), 28; A. Badiou and M. Gauchet, *Que faire?* (Paris: Philo, 2014), 50. I discussed this in detail in L. Chiesa, "The State of Communism: Badiou, Stalin, Lenin," in: D. Finkelde (ed.), *Badiou and the State* (Baden-Baden: Nomos, 2017), 127–150.

3. See for instance V. I. Lenin, *Selected Writings* (London: Lawrence & Wishart, 1937), vol., 228, 281, 316, 340, 376; *Selected* Writings (London: Lawrence & Wishart, 1938), vol. 10, 138.

4. Carr refers to *The State and Revolution* as "the most Utopian of [Lenin's] writings" (E. H. Carr, *The Russian Revolution. From Lenin to Stalin* [New York: The Free Press, 1979], p. 4); Žižek claims that in his later writings Lenin "renounced the utopia of his *State and Revolution*" (S. Žižek, "Introduction: Between the Two Revolutions," in: V. I. Lenin, *Revolution at the Gates: A Selection of Writings from February to October 1917* [London: Verso, 2001], 9); Jameson maintains that "there are wonderful utopian passages in The State and Revolution" (F. Jameson, "Lenin and Revisionism," in: S. Budgen, S. Kouvelakis, and S. Žižek (eds.), *Lenin Reloaded. Towards a Politics of Truth* [Durham, NC and London: Duke University Press, 2007], 64).

5. Badiou and Gauchet *Que faire?*, 50; A. Badiou, *Quel communisme?* (Montrouge: Bayard, 2015), 122.

6. V. I. Lenin, "The State and Revolution," in: *Essential Works of Lenin* (New York: BN Publishing, 2009), 272.

7. See for instance ibid., 274, 292–293, 298, 309, 312, 358.

8. V. I. Lenin, *Selected Writings* (London: Lawrence & Wishart, 1937), vol. 7, 117, 159.

9. Ibid., 7, 215.

10. Lenin 2009, 272.

11. Ibid., 285.

12. Žižek rightly highlights this point: "The key premiss of *State and Revolution* is that you cannot fully 'democratize' the State; that the State 'as such', in its very notion, is a dictatorship of one class over another; the logical conclusion from this premiss is that, *in so far as we still dwell within the domain* of the State, we are legitimately entitled to exercise full violent terror, since, within this domain, every democracy is a fake" (S. Žižek, "Afterword: Lenin's Choice," in *Revolution at the Gates*, p. 192).

13. Engels in Lenin, "The State and Revolution," 281.

14. Ibid., 281–282.

15. Ibid., 282. György Lukács praises Lenin for fully assuming it in no uncertain terms: "*The proletarian state is the first class state in history which acknowledges quite openly and un-hypocritically that it is a class state, a repressive apparatus, and an instrument of class struggle*" (G. Lukács, *Lenin: A Study on the Unity of His Thought* [London: Verso, 2009], p. 66).

16. Lenin, "The State and Revolution," 286.

17. Ibid., 294.

18. Ibid., 343 (my emphasis).

19. Ibid., 294.
20. Ibid., 299, 360, 295.
21. Ibid., 304, 301.
22. Ibid., 301, 303.
23. Ibid., 275–277.
24. Ibid., 301. See also p. 320.
25. Ibid., 306, 330.
26. Ibid., 307.
27. Ibid.
28. Ibid.
29. Ibid., 302.
30. Ibid., 348.
31. Ibid., 355, 360. It is very tempting to read the recent neoliberalist "restructuring" of labor in Western economies, especially in sectors still partly controlled by the state (e.g., education and health services), as a perversion of this Leninist (and, frankly, quite utopian) program: *everybody* must *become* bureaucrats (forced to micromanage useless tasks for an increasing amount of often non-remunerated time) so that *somebody* can forever *remain* a bureaucrat (as "privileged persons" who economically profit from managing precisely the imposition of micromanaging).
32. Ibid., 348.
33. Ibid.
34. Daniel Bensaïd argues that "in *The State and Revolution* parties do indeed lose their function in favor of direct democracy, which is not supposed to be entirely a separate state" (D. Bensaïd, "Leaps! Leaps! Leaps," in *Lenin Reloaded*, p. 156). I fully agree that the Bolshevik party has a marginal—or at best implicit—function in this pamphlet. Yet Lenin does not replace it with direct democracy (I will soon return to this question). Or better, direct democracy is central only to the extent that the socialist state is indeed *partly* a non-separate state, or a state that is no longer really a state (as the immanent dictatorship of the armed workers). However, the socialist state also remains separate (here as the employer of the same workers as salaried employees), and the party still looms in the background.
35. Marx and Engels in Lenin, "The State and Revolution," 2009, 286.
36. Lenin, "The State and Revolution," 345. 345.
37. Ibid., 302.
38. Ibid., 304–306.
39. Ibid., 306.
40. Ibid., 332.
41. Ibid., 337.
42. Ibid., 317.
43. Ibid., 364.
44. Ibid., 282, 338.
45. Marx in Lenin, "The State and Revolution," 286.
46. Lenin, "The State and Revolution," 341.
47. Ibid., 342.
48. Marx in Lenin, "The State and Revolution," 341.

49. Ibid. As Negri points out with regard to Pashukanis's Leninist theory of law, strictly speaking, "there is no proletarian law" (A. Negri, "Rereading Pashukanis: Discussion Notes," *Stasis*, 5 (2), 2017).

50. Lenin, "The State and Revolution," 341.

51. Ibid., 347.

52. Marx in Lenin, "The State and Revolution," 343.

53. Ibid.

54. Lenin, "The State and Revolution," 333.

55. Ibid.

56. Ibid., 333, 349.

57. Ibid., 333.

58. Ibid., 334, 344.

59. Ibid., 334, 338, 344. In an early essay on Stalin, Žižek proposes an anti-Stalinist resumption of the two phases of communism, which seems to be fundamentally in line with Lenin's original arguments. "We could nonetheless make the formula about 'the two phases of communism' ours, on condition of introducing a supplementary opposition. The 'first phase' is the negation of capitalism 'on its own level', the negation of the capitalist position *in the field of common presuppositions*, hence its specular negation. . . . On the other hand, the 'second phase' is the 'negation of negation'; it is not an opposition that is specular to the starting point, but the negation of the *presuppositions* shared by the thesis and the antithesis: not only the negation of *alienated* production, but the subversion of productive economy *as such*" (Žižek, "Essai sur 'l'herméneutique' stalinienne," in: A. Verdiglione (ed.), *Actes du Colloque de Milan, 1977: Généalogie de la politique*, 1977).

60. Karl Marx, *Critique of the Gotha Programme* (London: Martin Lawrence, 1933), pp. 44–45.

61. Lenin, *Selected Writings*, vol. 7, 119–120.

62. Marx-Engels-Lenin Institute, "Introduction," in: *Critique of the Gotha Programme*, 18.

63. Lukács, *Lenin*, 59.

64. Ibid.

65. Ibid.

66. Ibid., 12.

67. Lenin, *Selected Writing*, vol. 7, 119.

68. Engels in Lenin, "The State and Revolution," 278.

69. Ibid., 279.

70. Ibid., 280.

71. Ibid.

72. Ibid., 281.

73. Lenin, "The State and Revolution," 274. In a footnote to his greatly underestimated *Soviet Marxism*, Herbert Marcuse points this out in passing: "The continuation of the state in the first period of socialism is implied in the original Marxian conception" and also by Engels "as early as 1847." Yet "Engels's statement in *Anti-Dühring* . . . seems to contradict this notion" (Herbert Marcuse, *Soviet Marxism. A Critical Analysis* [London: Routledge & Kegan, 1958], pp. 87–88.

74. Lenin, *Selected Writings*, vol. 9, 9–10.
75. Ibid., 319.
76. Lenin, *Selected Writings*, vol. 8, 239.
77. Ibid., 240.
78. Ibid., 241. More specifically, the "communist Saturdays" are—in line with Marx's remarks in the *Critique of the Gotha Programme*—a "communism in fact" since, as Robert Linhart observes, they advance a concrete overcoming of the distinction between intellectual and manual labor. They keep "the old proletariat that had passed to the army and the administration in contact with productive work." Linhart's Maoist reading interestingly also dwells on the most evident limit of this phenomenon; while "intellectual workers promptly became closer to manual work," "there was no effort to elevate the intellectual content of manual work" (Robert Linhart, *Lénine, Les Paysans, Taylor* [Paris: Seuil, 1976], pp. 183, 189).
79. Lenin, *Selected Writings*, vol. 8, p. 241.
80. Ibid., 245.
81. Lenin, *Selected Writings*, vol. 9, 408 (my emphasis).
82. Lenin, "Lenin on the Critique of the Gotha Programme," in: K. Marx, *Critique of the Gotha Programme*, p. 83.
83. K. Marx and F. Engels, *The Communist Manifesto* (London: Penguin Books, 2002), p. 258.
84. Marx in Lenin, "The State and Revolution," 285–286.
85. Ibid., 286.
86. Ibid.
87. Ibid.
88. Lenin, "The State and Revolution," 290, 292.
89. Ibid., 289.
90. Ibid., 289–292.
91. Marx and Engels in Lenin, "The State and Revolution," 297.
92. Marx in Lenin, "The State and Revolution," 289.
93. Ibid.
94. Marx in Lenin, "The State and Revolution," 294.
95. Lenin, "The State and Revolution," 310.
96. Ibid., 312.
97. Ibid., 334.
98. Engels in Lenin, "The State and Revolution," 315, 319, 330.
99. Lenin, "The State and Revolution," 315.
100. Marx, *Critique of the Gotha Programme*, 40, 43.
101. Ibid., 31, 40.
102. Ibid., 43–44.
103. Ibid., 44 (my emphasis).
104. Ibid.
105. Lenin, "Lenin on the Critique of the Gotha Programme," 86.
106. Ibid.
107. Lenin, "The State and Revolution," 334.
108. Lenin, "Lenin on the Critique of the Gotha Programme," 86–87.

109. Lenin, "The State and Revolution," 346.
110. Ibid., 334.
111. Stalin's stance here does not so much correspond to an indefinite postponement of the passage from socialism to communism as to one for which, in Marcuse's words, "communism will be introduced as a [state] administrative measure" (Marcuse, *Soviet Marxism*, 139).
112. Marx, *Critique of the Gotha Programme*, 45.
113. Ibid., 31.
114. Lenin, "The State and Revolution," 339.
115. Lukács, *Lenin*, 70–71.

Chapter 8

The March of God or the Žižekian Theory of the State

Agon Hamza

A person must translate his freedom into an external sphere in order to exist as an Idea. (G. W. F. Hegel[1])

1. INTRODUCTION

We are in the midst of the pandemic COVID 19. While it is still too early to think of the consequences caused by corona virus, some short reflections are in order. I will limit those reflections on the spirit of the text, which was written well before its emergence.

It revealed—yet again—the structural shortcomings and impossibility of the market to deal with the massive catastrophes such as the ongoing pandemic. All the measures (as well as those that will be possibly taken in the future) take place outside of the market mechanisms and its coordinates. Corona successfully destroyed the (not so) smooth functioning of the global capitalist market.

More than ever, and perhaps even more so than during the last financial crisis of 2008–2009, the limits of the nation-states are becoming visible. Regardless from what a particular state does (or does not do), international cooperation, coordination, and solidarity are *sine qua non* for battling the pandemic.

Are not these two facts enough for our necessity to urgently reorganize the global economy so that it goes outside of the market mechanism and beyond the confines of the nation-states? The regulation and controlling of the production, as well as a mechanism that would limit the sovereignty of the nation-states (when needed!) and, at the same time, would create interstate forms of organizations, are the tasks that lie ahead of us, if we want to avoid Frederic Jameson's dystopia: a world in which humanity disappears, but capitalism goes on.[2] As Žižek recently put it, "Countries were able to do it in the conditions of war, and we are now effectively approaching a state of medical war."[3]

However, one thing seems to be certain: whenever the situation "normalizes," we will not go back to our old reality. A new reality will be created, and my fear is that that reality will be far grimmer: authoritarian far-right may exercise and spread its power, thus imposing new forms of "shock doctrine" as well as new political regulations which will turn the lives of the vast majority into a misery. The crisis is always an opportunity, but as always, the Left never misses the chance to miss all opportunities.

Frank Gehry is arguably one of the most important architects of our era. Once he called his work as "cheapskate architecture"—something which no viewer can miss. What is interesting about his work, as some have noticed, is the grandeur of his buildings is completely inappropriate to the age which announced the "death of the subject." Looking at his Guggenheim Museum Bilbao, one cannot escape the doubt that his extravagant spaces do not only function to overwhelm the subject, but simultaneously, while they pretend to be open for the people, they create a new form of elitism. What he takes as paragon might be our neo-Baroque nightmare.

Another bitter lesson that we have to learn from the COVID 19 pandemic consists in the ecological catastrophes. The worldwide response to the virus proves that we are thoroughly unprepared to deal with the forthcoming ecological catastrophes whose consequences will be much harsher than those of this pandemic.

A joke told by Žižek over a decade ago seems to have lost its "comical" dimension: indeed, we will meet either in hell or in Communism. And, this is what our crossroads are today!

Today's ideological space is structured by the signifier "totalitarianism." While its usage is presented as an operation that prevents all kinds of ideological and political excesses, in truth its effective function is to obfuscate the space of politics proper.[4] What is intended as a critical concept remains little more than an ideological notion. Subscribing to "totalitarianism" as an ideological and political foundation for thinking politics and the state cannot overcome the confines of the capitalist state form.

Throughout the previous century, Marxism provided perhaps the best theoretical orientation for both fighting and resisting the seizure of state power. Yet the twentieth century produced a theory of power, especially among French philosophers and theorists, that carved a space for emancipation in the *resistance* against power—but never in its exercise. In a sense, Michel Foucault became the spokesperson, or *the* theorist, of this orientation. Throughout its history, the Left has lacked a theory of power that would be active rather than reactive. A theory that, unlike the "deconstructive Marxism" of today, would be prepositive, not merely reactive and critical.

What characterizes the contemporary left is the constitutive principle of a refusal to assume state power and, as a consequence, to rethink the Communist State. Since this is an organizing principle, along with the notion of "totalitarianism," it appears that the left abhors nothing more vehemently than Hegel's definition of the state as the "march of God in the world."[5] The present chapter seeks to think the consequences of this idea (and for Hegel, philosophy is preoccupied only with the Idea, which it takes as its sole object) in an attempt to think the Communist State. This idea springs forth from the axiom that there can be no overcoming of capitalism without a rethinking of the state form.

2. CONTEMPORARY "YOUNG HEGELIANISM"

The "Communist State" cannot but appear as an oxymoron. The very idea of the state and its recuperation appears, in one respect, to be a non-Marxist position. But let us think through this, as a mode of laying the foundations for rethinking the state.

One of the predominant ideological and political positions on the left today is the tendency to rehabilitate socialism, which in itself implies an appropriation of the state form. Yet can socialism—in any of its iterations (democratic, "for the twenty-first century," etc.)—be the solution to the inherent deadlocks of contemporary capitalism? Leftist advocates of socialism are not alone in their call. The most efficient capitalists, say Elon Musk or Bill Gates, are increasingly eager to discuss the limitations of capitalism.[6] This unlikely alliance is not as strange as it might at first appear. Following Marx, who described socialism as "vulgar communism," I will propose that the historical failure of socialism was not due to state terror, authoritarian regimes, the violation of human dignity, economic backwardness, hunger, or any other of its "aberrations." All these were only the necessary products of socialism as such. The failure of socialism did not result from the betrayal of some noble idea; it was neither a consequence of distortions in its realization nor a question of producing "non-authentic" versions of socialism that were then cloaked in its mantle. Its failure, from the perspective of the present situation, allows us retroactively to think its essential/innate/foundational/and so forth limitations. Differently put, the failure of socialism—its "original sin"—is a result of the very *idea* of socialism itself.

One of the main theorists of the return to socialism is Axel Honneth, who, in his *Idea of Socialism: Towards a Renewal*, sets out to rethink the basic ideas of socialism, arguing that it contains the potential to be asserted as the ethical force of the future, as opposed to religion. Honneth maintains that socialism can become the force of the future if "only we can manage to extract its core idea from the intellectual context of early industrialism and place it in a new socio-theoretical framework."[7] Despite its current "retreat," Honneth remains convinced of the potency of socialism. He aspires to think "the conceptual changes needed to restore the vitality these ideas have lost," which would arise from the "need to reconstruct the original idea of socialism as clearly as possible."[8] Socialism can become a "source of political-ethical orientations," then, only if it is radically rethought. Honneth takes it from the beginning: the beginning of the idea of socialism, from which he sets out to extract the "true" potential for its renewal. The idea of socialism for the twenty-first century has to be a "project of harmonizing liberty, equality and solidarity in a way that overcomes liberalism from within" by way of abandoning "old" ideas of the proletariat as revolutionary subject and by extending the premise of freedom to all forms of social life. Above all, its renewal entails "replacing the vision of an economically administered society with the vision of a democratic way of life." Socialism should thus be rethought in such a way that "would make its main purpose and theoretical impulse unrecognizable to the majority of its previous followers."[9] Sounds good and promising, but does socialism have the power of the Hegelian concrete universality, that is, the ability to reinvent itself in each new historical period, as distinct from the Kantian regulative idea?

The elementary reproach to this should be Hegelian: consciousness cannot be happy with an old order. In the final analysis, socialism does not stand for the negation of capitalism. In the crisis of 2008, it was in fact socialism that ultimately *saved* capitalism (e.g., bailing out the banks). On the other side of the spectrum, China needs capitalism to maintain and push forward its own "socialism." This allows us to touch upon the main thesis of the complementary and correlative dimensions of capitalism and socialism. Socialism stands for "public" or "state" property, whereas in capitalism, property is (predominantly) of a "private" nature. Thus socialism is not the abolition of property as such (as I interpret Marx and Engels in their *The Communist Manifesto*). It merely represents the transformation of ownership—a shift from private property of the means of production (capitalism) to that of the state (socialism). Socialism is not the negation of property as such but rather the negation of one particular type of property, thus leaving untouched the field of social relations in which property (private or state) operates. Property remains the touchstone of existing social relations. In Hegelian terms, socialism is an abstract negation of property, that is to say, a negation of a particular type of property within the field of properties as such. In this regard, Žižek is correct to go against the belief that socialism represents the "lower stage" of communism. On the contrary; socialism is the true competitor and the greatest threat to communism. In the Marxism of the previous century, the name for this "lower stage," or transitional period, was the "dictatorship of the proletariat." The problem with successive historical stages toward a "higher" one (a fully realized Communism) is that the intermediary stages are inexhaustible: they are taken as a fetishistic substitute for the supposed utopia. As Étienne Balibar showed long ago, "a fetishism concerning the formal number of these stages is produced,"[10] which brings us back to a utopian ideology. Almost as in the previous century, many present-day "socialists" are ready to admit that after the construction of a "complete" socialism, which would therefore be its end, another stage will come. They are correct, with the difference that this "something else" will not be communism but socialism. The question of temporality comes into play here. The traditional linear notion of time, according to which the gradual evolution of history will lead us to socialism, should be opposed. Yet this opposition should not be a Leibnizean one, according to which History is an open process, with many possibilities open to realization. For in Leibniz, we recall, God created the best imaginable world out of many options. In contrast, the Hegelian dialectics of contingency and necessity offers us the possibility of thinking the notion of time anew.

Jean-Pierre Dupuy is among those theorists who have proposed a rethinking of the notion of time. He writes that we should aim neither to contend nor to reverse time (e.g., in the wake of ecological catastrophes); on the contrary, we have to reconfigure it. This "invites us to project ourselves into the future and to look back at the present from a point of view that we will ourselves have created."[11] In a Hegelian fashion, Dupuy argues that

> a catastrophic event not only belongs to the future as something that is fated to happen, but at the same time is contingent and accidental, something that might not happen—even if, from the perspective of the future perfect, it appears to be necessary.[12]

But let me go back to socialism as the elementary stage toward the realization of full communism. Analyzed from the matrix of Hegelian dialectics, the higher stage is not yet achieved once the lowest one is realized, or even overcome. We have to get rid of the idea that there is a higher stage toward which we are headed. What we are engaged in in our actuality will lead us there. We have to reject the Stalinist belief that our actual deeds will appear as legitimate when analyzed from the standpoint of the higher stage. There is nothing but the present stage.

Žižek has identified the "four horse riders" of the apocalypse, the antagonisms that cannot be controlled within capitalism.[13] Accordingly, he argues:

> Socialism wants to solve the first three antagonisms without addressing the fourth—without the singular universality of the proletariat. The only way for the global capitalist system to survive its long-term antagonism and

simultaneously avoid the communist solution, will be for it to reinvent some kind of socialism—in the guise of communitarianism, or populism, or capitalism with Asian values, or some other configuration. The future will thus be communist . . . or socialist.[14]

In Žižek's dilemma, if things will continue on their own "spontaneous" path, the future will be socialist. Unlike in the previous century, twenty-first-century socialism is being prepared for and planned by the capitalist class itself.

Advocates of socialism and of its state form tend to ignore one of the basic theses of Marx, according to which capitalism is not defined by the type of state—whether it be democratic socialist, socialist centralist, or otherwise. What defines capitalism as a mode of production are capitalist relations of production.

Another crucial element in the struggle against socialism, from the standpoint of the idea of Communism, is to counter the common belief that in socialism, feelings like jealousy, envy, and resentment will cease to exist. In other words—in an almost caricatured description—socialism claims to represent a higher dialectical synthesis of all the oppositional tendencies/contradictions of all existing societies, in which a harmonious order would emerge. Nothing proves this better than the famous formula from Marx's *Critique of the Gotha Program*: "From each according to his ability, to each according to his needs!"[15] But what if the exact opposite were true? That in a just (Communist) society, because of the abolition of exploitative, dominating and oppressive relations, a new set of relations will have to emerge? And what if this new set of social relations will not be based on solidarity and collective satisfaction, but rather on envy, jealousy, resentment—all of which would be very difficult, if not impossible, to control in the new society? These are the threats and imbalances we must take into account when we portray or think of the "higher stage."

This brings us to a crucial moment in Hegel's thought, one that would continue to haunt his philosophy and its aftermath: the division, or split, between the Old and Young Hegelians. Each group privileged a certain reading and assumption regarding that which they took to be the cornerstone of the Hegelian system. The Old/Right Hegelians appropriated the question of the state and Christianity from Hegel's philosophy, which, by contrast, the Young Hegelians deemed to be ideological remainders within his system. These latter focused instead on subjectivity and dialectics.

So; perhaps the correct path to take in this endeavor would be to follow the tradition of Žižek and others in rehabilitating or appropriating what is crucial in Hegel's philosophical system: the state.

3. REAPPROPRIATING "OLD HEGELIANISM"

In the *Philosophy of Right*, Hegel provides a series of definitions of the state. In the opening sentence of the chapter on the state, he writes: "The state is the actuality of the ethical Idea."[16] This can also be formulated as "the actuality of concrete freedom."[17] Philosophically, however, the most compelling definition is the one referred to earlier, which is worth quoting at length:

> The state consists in the march of God in the world, and its basis is the power of reason actualizing itself as will.[18]

This definition best epitomizes what the Young Hegelians abhorred most in Hegel. This can also be seen in the Marxist critique of Hegel's teleology, construed as a dialectical process that swallows everything and culminates in a rationalization of the present. Louis Althusser's anti-Hegelian Marxism stands as the best example of this. Althusser accused Hegel of a teleological understanding of both nature and society—taken to be the natural outcome of his metaphysical idealism. Althusser spoke against Hegel's pretensions to know the entire universe, the absolute, and thus of reaching/attaining an absolute knowledge (the truth of the Absolute). Perhaps Althusser would have been all too happy to "prove" his point with reference to a letter Hegel sent to his friend Niethammer:

> I adhere to the view that the world spirit has given the age marching orders. These orders are being obeyed. The world spirit, this essential, proceeds irresistibly like a closely drawn armored phalanx advancing with imperceptible movement, much as the sun through thick and thin. Innumerable light troops flank it on all sides, throwing themselves into the balance for or against its progress, though most of them are entirely ignorant of what is at stake and merely take head blows as from an invisible hand.

Žižek is right to argue, against Althusser, that "it is difficult to imagine a more 'arrogant' philosopher than Spinoza, whose *Ethics* claims to reveal the inner workings of God-Nature; if nothing else, it can be demonstrated that here Spinoza is much more 'arrogant' than Hegel."[19] Or, if one formulates his shortcomings in different way—one that, at the same time (albeit at another level) discerns the shortcomings of anti-Hegelianism—one can argue that what Althusser "was not able to think was the capitalist universe 'structured like the Spinozan absolute,' i.e., the reemergence of Spinoza as the paradigmatic thinker of late capitalism."[20]

But back to Hegel. The Hegelian theory of the concrete universal—of something which stands for the whole *within* the whole, even more so than the abstract apprehension of its totality—was fully deployed in Hegel's work, both in his understanding of Christianity and in his ontology, where the relation between a concept's extension and its exception turns out to be the relation between the concept's *formal* and *concrete* existences. In his social theory, however, Hegel took a more "formalist" perspective. He took the concrete establishment of social rules by the state—the means of regulating the interaction between private volitions in civil society—to be the expression and realization of the very concept of volition, and hence to stand for the concrete universal of society as such. This view, in which historical existence was as real as the rational existence of the state, was then subverted by Marx, who—in line with the materialist turn of his time—recognized an impasse in Hegel's deployment of the articulation between civil society and the state. Rather than taking the state to serve as the concrete measure for the concept of what humanity is at a given historical moment, Marx took up Feuerbach's theory of generic being to argue that it is in the very concrete activity of labor that men make their essence objective. This is a process that is extrinsically and formally deviated and deformed by state laws of property, which alienate workers from participation in and realization of their historical existence.

For the young Marx, then, it was not a matter of doing away with Hegel so much as pointing out that the logic of concrete universality, if properly followed through, should not lead us to recognize the state as "the march of God in the world"[21] but rather to recognize that there is a social class whose concrete existence stands in for the existence of society as a whole. In its debasement, the poor working class did not only speak to the true consequences of a society based on private property, but they also incarnated the very properties the ascendant bourgeoisie had sought to champion; if one wanted to defend the rights of man, irrespective of his particular identity or nationality, of his possessions and social standing, one could find this selfsame "abstract man" walking down the streets, "abstracted" due to social conditions from his identity, nation, social standing, and means of living.

But back to Hegel's conception of the state—once again! As Shlomo Avineri confirms, in Hegel, there can be no state that will be adequate to the one that was developed as a philosophical idea in his work.[22] The crucial question to be asked is: What does Hegel mean when he says that the state is something inherently rational? He does not follow the logic according to which everything in every state is rational (for Hegel, the state as actual is always an individual, not a particular, state; for the former is a moment within an Idea, whereas the latter always belongs to history in a general sense). On the contrary, for Hegel the phenomenon of the state, the "place" where people live under the same "promise," expresses the rationality or the rational aspect of human life. Hegel himself writes:

> It *is this very relation of philosophy to actuality* which is the subject of misunderstandings, and I accordingly come back to my earlier observation that, since philosophy is *exploration of the rational*, it is for that very reason the *comprehension of the present and the actual*, not the setting up of a *world beyond* which exists God knows where—or rather, of which we can very well say that we know where it exists, namely in the errors of a one-sided and empty ratiocination.[23]

Proceeding from this, Hegel formulates his infamous formula: "What is rational is actual; and what is actual is rational." This already scandalous sentence becomes even more monstrous in its English translation.[24] The German word for "actual" is *wirklich*, whose "specific connotation derives from its root in the verb 'to act' (*wirken*), which makes it clear that 'actuality' (*Wirklichkeit*) is not a merely passive, natural given."[25] Another important point should be noted here: Hegel starts this statement by saying that what is rational is actual, and not the other way around, as it is predominantly understood. The difference is not semantic. He puts forward the actuality of the rational, which means that what is rational has, in itself, the power to actualize itself. It has the potential to turn from potential into actuality. Hegel does not put forward the primacy of rationality in actuality. This is nothing but a corollary of the former. Actuality is that in which essence and existence concur, or as he puts it in the *Science of Logic:* "Actuality is the *unity of essence and concrete existence*; in it, *shapeless* essence and *unstable* appearance—or subsistence without determination and manifoldness without permanence—have their truth."[26] For this reason, actuality is rational. Hegel's dialectical process is not a closed process; it does not end with the reconciliation of all antagonisms. On the contrary, the properly Hegelian reconciliation "is not a peaceful state in which all tensions are sublated or mediated but a reconciliation with the irreducible excess of negativity itself."[27] This is why for Hegel, reconciliation is not a situation in which antagonisms are diminished, because antagonisms and contradictions are already part of the reconciliation. One good example of this from his own work is the necessity of war. This necessity is not only the way to assert universality again and again, against all forms of the organic organization of life, but ultimately, it speaks to the crucial argument that reconciliation itself is not possible, that an organic social state is not attainable precisely due to the force of negativity.

Let's move on to another dimension of this. In the preface to the *Philosophy of Right*, Hegel writes about recognizing reason. This condensed *sentence* is worth quoting:

> To recognize reason as the rose in the cross of the present and thereby to delight in the present—this rational insight is the reconciliation with actuality which philosophy grants to those who have received the inner call to comprehend, to preserve their subjective freedom in the realm of the substantial, and at the same time to stand with their subjective freedom not in a particular and contingent situation, but in what has being in and for itself.[28]

The "rose in the cross of the present" is Hegel's reference to Luther, used not only to criticize the position of the beautiful soul as the operation of inactivity but to recognize the present as the only domain where freedom can be realized. This is the Christian, or more precisely, Protestant dimension of Hegel's thinking.[29] Luther's emblem was the cross with roses encircling it, which was conceptualized by Hegel as "Reason apprehended as the rose in the cross of the present."[30] The point being that we have to participate in the brutality of the actual, as the place of actual freedom. Is this not the other definition of the state?

4. THE STATE

How can we conceptualize the state in a Žižekian-Hegelian orientation? If absolute knowing is the culmination of the dialectical process, then the absolute of politics is the state. That is to say, politics does not begin with the state, but it always ends with the state. And this is a crucial point. For Hegel, the exact form of regulation within a state is not the object of philosophical thought. What matters is the universal *form* of the state. We can even argue that politics should aim at taking over and transforming the state. It is in this manner that we should understand Hegel's affirmation of the state form not as a moment of conformity or capitulation to the Prussian Empire but as an affirmation of politics as such. Put differently, he does not regress from the position of active Consciousness to that of the Beautiful Soul.

For Hegel, as for Žižek, the state is the answer to the problem of internationalism as well as to the problem of the commons, neither of which fits borders or other "limitations" of this kind. Hegel was aware of this, and it is for this reason that the state is "the march of God in the world." His is a state which is ultimately not representative of a nation or community. For Hegel, the state was tied to the problem of dealing with multiple nations, as was the case with Prussia, that is to say, the pre-German state. His understanding of *Volkgeist* cannot be interpreted in the spirit of a national or romantic vision. *Volkgeist* does not create the character of a people, of a nation, but is ultimately a result of its religious, cultural, and other traits. The creation of the state based on the *Volkgeist* is not that of a national state. The state is at the level of self-consciousness. The modern world, in Hegel's view, contains a multiple of political units which are not held together by power but by Spirit. So how should we follow on from this, in revitalizing the Hegelian theory of the state from a Žižekian standpoint? The starting point should be an appropriation of Hegel's idea of *the ethical* state, a state which is founded upon a shared ethical order. Hegel writes that "the ethical order has been represented by mankind as eternal justice, as gods absolutely existent, in contrast with which the empty business of individuals is only a game of see-saw."[31] Or better still, the ethical order or ethical substance is "an absolute authority and power infinitely more firmly established than the being of nature."[32] In its Žižekian conceptualization, the state is not a representative one but is a strong body which does not only represent the people but includes everyone in itself. This *inclusion* is not, so to speak, an easy solution, but rather the crucial problem in every attempt to recuperate Hegel's theory of the state—a very difficult task.

When Žižek writes about the relationship between the state and politics, he says:

> The failure of the Communist State-Party politics is above all and primarily the failure of anti-statist politics, of the endeavor to break out of the constraints of the State, to replace statal forms of organization with "direct" non-representative forms of self-organization ("councils").[33]

Further, in responding to the prevailing leftist position which affirms distance toward the state as the only political option, Žižek argues:

> If you do not have an idea of what you want to replace the State with, you have no right to subtract/withdraw from the State. Instead of withdrawing into a distance from the State, the true task should be to make the State itself work in a non-statal mode.[34]

The crucial task remains doing this in a Hegelian manner. That is to say, how can we think of a non-national state, based on a common, shared ethical substance?

When we discuss the state in its philosophical aspect, the Idea of the state cannot be identified with any form of the modern state. The dictum quoted earlier, on the state as God's march in the world, continues as follows:

> In considering the Idea of the state, we must not have any particular states or particular institutions in mind; instead, we should consider the Idea, this actual

God, in its own right [*für sich*]. Any state, even if we pronounce it bad in the light of our own principles, and even if we discover this or that defect in it, invariably has the essential moments of its existence [*Existenz*] within itself (provided it is one of the more advanced states of our time). But since it is easier to discover deficiencies than to comprehend the affirmative, one may easily fall into the mistake of overlooking the inner organism of the state in favor of individual [*einzelne*] aspects. The state is not a work of art; it exists in the world, and hence in the sphere of arbitrariness, contingency, and error, and bad behavior may disfigure it in many respects.

When Hegel says that men become conscious of themselves only in the state, he thereby distinguishes between the three levels of family, civil society, and the state. The family exists at the level of feelings, with civil society as the field of self-interest. It is only within the structure of the state that there emerges a unity of subjective consciousness (intentions) and the objective order (actions). In short, this is what he means when he says:

The state is the actuality of the ethical Idea—the ethical spirit as substantial will, *manifest* and clear to itself, which thinks and knows itself and implements what it knows in so far as it knows it. It has its immediate existence [*Existenz*] in custom and its mediate existence in the *self-consciousness* of the individual [*des Einzelnen*], in the individual's knowledge and activity, just as self-consciousness, by virtue of its disposition, has its *substantial freedom* in the state as its essence, its end, and the product of its activity.[35]

The actuality of the state is reached only when the spheres of the public and the private are not one and the same. That is to say, contrary to civil society, where the individual can pursue his or her interests while taking no account of others and their interests/aims, it is in the state that duty and the right merge. This pits Hegel against both liberal and conservative positions. Of course, this in itself does not mean that Hegel is in the position of Communism. However, one can try to push him into it, by conceiving his idea of the state on non-national grounds, that is to say, a state which is not grounded on national *Geist*. The state as the rational whole can realize itself only if it is held together by the figure of the monarch, who is an ordinary human being, who becomes a monarch not by virtue of his abilities but by the sheer arbitrariness of his birth (biological contingency), and in this capacity guarantees the state as the ethical order of society and makes it an actuality. His or her dismissal is simultaneously the disintegration of the state. In his plea for a rehabilitation of the state, Žižek affirms the relationship between collectivity and the state, which is not bound to electoral mechanisms, but to a strong collective whose function is not representative but inclusive. The first thing to show is that Žižek is *very* clear in his remarks on the state, that "the state" is not an answer to the socioeconomic problems internal to a given nation.

At the crossing point of these two lines of argumentation lies the need to recuperate the "analytic" dimension of the Leninist Party-form—which Žižek has addressed in a series of "political thinking" texts, from *First as Tragedy, Then as Farce*, to his more recent *Like a Thief in Broad Daylight*—and the need to rethink the critique of the state in order to conceive of a paradoxical "non-statal State." In short, this is the premise of the Hegelian-informed theory of the state that Žižek has been trying to revitalize. In defining communism, he writes:

> In contrast to socialism, communism refers to singular universality, to the direct link between the singular and the universal, bypassing particular determinations. When Paul says that, from a Christian standpoint, "there are no men or women, no Jews or Greeks"; he thereby claims that ethnic roots, national identities, etc., are not a category of truth. To put it in precise Kantian terms: when we reflect upon our ethnic roots, we engage in a private use of reason, constrained by contingent dogmatic presuppositions; that is, we act as "immature" individuals, not as free humans who dwell in the dimension of the universality of reason.[36]

One of the issues/quandaries for the contemporary left is the question of representation versus participation. Hegel writes that "the ethical order has been represented by mankind as eternal justice, as gods absolutely existent, in contrast with which the empty business of individuals is only a game of see-saw."[37]

In the struggle against global capitalism, this Hegelian way is the only way to move beyond the bourgeois state form. In taking over the state and state power and transforming it in such a way that the social and political structures do not remain solely in the hands of the Party—the state effectively *becomes the non-statal state*. Such is our task today! Only through such a political structure can we move beyond all the obstacles and impossibilities that condemned the previous century's attempts to establish a new form of social organization via socialism to political, economic, and ethical failure.

At the end of his *Philosophy of Right*, Hegel explains:

> The history of a single world-historical nation contains (a) the development of its principle from its latent embryonic stage until it blossoms into the self-conscious freedom of ethical life and presses in upon world history; and (b) the period of its decline and fall, since it is its decline and fall that signalizes the emergence in it of a higher principle as the pure negative of its own.[38]

How should we read this? This whole section is worth rereading. Here, Hegel discusses the stages of history, that is to say, transitions into history.

For Hegel, there will always be states, and history is in fact the history of these very states. However, the puzzling aspect of this is to think the way in which (this) history relates to the history of the state form as such. Here one should remember that this form is also historically completed or overcome once it has been fully developed. In modernity, there is a specific state form, but simultaneously, there is a history of this form. One should take this into account when reading "God's march in the world" in a profane spirit. Reading this together with the passage of the (in)famous "owl of Minerva" can be productive. One way to read this consists in claiming that God is gone—in the same manner as is the stable state form. A worldly divinity can die; it therefore has a history and its further determinations depend upon us.

The present time challenges us to overcome the constraints of the nation-state and to move to a universal form of political organization. I maintain that Žižek's four riders of the apocalypse will be the driving force toward a transnational unity. Žižek's wager is that the only way to cope with the challenges of late global capitalism is to move beyond the nation-state form. And this is where Hegel is of crucial importance. He poses a penetrating challenge to the idea of the nation, from the perspective of the state as Idea. This is the challenge before which the good old socialism of the previous century failed and ended up succumbing to nationalism.

The "state" was the name Hegel had for a self-determining and objective organizational infrastructure. This makes it exceptionally challenging and hard to evacuate of a specific political reading when its logic is not so tied to praise of modern statehood. Therefore—yet again—what does Hegel mean by the "state?"

Every form of the modern state has very little, if anything at all, in common with the forms of political and social organization that Hegel calls the "state." This non-identification, or negative determination, of the idea of the state with individual states challenges the conservative understanding of the state. This position renders an understanding of Hegel's idea of the state rather difficult, as it does not side with any particular form of statehood, be it historical or actual. In Hegel's "political philosophy," there is little or no room for a positive determination of the "idea of the state," whose movement is both the material and historical existence of God, that is to say, God's march in the world. Thus, the following hypothesis can be put forward: what Hegel calls the "state" is the condition of historical existence. Wherever there is history, the organizational conditions for it can be called a state! In this historicizing manner, one can argue, for example, that if the Paris Commune made history, then, from this perspective, for a Hegelian, this should mean that the Parisian proletarians had a state. Yet in the Hegelian sense, in its capitalist forms of social organization, the state is not a state; for here, it is reduced to governmental structure, while its core remains the commodity form plus property laws.[39]

So how does this help us to conceptualize a state that would be neither the nation-state nor its mirroring in the previous century's socialist state? The mistake—one that is perhaps even fatal—of twentieth-century socialism and Marxist theory in general (including the work of many contemporary thinkers such as Poulantzas, Jessop, and Brock) is the reduction of the state to secondary apparatuses that are subordinate to the needs of capital for its reproduction. This position is strikingly similar to that of the neoliberals, as both orientations appear to underplay the crucial and active role of the contemporary state and its apparatuses in economic life. Sometimes it seems that capitalism not only controls the state, but that state apparatuses are at the very center of economic and capitalist reproduction, well exceeding the "traditional" description of their role as the legal and political guarantor for capitalist reproduction. The state serves as a direct agent for economic processes in various forms. This was also the case in twentieth-century state socialism, where the state was the sole agent and regulator of economic processes, the only difference being that there was no capitalist class.

Can we decouple the state from capital, as well as from the nation? Can there be a strong non-statal state, which would not be "reducible" to the logic of both nation and capital? In speaking of this we should not embrace the loosening up of state power into its administrative aspects, but should keep in mind the idea of the state as agent of absolute power. The state is not a closed end, but an open historical situation, full of antagonisms and possibilities, and is absolute precisely in this sense (as developed in the works of Comay, Žižek, and others).

The crux is thus to break the relationship between the state and capital, as well as its identification with the nation. The identification of the state with national identity is talk of identity, which as Hegel knew, contradicts itself:

> Talk of identity . . . contradicts itself. Identity, instead of being in itself the truth and the absolute truth, is thus rather its opposite; instead of being the unmoved simple, it surpasses itself into the dissolution of itself.[40]

The empowerment of the nation-state in contemporary global capitalism is extremely dangerous as it runs against the urgent need to establish a new relation to what Žižek refers to as our new "commons." Common dangers are a serious and urgent challenge to the totality of humanity, and for this reason, they cannot be reduced either to the nation or to (contemporary) states. The commons are not enclosed within particular determinations. The commons, as Marx has written, are the collective shared substance of our being, which are enclosed by privatization. Žižek, following Marx, identifies:

- the commons of culture, the immediately socialized forms of "cognitive" capital, primarily language, our means of communication and education, but also the shared infrastructure of public transport, electricity, the postal system, and so on;
- the commons of external nature, threatened by pollution and exploitation (from oil to rain forests and the natural habitat itself); and
- the commons of internal nature (the biogenetic inheritance of humanity); with new biogenetic technology, the creation of a New Man in the literal sense of changing human nature becomes a realistic prospect.[41]

This process of enclosure necessitates the resuscitation of two crucial notions: communism and the class struggle. Enclosure or privatization is the other name of proletarization, as Marx defined it, as a deprivation of a subject from his or her substance. Communism is the name of the collective appropriation of the commons. The difficult task is to identify ourselves, as agents of the class struggle, in this new figure. The class struggle is not reduced to an ontic level, as in the struggle of existing social classes, but is the name for the social antagonisms out of which these very social classes emerge. The reappropriation of the commons, that is, Communism, should be the name of the ethical substance, or in Hegelian terms, the name of the shared ethical idea.

Therefore, if the "state" is the term for the "presence of organizational conditions for the objective experience of people's self-determination," then the question to be asked is: what is the use of this politically?

If the declaration of "the end of Communism" as an Idea was simultaneously the "end of history," it becomes apparent that bringing about Communism back as an Idea also means bringing back history. In this sense, the Hegelian Idea of the state can be said to be the condition of historicity. What is it if not the set of conditions that allow a people, using whatever contingent means, to face their own history objectively ingrained in their objective life? There could even be an etymological claim within this argument. "State" connotes "*stare*," a stable segment of time (e.g., the "state" of a system). This is why it makes perfect sense to contend/posit that the possibility of conceiving states is a precondition for history (a time that alienates itself from itself).

This also means that bringing about a new theory of the state as the practice of the organization of objective conditions that we can create, then alienate ourselves from, and then also think and critique: in other words, the communist theory of the state should contain in itself the theory of the conditions and possibilities for the creation of the historical dynamics that can affect the people, rather than being yet another theory of "central government." The latter would be a theory of administration, which is a completely different domain.

This is why a Communist theory of the state is a theory of all the practices that can lead us to relate to the objective spirit, that is, to recognize in our objective concrete social existence some level of autonomy (God's march in the world), which until now remains hidden beneath the national and communal borders of national territories.

NOTES

1. G. W. F. Hegel, *Elements of the Philosophy of Right* (Cambridge: Cambridge University Press, 1991), p. 73, §41.
2. Fredric Jameson, "The Future City," *New Left Review* 21, May–June 2003.
3. Slavoj Žižek, *Pandemic! Covid 19 Shakes The World* (manuscript, forthcoming with OR Books, UK).
4. Cf. Slavoj Žižek, *Did Somebody say Totalitarianism? Five Interventions in the (Mis)Use of the Notion* (London: Verso, 2001).
5. Hegel, *Elements of the Philosophy of Right*, 279, §258.
6. Bill Gates argues that socialism is our only hope to save the planet reference, whereas Elon Musk has proposed universal basic income as a way to address the impact of automation on employment.
7. Axel Honneth, *Idea of Socialism: Towards a Renewal* (London: Polity Press, 2017), p. viii.
8. Ibid., 5.
9. Ibid., 106.
10. Étienne Balibar, *On the Dictatorship of the Proletariat* (London: NLB, 1977), p. 142.
11. Jean-Pierre Dupuy, *A Short Treatise on the Metaphysics of Tsunamis* (East Lansing: Michigan State University Press, 2015), p. 6.
12. Ibid., 8.
13. According to Žižek, these four riders are ecological crisis, biogenetic revolution, intellectual property, and new forms of proletarization. Slavoj Žižek, *Living in the End of Time* (London: Verso, 2010), p. x.
14. Slavoj Žižek, *First as Tragedy, Then as Farce* (London: Verso, 2009), p. 95.
15. Karl Marx, *Critique of the Gotha Programme* (London: Martin Lawrence, 1933), p. 31.
16. Hegel, *Elements of the Philosophy of Right*, 275, § 257.
17. Ibid., 282, § 260.
18. Ibid., 279, § 258.
19. Slavoj Žižek, *Incontinence of the Void: Sprandels: Economico-Philosophical Sprandels* (Cambridge, MA: MIT Press, 2017), p. 8.
20. Ibid., 10.
21. Hegel, *Elements of the Philosophy of Right*, 279, §258.

22. Shlomo Avineri, *Hegel's Theory of the Modern State* (Cambridge: Cambridge University Press, 1974), p. 116.
23. Hegel, *Elements of the Philosophy of Right*, 20.
24. Ibid.
25. Avineri, *Hegel's Theory of the Modern State*, 126.
26. G. W. F. Hegel, *The Science of Logic* (Cambridge: Cambridge University Press, 2010), p. 465.
27. Slavoj Žižek, *Sex and the Failed Absolute* (London: Bloomsbury, 2019), 351.
28. Hegel, *Elements of the Philosophy of Right*, 22.
29. Žižek is correct to portray Hegel as a philosopher of Christianity, or more concretely, of Protestantism. For Hegel, as he himself puts it, modern philosophy is Luther in the form of thought.
30. Žižek, *Sex and the Failed Absolute*, 395.
31. Hegel, *Elements of the Philosophy of Right*, 152.
32. Ibid.
33. Slavoj Žižek, "How to Begin from the Beginning?" in: C. Douzinas and S.Žižek (eds,), *The Idea of Communism* (London/New York: Verso, 2010), 219.
34. Ibid.
35. Hegel, *Elements of the Philosophy of Right*, 275, § 257.
36. Žižek, *First as Tragedy, Then as Farce*, 104.
37. Hegel, *Elements of the Philosophy of Right*, 152.
38. Hegel, *Elements of the Philosophy of Right*, 374.
39. Here I refer to a private conversation with Gabriel Tupinambá.
40. Hegel, *The Science of Logic*, 360.
41. Žižek, *First as Tragedy, Then as Farce*, 91.

Chapter 9

Democratic Corpses and Communist Specters: Between the Liberal Democratic and Post-Socialist State

Christian Sorace

Wherever one looks, liberal democracy appears to be in crisis. Aspirational dictators flaunt their disregard for the institutions that are supposed to bind them: Trump in the United States, Putin in Russia, Bolsonaro in Brazil, Modi in India, Duterte in the Philippines, Boris Johnson in the United Kingdom, to name only a few of the most familiar examples. In the United States, at several elite college campuses on Election Day in 2016, students were crying, classes were canceled, and classrooms were converted into makeshift triage centers for the collective political unconscious.[1] To many, it felt like someone intimate had died and that they were waking up to a barely recognizable and terrifying reality.[2]

The claim that liberal democracy is in crisis raises questions about the uniqueness of the conjunctural moment in which we live. Mainstream liberalism regards Trump's electoral victory in 2016 as a catastrophe, which it has frantically attempted to displace through the explanation of Russian interference, a tactic which ironically mirrors the tendency of both Russia and China to blame the United States for their own domestic crises. Even after the revelations of the Mueller report, it is clear that the *fact* of Russian interference in U.S. elections is not an adequate explanation of the *cause* of democratic crisis (one can fire numerous "smoking guns" without hitting a target). The anxious proliferation of crisis discourses results from the sense that crisis has moved from the periphery (where it is normalized and expected) to the heart of the democratic imaginary and institutions. From the model of democracy, the United States has become its cadaver.

What I call the *democracy autopsy genre* contains academic and journalistic writing diagnosing the causes of death of liberal democracy. In the cases where liberal democracy is in critical condition, remedies are prescribed. To provide a sense of the funereal atmosphere of political discourse, a few examples should suffice. In February 2017, *The Washington Post* controversially changed its masthead to the ominous phrase: *Democracy Dies in Darkness*. Nearly one year later in January 2018, political scientists Steven Levitsky and Daniel Ziblatt published *How Democracies Die*, which appeared on *The New York Times* Best Seller list. On May 17, 2019, *The Wall Street Journal* featured political scientist Larry Diamond's essay "The Global Crisis of Democracy"[3] based on his most recent book. Another titan of the field, comparative political scientist Adam Przeworski, offered an overview of the "shaky state of democracy around the world" in his new book *Crises of Democracy* published in September 2019.[4] In the same year, a top-ranking research university in the United States posted a job description for a candidate, "Who will advance the substantive commitment of the department's strategic plan: to investigate 'Democracy Under Threat.'" It is not only academia that is obsessed with democracy's death. During Trump's presidency, mainstream media in the United States flood the public sphere with op-eds and think pieces on the shibboleths of democracy, crisis, and death, which might as well have been algorithmically generated.[5] Most notably is former secretary of state and presidential candidate Hillary Clinton's article "American Democracy Is in Crisis" published on September 16, 2018, in *The Atlantic* with a background photograph of an American flag attached to a burning match flagpole.[6] The fact that it is mainly members of the elite political class and intelligentsia who are engaged in public mourning over democracy's demise raises the suspicion that what is being mourned may not actually be democracy.

The question "is democracy in crisis" misleadingly presumes that we are already living in a democratic state. Paradoxically, the discourse of democracy in danger calls on us to save and defend parliamentary institutions which have been drained of democratic vitality. Rescuing liberal democracy from the clutches of death dialectically prevents other modes of democracy from being born, such as the collective process of decision-making and mass participation in the affairs of the state. The genre of democracy in crisis is a *plea for the world to remain as it is*.

At the margins of political and social theory, a revolt against crisis language has been gaining momentum. In a presentation titled "Whose Crisis? Whose Democracy? Notes on a Political Conjuncture," Andreas Kalyvas pointed out how the crisis of Trump has made the war-criminal George W. Bush retroactively appear presidential and even likable—an observation recently both confirmed and challenged by the public backlash against media star Ellen DeGeneres for defending her friendship with the former president.[7] Written in the context of the 2008 global financial crisis, anthropologist Janet Roitman's book *Anti-Crisis* theorizes the norm-stabilizing properties of crisis as a performative genre. In Roitman's words: "Crisis always aims at and implicates a norm, what went wrong assumes a normative account of what ought to have happened."[8] Despite its deceptive negativity, the language of crisis operates as a mode of affirmation through which a norm is constituted, idealized, and affectively invested in. Rather than creating conditions for "radical change," Roitman suggests that the language of crisis results in "the affirmation of long-standing principles, thereby precluding certain thoughts and acts." In a crisis, one must do as told, whether by voting for the Democratic Party candidate, regardless of their politics, or having to "stay the course," regardless of where it is set for.

Although it acknowledges the reality that there are serious strains, fractures, and contradictions within liberal democratic institutions, the narrative of democracy in crisis narrowly frames how they can be investigated, talked about, and explained. It conveys a normative demand to shore up political institutions rather than interrogate, contest, reimagine, and constitute them. Under these conditions, the discourse of *crisis* is the dialectical opposite of the practice of *critique*, despite their shared genealogy.[9] A perfect example of how the crisis genre reinforces the status quo of liberal democracy is Levitsky and Ziblatt's *How Democracies Die* mentioned earlier. According to the authors, the gravest threat to democratic institutions comes from closet authoritarians who are democratically elected to office and then dismantle democratic institutions from within. "Democracies may die at the hands not of generals but of elected leaders—presidents or prime ministers who subvert the very process that brought them to power."[10] Levitsky and Ziblatt diagnose the problem as a breakdown of the "gate-keeping" function of political parties and institutions anchored in a "commitment to keep extremists out of power."[11] In their demarcation and defense of the center, political distinctions and ideological differences fall away: the Venezuelan communist leader Hugo Chávez and Hungarian rightist prime minister Viktor Orbán fall into the same category of populist demagogues. *How Democracies Die* is not concerned with democratic species extinction but with preserving the status quo of liberal democracy.

Levitsky and Ziblatt offer a more sophisticated gloss of the logic of displacement than blaming Putin for Trump's victory. For them, today's crisis does not originate from within liberal democracy but is a consequence of the gates to it coming unhinged and allowing the outsider inside. The selection of who is qualified to rule needs to be determined before the people are summoned to vote on their preferred candidates. The antidemocratic implication of their argument is that the people should not be allowed near the gates of power because "What if the people choose a demagogue?"[12] This sentiment could not find a more vivid portrayal than nineteenth-century French author Gustave Flaubert's reflections on academia, "I have always tried to live in an ivory tower; but a tide of shit is beating at its walls, threatening to undermine it."[13] In Jacques Rancière's updated version: "There is only one good democracy, the one that represses the catastrophe of democratic civilization."[14] What is not considered in their account is that the liberal democracy is in crisis because it is undemocratically founded on the exclusion of the masses from participation in the administration of the state power.

In this chapter, I will argue that the *democratic necrophilia* we are witnessing today is an investment in avoiding the lack of democracy in democratic institutions under global capitalism. Our anxiety about losing democracy reassures us that it was something we once inhabited. Mourning democracy does not commemorate a rupture with the past but is an affectively charged continuation of *democratic liturgy* through which democracy is celebrated and consecrated as the hegemonic secular religion of our times. As Wendy Brown puts it: "Democracy has emerged as a new world religion"[15] sanctioning foreign interventions in its name, which are the contemporary avatar of "imperial crusades." For Brown, the exaltation of democracy has occurred alongside and contributed to a process of de-democratization and a retreat from public engagement into private, commodified life. "Democracy is exalted not only across the globe today but across the political spectrum . . . we are all democrats now. But what is left of democracy?"[16] To answer Brown's question, what remains is the decayed aura of *democratic liturgy*.

The concept of *democratic liturgy* derives from Giorgio Agamben's genealogical investigation into the secular production of glory. Writing in the vein of political theology, Agamben argues that "the sphere of glory . . . does not disappear in modern democracies, but simply shifts to another area, that of public opinion."[17] For Agamben, public opinion is a site of "acclamation" through which democratic legitimacy is produced. From cable news, university classrooms, informal conversations, online discussions, I voted stickers, to obituaries of democracy's death, sermons saturate discursive space. Even democratic deliberations starts to sound like hymns of the faithful. Far from being a practice of collective self-determination, democracy has become an instrument of self-exaltation. As soon as anyone begins to challenge parliamentary democracy, they are sternly reminded of the catastrophe that lurks beyond the horizon. Those who do not identify as democrats are treated as heretics and threatened with conversion, excommunication, or death.[18] The mainstream discourse of *democratic crisis* is a liturgical attempt to preserve its aura. In a state of danger, its aura starts to glow again. The imagined task of liberal democratic resistance is to heroically drive the barbarians from the palace rather than to dismantle the palace.

This chapter submits that the present impasse of politics is the attachment to parliamentary democracy, not to mention the violence mobilized to defend it, which prevents people from living democratically. Paradoxically, in order to act democratically, it is necessary, in Étienne Balibar's words, to "openly confront the *lack of democracy* in existing institutions and transform them in a more or less radical manner."[19] For Alain Badiou, this confrontation entails not only calling out the absence of democracy but our investment in the concept of it. "The only way to make truth out of the world we're living in in is to dispel the aura of the word *democracy*."[20] The question that must be asked is: *What does liberal democracy look like without its aura?*

1. BEGINNINGS AND ENDINGS

Although these problems are global in scope, this chapter is based on the assumption that the post-socialist context offers a unique window into the production and disenchantment of the aura of liberal democracy. Post-socialist democratization was not simply another ripple or "wave of democratization" but the end of any conceivable *progressive* alternative.[21] From that point forward, liberal democracy can *regress* into authoritarianism but after the disintegration of the Soviet Union what could no longer be conceived was its replacement by a higher, democratic, communist form. For Western public opinion, the early 1990s was a time of liturgical ceremony, celebration, and dissemination of the "good news" and "gospel" of liberal democracy.[22] Despite the reality that many post-socialist nation-states did not survive the perilous "transition,"[23] the historic-symbolic significance of the period generates a democratic aura.[24]

After the collapse of socialism, there was no real question of experimentation with alternative models. Despite regional, national, and intra-national variation in outcomes which would emerge over time, new parliaments and constitutions were designed and founded according to the principles and blueprints of developed Western democracies under the guidance of international organizations. As political scientist Valerie Bunce starkly writes: "With the collapse of the Cold War order in 1989–1990, and the decisive defeat of its 'other,' liberalism came to occupy—for the first time in its life, either in theory or practice—the position of an ideological monopoly."[25] Post-socialist liberal democracies are not anomalous or marginal cases but carry the congenital defect of their origins.

Instructive in this regard is anthropologist Katherine Verdery's suggestion that post-socialist transformation offers a rare opportunity to engage in

> a broader critique of Western economic and political forms by seeing them through the eyes of those experiencing their construction. The forced pace of privatization, for example, reveals with special clarity the darker side of capitalism. . . . "Democracy" is being unmasked too, as the export of Western electoral practices makes their failings transparent.[26]

Verdery challenges the dominant assumption of the "transition paradigm" that post-socialist nation-states are failing to live up to the ideals of liberal democracy and capitalism and reverses it by suggesting that maybe the models are failing post-socialist nation-states and their citizens.[27] In these cases, we are not looking at a failed attempt, marginal outlier, or defective knock-off, but the *real thing*, parliamentary democracy in all of its noumenal glory.

Taking up Verdery's challenge, I will focus on the democratic history of Mongolia, an Inner Asian country with a population of slightly over 3 million people and shared borders with Russia and China. For the past several years, I have been conducting research in Mongolia's capital Ulaanbaatar for a cumulative eleven nonconsecutive months on the links between urban redevelopment, air pollution, and the political system. In that time, I have interviewed over fifty people, including ministers of government, members of parliament, urban planners and architects, nongovernmental organization workers, academics, and ordinary citizens. What has captured my attention is the conspicuous dissonance between Mongolians' proud commitment to the abstract notion of democracy (it is, as political scientists like to say, "the only game in town"), and their lack of trust and faith in political elites, parties, the state and political system in general. One of my guiding assumptions is that *political cynicism* and *democratic commitment* do not only simply coexist but also dialectically condition each other. Rather than accepting assertions of democracy at face value, this chapter poses the question: *What does it mean for people to be powerless in a democracy*? Part of the answer has to do with Mongolia's status as a post-socialist state and the effect of democratic liturgy in shaping people's beliefs, attitudes, and imaginations of political possibility. But the main hypothesis that I will explore is that parliamentary democracy is crisis-prone because it grants the people sovereign power without allowing them to exercise it. As a result, it is susceptible to being pulled in directions that undermine it.

This chapter does not provide a detailed, comprehensive account of all of the dimensions of Mongolian politics but aims to offer insight into the dynamics of its political system and what it can tell us about parliamentary democracy. If one brackets the different context and culture, the patterns in Mongolia should be familiar to any reader in United States. As either a warning or an enticement depending on the reader's proclivities, the chapter will weave in and out of and hopefully together, general theoretical observations, empirical analysis of Mongolia, broader patterns of post-socialism, commentary on democracy globally, and conclude with a discussion on the exorcism of Lenin who must remain consigned to the past for parliamentary democracy to appear as the only legitimate horizon of politics.

2. DEMOCRATIC OASIS OR MIRAGE?

By most definitions, Mongolia appears to be a successful example of peaceful democratic transition, institution-building, respect for rules of the game, open media, and active civil society. During his 2016 visit to Mongolia as secretary of state, John Kerry praised the county as an "oasis of democracy" stranded between two authoritarian neighbors: Russia and China.[28] Further validating Mongolia's democratic status, political scientists M. Steven Fish and Michael Seeberg glow: "In postcommunist Eurasia, a region littered with failed democratic experiments and frozen autocracies, Mongolia stands out."[29] For writers such as Fish and Seeberg, Mongolia is a beacon of democracy in a bleak political landscape. And yet—or maybe this is why—among Mongolian people, there is public disquiet with the political system. Even though most Mongolians remain committed to the ideal of democracy, they perceive it to be *lacking* in their own political institutions and society.

Consequently, Mongolia is said to have joined the ranks of countries on a path of "democratic backsliding."[30] On July 1, 2019, "independent economist and media representative of Mongolia" Mr. Jargalsaikhan Dambadarjaa (known as "Jargal DeFacto") observed: "If we look at what's been happening in Mongolia for the last 2–3 years, we can also say that we're moving backwards on democracy."[31] A former martial arts champion, business mogul, and populist outsider, Mongolia's President Khaltmaagiin Battulga (Democratic Party) seems to be the kind of politician they had in mind. Taking a "page out of Trump's playbook,"[32] Battulga's 2017 presidential campaign slogan "Mongolia Will Win" (*Mongol Yalaan*) appealed to a romantic conception of "Mongol-ness," cultural purity, and national pride.[33] In Mongolian political discourse, an undercurrent of Sinophobia is also never far from the surface.[34]

So far, Battulga's record in office seems to have confirmed people's initial anxieties over his "behavioral warning signs"[35] of incipient authoritarianism. On March 27, 2019, the Mongolian parliament passed legislation authorizing the National Security Council (composed of the president, prime minister, and speaker of Ikh Khural [parliament]) "the power to dismiss judges and other officials in the judicial system on request of the Judicial Council. The Judicial Council is appointed by the president, of course."[36] Despite the fact that a large number of Mongolians approve of these measures, "many foreign observers and some Mongolians" fear that executive control over judicial appointments will undermine anticorruption investigations and judicial independence.[37] As a result, a flurry of English and Mongolian language articles anatomizing Mongolia's fragile democratic health were published.[38] On March 29, 2019, Anand Tumurtogoo published in *Foreign Affairs* an article titled "Mongolia's President Is Slicing Away Its Hard-Won Democracy" condemning the president and Prime Minister Khurelsukh as "another aspiring strongman who idolizes Putin and has little time for democracy."[39] But the editorial also adds: "Many Mongolians are eager for a strongman. . . . They've been hoping for one man to bring an end to all the bad things in Mongolia, and democracy seems a small price to pay for that." In this version, the democratic desire for strongman results in the nullification of democracy. It is the people who are failing democratic institutions and not the other way around. On April 3, 2019, *The Washington Post* published an editorial by Boldsaikhan Sambuu and Aubrey Menarndt titled "Here's How Democracy Is Eroding in Mongolia"[40] evincing a similar argument on the populist appeal of strongman politics. In an idiotically titled article published by *Bloomberg Businessweek*, President Battulga is referred to as the "Genghis Khan-Idolizing Trump of the Steppe."[41] Evidence of Battulga's authoritarianism is based on his "bond" and "cozy" relationship with Putin. Rather than investigating the underlying reasons for the "anti-establishment anger" that Battulga's campaign tapped into, one is left with the sense that Putin's authoritarianism is a contagious disease that infects anyone who talks to him.

This dominant narrative of the desire for strongman rule overlooks the underlying conditions which make would-be authoritarians desirable. The liberal response is to blame the people for their ignorance and repair the institutions that keep them, and the populist demagogues who speak for them, out of power. Unless one is satisfied with the complacent conceits of liberalism, another explanation is needed in order to extricate us from this circular logic. In this chapter, I propose that people can't live on liturgy alone. The global crisis of democracy is caused by people's lack of sovereignty over the conditions in which they live. Returning to the mythically imbued origins of post-socialist democratization, in what sense did political power transfer to the hands of the *demos*?

Peaceful demonstrations began on Human Rights Day on December 25, 1989 in the capital city Ulaanbaatar and spread throughout the country. People gathered in the main square under slogans, such as: "New times have come, wake up!" (*shine tsag irlee, sertsgee!*).[42] Democratic legitimacy was founded in a wholesale rejection of the socialist past. This rejection provided a shortcut between the democratic present and the imagination of a pre-socialist past based on Mongolian traditions and cultural patrimony. According to Christopher Kaplonski, in the unfolding of democratic revolution, a nationalist historiography emerged in which socialism was recoded as a foreign (Soviet-led) imposition and detour from Mongolia's nationalist identity and development. The democratic protests marked "the end of an era that was in turn seen as a foreign imposition. They signal a return to the true destiny of the Mongolian nation."[43] On the banners calling for democracy and denouncing one-party rule were also images of national icons, including the now ubiquitous image of Chinggis Khaan.⁴⁴ Since the 1990s "rituals of the state" have been invented and revived in order to "build a distinctive national brand of public culture."⁴⁵ Nationalism dominates Mongolia's political landscape today.

As democratic protests spread throughout Mongolia, the ruling Mongolian People's Revolutionary Party (MPRP) pledged nonviolence but were also unresponsive to the protestors' demands. Hunger strikes were declared in the Ulaanbaatar and Khuvskgul Aimag (province) catalyzing the process of the disintegration of the political system. Shortly after the Politburo collectively resigned in an "Extraordinary Meeting," the Constitution was amended to excise reference to the leading role of the MPRP and of Marxist-Leninist ideology in society.⁴⁶ Mongolia's first democratic elections were held on 22 July 1990. On 14 February 1991, Mongolia joined the International Monetary Fund and World Bank, and on August 2, 1991 U.S. secretary of state James Baker visited Mongolia to consecrate its democracy. Only months after Baker's visit the U.S. Congress pledged its support for the "democratic reconstruction" (*ardchilalyn shinechlel*) of Mongolia. A few years later in 1996, in a conscious effort to help the opposition defeat the incumbent MPRP, and intensify the privatization already underway, the International Republican Institute (IRI) helped the Democratic Union author a "Contract with the Mongolian Voter" copied nearly verbatim from the playbook of the U.S. Republican Party.⁴⁷ For the first time in Mongolia's history, power democratically "changed hands."

If viewed on its own, Mongolia's political transformation appears democratic. When refracted through Mongolia's post-socialist economic transformations, however, a much different picture of democratic politics emerges. According to the hegemonic narrative of liberal democracy, the socialist state stifled market competition and the entrepreneurial spirit of individuals. Policy recommendations which "reflected a neoliberal discourse in which the economy should be emancipated from the political structure, permitted to assume its latent 'natural' form, composed of private property and the market."⁴⁸ The program of economic "shock therapy" was not a matter of democratic deliberation but the result of conjunctural effects stemming from the Mongolian state's dependence on international finance,⁴⁹ and a belief in free-market ideology among its democratic reformers and even some members of the former Communist party.⁵⁰ To give an idea of the spirit of reform, a proposal was floated to erect a statue of Milton Friedman in the place where a statue of Stalin was recently toppled.⁵¹ Elite discourse assured Mongolian citizens that austerity and short-term sacrifice would generate prosperity in the long term. In political scientist John Gould's observation, across the post-Soviet world, "many economists compared themselves to doctors, who had professional access to the scientific knowledge to cure a sick patient. This was vaguely similar to the hyperrational Bolsheviks of Lenin's day. Both saw regrettable short-term means as necessary to achieve desirable long-term ends."[52] On the "advice" of international financial agencies—which were in reality more like *commands* if one considers the leverage of international lenders and creditors over the local economy[53]—instead of building on the gains and state capacity developed under socialism, Mongolia's liberal democratic state began to dismantle it. Like other countries in the post-socialist world, Mongolia's parliamentary democracy came into being at the height of what David Harvey refers to as the "neo-liberal turn" that was also taking place globally, including in the People's Republic of China under the rule of a nominally Communist party.[54] Under these global conditions, ordinary citizens throughout the post-socialist world had little chance of democratically exercising state power.

The state does not disappear under neoliberalism but proliferates in different guises. Anthropologist Morton Axel Pedersen argues that, in Mongolia, the post-socialist state became "shamanic" resembling the fluidity and unpredictability of markets and spirits, which were kept at bay under socialist rule.[55] The decomposition of the socialist state's "benevolent paternal, authoritarian sovereign body"[56] did not mean that the state disappeared but only changed shape. For Pedersen, the post-socialist state's power is dispersed across multiple sites and shifting vantage points that are impossible to contain in a recognizable and predictable form. The various examples he gives range from the "multitude of spectral political faces"[57] on electoral campaign posters to the phenomenon of local strongman known as *ataman* who are "imbued with the capacity to harness the forces of the market and democracy into political capital."[58] The ontology of post-socialism is a permanent state of transition and powerlessness "in the face of occult forces that take the form of spirits, the market, and democracy."[59] As a result of democratization, the "shamanic state" slipped further beyond the reach and control of the people.

The different faces of the post-socialist state can be explained by the countervailing pressures placed on it by global capitalism. During the process of transformation, the state's positive functions developed under socialism (such as public goods provision, regulatory capacity, and solidarity-building), were scaled back, while the state's repressive, legalistic, and ritualistic functions were gradually reassembled.[60] For example, Historian Morris Rossabi describes Mongolia's post-socialist transformation as a process of deterioration. "Education had been one of the glories of the communist era, when the state devoted considerable resources to it. . . . The postcommunist era has been characterized by steady deterioration in the educational system."[61] The commitment to universal literacy, cultural transformation, and the raising of educational standards was common throughout the socialist world. On the other hand, socialist educational systems also were "rigidly bureaucratized, and narrowly and involuntarily vocational"[62] and viewed as lagging behind Western educational standards. Despite its limitations without the socialist state's commitment and investment in education, the quality of education throughout the post-socialist world became erratic and less accessible to poor and marginalized communities.

Accompanying political and economic transformations were changing conceptions of state-society relations, authority, responsibility, and expectation. Post-socialist democracy came into being through an assault on the concept and resources of the public, which was identified with the socialist state. On a philological level, the Mongolian words for *private* and *privatization* denote being carved out of collective entities—an understanding that runs counter to the ontological and methodological individualism of liberalism (although English contains a similar etymology in the derivation of the word *private* from the Latin *privatio*, meaning privation, the Lockean definition of private property based on an understanding of possessing "*property in one's own person*" that authorizes "*exclusive rights*" to natural resources and objects elides the sense of loss and withdrawal from relationality in the formation of the individual). David Sneath explains, "*Khuv*' is the term used for the concept 'private' and means a share, portion, allotment, as well as personal or individual. The verb *khuvaah* means to divide or apportion. So, items of personal property are explicitly part of wider fields—be they domestic, district or state political economies."[63] Linguistically and economically, the Mongolia case reveals privatization to be a mode of dismemberment. Similarly, the shift in meaning of the Mongolian word *archilal*, which is the closest translation of *democracy*, also outlines a process of atomization. Rebekah Plueckhahn and Dulam Bumochir note:

> The word *archilal* does not completely evoke the same meaning and definition of the Euro-American word "democracy." In Mongolia, there are two versions of what it can mean. One rests on the historical revolutionary Mongolian word *ard*, which means subject, proletarian, people, commons and the masses from which comes the word *ard-chilal*, literally "people-ization." This "people-ization" is heavily linked to the making of capitalism in Mongolia, where after 1990, the political system and also Mongolia's market, finance trade, industry, agriculture and economy in general, became democratized and made up of individual actors. . . . However in the 2000s, *ardchilal* (and Mongolia's desire for an alternative society other than capitalism) started to losing its earlier meaning and has grown to be more understood in line with the 'democracy' that is implicated in perceptions of "capitalism."[64]

Democratization engineered the ideological transformation of the collective people (*ard tümen*) into atomized, interest bearing citizens in their dual role as market actors and voters. As a result, survival was transferred from the purview of the state to the realm of individual responsibility, initiative, and fortune.

Mongolia's capital Ulaanbaatar has witnessed an explosion in population growth as herders leave the countryside for the city. One of the main reasons for the waves of migration to Ulaanbaatar is the post-socialist transformation of the pastoral political economy, which benefited from the planning, scale, subsidies, and infrastructures of socialist collectivization. The decollectivization process resulted in a return to subsistence economies. Without state support, herding families were vulnerable to market fluctuations and winter storms during which many lost their animals and fell into debt. In Sneath's haunting words, "The most striking transition that rural Mongolia has experienced has been from a middle-income to a poor country, as if the process of development had been thrown in reverse."[65] To further obliterate the teleological fantasy of "transition," Katherine Verdery poses the intentionally hyperbolic and provocative question: "What if we were to think, then, of a transition from socialism not to capitalism but to feudalism?"[66]

In the 2000s, the mining boom catapulted Mongolia into a resource-extractive economy, exporting copper, gold, coal, molybdenum, and uranium mines. When revenue from mining flowed into state coffers, it allowed the state to increase its expenditure of welfare in the form of popular subsidies. The state's dependence on mineral exports, however, has also worked against its capacity-building, as Mongolia's economy nosedived in tandem with the plummet of global commodity prices in 2012.[67] Although numerous jobs have proliferated around the mining economy, they have not translated into improved living conditions for ordinary Mongolian.[68]

Overall, the accumulated legacies of Mongolia's post-socialist transformation continue to shape the wealth disparities of the present. Anyone who has been to Mongolia's capital Ulaanbaatar cannot miss the sense of a city divided in two: on one side are the luxurious homes and shopping centers in the Zaisan area and sprawling suburban developments south of the Tuul River, and on the other side are *ger* districts, where over 60 percent of the urban population live, unconnected to central heating and sewage infrastructure. The ubiquity of pawn shops (*lombard*)[69] is a symbol of how the majority of citizens survive "from debt to debt" (*örnöös öröund*)[70] and rely on tenuous access to disparate material resources, social networks, creative use of land, and capitalist practices as strategies for survival.[71]

Although Mongolians still turn out in high numbers for elections, and remain attached to democratic ideals, people have lost faith in the political system's willingness and capacity to address their demands. Data from a nation-wide survey of 5,000 people conducted by the IRI in August 2016 support this assessment.[72] A majority of respondents believe that the country is "headed in the wrong direction" with 39 percent of respondents citing the reason of "economic instability and income inequality" and 26 percent upset with "failed government policies." The lack of faith in state capacity is especially acute when it comes to the state's failed attempts to mitigate Ulaanbaatar's deadly winter air pollution crisis. According to the IRI survey, 52 percent of respondents characterized the results of state efforts to address pollution as *very bad* and 28 percent *somewhat bad*, meaning a total of 80 percent view the government's handling of air pollution in a negative light. In December 2018, the National Audit Bureau released a detailed report on the state budget allocated to air pollution reduction between 2008 and 2016, a total expenditure of 550 billion MNT (US$205,992,509 based on exchange rate as of October 15, 2019). The released budget compared with the fact that air pollution seems to only be worsening triggered a public outcry. One newspaper editorial directly blamed the electoral system: "From October until April, it is by now prosaic, we complain until the warm season come and we rest, we hike and forget. What a lovely idea if we held elections and could vote during the winter months."[73] Later in December, a petition was circulated which appealed to the United Nations to intervene against the Mongolian government on behalf of ordinary Mongolian citizens suffering from the "Human Rights Violation propagated by our own #Government & #Parliament who have failed to solve this issue for years and years."[74]

The crisis of faith in Mongolia's political system derives in part from the fact that it has been unable to guarantee its citizens breathable air.[75] But it is not only the air which is experienced as unbreathable but also the "political atmosphere."[76] Most Mongolians view political elites and business people to be conducting business in a "fog" of corruption.[77] The Mongolian word for *fog* MANAN is an acronym for the two major political parties, the Mongolian People's Party (MAN) and the Democratic Party (AN). Not only are politicians corrupt, but the two major political parties are viewed as interchangeable. "When you line up the MPP policies and compare them to DP policies, there is no ideological pattern to be found in either and voters would be unable to guess what position these parties would take on particular initiatives or challenges in the future."[78] A local researcher at a think tank who specializes in political parties explained that "there is no political ideology anymore. Both parties came out with their programs last year before the election, but they are meaningless. Nowadays the political parties no longer stand for anything. They are just 'pragmatic'."[79] In the bleak prediction of Jargal DeFacto: "Both of the main political parties are dead. How long they survive depends on how long the people will tolerate them."[80] Party interchangeability implies that election outcomes do not matter. In this context, fog takes on an additional meaning of that which obscures the promise of a future.

Anthropologist Rebecca Empson captures this idea in her description of the atmosphere surrounding 2016 parliamentary elections:

> In this atmosphere politics, as we might imagine it, appears as a kind of empty shell. People feel they are living in an economic system (capitalism) rather than a political one (democracy now appears jaded and opaque). And because the economic system persists, regardless of who is in charge, politics itself appears defunct, a point that makes attaching the term "crisis" to the word "economic" a kind of political parody.[81]

When people lack the decision-making power to intervene in and shape their own lives, in what sense do they live in a democracy? If regardless of who is elected, business continues as usual, in what way are elections meaningful apart from their liturgical function? This point calls into question the accepted wisdom that the development of democracy and capitalism are mutually imbricated.[82] In the words of media theorist Hito Steyerl, democracies are in crisis precisely "because whatever the people want, whoever they are, and regardless of who represents them, the contemporary sovereigns are mainly the 'markets.' The markets, not the people, are to be appeased, satisfied and pleased by the political class."[83] As Žižek puts it, "Today's democracy is no longer the place where crucial decisions are made."[84] Throughout today's world, people sense their own powerlessness; authoritarianism and populism are reparative fantasies of an underlying feeling of dispossession.

During the 2017 presidential elections in Mongolia, in which neither of the three candidates represented genuine ideological differences, a protest movement emerged that encouraged citizens to cast "white ballots" (*Tsagaan songolt*) based on a provision in the electoral law that if no candidate receives at least 50 percent of the valid votes, new elections will be called that exclude the candidates nominated in the failed first election.[85] The hashtag #*Songoltryi songogch*, literally meaning "Voters without a Choice," went viral on social media.[86] Although the "blank ballot" movement in Mongolia only garnered a single-digit percentage of the total votes, its radical potential can be glimpsed in the novel *Seeing* by Nobel Prize–winning author José Saramago.[87] In the country imagined in Saramago's novel, only blank ballots are cast resulting in a breakdown of political legitimacy. The defense minister labels the refusal to vote an act of terrorism and declares a state of emergency to combat it. In her review of Saramago's novel, Ursula K. LeGuin reflects that "it comes hard to me to admit that a vote is not in itself an act of power" and to see the radical potential of a general strike against voting until realizing the kind of response it provoked in the government.[88] What Saramago's novel reveals is how the state mobilizes violence to protect the aura produced by the liturgical machinery of the democratic state.[89]

Democratic liturgy elevates democracy as a ritual object of belief and exaltation. In times of "crisis," rituals and sermons are mobilized to shore up wavering faith. In July 2018, the Independent Research Institute of Mongolia hosted an international conference titled "Democracy in the 21st Century: Challenges and Ways Forward." At the conference, the U.S.-based democracy-promotion IRI handed out glossy brochures in Mongolian and English retelling the narrative of how "Democracy Was Born in Mongolia."[90] When asked why it was important to commemorate the democratic revolution, one of the organizers answered that *"Mongolia's democracy is in need of re-enchantment."*[91]

3. COMMUNIST SPECTERS

When *re-enchantment* does not work, *exorcism* becomes the liturgy of last resort. As Ilya Budraitskis argues, "The specter of communism will come to the rescue of the government every time it needs to explain away its own mistakes or crimes."[92] This process "strives to displace any explanation of contemporary social and political conflicts, and this leads to a dematerialization of reality. The remnants turn into an elusive and restless spirit, which can just as easily take root in institutions, people, or stones as it can abandon them."[93] The immaterial properties of the specter enable the body to appear as if it is possessed by something external to it; the rite of exorcism, therefore, (re)establishes boundaries between inside and outside. Exorcism purifies the body politic.

Exorcism continues to be performed at the bedside of Mongolia's ailing democracy. As a post-socialist state, Mongolia's democracy is haunted by its socialist past. This idea was recently put forward in an article by the political scientist Munkh-Erdene, which characterizes Mongolia's parliament as a "Frankenstein" hybrid of parliamentary and socialist systems. Munkh-Erdene blames the problems of Mongolia's parliamentary democracy as a "direct inheritance of the Communist father."[94] When I interviewed a liberal Democratic Party representative of parliament and former minister, he complained that Mongolia's "problems are in part due to the Communist mentality. There is only planning and no respect for citizen's property rights and no understanding of the market economy."[95] In a public lecture delivered at the Harvard Kennedy School in March 2018, Jargal DeFacto declared: "We have yet to learn how to develop our democracy and work the free market economy."[96] The shared logic of these positions is that today's crises are not failures of liberal democracy and capitalism because Mongolia is still living in the remnants of state socialism.

As Mongolia struggles with its political identity, crisis discourse alerts the public that the country is about to slide back into the darkness of communism. Political commentator Boluskha observes that "it is not accidental that posts are being written day and night about returning to Communism and how the populists are going to destroy our country."[97] The threat of a "regression" to communism is an engrained "habit of telling a story you have repeated your whole life." This raises the question: *What is democracy warding off?* It is the wager of this chapter that democracy is not protecting itself from the dark past of communism but from the abandonment of its future.[98]

In the famous opening lines of *The Communist Manifesto*, Marx and Engels similarly argue that "the specter of communism" is internal to the dominant structures and ideologies of power:[99]

> All of the powers of old Europe have entered into a holy alliance to exorcise this specter. . . . Where is the party in opposition that has not been decried as communistic by its opponents in power? Where is the opposition that has not hurled back the branding reproach of communism against the more advanced opposition parties, as well as against its reactionary adversaries?

Communism is a specter in a dual sense. On the one hand, communism is a "nursery tale" that the ruling classes tell themselves. On the other hand, communism is an immanent future that Marx and Engels trace in their Manifesto. After this future failed to come to fruition, most people focused on the former sense while forgetting the later—the attempt to give the specter a body. When analyzing today's crisis of democracy, it is absolutely necessary to superimpose them once again. The specter of communism indices both the decomposing body of parliamentary democracy and the need for something to replace it. Communist spirits are both the discursive figments of the ruling classes and the bearers of a promise "in which the free development of each is the condition of the free development of all."[100] As emissaries from the future which has already been traced in the present, they haunt the "empty" throne of liberal democracy.[101]

In *Specters of Marx*, written at the height of liberal democratic self-intoxication in the early 1990s, Derrida mourns the loss of what he describes as a "certain emancipatory and *messianic* affirmation, a certain experience of the promise"[102] of Marxism absent from the world being celebrated.[103] Liberal democracy was not the "end of history" but the abandonment of the future. This abandonment/betrayal injected a sense of fragility and nervous energy at the heart of liberal democracy, which requires constant liturgical attention.[104]

> This dominating discourse often has the manic, jubilatory, and incantatory form that Freud assigned to the so-called triumphant phase of mourning work. The incantation repeats and ritualizes itself, it holds forth and holds to formulas, like

any animistic magic. To the rhythm of a cadenced march, it proclaims: Marx is dead, communism is dead, very dead, and along with it its hopes, its discourse, its theories and its practices. It says: long live capitalism, long live the market, here's to the survival of economic and political liberalism![105]

For post-socialist democracy to survive, Lenin's spectral remains need to be repeatedly exorcised. Nothing else can explain the revival of anticommunism almost thirty years after the "Leninist extinction"[106] and collapse of the larger part of the world's Leninist Party-states (apart from the historically inaccurate association of Lenin with Russian imperialism, which depends on the erasure of Lenin's unwavering position of anti-Russian chauvinism). The examples are numerous and traverse different regions. In 2015, the Ukrainian government passed a legislation authorizing a "decommunization" process, including the demolition of Lenin statues and "criminalized historical questioning"[107] by deeming that "any suggestion in a newspaper or magazine that the era between 1917 and 1991 had some redeeming qualities was unacceptable."[108] In Mongolia after the election of the liberal Democratic Party in 2012, Lenin's statue in front of the Ulaanbaatar Hotel was removed and sold to a private investor and relocated to a five-star hotel in a national park; in 2013, the Lenin Museum was converted into the Central Museum for Mongolian Dinosaurs. In 2011, in Khujang, Tajikistan, the largest Lenin statue in Central Asia was toppled. In most of these cases, Lenin has been replaced with statues of *nationalist heroes* supporting the ethnographer Kristen Ghodsee's observation that "anticommunism legitimates resurgent nationalisms."[109] Ghodsee dates the resurgence of anticommunism to the 2008 global financial crisis, as people begin to seriously consider the need for alternatives to capitalism. Lenin needs to be continually killed as a reminder that there can be life outside of capitalism.

In Žižek's interpretation of Trotsky's dream, in which Lenin unaware that he was already dead pays a visit to Trotsky: "There is, however, another sense in which Lenin is still alive: he is insofar as he embodies what Badiou calls the 'eternal idea' of universal emancipation, the immortal striving for justice that no insults or catastrophes will manage to kill off."[110] No matter how many synthetic fluids are drained from and injected into Lenin's embalmed corpse, its "spectral flesh" is a congealed index of an international and universalist dimension pulsating with collective self-creation that is bereft in post-socialist liberal democracy.[111]

This is not to evince a nostalgia for Lenin but for the frozen revolutionary potentials of 1917 and 1989: the missed historical chance to invent new forms of democracy from the collapse of the moribund structures of state socialism and the failure of imagination and nerve to democratize the state and economy.

4. DIALECTICAL (RE)TURNS

We are left with a liberal democratic state power that is inaccessible to the people.[112] The status of being a citizen in a democracy may (depending on one's skin color) afford constitutional rights and protections against arbitrary violence but it does not translate into the exercise of power. The difference between parliamentary democracy and authoritarianism is not to be found in the exercise of sovereign power—in neither case do the people rule—but in the system of legal and institutional constraints placed on the state. The reason for today's crisis is not the loss of democracy but the damage to its aura, which has revealed the state as cold, indifferent, monstrous.

The conceptual and discursive separation of democracy from the state enables a mystification of how power operates. The state must "get out of the way" for democracy to flourish. This leads to the incoherent position that democracy exists in an inverse proportion with state power—the *less* state power, the *more* democracy—whereas precisely the opposite is the case. The idealization of democracy and demonization of the state means that we are stuck, like the victims of Pompeii, forever in a posture of resistance, cringing as the shit rains down on us. Generations have been trained to think and write according to a grammar of resistance, imprinting on an unconscious level a taboo against reflecting on how to transform state power.

The erasure of Lenin from political theory speaks volumes on the desire to resist rather than revolutionize. This is not to argue that Lenin's texts contain ready-made solutions that would make sense in today's circumstances but that he offers an unsurpassed diagnostic of the relationship between parliamentary democracy and the state and the need to dialectically and qualitatively transform them.

Lenin's argument in *The State and Revolution* that parliaments function as "talking shops" whereas "the real business of 'state' is performed behind the scenes" casts light on what I have been referring to as the separation of parliamentary democracy and the state.[113] In Lenin's account, the primary domain of parliaments is public discourse and liturgy. Central to Lenin's argument is Marx's distinction between "talking shops" which are a screen for class rule and "working bodies" which have to "execute their own laws . . . test the results achieved in reality, and to account directly to their constituents."[114] Lenin develops this idea by polemically targeting the divergence of representation from reality enabled by the parliamentary form. Lenin cites the example of women's suffrage, writing on November 6, 1919, in *Pravda* that "bourgeois democracy is a democracy of pompous phrases, solemn words, exuberant promises and the high-sounding slogans of freedom and equality. But, in fact, it screens the non-freedom and inferiority of women, the non-freedom and inferiority of the toilers and exploited."[115] At that time in the

United States, the Nineteenth Amendment granting women the right to vote was still a year from being ratified (Wyoming Territory granted women the right to vote as early as 1869 before it was incorporated into the Union; however, other states such as Mississippi ratified the Nineteenth Amendment only as late as 1984);[116] in the developed democracy of France, it would arrive in 1944, and in Switzerland in 1971. Lenin's point is not that words are meaningless or that liberal democracies are immune to change but that progress is the result of extra-parliamentary struggles and social movements putting pressure on the government.

In a letter dated August 15, 1920, to Australian Communists who boycotted elections, Lenin urges them that as long as workers have "confidence" in parliaments, Communists are "duty-bound" to participate in them and use these "rostrums of deception" to "unmask" their functioning and spread the communist message.[117] Although Lenin encourages comrades to use the parliamentary form against itself, he does not believe that holding seats in parliament translates into actual political power, let alone democracy. In the ideal case scenario when a parliamentary body is representative of the will of the people, it will run up against an internal limit, which separates it from state power. Despite electoral victory, sovereign power continues to remain elsewhere, which is a formula for political disillusionment. This point is confirmed by numerous examples of "socialist" governments that once elected have had no other "option" than to submit to financial discipline and "act like a state," the Syriza government in Greece being the latest casualty.

From these experiences, it requires only a short step to draw the conclusion that state power extinguishes any flickers of democracy. Lenin opposes this move insisting on the need for a dialectical reinvention of both democracy and the state. Although anachronistic and unsettling to contemporary ears, what Lenin calls the "dictatorship of the proletariat" was intended to reconfigure the state apparatus and usher in an "immense expansion of democracy, which *for the first time* becomes democracy for the poor, democracy for the people, and not democracy for the money-bags."[118] For Lenin, the *democratization of the state* requires a simultaneous *transformation of democracy*—one cannot exist without the other. "We cannot imagine democracy, even parliamentary democracy, without representative institutions, but we can and *must* imagine democracy without parliamentarism."[119] Without such a dialectical transformation, we will remain forever stuck in the uninhabitable non-space between the state and democracy.

In *"Left-Wing" Communism: An Infantile Disorder*, Lenin posits a transitional temporality in which parliaments are "'historically obsolete' from the standpoint of *world history*" but are not yet "politically obsolete."[120] The argument offered in this chapter confirms Lenin's intuition that the parliamentary form is already dead as a form of political transformation but still alive in people's beliefs and "politico-ideological attitudes." We are still living in the gray expanse between the democratic corpse and communist specter.

It should not be a surprise that the crisis of liberal democracy has elicited a militarized policing of its borders. It is not only racialized and "excess" bodies[121] that it is trying to keep out but also spirits, to which it responds: "Quick, a vault to which one keeps the keys!"[122]

The gate is once again coming unhinged, as the dialectical screw, with uncanny familiarity, returns to where we began—the global crisis of parliamentary democracy.

NOTES

1. Nikita Vladimirov, "Cornell Students Host 'Cry in' after Trump Victory," *The Hill*, November 10, 2016, https://thehill.com/blogs/ballot-box/presidential-races/305526-cornell-students-host-cry-in-after-trump-victory; Melissa Korn and Douglas Belkin, "Colleges Try to Comfort Students Upset by Trump Victory," *The Wall Street Journal*, November 9, 2016, https://blogs.wsj.com/washwire/2016/11/09/colleges-try-to-comfort-students-upset-by-trump-victory/; naturally, *Fox News* had their own patronizing take: Brook Singman, "Coddling Campus Crybabies: Students Take Up Toddler Therapy after Trump Win," *Fox News*, November 17, 2016.

2. This, of course, disavows the fact that Trump is the product of a world that should be familiar to anyone who has spent time in the United States and has continued many of the policies of his predecessors, albeit in an "unpresidential" style. See China Miéville, "'One Thinge that Ouerthroweth All that Were Graunted before': On Being Presidential," *Salvage* October 5, 2017, http://salvage.zone/in-print/one-thinge-that-ouerthroweth-all-that-were-graunted-before-on-being-presidential/.

3. Larry Diamond, "The Global Crisis of Democracy," *The Wall Street Journal*, May 17, 2019. https://www.wsj.com/articles/the-global-crisis-of-democracy-11558105463; see Larry Diamond, *Ill Winds: Saving Democracy from Russian Rage, Chinese Ambition, and American Complacency* (New York: Penguin Press, 2019). Larry Diamond and Marc F. Plattner (eds.), *Democracy in Decline?* (Baltimore, MD: Johns Hopkins University Press, 2015).

4. Adam Przeworksi, *Crises of Democracy* (Cambridge: Cambridge University Press, 2019). Quote from endorsement by Mitchell A. Seligson.

5. "Democracy Is in Crisis around the World. Why?" *The Washington Post*, November 12, 2018, https://www.washingtonpost.com/opinions/global-opinions/democracy-is-in-crisis-around-the-world-why/2018/11/21/ccb6423c-ecf4-11e8-8679-934a2b33be52_story.html; Kenneth Rapoza, "Democracies in Crisis: Has the West Given Up on Democracy?" *Forbes*, January 9, 2019, https://www.forbes.com/sites/kenrapoza/2019/01/09/democracies-in-crisis-has-the-west-given-up-on-democracy/#23f53ac11242; John Feffer, "Democracy Faces a Global Crisis," *Counterpunch*, June 17, 2019, https://www.counterpunch.org/2019/06/17/democracy-faces-a-global-crisis/; for a conservative rebuttal, see Kyle Smith, "Our Democracy

Is Not in Crisis," *National Review*, July 23, 2019, https://www.nationalreview.com/2019/07/american-democracy-is-not-in-crisis/.

6. Hillary Clinton, "American Democracy Is in Crisis," *The Atlantic*, September 16, 2019, https://www.theatlantic.com/ideas/archive/2018/09/american-democracy-is-in-crisis/570394/; see also Devin Cole's coverage of Clinton's speech in Selma for CNN, March 3, 2019, https://www.cnn.com/2019/03/03/politics/hillary-clinton-selma-crisis-democracy/index.html.

7. Andreas Kalyvas, "Whose Crisis? Which Democracy? Notes on the Political Conjuncture," Paper delivered at the Radical Critical Theory Circle Workshop in Nisyros Greece, June 7–11, 2019.

8. Janet Roitman, *Anti-Crisis* (Durham, NC: Duke University Press, 2013).

9. Ibid., 22–31; see also Reinhart Koselleck, *Critique and Crises: Enlightenment and the Pathogenesis of Modern Society* (Cambridge, MA: MIT Press, reprint edition, 1998).

10. Steven Levitsky and Daniel Ziblatt, *How Democracies Die* (New York: Crown Publishing Group, 2018), p. 3.

11. Ibid., 68.

12. Ibid., 41.

13. Gustave Flaubert, quoted in Simon Leys, *The Hall of Uselessness: Collected Essays* (New York: New York Review of Books, 2011), p. 462. An intransigent critic of Maoist China, Leys's fondness for this quote is not surprising.

14. Jacques Rancière, *Hatred of Democracy*, translated by Steve Corcoran (London and New York: Verso, 2006), p. 4.

15. Wendy Brown, "We Are All Democrats Now . . . ," in: *Democracy in What State?* (New York: Columbia University Press, 2011), 44–45.

16. Ibid., 45.

17. Giorgio Agamben, *The Kingdom and the Glory: For a Theological Genealogy of Economy and Government*, translated by Lorenzo Chiesa (with Matteo Mandarini) (Stanford, CA: Stanford University Press, 2011), p. 255.

18. As Badiou puts it: "A democrat loves only a democrat. For the others, incomers from zones of famine and killing, the first order of business is papers, borders, detention camps, police surveillance, denial of family reunion. One must be 'integrated.' Into what? Into democracy, clearly." Alain Badiou, "The Democratic Emblem," in: William McCuaig (trans.), *Democracy in What State?* (New York: Columbia University Press, 2011), 7.

19. Étienne Balibar, *Citizenship*, translated by Thomas Scott-Railton (Cambridge: Polity Press, 2015), p. 124.

20. Badiou, "The Democratic Emblem," 7.

21. Samuel P. Huntington, "Democracy's Third Wave." *Journal of Democracy* 2.2 (Spring 1991): pp. 12–34.

22. Jacques Derrida, *Specters of Marx: The State of the Debt, the Work of Mourning and the New International*, translated by Peggy Kamuf (New York and London: Routledge, 1994).

23. Thomas Carothers, "The End of the Transition Paradigm." *Journal of Democracy* 13.1 (January 2002), pp. 5–21.

24. Kristen Ghodsee's short story "Post-Zyvarism: A Fable about Animals on a Farm" offers a vivid account of the liturgical dimensions of liberal democracy. The story takes place on a farm on the verge of post-socialist decollectivization and democratization, where excited sheep bleat the word "elections." After the first election, however, conditions on the farm begin to deteriorate: workers are laid off, privatization vouchers lose their value, crime skyrockets, and a shady decision is made to sell the collective farm to human buyers. "When the humans came to bulldoze the buildings and flatten the farmland, the sheep wandered around in a daze, bleating the word 'elections' to no one in particular." In Ghodsee's parable, democratization brought neither collective self-rule nor common prosperity, but only dispossession and disappointment. Still, it is given an aura through the mantra of "elections." Kristen Ghodsee, *Red Hangover: Legacies of Twentieth-Century Communism* (Durham, NC: Duke University Press, 2017), pp. 150–166.

25. Valerie Bunce, "The Political Economy of Postsocialism." *Slavic Review* 58.4 (Winter 1999): p. 757.

26. Katherine Verdery, *What Was Socialism, and What Comes Next?* (Princeton, NJ: Princeton University Press, 1996), pp. 10–11. See also Jean Comaroff and John L. Comaroff, "Theory from the South: Or, how Euro-America Is Evolving toward Africa." *Anthropological Forum* 22.2 (July 2012): pp. 113–131.

27. In the definition of Thomas Carothers, one of the core assumptions of the transition paradigm is that "any country moving *away* from dictatorial rule can be considered a country in transition *toward* democracy." Carothers, "The End of the Transition Paradigm," 6.

28. Yeganeh Torbati, "Kerry Hails Mongolia as 'Oasis of Democracy' in Tough Neighborhood," *Reuters*, June 4, 2016, https://www.reuters.com/article/us-usa-mongolia-idUSKCN0YR02T.

29. M. Steven Fish and Michael Seeberg, "The Secret Supports of Mongolian Democracy." *Journal of Democracy* 28.1 (January 2017): pp. 129–143.

30. On "democratic backsliding," see Nancy Bermeo, "On Democratic Backsliding." *Journal of Democracy* 27.1 (January 2016): pp. 5–19; David Waldner and Ellen Lust, "Unwelcome Change: Coming to Terms with Democratic Backsliding." *Annual Review of Political Science* 21 (May 2018): pp. 93–113; Yascha Mounk, *The People vs. Democracy: Why Our Freedom Is in Danger and How to Save it* (Cambridge, MA: Harvard University Press, 2019); Pippa Norris, "Is Western Democracy Backsliding? Diagnosing the Risks," *Harvard Kennedy School Faculty Research Working Paper Series*, March 2017; "Democracy in Retreat: Freedom in the World 2019," *Freedomhouse Report*, https://freedomhouse.org/report/freedom-world/freedom-world-2019/democracy-in-retreat; For a different approach, see Dan Slater, "Democratic Careening." *World Politics* 65, 4 (October 2013): pp. 729–763.

31. D. Jargalsaikhan, "We're Going through Democratic Backsliding," *Jargal DeFacto*, July 1, 2019, http://jargaldefacto.com/article/we-re-going-through-democratic-backsliding.

32. Justin Higginbottom, "Mongolian Martial Arts Champ Takes Page Out of Trump Playbook," *Ozy*, May 3, 2018, https://www.ozy.com/rising-stars/mongolian-martial-arts-champ-takes-page-out-of-trumps-playbook/85516.

33. Julian Dierkes and Mendee Jargalsaikhan, "Election 2017: Making Mongolia Great Again?" *The Diplomat*, June 20, 2017, https://thediplomat.com/2017/06/election-2017-making-mongolia-great-again/.

34. Franck Billé, *Sinophobia: Anxiety, Violence and the Making of Mongolian Identity* (Honolulu: University of Hawaii Press, 2014).

35. Levitsky and Ziblatt, *How Democracies Die*, 21.

36. Julian Dierkes, "Not the End of Democracy?" *Mongolia Focus blog*, April 19, 2019, https://blogs.ubc.ca/mongolia/2019/different-perspectives-judicial-appointments/.

37. Ibid.

38. Political analyst Sanchir Jargalsaikhan notes how it is mainly the Western media amplifying the sense of democracy in peril. He writes, "In the last few weeks, Western publications have been howling about Mongolia's perishing democracy" (*Süüliin kheden doloo khonogt Mongolyn ardchilal sönöj baigaa talaar gadny khevlel medeellüüd nileen ikh shuugiad avlaa*), skeptical of the claim of a return of the all-powerful "autocrats" (*daranguilagch*), instead viewing the present conjuncture as a moment of productive re-politicization. Sanchir Jargalsaikahn, "*Ardchilal ayuld orson uu*?!" ("Is Democracy in Danger?), *Medium*, April 20, 2019, https://medium.com/@sanchirjargalsaikhan/ардчилал-аюулд-орсон-уу-aedd93771385.

39. Anand Tumurtogo, "Mongolia's President Is Slicing Away Its Hard-Won Democracy," *Foreign Policy*, March 29, 2019, https://foreignpolicy.com/2019/03/29/mongolias-president-is-slicing-away-its-hard-won-democracy/.

40. Boldsaikhan Sambuu and Aubrey Menarndt, "Here's How Democracy Is Eroding in Mongolia," *The Washington Post*, April 3, 2019. https://www.washingtonpost.com/politics/2019/04/03/heres-how-democracy-is-eroding-mongolia/.

41. Matthew Campbell and Terrence Edwards, "Mongolia's President Is a Genghis Khan-Idolizing Trump of the Steppe," *Bloomberg Businessweek*, September 25, 2019, https://www.bloomberg.com/news/features/2019-09-26/mongolia-s-president-is-the-trump-of-east-asia.

42. *Mongold ardchilal ekhelsen tüükh* (*How Democracy Was Born in Mongolia*) published by the Zorig Foundation and International Republican Institute, Ulaanbaatar, 2018.

43. Christopher Kaplonski, *Truth, History, and Politics in Mongolia: The memory of heroes* (London: Routledge, 2014), p. 80.

44. Uradyn E Bulag, *Nationalism and Hybridity in Mongolia* (Oxford: Oxford University Press, 1998), p. 232.

45. David Sneath, *Mongolia Remade: Post-Socialist National Culture, Political Economy, and Cosmopolitics* (Amsterdam: Amsterdam University Press, 2018), p. 179.

46. *How Democracy Was Born in Mongolia*.

47. Branko Marcetic, "How Washington Hacked Mongolia's Democracy," *Jacobin*, November 2017, https://www.jacobinmag.com/2017/11/mongolia-elections-mccain-international-republican-institute.

48. Sneath, *Mongolia Remade*, 132.

49. Verena Fritz, "Mongolia: Dependent Democratization." *Journal of Communist Studies and Transition Politics* 18.4 (2002): pp. 75–100.

50. Morris Rossabi, "Mongolia: Transmogrification of a Communist Party." *Pacific Affairs* 82.2 (Summer 2009): pp. 231–250.

51. Morris Rossabi, *Modern Mongolia: From Khans to Commissars to Capitalists* (Berkeley: University of California Press, 2005), p. 82.

52. John Gould, *The Politics of Privatization: Wealth and Power in Postcommunist Europe* (Boulder, CO: Lynne Rienner, 2011), p. 32.

53. "After 1989, any government or party that talked convincingly of privatization increased its likely access to aid, credits, and investment, especially from international organizations like the World Bank and International Monetary Fund." Verdery, *What Was Socialism, and What Comes Next?* 210.

54. David Harvey, *A Brief History of Neoliberalism* (Oxford: Oxford University Press, 2007).

55. Morton Axel Pedersen, *Not Quite Shamans: Spirit Worlds and Political Lives in Northern Mongolia* (Ithaca, NY: Cornell University Press, 2011), p. 44. See also Manduhai Buyandelger, *Tragic Spirits: Shamanism, Memory, and Gender in Contemporary Mongolia* (Chicago, IL: University of Chicago Press, 2013); Anya Bernstein, *Religious Bodies Politic: Rituals of Sovereignty in Buryat Buddhism* (Chicago, IL: University of Chicago Press, 2013); Nicholas Thomas and Caroline Humphrey (eds.), *Shamanism, History and the State* (Ann Arbor: University of Michigan Press, 1996); Caroline Humphrey, "Shamans in the City." *Anthropology Today* 15.3 (June 1999): pp. 3–10.

56. Pedersen, *Not Quite Shamans*, 57.

57. Ibid., 67.

58. Ibid., 71.

59. Ibid., 5.

60. Sneath, *Mongolia Remade*, 178.

61. Rossabi, *Modern Mongolia*, 160–161.

62. Iveta Silova, "Varieties of Educational Transformation: The Post-Socialist States of Central/Southeastern Europe and the Former Soviet Union," in: Robert Cowen and Andreas M. Kazamias (eds.), *International Handbook of Comparative Education* (Heidelberg, Germany, the Netherlands: Springer, 2009), pp. 295–320.

63. Sneath, *Mongolia Remade*, 88.

64. Rebekah Plueckhahn and Dulam Bumochir, "Capitalism in Mongolia—Ideology, Practice and Ambiguity." *Central Asian Survey* 37.3 (2018): p. 346.

65. Sneath, *Mongolia Remade*, 72.

66. Verdery, *What Was Socialism, and What Comes Next?* 205. For a thought-provoking account of what comes after capitalism, see Jodi Dean, "Communism or Neo-Feudalism?" Paper presented at the Radical Critical Theory Workshop, Nisyros, Greece, June 7–11, 2019.

67. "Mongolia's resource economy gives rise to senses and experiences of precarity, in that it is fundamentally dependent on fluctuating commodity prices and speculation-fuelled foreign direct investment." Plueckhahn and Bumochir, "Capitalism in Mongolia," 353.

68. One of the economic survival strategies among Mongolians has been to engage in the dangerous work of illegal mining operations, earning them the

pejorative nickname of "ninjas." See Mette M. High, "Polluted Money, Polluted Wealth: Emerging Regimes of Value in the Mongolian Gold Rush." *American Ethnologist* 40.4 (2013): pp. 676–688; Andrew Rowat, "The Ninja Gold Miners of Mongolia," *The New York Times Magazine* photo essay, December 2, 2011, https://archive.nytimes.com/www.nytimes.com/interactive/2011/12/04/magazine/ninja-gold-miners-mongolia.html; Rebecca Empson, "Claiming Resources, Honouring Debts: Miners, Herders and the Land Masters of Mongolia," University of Oxford Podcast, April 29, 2014, http://podcasts.ox.ac.uk/claiming-resources-honouring-debts-miners-herders-and-land-masters-mongolia.

69. Sneath, *Mongolia Remade*, 127.
70. Interview with local resident, Ulaanbaatar, June 2018.
71. Rebekah Plueckhahn and Terbish Bayartsetseg, "Negotiation, Social Indebtedness, and the Making of Urban Economies in Ulaanbaatar." *Central Asian Survey* 37.3 (2018): pp. 436–456.
72. "Mongolia: New Poll Shows Declining Optimism, Continued Economic Concerns," International Republican Institute, March 22, 2017, https://www.iri.org/resource/mongolia-new-poll-shows-declining-optimism-continued-economic-concerns.
73. "*10 jil utaatai ingej 'temtssen', ür dün khaana baina?*" (Ten Years of Struggle Against Pollution: Where are the Results?) news.mn, December 18, 2018 https://news.mn/r/2061649/.
74. B. Bat-Enkh, "Death from Smog in Mongolia #HumanRights," December 2018, https://www.change.org/p/united-nations-death-from-smog-in-mongolia-humanrights.
75. Chisato Fukuda, *Breathing Uncertainty: Politics of Harm in Mongolia's Air Pollution Crisis*. Dissertation, University of Wisconsin–Madison, 2017.
76. Rebecca Empson, "Political Atmospheres in the Lead-up to the Parliamentary Elections, 2016," Emerging Subjects Blog (UCL), August 17, 2016, https://blogs.ucl.ac.uk/mongolian-economy/2016/08/17/political-atmospheres-in-the-lead-up-to-the-parliamentary-elections-2016/.
77. Christian Sorace and Sanchir Jargalsaikhan, "Lost in the Fog," *Jacobin*, January 29, 2019, https://jacobinmag.com/2019/01/mongolia-protests-corruption-pollution.
78. Julian Dierkes, "Party Implications of SME Fund Scandal," *Mongolia Focus Blog*, November 20, 2018, http://blogs.ubc.ca/mongolia/2018/political-parties-жду-implications/.
79. Interview, Ulaanbaatar, June 2018.
80. Interview, Ulaanbaatar, June 2018.
81. Empson, "Claiming Resources, Honouring Debts."
82. See: Seymour Martin Lipset, "Some Social Requisites of Democracy: Economic Development and Political Legitimacy." *The American Political Science Review* 53.1 (March 1959): pp. 69–105; Gabriel Almond, "Capitalism and Democracy." *PS: Political Science and Politics* 24.3 (September 1991): pp. 467–474.
83. Hito Steyel, *Duty Free Art: Art in the Age of Planetary* Civil War (London and New York, Verso 2019), p. 172.

84. Slavoj Žižek, "Repeating Lenin," https://www.marxists.org/reference/subject/philosophy/works/ot/zizek1.htm.

85. Julian Dierkes, "Blank Ballots as Protest," *Mongolia Focus* Blog, June 17, 2017, https://blogs.ubc.ca/mongolia/2017/voting-but-not-voting-empty-ballot/; Terrence Edwards, "Amid Apathy, Mongolians Vote Again to Choose New President," *Reuters*, July 6, 2017, https://www.reuters.com/article/us-mongolia-election/amid-apathy-mongolians-vote-again-to-choose-new-president-idUSKBN19R38M.

86. Julian Dierkes, "The Mechanics of a Blank Ballot," *Mongolia Focus* Blog, July 4, 2017, https://blogs.ubc.ca/mongolia/2017/цагаан-сонголт/.

87. Jose Saramago, *Seeing*, translator Margaret Jull Costa (New York: Harvest Books, 2007).

88. Ursula K. LeGuin, "The Plague of Blank Ballots," *The Guardian*, April 15, 2006, https://www.theguardian.com/books/2006/apr/15/featuresreviews.guardianreview16.

89. In August 2016, I attended a lecture in Ulaanbaatar by a former government minister, which contained a litany of complaints about the inefficiency of Mongolian democracy. During the Q&A, I asked him (not intending to be sarcastic): "If you are so clearly dissatisfied with parliamentary democracy, why not try something else?" Infuriated, his response was as follows: "Democracy is a *national security issue*. If we lose our democratic status, we lose support from the US, Europe, Japan, international organizations, and the funding and protection that comes with," implying that Mongolian would be left to fend for itself against China and Russia. The symptomatic point raised by this exchange is how democratic procedures and institutions are abstracted from their surroundings and results. For the speaker, democracy was both *not working* and *absolutely necessary*. These remarks indicate that democracy has "no positive support of its own" but to translate it into Lacanian terminology is *the signifier which represents the subject for another signifier*. Democracy is the recognition of democratic status by other democracies and not determined by the actual distribution and practice of power (as long as the United States regards a country as a democracy, it is a democracy; and conversely, even if a country is democratic, it does not count as a democracy if the United States withholds its recognition—necessary to this operation is the untouchable status of the United States as the guarantor of democracy). The logic of this speech is also repeated in U.S. discourse toward Mongolia. As tensions between the United States and China increase, Mongolia's democracy has started to be viewed as a strategic asset to the United States. In a recent op-ed Michael Green, a former senior National Security Council official in the George W. Bush administration, writes: "Washington has a stake in Mongolia's sovereign democracy surviving Chinese pressure." Michael Green, "The United States Should Help Mongolia Stand Up to China," *Foreign Policy*, September 26, 2019, https://foreignpolicy.com/2019/09/26/the-united-states-should-help-mongolia-stand-up-to-china/.

90. *How Democracy Was Born in Mongolia*.

91. During the keynote delivered by a foreign democracy expert, my friend remarked that the repetitious praise of democracy reminded him of Soviet-style propaganda and CNN media coverage.

92. Ilya Budraitskis, "The Eternal Hunt for the Red Man," *e-flux journal* #70, February 2016, https://www.e-flux.com/journal/70/60563/the-eternal-hunt-for-the-red-man/.

93. Ibid.

94. L. Munkh-Erdene, "*Ulysn Ikh Khural bas Zövlölt Zasaglal*" ("The Great State Khural and Soviet Governance"), December 24, 2018, https://www.n24.mn/a/1305.

95. Interview, Ulaanbaatar, January 2017.

96. D. Jargalsaikhan, "Harvard Kennedy School: Lessons from the Democratic Transition in Mongolia: 25 Years after Revolution," April 4, 2018, http://jargaldefacto.com/article/harvard-kennedy-school-lessons-from-the-democratic-transition-in-mongolia-25-years-after-revolution.

97. Bolor Erdene, "*Kommuninizmoos tom ayuld*" ("To the Larger Danger than Communism"), July 1, 2019, https://www.trends.mn/n/9024.

98. Jodi Dean, *The Communist Horizon* (London: Verso, 2012).

99. Karl Marx and Frederick Engels, *The Communist Manifesto: A Modern Edition* (London and New York: Verso, 2012).

100. Ibid.

101. Claude Lefort, *Complications: Communism and the Dilemmas of Democracy*, translated by Julian Bourg (New York: Columbia University Press, 2007).

102. Derrida, *Specters of Marx*.

103. Ibid., 111.

104. Ibid., 70–71.

105. Ibid., 64.

106. Ken Jowitt, *New World Disorder: The Leninist Extinction* (Berkeley: University of California Press, 1992).

107. Ghodsee, *Red Hangover*, 129.

108. Ibid., 130.

109. Ibid., 134. Making a similar argument, Owen Hatherly observes: "In Ukraine, there is a near-identical relation between those who are most committed to erasing Lenin statues and those who are most intent on raising those of Stepan Bandera" who was a Ukranian nationalist as well as Nazi collaborator. Owen Hatherly, "On the Heritage of Totalitarianism," *New Socialist*, May 4, 2018, https://newsocialist.org.uk/on-heritage-totalitarianism/.

110. Slavoj Žižek, *Absolute Recoil: Towards a New Foundation of Dialectical Materialism* (London and New York: Verso, 2014), p. 214.

111. Eric L. Santner, *The Weight of All Flesh: On the Subject-Matter of Political Economy* (Oxford: Oxford University Press, 2016). See also Alexei Yurchak, "Bodies of Lenin: The Hidden Science of Communist Sovereignty," *Representations* 129 (Winter 2015).

112. Artemy Magun, chapter 10 of the present book, "*Civitas Paradoxa* or: A Dialectical Theory of the State."

113. Vladimir Lenin, *The State and Revolution*, in: Robert C. Tucker (ed.), *The Lenin Anthology* (New York: W. W. Norton & Company, 1975), p. 343.

114. Ibid.

115. Vladimir Lenin, "Soviet Power and the Status of Women," *Pravda* No. 249, November 6, 1919, https://www.marxists.org/archive/lenin/works/1919/nov/06.htm.

116. It is important also to note the racism rampant in suffragette movement, which was epitomized in Susan B. Anthony statement: "I will cut off this right arm of mine before I will ask for the ballot for the Negro and not for the woman." I owe

this point to Heidi Lewis. See Evette Dionne, "Women's Suffrage Leaders Left Out Black Women," *Teen Vogue*, August 18, 2017, https://www.teenvogue.com/story/womens-suffrage-leaders-left-out-black-women; Brent Staples, "When the Suffrage Movement Sold Out to White Supremacy," *The New York Times*, February 2, 2019, https://www.nytimes.com/2019/02/02/opinion/sunday/women-voting-19th-amendment-white-supremacy.html?module=inline.

117. Vladimir Lenin, "Letter to the Austrian Communists," August 15, 1920, published in Gerrman in *Die Rote Fahne* (Vienna) No. 396, https://www.marxists.org/archive/lenin/works/1920/aug/15.htm.

118. Lenin, *The State and Revolution*, 373.

119. Ibid., 344.

120. Vladimir Lenin, "'Left-Wing' Communism: An Infantile Disorder," in: Robert C. Tucker (ed.), *The Lenin Anthology* (New York: W. W. Norton & Company, 1975), p. 579.

121. Achille Mbembe, *Necro-Politics*, translates by Steven Corcoran (Durham, NC: Duke University Press, 2019), p. 12.

122. Derrida, *Specters of Marx*, 120.

IV

EX PLURIBUS UNUM

Chapter 10

Civitas Paradoxa or a Dialectical Theory of State

Artemy Magun

1. INTRODUCTION

The state invites one to use statist language when describing it. Hence the predominance of technical, bureaucratic, and positivist language in the contemporary discussions of state. In many political cultures outside liberalism, the state has also presented itself as an object of a secular cult, a "myth" (in the parlance of Cassirer). In contrast to both ways of ideological self-presentation, here I will offer a *philosophical* and dialectical perspective, which takes state for more than what it would like itself to be.

Today, there are four main aporetic oppositions inside the concept of state.

The first is the tension between the state as an authoritarian vertical structure of power, and the democratic, republican context, which accompanied the Modern state since the moment of its emergence. Of course, it is the *absolutist* state that subsequently got democratized. But the impersonality of state did from the start allow for a republican interpretation. The late modern state, with its representative role, national identity, and its division between the elected and unelected officials, is unthinkable without the appeal to popular sovereignty. The top-down and the bottom-up logics coexist, but, when taken in absolute terms, pose a contradiction. The inability to honestly account for the top-down constitutive logic makes a lay observer ideologically blinded and generates the false "technical" appearance of state.

The second is the opposition between the state as a system of technical and instrumental governance and the state as *polity*. As we have seen in the Introduction chapter, scholars usually distinguish the state from polity but do not offer any alternative concept, so that the place of a generic concept of polity remains vacant and the common meaning of state as polity repressed. In truth, however, this ambivalence is a sign of a genuine contradiction between the state as a political unity of a people and the state as an apparatus that holds it together through force and command. The need for force and machine-like mechanisms means that the unity would not hold by itself: the "despotic state" (to use Michael Mann's term) is a reaction to the internal divisions of the people, but it also reproduces and aggravates these divisions. Marx and his followers saw this well, but it is important to remember that the state as "the executive committee of the bourgeoisie" is a critical notion that is only thinkable, in Marx, against the horizon of Hegel's State being "God's march on Earth."

The third opposition is that of form and content. State is a form of political organization, and it spreads and promotes liberalism. The essence of state as political power is its abstract character: an official never acts here in his or her individual, personal function. "Nation," often used as a synonym of state as a unit, is, in liberal democratic states, purified of any substantive meaning of ethnicity, and the "people" is only conceived as a totality of citizens, not in the old terms as a poorer strata of society. Such large-scale effort of formalization is doubtlessly emancipatory, but it is increasingly put into doubt by the social movements from far right and far left, which acquire a nomination of "populism," which sounds strange in a nominally democratic country. Formalism also goes against the *personification* of politics, which is pervasive in our age of electronic and digital media but does not really fit the formal idea of state power as impersonal bureaucracy.

The fourth and final opposition is that between the local and the global. Being formal and abstract, a constitutional state does not have almost anything specific to a particular time and space. Constitutions differ in details, but they all impose on a society a universal form. There is no reason then, why this state should remain bound to a nation or a region. A state worthy of its notion should be a world state. But such state does not exist; states are essentially plural and sovereign, as they emerged as a reaction to the universalist ambitions of the empire and the Church in the Middle Ages. This creates a tension because, on the one hand, the form of reason, which any state is, implies imperial ambitions and allows, in principle, to infinitely expand its scope or accept an infinite number of immigrants. On the other hand, the state, in its formal, constitutionalist and legalist features, is perceived, from inside the society, as a globalist imperialist agent imposing itself on the specific substance of people and their situations.

This is a very brief statement of what will be unraveled below in a more systematic fashion. Of course, the dialectical theory of state is nothing new: one such theory was proposed by Hegel early on in the history of the notion. Hegel's theory, which I will gloss below in more detail, points at some of the oppositions I have delineated, such as the tension between the formal and the substantive, and the contradiction between unity ("state") and division ("civil society"), which for him generates the tension between technical "understanding" and reflexive "reason." However, Hegel lives before the epoch of the democratization of state and therefore does not see the dialectic related to this. For the same reason he sees state as a *resolution* of oppositions rather than their problematic knot, knowing yet not that it would be historically torn, as it is now, between imperial peace and permanent revolution. Therefore, if the state is indeed the site where we have to resolve problems, its current form and idea should be transformed in the *future*. This, in turn, signifies that the dialectic, being an efficient instrument of criticism, contains in its form the contours of an *ideal*. The state is implicitly dialectical, but this means that it is only redeemable if dialectic becomes the very form of its constitution: I suggest a sketch of such dialectical constitution in the conclusion of this chapter. Now however, I start with a methodological, philosophical exposition of dialectics—not a very common or a very clear method to use in today's social theory, which is why it requires explanation.

2. THE DIALECTICAL APPROACH TO THE STATE

2.1. Dialectics What

It is relatively normal even today, after a general dismissal of dialectic in the mainstream, the social sciences, to invoke "dialectic" with regard to the notion of state. Thus, several authors[1] speak, in passing, of the dialectical relations between state and civil society. Benjamin Barber[2] sees a dialectical relation between participatory and representative democracy. Richard Sakwa speaks of a "dialectic of international adaptation and exceptionalism" in Russian foreign policy.[3] None of these authors, however, elaborates on these references to dialectic: they give the impression that this is the name of an all-too-familiar type of relationship, mostly involving the mutual determination of correlative phenomena. This is strange, given that dialectic is not an accepted type of reasoning in Anglo-American academia and more importantly, has not been often elaborated since the times of Bradley and Greene, with a notable but isolated exception of Roy Bhaskar and his school (who shared the orthodox Marxist dismissal of state, in favor of *social* transformative praxis), and of the literary theorists like Fredric Jameson. This, in turn, threatens with trivialization of dialectic where it is mentioned in passing. Dialectic is not just a coincidence or a correlation of polar opposites. It is a relationship in flux, which sets free the element of negativity, allows for a game of cheat and bluff, and ultimately collapses in—sometimes—moving to a higher level.

Dialectic is a methodology that obtained its name in the early nineteenth century from Schelling and Hegel. The idea of a gradual development of concepts that show *internal* contradictions and thus have to be abandoned in favor of other, more complex ones, and the critique of Kant's criticism, which leads one to pose a contradictory *identity* between the concept and the reality it describes, have as of then been called "dialectic." Yet Hegel did not invent the method itself, he just gave it a name. The method derives from Plato and his disciples, the Neoplatonists. In *Parmenides*,[4] Plato had already, long before Hegel, built a scale of internally contradictory concepts, which pass from the purely intellectual "one" to material existence.

Dialectics, understood as a method of inquiry, is more productive than common sense reasoning or the testing of hypotheses. Yet this method should be thought through: much time has passed since Hegel and his dialectical system, not to speak of Plato.

For our purposes, dialectics turns its somewhat unusual head. What strikes us as counterintuitive and paradoxical in the current state of the state is not only contradiction and opposition but, first of all, tautology and identity. States run into state-like units and reflect themselves within them. Negativity and opposition are only the next steps in the logical development of reflection. All great authors, particularly Hegel and early Schelling, agreed on the priority of identity in dialectics. "Negative" dialectic is a twentieth-century modernist interpretation. I will briefly spell out the dialectical method as I see it for practical purposes.

2.1.1. Guideline 1

Methodologically, any dialectical investigation starts with taking seriously the *principles* that characterize a certain historical situation. Usually, we qualify these principles by space and time or endow them with an accidental existence, and therefore remain blind to contradictions. But when we take a principle absolutely, we see that it coexists with one that is opposed to it. For example, my chapter shows that democracy, taken seriously, contradicts the idea of the state. Moreover, if we take democracy absolutely, we see that it is a principle that risks completely undermining the current liberal democratic state: international democracy would have destroyed the nation-state, and economic democracy would have destroyed capitalism, so an actually democratic polity would have looked entirely different to the current one. This does not mean that we necessarily need to implement this absolute democracy, at least in politics: this would probably lead to a state of permanent self-dissolution. But it does mean that we have to see the insistent potential of the democratic notion, and its contradiction with the state apparatus that is supposed to embody it.

2.1.2. Guideline 2

The dialectical method discerns the underlying *unity* and *identity* of all entities, particularly those that are supposed to be parts or substructures of each other. The reason why reality contradicts itself, and why contradictions turn into contraries, is, paradoxically, its excessive *unity*. In Hegel, master and bondsman positions are contradictory and contrary because *both* are characteristic of humans who can potentially be both masters and slaves. State and civil society are contradictory because civil society is a *"state* of need and understanding," a false pretender to the universal position of the state. An idea or substance, if taken absolutely, redoubles in reality, and this is the reason why it contradicts itself as two versions of the same absolute.

2.1.3. Guideline 3

The other side of this unity is the presumption of *totality*. We have to consider together phenomena which are discrepant and seemingly unrelated but that contradict each other on the level of principles and projects. For example, progress in Western countries must be taken in conjunction with the abyssal poverty of other regions, not as stages of temporal development but as structural complementaries. The same is true of the technological instrumentalization of humans and the modern emancipation of individuals: they happen simultaneously and the one is not a mere negative default of the other.

2.1.4. Guideline 4

The most familiar presumption of dialectic is the contradictory nature of reality from which there follows the precept of uncovering contradictions at each step of conceptualization. Internal *contradiction*, which first appears as a confusion or inconsistency, develops into an opposition between *contraries*. There emerge two contrary principles through which reality begins to openly contradict *itself*. *Reflection* converts mere differences and disjunctions into reciprocally defined and mutually polemical *contraries*, which are defined by a negativity, negative energy, and may lead to war or apathetic decay. However, it is possible to *recognize* the tension and elaborate a creative *synthesis* between internal elements. A dialectical synthesis usually appears as a distribution of contradictory principles into *content* and *form*. For instance, according to Kojève, the modern state aspires to synthesize and reconcile the emancipatory and enslaving elements of capitalist society: a subservient worker appears in the dignitary form of *citizen*.

2.1.5. Guideline 5

The fifth guideline of dialectic is *tolerance* for wrong or contradictory statements, which are never merely mistaken but always contain a real 'moment' of contradictory but real phenomena, an existing subjective perspective. All historical phenomena are formed through a series of sublations (*Aufhebungen*): negativity, which is an active and destructive force of history, never destroys anything completely and leaves behind the hard results, or the indestructible remainders, of the *negation of negation*. Thus, the Hegelian dialectical state does not claim to dissolve the family, which it supersedes, but preserves it within its structure. The same is true for the market economy, and the like.

2.1.6. Guideline 6

Dialectics is also a critique of ideological *false consciousness*. The latter can in turn appear in two forms:

(a) If a complex phenomenon is viewed and presented *unilaterally*, without regard for the implicit point of reference to which the official stance polemically refers, without recognizing the negativity that is required to keep seemingly external or peripheral issues at bay. For instance, "democracy" is an ideological notion, as it dissimulates the full definition of the contemporary regime as a *liberal constitutionalist oligarchic republic with an inclusive and engaging social policy that also gives space to the protest voice of self-organized citizen groups*. Democracy is a part of this regime, but it is its negative part, which ideologically stands for the whole and appears as its positive defining feature.
(b) Unilateral ideologies can also allow for a cynical play on the two opposite poles of a phenomenon: when needed (for fiscal discipline), we emphasize the ascetic, and when needed (for advertising), the hedonistic principles of capitalism, without envisioning their complex unity. Hegel illustrates this dialectical ambiguity speaking of arithmetic: when necessary, a positive number is taken in the neutral sense of positivity ($-x \times y = -xy$), and when necessary, positive sign $+$ is taken as correlative to the negative sign, minus ($-a + a = 0$):[5] thus, taken as a closed region of mathematics, arithmetic is organized as ideologically as politics. In political science, it is the notions of state and democracy that play a similar role. When we need, the state is a hierarchy of sedentary mafia responsible for physical violence, and when we need otherwise, it becomes a neutral apparatus of impersonal power indispensable for the "rule of law." "Democracy" is not just officially used as a shortcut description of the reigning regime but is also presented, simultaneously and depending on one's need, as a rule of passive populace by competitive elites *and* as a normative model of popular power the (authoritarian/autocratic) departures from which are considered as anomalous.

2.1.7. Guideline 7

Dialectics is not only a method to discover things nor is it a realistic objective description of nature, Soviet style, but it is also a *normative* doctrine relevant to social practice. A dialectician is critical of unilateral judgments and tolerant of false and deniable phenomena; therefore he or she represents not just a method but also an *ideal*: ideal of a strained structure, of a self-dividing identity, and of a unity in conflict. This will allow me further to speak of a dialectical state (or *"civitas paradoxa"*).

2.2. Dialectical Theories of State

This is not the place to give a detailed historico-philosophical overview of the dialectics of state. I will briefly evoke the key theories, which can give us insight today. It is not by chance that most of them come from Germany. The German culture gave the state its most abstract and universal meaning, but the very conjunction of bureaucracy and police with the ideas of reason and the good constituted a problem, which dialectical philosophy attempted to resolve.

Here, closer to the German tradition, I will define "state" not in the narrow terms of modern impersonal power, but more generally as a system of abstract and reflexive power that acts through the intermediary of officials and that autonomizes itself from the everyday activities of "society." Political philosophy has since its inception given rational and ontological theories for why and how such an institution (polity, *civitas*, republic, state) can exist.

The state is a polity that is concentrated and thus distinct from the material association of people for mutual interest. It is not just a human community as such, but a human community that is distinct from itself. Its rule is therefore reflexive, abstract, and formal. It is a society that rules itself via a system of representation or, from an idealist point of view, it is a sovereign collective subject that rules and owns its plural, dispersed, individualized body of existences and activities. It was Hegel who first elaborated this distinction conceptually, and after him it was accepted by most writers on the state (including those who chastised the "totalitarian" state for absorbing society into itself). Marx, by turning Hegel on his head, insisted, on the contrary, that it was society that was prior to the state, but he agreed that the cleavage between the two was definitive for the current, bourgeois state.

Long before Hegel, the intuition of the double character of the human community had been present in the history of political thought. Plato starts his reconstruction of the polity with a "city of sows," an association created for material needs, which is then superseded by the portrait of a *"Kallipolis,"* which includes the monetary economy and war.[6] Aristotle, for his part, draws the line between family-like "communities" and other groups based on material interests, and the polity, whose task is to provide the "good life."[7] Liberals such as Locke define the state ("government," in his parlance) as an outgrowth of society ("state of nature"), which had been united already before the emergence of government through social contract.[8] What Hegel adds is that civil society is already an unaccomplished state (state of need and understanding), which suffers from internal contradictions and requires that the actual state, above it, continue to exist.[9] The state rules over preorganized, organic groups, which may claim a universality for themselves. Alain Badiou expresses this with a mathematical formula: he defines the state as the "set of all subsets" for a given set: it is a metastructure that can recognize and coordinate only elements that have already been counted, united, and constituted.[10]

The dominant language to describe the polity was for a long time the Aristotelian one. In it, the state is defined normatively, teleologically, and structurally. The state is not a family and thus not an economic association. In medieval Aristotelianism, most prominently in Thomas Aquinas, it was emphasized that the polity (republic) was based on natural and divine law, was a part of a system of analogies (universe/state/family, God/king/father), and required certain virtues from its rulers. Aristotle allowed for some vaguely dialectical elements, for example his insistence on alternating the roles of ruler and ruled, but the general approach was rather structuralist.

2.2.1. From Plato to Spinoza

Dialectics was, in contrast, developed by Plato and in the Neoplatonic tradition. Plato's own allegorical account of the "just" polity is structural (kings, guardians, artisans). But there is a negativity in this order, which is embodied in the *"thymos"*: a complex word signifying spiritedness, anger, intuition, and desire for recognition. The guardians need this affect to be able to suppress material interests to the benefit of higher goals, and to divide outside subjects into friends and enemies. Negativity also surfaces in Plato's portrait of democracy, which is presented as a "many-colored" chaos, the revolt of lowly desires.[11]

The Neoplatonists pursued a dialectical vision of the world, but they rarely took the sociopolitical sphere seriously, and where they did, produced idealistic apologies of virtuous monarchy. The situation changes in the Renaissance period, where the Neoplatonists insist on a continuous unity of the world (nature, man, God) and therefore on the rehabilitation of matter and of the common folk as lower steps to perfection.

In the seventeenth century, Thomas Hobbes, a nominalist Aristotelian and a Cartesian, actually describes state as the dialectical outcome of the untenable antagonisms that afflict human society.[12] By nature, society is not possible at all, as humans are naturally opposed to one another. Only the state ("commonwealth," as Hobbes calls it) retrospectively provides the conditions and definitions under which a social consensus becomes possible. Hobbes does not use the words "society" or "dialectical." But he does oppose the new polity to the state of nature and hints that the "Leviathan" would further reproduce those conditions—"nasty, brutish, and short"—wherever it does not have full control and that it produces them retrospectively.

The negative, materialist quasi-dialectics of Hobbes and some other Cartesians stands in contrast with the affirmative dialectics of the Neoplatonist humanists. Here, the internal inconsistency of the lower levels of being does not serve to discredit them: thus the Hobbesian competition of individuals for glory and power would only raise the stakes of glory and power as embodied, on a higher level, in a monarch and in God.

As I mentioned, "dialectics" does not necessarily mean a full-fledged theory of contradiction and negativity. It starts with the *paradoxes* that emerge from unity and identity, from the reduplication of the world that emerges whenever one divides it into truth and appearance. The Neoplatonic school (which for a period became dominant and then remained influential throughout modernity) usually emphasized this overflow of unity more than the *via negativa*. Nicholas of Cusa, arguably the greatest Neoplatonist philosopher of the Renaissance, in his implicit polemic against Plato himself, called the animating principle of his dialectics the *"non-aliud,"* the "Not-Other."[13] Negation emerges but immediately annuls itself as subjects and ideas identify with each other: x is *nothing else but y*, God is nothing else but man, maximum is nothing else but the minimum, and the city is nothing other than its people. Nicholas, like many Italian Neoplatonists, combined a preference for monarchy with discernable democratic tendencies, as evident in his principled defense of Church conciliarism.[14] In the modern spirit, Neoplatonists used the Platonic ideas of justice to insist on a bottom-top emanation of power that we would call "democracy," even though in Cusanus, it takes the form of conciliarism, of the election of the monarch, and of rule by consent; in Leibniz, similarly, it takes the form of the electoral nature of monarchical power and of proto-federalism, and only in Spinoza, literally, does it take the form of "democracy." God's power is not monopolized but dissolved in the universe, so that everyone is its holder, even if perhaps only in microscopic quantities.

In the seventeenth century, Spinoza introduces the Neoplatonic way of thinking into Cartesian Aristotelianism. His doctrine of the overflowing *"potentia"* is the same in his ontology and in his political theory: the law of the land is simply the sum of everyone's actual powers, which allows them to act in concert. This theory uses a tautological paradox: everyone "has as much right as the power he possesses," and even if the state unites individual powers and returns them as rights, its formal right simply expresses the collective power and the factual balance of forces.[15] Why would one then have right and power as distinct notions? This is the same problem as in Spinoza's doctrine of *Deus sive natura*, or the identity of extension and idea. The case is actually an instance of Neoplatonic dialectic, or what I would call *affirmative dialectic*. The proclaimed identity of obviously distinct phenomena creates an implicit tension, which, in Spinoza's conceit, negatively affects the outdated, materially unfounded power of nobility, and the subject-sanctioned formal knowledge of the Cartesians.

In the context of the present study, Spinoza's holistic version of Neoplatonism anticipates the redoubled and redundant nature of the modern state that counts itself *twice*, as a material and formal unity. What Spinoza does not see is the potential for a *dialectical* twist, in which the seemingly formal and derivative nature of the state takes over its seemingly material productive forces, and itself becomes a material power, to compete with the merely economic actors who appear as naturally strong.

The formal/material duality outlined by Spinoza allowed Hegel and other nineteenth-century thinkers to inscribe the internal rupture of the state into the state proper, and into the "external" state of the so-called civil society. Today, we see a proliferation of isomorphic "states" *qua* civil unions: self-organizing movements, nongovernmental organizations (NGOs), business corporations, and the former bureaucratic state proper. Weber's monopoly of violence is insufficient to explain why the latter has a right to stand for all others. Today's concealment of the state derives from a confusion between the multiple levels of statehood in Spinoza's benevolent sense of maintaining a political unity. In the harmonious world of Neoplatonic optimism, the multiple states would act in concordance by shifting gears among each other. However, if we delve into the more dialectical and paradoxical method of Platonism, we have to see the internal inconsistency of any summarizing wholes: the *one*, Plato and Plotinus teach us, is transcendent of any alliance or coalition.

2.2.2. Leibniz

Famously, it was Leibniz who inverted Spinoza's theory by recentering it around the principle of the individual unit (monad): a principle of individuality and a center of agency, rather than a complex whole. Like Spinoza, Leibniz combined Neoplatonism with Aristotelian scholasticism, but in his case, the Platonic influences were direct and consciously recognized, even if at one juncture he contests the Neoplatonic interpretation, siding with the "original" Plato.[16] The early Platonic and Neoplatonic roots of Leibniz's thinking, which start with his studies in Leipzig, have been well discussed in the literature.[17] The monadology of the infinite scale of homologous creatures that enclose each other and "represent" each other vividly recalls the Neoplatonic theory of emanations.

Leibniz wrote at a moment and in a place where the modern state was still *in statu nascendi*. What interested him was the notion of sovereignty. He concluded that sovereignty did not have to be monopolistic: there could be a sovereign under a sovereign, and a sovereign above sovereigns: the way it was organized in the German "Roman Empire." Leibniz used his monadology to present the political world as a system of mutually enclosed analogous units, which aims to perfection and develops from bottom to top. But then there arises the paradox of how there can be several sovereigns within one polity. Leibniz thought that his system would make clear enough the hierarchy among the analogous levels. He distinguishes between the "sovereign of territory" who disposes of a standing army, and the "sovereign of jurisdiction," who has also the supreme right to judge: in Leibniz's context, this is the Holy Roman Emperor. What was important was the international standing that was accorded to "sovereigns" of a lower order (such as a duke and, by extrapolation, any significant political actor). Leibniz devised his theory on the pragmatic occasion of proving the standing of the Duke of Hannover at the Nijmegen peace conference (1677–1679). While Leibniz's Germany was not yet a full-fledged state, but rather an empire—with loose subordination and with many feudal remnants—his analysis is nonetheless highly relevant for determining the *task* of the state: to replace the delegation of discretionary power with a vertical line of power consisting of dependent functionaries. This homogeneous analogical structure of power is as true of state bureaucracy as of imperial nobility. What Leibniz did not see was the inevitable *tension* between the different levels of sovereignty. He probably thought that a proper understanding of this structure would help to avert the civil wars.

Leibniz believes in the continuity and ubiquity of power, albeit in unequal proportions. Even though his political theory is an *ad hoc* statement, it contains a crucial intuition, which could be further extrapolated into a general structure, stretching from the emperor to what Kyle McGee calls 'nanosovereign' contemporary individuals[18] (even though the latter then takes a replace by: an anarchist Foucauldian take on nanosovereigns as instances of extra-legal governmental power), from the smaller societies like families to the larger political "monad" which in Leibniz's times was still called a "Res Publica Christiana": Leibniz frequently appeals to this higher unity of Europe in his political texts.

All of this is not a dialectic in Hegel's sense, and not even a Platonic dialectic of ontological levels. However, it contains a tautological paradox: how can a supreme authority command another supreme authority? This paradox reflects the ideological reality of modern times: if sovereignty exists on Earth, then there is no reason why any subject cannot aspire to it, and, moreover, sovereignty *is* the principle of subjectivity. Leibniz recalls that a lower sovereignty is still *sovereignty*, and that God is everywhere. Modern international law draws a distinction between national sovereignty and the human rights of an individual. However, both are forms of sovereignty as absolute right,[19] even if they are realized in polar, complementary ways. The border between the two is blurred in cases of revolutions and secession movements. The contemporary state rules over state-like structures that have become increasingly isomorphic to states:[20] corporations, NGOs, and households. On the other hand, international law weakens national sovereignties while preserving them. There is no global sovereign but an increasing number of global and regional institutions with a transnational authority.

Generalized, Leibniz's theory of monarchy contains a potentially *democratic* normative element: democracy is not only a system of popular unity, but it is also a coordination and mutual recognition of subjectivities on multiple levels: individual citizens, families, corporations, and NGOs.[21] Optimistically enriching each other in an impressive stream of Leibniz's "living force" ("*vis viva*"), these levels will be expected to clash, but this should not lead us to nihilistic theories of a Hobbesian type. Sovereign against sovereign, state against state: this is the formula of political dialectic that Hegel and Leibniz teach us together. Carl Schmitt expressed the same thought by a citation from Goethe: "*Nemo contra deum nisi deus ipse.*"[22]

Today, in the Anglo-American century, it would seem that Leibniz's political theory was a dead end. He is not on the syllabi. But, it was not so in the eighteenth century, when Leibniz, particularly in Germany, had a huge influence in all areas. Christian Wolff rendered Leibniz's heritage more systematic and less radical, thus adapting it for academic use. Late in his life, in 1749, Wolff wrote a treatise on international law, "On the Law of Nations Treated in a Scientific Way,"[23] where he developed a notion of world polity, 'Civitas Maxima,' as an inherent higher standard of international law. No law without a respective authority, he thought, so even if we do not see a functional world state, we should suppose the existence of one if we would like to seriously speak of international law (*ius gentium*). We should even suppose the existence of a leader, "rector," of such state. There is an analogy between different levels of social organization, from families to federations, at the top of which lies the world polity.[24] *Civitas maxima* is "the largest State" (in the sense of size and importance), but the language of "maximum" also connotes the scholastic and Leibnizean theme (think of Cusanus' "maximum!") of a teleology of perfection. The world state is not just a regulative idea of sorts (as Kant, Wolffian in this regard, would later formulate), but it is also an ideal of progressive development.

2.2.3. Hegel

When we say "dialectic of state," we immediately think of Hegel. He invented the new meanings of both dialectics and the state. Dialectic started to mean the real process of overcoming internal contradictions, and the state not merely an administrative and military apparatus, but an institution of human freedom, a "hieroglyph of reason." In his late lectures on the *Philosophy of Right*, Hegel was the first to strictly distinguish state from "civil society," and presented a dialectical structure which included family, civil society, and the state. Civil society is here the negative "middle term," the dissolution of an organic social whole. It is an association of individuals driven by material interests, and as such it requires the state to provide it with a higher unity and sense of legitimacy, in a reflected and mediated way. The state resolves the contradictions of civil society (among individuals, between rich and poor) by returning them a sense of common identity and cause. As such, a state is a kind of 'synthesis' between family and civil society, to use the Fichtean term (which Hegel did not use in this sense). It contains a contradiction between the (positive) family and (negative) civil society, but the contradiction is sublated (*aufgehoben*) within it and is no longer relevant.

The state also sublates the opposition between the impersonal rational machine and free personal will, between what Hegel had previously called "substance" and "subject." The merely symbolic figure of the sovereign who only signs the laws prepared by his advisors, "dots the i's," is an insertion of arbitrary will and subjectivity into the very core of the bureaucratic apparatus of power, which thereby gives it a human face, "represents" it and thus allows it to be representative of its individual subjects, in their freedom (Hegel does not however, explicitly acknowledge to what extent such "dialectics" is useful in providing the state with an alibi: when needed, personal whim may be covered by the projection of impersonal bureaucracy, and when needed, technocratic and blind bureaucracy can hide behind the theatrical figure of a 'charismatic' president who need not make any decisions).

There is, thus, a dialectic of state and society in Hegel, but not one we can easily use today. The state is here taken as a higher term and is barely affected by the dialectical process. It is society that is truly dialectical, whereas the state is "speculative," a spiritual and institutional solution to society's troubles. This puts the state out of the historical game and leaves open the question, why would civil society preserve its significance in a developed state? If the state is a higher form, it could just as well reconcile and consolidate society, let us say in a 'totalitarian' or at least in a social-democratic way. The fact that the state withdraws and actually allows the negativity of civil society to play out seems to be a fact of regression or experiment.

To develop Hegel today, one would need to introduce a dialectic of *state and society*, not just a dialectic of society and family, which the state would somehow resolve. Hegel alludes to it when he warns against the confusion between civil society and state and designates civil society as "the state of need and understanding." By extrapolation, today's state is a state that comes dangerously close to its two Others: family, and then we understand state as nation, and society, and then we understand the state as a large economic corporation that competes with other states.

What is productive is the way that Hegel posits the question of subjectivity and sovereignty. His solution (the minimal sovereign) might seem naïve, but he perceptively recognizes the core problem of the modern state in its oscillation between the sense of impersonal bureaucracy and that of the rule of persons. Moreover, to resolve it, Hegel draws a connection between sovereign and individual. Both are subjects, at a different level. Hegel, thus, makes a Leibnizian move of relativizing and universalizing sovereignty, alluding to the isomorphism between the lower and higher levels of the state. Today, this isomorphism touches not only the structures of personal power but also the reproduction, throughout society, of state-like bureaucratic structures in their impersonal form.

2.2.4. Marxism

The next largest dialectical theory of state, elaborated in direct reaction to Hegel, was Marxism. Both Marx and Engels gave the state a great deal of attention. Following the German precedent, both—and particularly Engels— understood 'state' broadly as including also the premodern polities. They rightly saw the insufficiently problematic character of Hegel's theory of state, and its unilateral idealism: the state, for Hegel, logically preceded and retrospectively justified its own material components (family and civil society). But since the materialist logic of civil society continued to exist, the state stood in constant danger of being subsumed by the powerful self-serving actors of civil society.

However, the solution of Marx and Engels bears essentially the same form as that of Hegel's state theory: they just invert it by saying that the state is an outgrowth of the contradictions in which civil society is entangled. The state is not a part of genuine dialectics, as in Hegel, but a "superstructure" which topples the social world. It claims to resolve and sublate its contradictions, but this claim is false, since the proposed solution is merely symbolic and ideal.

For the Marx of *The 18th Brumaire of Louis Bonaparte*,[25] the state is a relatively autonomous institution which draws its power from the fragmentation of class structure and from the structural passivity of the most numerous class, the "parcel peasants." For Engels in the *Origins of Family, Private Property, and State*, the state "is a product of society at a particular stage of development; it is the admission that this society has involved itself in insoluble self-contradiction and is cleft into irreconcilable antagonisms which it is powerless to exorcise."[26]

Marx and Engels believed that the way out of the deadlock of bourgeois society would be the transformation of *society* in the same way that Hegel had earlier outlined for the state. The state should thus fall back into civil society and dissolve in it. What remained unclear was the role of revolutionary authority, the party, and the 'dictatorial' proletariat in this process, and whether the latter would not become a new version of the Hegelian universalist state.

It was Lenin who answered this question in his seminal *State and Revolution*, where he described a transitory state emerging after the victory of socialist revolution. As we see so well in chapter 7 of the present volume, this would be a genuinely dialectical state, because its task would essentially consist in *dismantling itself*. The supersession of the bourgeois state by the proletarian state is impossible without a violent revolution. The abolition of the proletarian state, that is, of the state in general, is impossible except through the process of its gradual "withering away."[27]

This "semi-state"[28] would fight against the former state elites and would rely on the seemingly technical institutions of control and accounting. The transformation can be considered to be a vision of the socialist future (as in Chiesa), but it is also surprisingly similar to the one happening to the state today, when it is attacked, not by socialists, but by neoliberals, who also see it as an outgrowth of society.[29]

2.2.5. Jellinek and Schmitt

As mentioned earlier, the last philosophical theories of state, coming from Germany, interpreted Hegel in neo-Kantian, dualist ways, but, without saying so, had recourse to dialectic. The purpose of this crypto-dialectical argument was to show how the state, being a horizon of universality, can coexist with a capitalist society; how it can be democratic, in spite of the obvious monarchical legacy in its history and definition; and how it can combine police power and solidarity. Notably, these are the same questions that remained unresolved between Hegel and Marx: the universality of the state contradicted its force-like, material rule: a materialized God that appeared to be too despotic.

Georg Jellinek asks the question: how can a state abide by the rule of law if it hinges on the condition of *sovereignty*: a political unity that exists without external arbiters above it. It is fundamental, however, that the modern state is a legal system whose leaders act only by and through law. But, unlike Montesquieu and his Anglo-Saxon followers, Jellinek is not prepared to resolve this issue pragmatically, via the "division of powers": any division of powers does not bypass the question of the decision in the last instance.

Therefore, he gives a paradoxical solution, which goes back both to scholastic theology (Aquinas, for instance), and to German idealism (to Fichte rather than Hegel): the modern sovereign state rules by *auto-limitation*. Already in his early essay on state treaties, Jellinek writes:

> The essence of sovereignty consists not only in the highest power projected outside, but above all in self-mastery, in the power to give injunctions to its own will, in the capacity to create law for itself. Lorenz von Stein very profoundly saw self-mastery as the legal principle of state which distinguishes it from all other forms of personhood.[30]

The civil rights, in their negative nature, in declarations of the state's power that pledge not to hinder the freedoms of its subjects, essentially rely on the narrowing down of the jurisdiction of state power, *through this very power*.[31]

Legal statements on rights of political freedom are of course norms of the governmental activity of the state, but they are also limits on legislative power, in the sense that their disregard is only possible through a constitutional rejection of a part of fundamental law. Thus, any act of state will is also a limitation of state will, which is not pressed on it from without but derives from the inner nature of this will, as self-limitation. And this self-limitation of the state is not an accidental, passing condition.[32]

Jellinek adds that the limitations are *forms*, without which the law is not a law.[33] Constitutional law is a formula of such auto-limitation. There is the state, and then there is the voluntary submission of the state to its own rules.

To what extent can we call this solution dialectical? We can, only to the degree that such a model allows us to discern a *tension* within the modern order, a tension between the principle of the all-powerful state and the principles of limited power and of the subject's autonomy. This is what we sometimes call today a tension between democracy (or popular sovereignty) and liberalism. Self-limitation, which is understood by Jellinek unilaterally as a legal fact, may be seen from the social, 'material' side, as an actual policy and the virtue of a ruler. Or, in between the two, as the virtue of a particular constituent assembly.[34] As such, it may appear invisible and manipulable (one can declare self-limitation to the extent where one cannot do anything). And it may lead to disaster, to an actual self-destruction of the self-limiting instance. This is what happens, both from the legal and material points of view, in revolutions: a relatively mild leadership abstains from violence and is forced by the masses to abdicate, sometimes on constitutional grounds, for example of the right to secession, as in the USSR in 1991.

Carl Schmitt, Jellinek's most important and most famous follower and (indirect) disciple, offers his solution to the dilemma of the rule of law, and its relation to material power. Schmitt's answer is, as we know, the right to declare a *state of exception* as a mark of sovereignty. This seems to go in the direction opposite to Jellinek's, as this norm does actually allow for an unlimited use of power in the material sense. But the formula itself is similar to Jellinek's; it simply presents the connection between sovereignty and law from an inverted perspective. It is the law (and not the sovereign will) that limits itself, so as to give space for a moment of discretion and thus to establish a paradoxical suture to factual reality.

Schmitt's definition of the political as the sphere of the "distinction between friend and enemy"[35] follows the same logic: standards of legality and legitimacy in politics are not universal, they hinge on the question of political membership, and the recognition of someone as a friend or enemy can change the recommended ethical and legal behavior of a state from one to its opposite. The friend-enemy judgment is a dialectical operator that converts the opposites of modern politics one into the other.

Strangely, I have not found in the literature any reference to this filiation of Schmitt's "political theology." The influence of Jellinek on Schmitt has been discussed only in regard to the role of material constitution,[36] and then there is Schmitt's explicit polemic with Jellinek on this very subject: Schmitt reproached Jellinek for his overly normativist, idealistic understanding of the constitution.[37]

In fact, Schmitt develops the same implicitly dialectical logic that Jellinek had, makes it more explicit by referring to Kierkegaard, a Hegelian, and inverts its perspective. Does Schmitt invert the liberal meaning of Jellinek's formula into a more authoritarian principle? Perhaps, but not quite. Jellinek starts with the presupposition of infinite sovereignty and makes the rule of law depend on its goodwill (even though he does it all in the space of a legal fiction). Schmitt, conversely, presupposes the rule of law, equates sovereignty with this rule of law, and shows how this rule of law can found itself only by making exceptions and allowing for an unlimited use of power in special cases (here, Michael Hebeisen's[38] position that puts Schmitt on the side of concrete material institutions preceding laws, as in Hauriou and Duguit, strikes me as incomplete). Of course, it is not a pure opposition, because Jellinek explicitly put sovereignty itself on the side of legal, ideal reality, not in the sociological sphere. However, as David Dyzenhaus argues, there was an ambiguity on this point in Jellinek: he conceived the two spheres as interconnected, since he did not question the factual power of normative authority.[39] Sandrine Baume concurs, saying that, for Jellinek, "the self-limitation of the state presupposes that a sovereign power transforms itself in a *Rechtsstaat* through the limits it forces upon itself."[40] Given that Jellinek was even accused of dictatorial tendencies because he presupposed absolute sovereignty,[41] Schmitt's position seems to be, paradoxically, *more legalistic*. He wants to include reality into law, not law into reality, and not law into an all-powerful sovereign entity. This is what Agamben, from his anarchist position, reproaches Schmitt for[42]—but in fact, this concern for the survival of the law rather speaks to the latter's credit.

Now, what would turn Schmitt's sovereign exception from a paradox into a dialectical model? It would be possible if we combine his model with Jellinek's into one dialectical sequence, in the spirit of Hegel's stages of reflection. First, we limit our power, mainly to empower another subject (this is my correction to Jellinek: empowerment and not rule-legislating is the essence of democratic law). Second, when this subject revolts and proclaims his or her sovereignty, we announce a state of exception, which could seem to be a return to the former, unlimited sovereignty but is in fact a new stage, the result of a *negation of negation*. The sovereign who had limited himself or herself reclaims his or her power only exceptionally, to limit another potentially unlimited power and to reach a balance of subjectivities. What is this but Hegel's dialectical culmination, his "determinate reflexion?"

The meaning of this dialectical understanding is that a liberal state must reenact the movement *auto-limitation/exception/auto-limitation*, by probing outside of its boundaries in both the permissive and restrictive dimensions. Recognized social movements that do not pose a risk of subversion would become boring and lead to social apathy (the prognosis of Kojève, who had a tame understanding of the state), while the more radical movements would pose an actual threat to the existence of state.

It also follows from this dialectical interpretation that the social movements the state deals with would more often than not have a negative, 'subversive' agenda. In the moment of recognition, the state (like Hegel's master) encounters its own potential death, which revolutions, happening at "another stage," illustrate. And for a while, the movements take on themselves the aspect of negativity inherent in the limitation of power. However, this very negativity, threatening as it does catastrophe, allows all the involved actors to practice self-limitation and to proceed from antagonism to agonism.[43] The state reflects the violence back and becomes functionally analogous to agents lower than it in the hierarchy. The result is not simply a democracy, but a federal Russian doll-like structure of sovereigns subordinate to one another, as developed for instance by Leibniz.

2.3. The Dialectic of State and Society

What interest me are the paradoxical, dialectical relations that tie and intermingle the state with its complementary others:[44] democracy (people), personal rule, and international society (as opposed to the nation-state). The overarching couple is here: state and society. The state is defined as the other of society, as the society's *form:* its autonomous and reflexive shell which gives it order and representation.

Today, the division of state from society often serves as an argument for the crisis of state and for its deficiency. Precisely *because* the state is separate, it embodies alienation, oppresses society, and creates the false image of universality (or of representation) being in fact a symptom of society's internal contradictions and injustices. The claim of the state to efficiently represent and govern society is therefore not quite legitimate. The state increasingly loses power to vested interest groups and to international institutions.

But in spite of these critical moments, the state today preserves its force and legitimacy in a new way: by pursuing its policies *through* society, thereby both maintaining the division state-society and covertly subverting it. This gives the contemporary state an alibi but does not usually weaken or subvert its power, as long as the society is ideologically consensual and politically dispersed. However, this produces the specter of a "deep state," where the state itself, which is in principle a formal institution, is dislocated and reduced to a group of unelected elites who manage to dictate policies through informal channels. Another, contrasting perversion that one can fear, then, is 'state capture': the long-term occupation of top state offices by a group of people tied together by informal ties, using these ties to pursue their private interests through public means.

Society is, however, an overly broad term. Within the large umbrella dichotomy of state and society, there exist other, more concrete conceptual distinctions, such as the state and democracy (or state and nation), state and economy (or state and capitalism), state and person (in the sense both of legal personality and political actor), and state and international society (the latter mostly referring to other nation-states and international organizations).

2.3.1. *State and Democracy*

1. In the framework of the first dilemma, there are the pairs "state-democracy" and "state-people." To us, on the one hand, the state seems to be teleologically destined for democracy. Spinoza calls democracy the "most absolute" form of power, while Marx says that a democratic state is the ideal of the state, the state as such.[45] This is because the state has to represent society and be an organ of its self-rule. It is logical then that it must be all-inclusive. Democracy is the first virtue of today's state. But this has not always been the case. Before the nineteenth century, democracy seemed, conversely, to be a great danger for statehood. This was rejected, the first point of view triumphed, but it remains for us to see what, in democracy,

opens the way to the subversion of order and renders state officials wary of excessive participatory democracy. Whereas in most Western countries, democracy is a synonym of peace and stability, in non-Western countries, the democratization efforts of the United States and Europe are realized via "revolutions of color," which sometimes lead to civil wars or to "state failures." The task of reinforcing a liberal state often runs counter to the interest of democratic movements.

2. In the twentieth century, the understanding of democracy shifted from a social to a political understanding, elections becoming its core. However, historically speaking, the representative government of the British type began to be called "democracy" because the electoral system was extended to the poor,[46] and because *society* became more equal.[47] In the early twentieth century, "democracy" was contested between its liberal, representative, and electoral meanings[48] and the social-democratic meaning of inclusiveness.[49] Many distinguished between a democratic *regime* (which includes social institutions) and a republican form of government.

Scholars differ as to the understanding of the relationship between democracy and state. Some[50] do not see any problem in combining them and, moreover, do not conceive of a democracy that would not represent a state. Without statehood, democratic institutions such as elections, parliaments, and courts would not be able to sustain themselves. Some others, Marxist in inspiration, agree, but from a critical point of view: since democracy is a form of the state, it is a suspect institution, responsible for maintaining capitalist hierarchies, and thus cannot serve as a normative ideal.[51] But increasingly, many authors point to a *tension* between a hierarchical and unitary state and democracy, with the latter's horizontal ideals, its contestatory, often anarchic, social spirit, and decentralizing tendencies.[52] For some, such as the French social theorists Pierre Clastres and Miguel Abensour, democracy is defined and valorized as the side of 'society' in its irreducibility and opposition to the state.[53] Whoever is right, it is clear that the alliance of state and democracy is not innocent: even if democracy is an organic part of the contemporary state, it is there as a germ of "agonistic" imbalance and self-criticism. As I mentioned in the introduction to the chapter, the very concept of state is split between the logics of top-down (authoritarian) and bottom-up (democratic) legitimation. Because historically, state started as an authoritarian institution, this dilemma figures today as an opposition between democracy and state, but there is equally a malaise in the very existence and legitimization of the authoritarian apparatus, which gets caricatured as an order of physical violence.

Some, in recent times, have resurrected Siéyes's language of "constituent power."[54] They view the people's direct action movements as a kind of flashback to the founding moment of the liberal-democratic polity: there is a vibrant participatory democracy at this moment, which then is lost but is capable of periodic return, legitimized by virtue of the regime's revolutionary descent. I share the admiration for revolutionary power structures, but I think that this notion excessively plays into the liberal democratic fiction of a sovereign *demos* somehow authoring the state's decisions. This is an important normative myth, but we do not have to confuse it with reality. Olga Bashkina, in chapter 3 of this volume, recovers some convincing arguments against the notion of constituent power from the *liberal* side (real-life popular movements are negative and partial, they don't stand for the whole), but similar arguments can be used from the leftist or radical democratic point of view. In reality, most social movements are *contentious*;[55] they are in dialogue with the state, sometimes against the state as such, but they rarely aspire to a re-founding of the polity, and even if so, this rarely happens as a consequence of protesting. Therefore, when speaking of the movement component of today's democratic state, we must not mistake the powerful *negativity* of revolt for a god-like institutional creativity. The movements are reactive rather than active, have more in common with a *destituent* rather than constituent power,[56] and their negativity itself is what produces their carnivalesque enjoyment.

While Western countries manage to maintain a balance between state order and unruly rebels, 'democracy-building' in democratizing, non-Western countries often falls prey to the aforementioned contradictions. These countries face a risk of imbalance in the face of antagonism. Russia was considered democratic in the 1990s, when the parliament rarely agreed with the president, the media was free, and oppositional parties openly contested the ruling regime. However, democracy thus understood was characterized by *polarization*, explained in part by the key substantive issue of a possible (feared) return to the past "totalitarian" model, and in part by the very *dispositif* of parliamentary democracy. 'State capacity' was becoming weak in the face of direct sabotage. Most international observers, such as Larry Diamond or Michael McFaul, saw the Russia of the time as a democratic society lacking a *consolidation*, a reinforcement of the state.[57] It is with this program of state reinforcement that Putin came to power in 1999, and was widely supported by both the Russian and Western policy elites. However, as we know, Putin neither wanted nor managed to keep the balance and gradually dismantled democracy, seeing it as too divisive in the face of the anti-secession war in Chechnya, and as too open in the face of potential meddling by the United States into Russian politics via its support of mass movements.[58]

Conversely, in cases like Libya and Syria, Western interventions aimed at democratization led to the opposite result and induced civil wars, for the simple reason that democratic disagreement and the right to dissent fell on a ground imbued with substantive antagonisms, such as religion and foreign allegiances. In the absence of resources available to the Russian leadership (size and a relatively apathetic population), leaders of these countries were unable to block democratic developments, and the countries descended into civil wars.

In the 2000s, based on this experience, political scientists understood the nonlinear nature of the relationship between democracy and state capacity. Hadenius and Bäck suggested a model of a "J-shaped relationship" between democracy and the state's administrative capacity: state capacity is relatively high at the lowest levels of democracy (understood here as the liberal, rights-based representative system), lower at the medium level, and highest at the highest levels of democratic development.[59] Dynamically speaking, in many instances, "the attained quality of state capacity in authoritarian regimes may work as a powerful disincentive to democratization."[60] The quantitative "J-shaped" correlation, theoretically speaking, points to the contradictory, dialectical relation between the concepts of state and democracy.

We see that one and the same model turns into its dialectical opposite in a changed environment, which means that it lacks universality and has to be rethought. A sustainable and expandable democratic state can only exist as a model that includes the differential of power: somewhere between a democratizing and an already democratized country. Lacking this, the relationship United States/Syria or Germany/Russia is homologous with the internal relationship "elites/contentious movements" that exists inside a state. The agent of democratization is at the same time a potential target of discontent and a military opponent, and therefore democratization, on both levels, must be a sustained effort, not a one-time "revolution."

In many ways, the question of the state's role in society hinges on its capacity to control and sustain social movements. Both the pluralist and radical democratic accounts tell us that the state should not play the despotic or totalitarian role of micromanaging society, that the state is an autonomous institution with its own agenda. Moreover, the state cannot artificially create the sphere of civil society: people would not be interested in participating in it. It cannot efficiently control the existing civil society either. What it can do, is formally regulate and support spontaneously emerging clubs, action committees, and foundations.

The problem with this argument is the existence of successful means for the control and limitation of social movements when they become "radical." The U.S. and European Union (EU) governments do dissolve peaceful demonstrations (a recent case would be Occupy in New York), or authorize them on demand. Both the United States and the EU provide tax relief and grants to NGOs: NGOs require funding that only a wealthy corporate donor or a state can provide. And, there is the negative example of states such as Russia, Turkey, and China, which successfully limit liberal NGO and demonstration activities in their countries, through a combination of legal restrictions and police violence, and support NGOs of a patriotic, religious, or conservative orientation. Against their background, it is clear that the developed civil society of the United States and Europe exists, if not *because* of the state, then with its sanction and active support. The potential for *negative* measures, which largely remains with the state because of its official role as security monopolist, often remains unseen (unlike any positive measures) but is nevertheless vital in the establishment of relations of control and of hegemony.

Taken together, these arguments add up to an important theoretical argument: a *democratic state* is not a state created from below as a function of society. It is an intersection of two series and two principles: civic participation and self-organization, *and* the responsiveness and democratic interest of the governing bodies. Even if they are not all-mighty and remain formally responsible to the "people," they are endowed with legal and material power and therefore must play a role in the empowerment of the much less resourceful "common people." The moral *desideratum* of equality should not close our eyes to the actually existing inequality of power.

Another aspect of the dialectic of state and democracy is the question of the *nation*. Since the nineteenth century, the state has been understood as a *nation*-state. The "people" of democracy is not humanity at large but a *definite* people, which was originally understood in ethnic terms, and was later interpreted as a civic, color-blind community of people. Who integrates this heterogeneous community into one but the state, with its formally unifying program? It is top-down institutions such as school education, citizenship tests, the "affirmative action" of the U.S. or Soviet models, which build up a nation out of different ethnicities and assimilate newcomers. Thus, the state builds its sovereign identity, tautologically, on the material it constructs.

In the introduction to the chapter, I mentioned the tension between the formal and the substantive aspects in the definition of Modern state. The nation remains a *substantive* ground of the formal sovereignty of the state, and of the formal structures of representative democracy. Yet nationalism is an ideology that has a bad name and is rarely recognized officially by the governments of major countries, because of globalist and universalist tendencies in politics, as well as the lack of legitimate substantive criteria for citizenship. Germany was recently one of the last countries to abandon an exclusively 'blood' criterion for political membership. In France, the birthplace of the concept of the nation, it has evolved to become a near-synonym of the state. Bashkina shows in her chapter how Carré de Malberg, a great French liberal jurist of the mid-twentieth century, used "nation" to express the abstract, non-empirical essence of the "people" on behalf of which democracy claims to rule. Through the "nation," the "people" become statized. But, generally speaking, the situation is paradoxical, because the state depends on the nation for its legitimacy and yet, in the liberal, democratic Western countries, does not dare to avow it, so that nation and nationalism remain its repressed *unconscious*, reemerging in the party programs of the far right. However, nation, just as literal revolutionary democracy, is alive and well at the global periphery, where the politics of secession and ethnic self-determination are presently active as ever: enough to recall the cases of Kosovo, Kurdistan, Palestine, where separatism is generally backed by the West, and Abkhazia and South Ossetia, as well the irredentist secession of Crimea, all backed by Russia.

To conclude, the relationship of state and democracy is indeterminate. If we limit our view to the leading Western capitalist societies, then the democratic state would be the same as the liberal state; the state would be more or less representative of the structure of society and become concealed, almost transparent, in its functions of authority and subjective will. The state half-dissolves into society. This does not lead to a happy synthesis but to an uneasy contradiction between a statized society of responsible citizens-bureaucrats and the increasing pressure to ground state policy in identitarian, substantive subjects—the nation and multiple ethnicities. The blistering negativity that is still needed to re-formalize all substantive issues and to reindividualize an increasingly communitarian society is expressed in loose antiauthoritarian and identitarian social movements, which remain firmly under the control of the state-society consensus.

But if we go beyond the West, the relationship flips. Society, replete with private powerful actors, claims actual power, and the state reacts by reconsolidating its hold violently, and with reliance on identitarian nationalism. The "democratic" forces of civilizing liberalism emerge here as globalist revolutions and, potentially, as civil wars. The nation, which in the West is an ascriptive category, is essentialized as ethnicity, form becomes content. A framework that is merely symbolic at its core becomes "real" outside it.

2.3.2. *State and Economy*

The neoliberal wave of "deregulation," which was originally seen by its ideologists as a limitation of the state in favor of private business, quickly led to the growth of a transformed state: the number of controlling agencies, of paperwork needed to keep track of the new "private" sector, was enormous.[61] Moreover, even as it privatized, the state often preserved its leverage, particularly in planning and investing in industries with long-term effect, as with Finland's investment in Nokia, or the U.S. extensive investment in Apple.[62] Privatization was in many ways a symbolic measure that allowed elites to privatize the rewards while socializing the risks, in Mazzucato's terms. One could argue that unconsciously, neoliberal elites might have also used the situation to send a false signal to developing countries: neoliberal reforms in semi-peripheral countries have almost universally been a disaster,[63] while in the United States and Europe their application has at times generated growth. In response to this ruse, the behavior of the large non-Western countries (BRICS) changed in the 2000s. A tendency toward state capitalism became predominant, where the state complies with the ideology of privatization and market mechanisms by creating, in key sectors of economy, companies with control or minority packages of state-owned stocks (in Russia, Gazprom, Rosneft, Aeroflot, and Sberbank; in Brazil, Petrobras, Electrobras, and Vale). A much more widespread, weaker form of the same is the "public-private partnership," a capitalist corporation that operates with state support for an *ad hoc* project. Such forms flourish in central Western states (such as the United States and Canada), as well as in China and Russia, and do their share of disguising state power under the form of market relations.

Jason Royce Lindsey, in an excellent and under-reviewed recent book, *The Concealment of the State*,[64] shows how the contemporary state (which he calls "postmodern") plays on its distinction with society in withdrawing its responsibility from the operation of institutions it presents as entirely autonomous from itself. The main institution that Lindsey focuses on is the *market*. The state plays its part in the "neoliberal" economy by preserving control, in various ways, over major industries that are nominally private or—to boot— that are privatized *by* the state and on its conditions. Therefore, the presumed weakening of the state in an era of neoliberal deregulation latently turns into its own opposite: the state, which seemingly reduces its scope to oversight of the market, in fact keeps an invisible hand on the major economic actors, while divesting itself of any responsibility or accountability.

> For these various reasons, the postmodern state is an institution which attempts to conceal its agency. By denying it has the power to act, the postmodern state makes the continuing development of globalized capitalism appear inevitable. The postmodern state also claims that the market it has created is now an autonomous entity. This claim allows the state to avoid responding to democratic demands to modify the rules and outcomes of the market. Finally, by concealing its agency, the postmodern state can continue to neglect the ossifying modern political system it inherits from the past.[65] The existence of the state lulls society into accepting that it is dependent on it.[66]

One subdivision of market ideology covers a change in the use of violence, which was once supposed to be the exclusive domain of the state. Today, violence is often outsourced and counted as a security "service." This, paradoxically, produces a situation of totalized and accepted coercion.

This empirical account rhymes with a political theory Lindsey does not cite: that of Giorgio Agamben who, in his *The Power and the Glory*[67] characterizes the modern liberal state as a system of sovereign *alibi*: sovereign bodies delegate actual operations to "technical" governments and thus divest the people of their control of the nominally 'democratic' polity.

Lindsey draws anarchist hypercritical conclusions from his analysis: he suggests "exposing" state power by opposing it but also warns against the facile choice of voluntary activism by civil society, because this is arguably a way in which the state conceals itself through the outsourcing of various tasks.

However, because the state alternately presents its power as "state" or "society," we actually deal with an *internal contradiction* of the notion, which points to the possibility of either a radical transformation, or a conscious *synthesis* of what had previously been disjunct and unconsciously united.

The state/economy divide is not only dubious in the direction of the state but also fallacious in its presumption of the non-statist nature of the market society *as such*. Marxist-inspired political economy presents society as a more or less autonomous functioning of economic exploitation, which the state regulates and facilitates. This argument builds on Hegel's distinction between civil society and state and exaggerates it. Moreover, as in the case of social movements, it presents society as something organic and heterogeneous to the state. But this is not a fair picture. The so-called society is penetrated by power relations. One of the functions of the strong modern state has always been to limit the authority of strong power holders within a society (fathers, professors, prison guards, train conductors, all of whom could potentially exercise an uncanny power over an individual). Michel Foucault wrote much on this subject, even though at an early stage he erroneously presented his findings in the familiar pattern of pitting material societal processes against a supposedly fictional public law (a position he revised later in his life to include Weber-like considerations on the violent and bureaucratic state[68]). In truth, while the state is certainly a semiautonomous set of institutions, society is not a formation of an entirely different nature from the state. It is built not just on self-organization, but on a system of ubiquitous power relations that have both a material and a symbolic dimension. It would be wrong to contrast the symbolic power of the state with the somehow more physical or material power of father, of employer, or a doctor. The latter are also symbolic authorities whose power is built on prestige and charisma, on contract, and, in many cases (like doctors and teachers), on the direct choice and consent of their clients. It is not that a representative public authority of the state an authoritarian leaning society of "elites," nor that a bureaucratic violent authority of the state rules over an element of societal self-organization. The state and society form one, if subdivided, whole, which is isomorphic on all its levels[69] and exists in a tension between the system of correlated hierarchies of "nanosovereigns"[70] and the system of solidary collectivities, which support *or* contest their leaders. This seemingly homogenizing view leads us to view the life of economic society as a development of *internal* contradiction between authority and freedom, between personalistic and collective rule.

2.3.3. State and Person

State is by definition an *impersonal* form of authority, power abstracted from the figure of its holder. I have mentioned Skinner's historical account that emphasizes this function of the concept as essential to its rise. Harvey Mansfield agrees.[71] Claude Lefort famously calls democratic state power "disembodied," which means depersonified.[72] Some connect the impersonal nature of the modern state to the supposedly impersonal nature of *capital* in economics.[73] But this reality of the notion contradicts what it describes. In the introduction, I evoked the contradiction between this impersonal formalism and the substantive figure of personality that is built into the reality and the normative expectations of how the state functions. The absolutist period, when the notion of the state was gradually elaborated, was person-centered, and the phrase, later attributed to Louis XIV, "*l'état, c'est moi!*," captures at least something of how the state of the period was perceived. The representative governments of the nineteenth century did try to reduce the personal factor, through the *rotation* of officials, but the very idea of *electing* representatives made politics more, not less, personified. Election is above all a competition of personalities for popular sympathies. Today, alongside the triumph of the faceless network of global bureaucracy, we see its opposite, a worldwide fixation in politics on the persons of state leaders, whoever they may be. This has been recognized as a contemporary tendency toward a "personalization of politics."[74] The recent U.S. elections, and particularly the media campaigns for and against Donald Trump, are the most vivid example. Even as they reject monarchy, the creators of modern states have in many cases replicated a king-like figure to be a *representative* of the people, in a new sense. Both the words "state" (*état*) and "representation" connoted, particularly in French, not just a political corporation, but also glamour and the awe of a ruler.

The concept of representation embodies the dialectic that I speak of. When Hobbes introduces his theory of monarchic representation, he shows this dialectic without naming it: he speaks of a sovereign as of an actor who plays a role, a person who is authorized by each subject to act on his behalf, in the same way that we would authorize someone to be our representative in court or our envoy to a foreign country. He thus plays on the two senses of the word "representative": someone to whom we would delegate our authority and seems to be our subordinate (first meaning) but, against this appearance, within the commonwealth, turns out to be our superior, someone who embodies the state (second meaning). And, from then on, all political power is conveyed from the sovereign downward. What Hobbes does not underline, but what follows from his theory within a democratic and/or federal state, is that all persons endowed with the power of authority wield powers of discretion: the government is authorized by the society in the same way that the officials and agents of social power are authorized by the government. There is a structure of mutual and reciprocal delegation. The picture of a machine-like and vertical state bureaucracy is a myth: in fact, any appointment implies a discretion within certain limits, otherwise, institutional leadership (which is necessary in almost any organization) would not have made sense. The Leibnizian and Hegelian world of many sovereigns does not just describe an archaic empire, but the unconscious of any functional state.

Today, the democratic principle has little penetrated business corporations, which are more often than not ruled vertically, by a CEO responsible to a Board. The CEOs of large corporations have become famous like media stars (Steve Jobs, Elon Musk, Mark Zuckerberg, to name a few). These fetishistic tendencies are not easy to dismiss as naïve, so central are they to today's politics. It may be argued that both state and capitalism conceal their person-centered universe behind the bureaucratic screen of impersonality, or that personality and formal anonymity are two dialectically intertwined instances.

Personalized power exists, moreover, inside the state. Weber's state might have monopolized violence, but not all power or authority. Therefore, the modern state is reflected in modern society, which abounds with instances of "natural" yet formally limited power: the taxi driver (only) while he or she drives you, the corporation boss as you work for him or her. The task of the state is to restrict those elements of personal power which potentially undermine its authority. The recent campaigns against abuses of societal power such as sexual harassment are instances of these antiarchic policies that the state supports and helps to implement. Another typical instance of power abuse is the corruption of officials. The state does not see these lower powers as similar to state power, but they are nevertheless an authority that humans possess and like to exercise, sometimes in cruel ways that offend one's sensibility. The state has not directly monopolized this power, since it is not violent, even though it may well be despotic and even erotic. Yet the state tries to indirectly monopolize or at least control it, by fighting abuse or even the use of authoritarian discourse by dominant actors in politics (such as men). This is a difficult fight, because power hierarchies and the inevitable discretion of the officials penetrate all institutions, both public and private, so that the limits between coercion and authoritative persuasion are often fragile. The self-aggrandizement of petty bosses and the rude behavior of policemen and bus drivers are, paradoxically, both the sign of a weak state—because the state is unable to monopolize its authority—and simultaneously an expression of the strong state power with which these actors identify. Thus, the task is to maintain a fragile balance between the empowerment and limitation of authority. A better way to resolve this issue would be to democratize society by establishing rules of election and rotation universally throughout it, on all levels—including business structures—but no one has attempted this since ancient Athens.

2.3.4. State and International Society

In the international context, as in the domestic one, there has been a talk of sovereignty becoming fragile in the face of globalization and neoliberal reform, which foster non-state actors as international players. What we observe in recent years, however, is a complex play on the state/society divide, which both states and non-state actors engage in. In wars such as the Iraq war, governments increasingly use private companies for both combat- and non-combat-related military tasks. The recent operations of Russia and Russia-backed separatists in the Ukraine have contributed to the popularity of the discourse of "hybrid warfare." A hybrid war is one that is conducted not only through combat but also through propaganda campaigns and by support of subversive social movements within the "enemy" country.[75]

This "hybridity" generates an atmosphere of suspicion with regard to all critically oriented social movements and media. Russia accuses the United States and EU of having been engaged in hybrid wars during the "color revolutions" of Eastern Europe and the "Arab Spring" revolutions of the Arab world. Non-state institutions, such as the Soros and MacArthur foundations, are accused of supporting these uprisings, along with state-affiliated U.S. institutions such as National Endowment for Democracy and National Democratic Institute. Private media such as *Le Monde* and *The New York Times* are widely seen to be shaping the course of their countries' foreign policy and to be influencing public opinion in favor of revolutionary movements across the globe, so that their enormous policy effect is often attributed to the nations where they are published.

This perspective is, of course, biased and unfair, but it does reflect an objective issue: a social or business organization can in principle be allied with government, particularly in the international context. This is also true for international organizations whose policies often align with those their country of origin. Moreover, even an organization that is critical of government policy may be seen from without as part of this policy in what concerns international affairs (as it is the case with many human rights organizations, such as Amnesty International and Greenpeace, whose criticism of non-U.S. governments is often seen as a part of the U.S. and EU's hegemonic expansion). As I have discussed earlier with regard to democracy, the contemporary democratic state draws its legitimacy, to a large degree, from its tolerance of, and reliance upon, contentious social movements. It is a risk, because these movements can potentially threaten the political regimes themselves, though this does not normally happen in the stable liberal democracies of the North. However, the democratic legitimacy of social movement states should be seen in an international context, where the United States and EU appear as two-tiered structures. The principle of tolerating and encouraging social movements, when applied in the politico-economic peripheral and semi-peripheral countries, leads to results *opposite* to those applied in the metropolis: here, social movements risk subverting regimes that are seen as too authoritarian.

Recent Russian strategic operations, such as the regime's support of the separatist movement in Ukraine and its alleged campaign of influence during the U.S. elections of 2016, are based on the theory of latent, or hybrid, imperialism of the United States and EU, that the latter accomplish through NGOs and the media. The Russian tactic consists in mimicking this policy, while making its own more organized and coordinated, and thus more obvious.[76] The Russian state appears to have directly coordinated both the Donbass separatist movement and the internet activity of bloggers supportive of Trump, while the United States and EU rely, in their support of foreign insurrections, on the spontaneous goodwill of democratic movements that they support or help to educate.

Perceiving a threat to its sovereignty in the existence of foreign-funded NGOs and media, Russia restricted their activity and officially labeled them "foreign agents," using a precedent from the U.S. FARA law (1938). Currently, the United States, faced with the Russian "hybrid" counteroffensive, is in turn mimicking some of Russia's actions, by applying its own "foreign agent" categorization (as in the case of *Russia Today*), or as with the sustained media campaign against the Russian government in *The New York Times* and *The Washington Post* in 2017–2018.

Clearly, this constellation is a continuation of the latent state power described by Lindsey, with a significant *gain* in power of states, derived from the alibi effect. Unlike domestic socioeconomic policy, foreign policy makes it difficult to effectively conceal the state from one's opponents, so the concealment retains a formal, legal, and propagandistic value but does not exist from the point of view of the opponent country, for example, Russia. Here, both the media and experts tend toward the other extreme and declare the border between Western states, big business, and civil society to be illusory, given the impressive solidarity they demonstrate in international politics.

Let me now summarize. In the introduction, I briefly explained why the global and universal ambition of Modern state contradicts its constitutive sovereignty and makes the state a potentially globalized actor, imperial or colonized, even where the circumstances do not allow it to expand and/or allow it to remain autonomous. Today, the dialectic of state and the global system seriously complicates the ideal "Westphalia/Yalta" picture of an international order consisting of unitary states as its elements. What complicates it are the power of non-state international actors (most importantly, capitalist corporations); the growth of regional supra-state organizations; and the in-built temptation for the regions to secede, which is reinforced by the democratic understanding of sovereignty. The ideal of global governance, which was shared by both liberals[77] and postmodern leftists,[78] seemed, for a while, to weaken sovereignty and supersede the nation-states. But history went otherwise. What we observe is the *reaction* of the state to the forces of its dissolution and the *imperialist* expansion of many states, all profiting from ongoing globalization. Even regional organizations such as the EU currently display internal tensions of an imperialist/colonial nature.

Against the naïve conspiracy approach that can only discern the actions of the unitary state everywhere, the division state/society exists, and is highly significant. But in today's world, it is this very border that constitutes power and a new form of sovereignty. One would hesitate to whom to attribute agency in the hybrid policy in question: it may be seen as an operation of the state, after having successfully hegemonized civil society, or alternatively, as an expansion of a social force that democratically controls the state but goes beyond national boundaries (cosmopolitan liberalism in the case of the United States, and pan-Russian or ex-Soviet society exceeding nation-states in the Russian case). However, this shows, in any event, that the stereotypes of decentered "network societies," or even a network empire in the spirit of Negri and Hardt, do not describe the situation well enough. It is precisely the existence of extended socioeconomic networks that facilitates the formation of large scale, super-sovereign "fists," which inevitably happens in selected nation-states or supranational entities like the EU.

Capitalism, which had seemed to be a globalizing force with its interest in peace, open markets, and the free flow of money, turns its other side—that of restricted competition and a tendency to monopolization. Russia, China, and Turkey return to neo-mercantilist policies in their political protection of sale markets, at home and in their allied countries. Recent years show that even economic leaders, such as the United States, turn to aggressive trade protectionism. Large corporations depend on states in their functioning, as the crisis of 2008 widely showed. It is in their interest to make corporatist deals with the state, and to consolidate their power by creating a block with other capitalists, which is most easily done on the basis of nation and citizenship. The globalization of states turns them into huge corporations *sui generis*, so that their defense of sovereignty is at times indistinguishable from competitive profit maximization and even survival, by all means. In a dialectical twist (the one I touched upon earlier when criticizing Spinoza), the seemingly formal, legalistic power of sovereign states in many cases subsumes the material, productive power of capitalist industries, but this is not a gain in transparency and democracy: instead, public power itself operates, essentially, as a semi-private unit of the business kind.

Democracy, which would also seem to be a globalizing force (states are structured according to near-identical constitutions, minorities' rights encourage migration, etc.), now also appears—as it used to be traditionally—as a factor legitimizing sovereignty. Migration challenges the basic premise of national democracy by increasing and dissolving political membership. The experience of globalization and/or international integration usually brings with it neoliberal elements of austerity and restrictions on production, which are easily attributed to foreign causes. Therefore, the national democratic vote often supports nationalist leaders. Again, the cognitive scheme of *capitalist* individualism and competition is transposed by voters to the level of their imaginary community, the nation.

The result is the *crisis*, in which the universalizing tendencies of both democracy and capitalism seem to be 'irrationally' frustrated by the increasing number of elected populist, nationalist governments. This tendency toward sovereignization appears archaic and irrational and provokes a bitter overreaction from ideologically minded Western elites who believe in Enlightenment. As always in a dialectical situation, a clash of *internal* contradictions produces an outburst of *negativity*, which tends to reinforce itself in spirals. As we will see below, a way out, in fidelity to the universalist principles of modernity and the Enlightenment, is possible, but for such a project we need a very clear, dialectical picture of what actually goes on.

2.4. Coda

The abstract legal framework, with its non-dialectical instrument of *understanding* (as opposed to reason), does not perceive the state-like and sovereign-like structures of domestic and international society. This omission leads to the ideological concealment of the state and the mythology of "impersonalism," to the nihilist and anarchist dismissal of the state that undermines the civic virtues of its officials, and to the unresolvable international crises around revolutions and secessions.

The alternative would be an international and extended deliberative democracy, which would recognize and encourage *all* civic autonomous structures, give them a standing, and organize a rotation of power between them (without the hypocritical fiction of the "empty place" of power). However, because this would be a *dialectical* constitution, it cannot be blind to the potential *conflicts* among pretendants to the sovereign position. Use of violence would be allowed, but only in extreme cases of a threat to national security. Unfortunately, democratization goes together with a quasi-dictatorial prerogative (as both Locke and Schmitt remind us). This in turn means that such a state is not salvageable as a purely impersonal enterprise: the capacity for a risky recognition of opponents up to the point of rupture, without an *a priori* recipe for when to apply violence, requires prudence and personal virtue, from below and from above. The proper modern state would be a mixture of personalized and impersonal institutions, in which supposedly virtuous persons would rotate in power on the basis of lot.

Dialectic is both about internal tension and about a historical movement whereby opposites reflect in each other and switch places. In our time, the dialectic of state and democracy produces a democratic state in which democracy is in an unfinished process of "statization," while the state is in a constant process of democratization.

What this means, first, is that social movements, if they want to make a difference, must institutionalize and aspire to political power, instead of functioning, like now, as *ad hoc* explosions of protest energy. But as they do so, state would itself acquire the characteristics of mobilized enthusiasm, equality, and radical democracy. There have been historical precedents for this, as with the Communist Party that became the state. It ended badly, since the state element quickly subsumed the "movement" structure, while the Soviet state exploded, in the 1930s, by the internal fraternal struggles characteristic of a democracy facing its own end. The superimposition of movement and state did not pass smoothly but generated an outburst of *negativity* ("terror" as some have called it), since both the logic of state and the logic of movement were threatened by an intrusion. Similarly, in our time, the process of reflection and chiasmic exchange between state and democracy is simultaneous with violent reactions against such mixture: authoritarian counterrevolutionary states and the exaggerated anarchism of grassroots political organizations. But the dialectical process need not end in antagonisms and abstract polarizations if it is conscious, if it is kept in check by the public legal framework of the state, and by the participatory morals of the populace.

Reciprocally, the state democratizes and has to democratize: not only in the representative sense of appealing to the citizens who had supposedly "delegated" it authority to rule but also in the reverse sense of self-limiting and delegating authority to the structures of civil society, including to social movements. The "democratic," cooperative, polite, and open behavior of state officials, which Pierre Rosanvallon calls a "democratic art of government,"[79] is a no less important condition of democracy, as is the grassroots activity of civil society organizations. The dialectical process of the democratizing state started long ago and led, already in the nineteenth century, to the internalization and *Aufhebung* of democracy by the state. Michael Marder, in his chapter of this book, formulates this as a general rule: "The state is the substantivizing stabilization of conflict and antagonism.... In the state, *stasis* acquires its form (in another possible formulation: the state is *stasis* hypostatized)."[80] In our time, the coexistence of state power and conflictual movements continues, but is affected, since the 1970s, with a new turn of dialectic (*determinate reflection*), where the state that had "swallowed" democracy to become internally democratic now re-externalizes democracy by projecting it outside, in the form of movements and democratic revolutions.

Methodologically, one must recall at this juncture that the familiar picture of dialectical "synthesis" (usually attributed to Hegel but in fact used only by Fichte and Schelling) is not quite accurate. There is certainly such a thing as a dialectical synthesis, whereby an element denied in the content returns in the very form of that which had denied it. It may be a fortunate coincidence, like Kojève's bourgeois-citizen who unites in himself or herself the roles of master and slave, being a slave in the form of a master. Or it may be a monstrous superimposition, like Adorno's subject of Enlightenment, who defeats the myth by taking on the mythic lust of power in the very form of its rationality.[81] However, synthesis is never the end of a development, since there may be at least two syntheses, master-as-slave and slave-as-master: history may proceed with its positive and negative sides. The two syntheses can coexist in a tension, and this, I would say, is a normatively appealing picture, albeit an unstable one. But they can also generate antagonism, negativity, and dissolution. The dialectical landscape of a contradiction x versus y thus consists of five elements: $x(y)$, $y(x)$, anti-x (or exaggerated y), anti-y (or exaggerated x), and the form of universal dissolution $\neg x \neg y$. In our case, this is (1) the statist society, society which is bureaucratized and filled with state-like groups and individuals, (2) the socialized state, the corporatist state that is a hegemonic vector resulting from the pressure of pluralist groups, of business-driven and ideologically driven interests, (3) the radical-democratic society that contests and blocks the state, (4) the authoritarian state that attempts to subsume society and deny its autonomy, and (5) the revolution or international crisis in which the state perishes as an autonomous unit.

Our task, however, is to make a logically coherent, even if empirically contradictory, *normative* rule that would be preferable to the current lack of logical coherence. According to both Hegel and Schelling, dialectical development has as its hidden premise a split *identity* so that, for instance, both state and democracy are expressions of the idea of sovereignty/subjectivity.

Thus, what the dialectical theory of state needs is a new, nonlinear construction of public law as a law of *subjects*, not rules or norms. Or rather, norms consist in the ideal *relations* between the subjects involved, plus the analogy which, in this construction, plays a central part in the legitimacy of law. Each subject embodies these norms but may see them from its partial perspective, so that there is a set of norms authorizing and regulating the subordinates (rights, recognition, multiculturalism, respect of opposition) and a set of norms regulating and guiding the superiors (building a synoptic picture, centralizing power, enforcing the norms of democracy on intermediary quasi-sovereigns, appointing good officials, limiting themselves in routine control).

This is not such an unfamiliar system: it is close to the institutional view of law first formulated by Montesquieu (who derived law from *liens*, interpersonal ties), and later developed by such legal scholars as Duguit and Hauriou. Moreover, since it is a system of legal subjects, it is also in a way a system of *rights*. Yet these rights are dialectically stretched, from a passive right to be defended, to the minimally active right to vote (or consent)—which exists only in an imperfect, "strict" law that lacks a better option—to the right to lead and command, which ideally ("perfectly," in Leibniz's parlance) would belong to *all*. The development of right and growth of a person in rank dialectically inverts the sense of "right" from a passive to an active role.

To the ascending order of representation, in which a multitude is represented by small groups and by the persons of elected leaders, there corresponds a descending order of mutually authorizing sovereigns and institutions (if this may sound blasphemous, enough to look at the global functions of the United States and EU), including those aspiring newcomers who eventually obtain (or not) recognition. The dialectical theory of the state is inevitably a theory of *international* law. The contradictions and tautologies of the democratic state are simply not resolvable at the level of the single nation-state: they can be overcome only if we understand and modify the entire system.

There is a *tautology* and a *conflict* in the proposed order, because each new sovereign is limited by his or her superior, but also potentially contests him or her, because analogous to his or her on his or her own level. This is true both of personal leaders, and of the councils at different levels, if we envision a hyper-federal council democracy. Therefore, the law comes to limit the superior instance, too. The formula is a potentially infinite series ($x(x(x(x. \ldots)$), at the end of which arguably stands the individual who attempts to govern himself or herself but encounters his or her unconscious. The truth of the sovereign state is thus not an entity but a circular *relationship*, in which a sovereign x authorizes a quasi-sovereign, who subsequently reauthorizes him or her as his or her "representative." Schelling would probably call it "an indistinct identity of sovereign and democratic authorizations."

How can the law accommodate this tautology and paradox? Clearly, both the state and the demotic assemblies have to learn how to live in symbiosis with their opposites. Siéyes's extraordinary constituent moment and Schmitt's state of exception are just a few instruments to think them, but they are far from being perfect. A workable way to resolve these contradictions would be possible only in a world federal state, in which the same laws of sovereign democracy would be applicable at each level. Lacking such a state, there may be simply a mode of soberly recognizing the existing reality of global democracy, without nationalist limits on citizenship, and without trust in the pseudo-democratic fictions of ascending "representation."

Let us apply this logic to real-life international statutory collisions such as the Ukraine and Syria. In both typical cases, the states encountered social movements that they could not accommodate, which led to partial state failures, loss of the monopoly of violence, and to the emergence of internal friend-enemy groupings. Arguably, the Syrian state did not even aspire to be 'democratic' and dissolved peaceful demonstrations, and the Ukrainian government, in Donbass, reacted to an already violent revolt of the Russian-speaking minorities (after having come to power as a result of another violent revolt against the government). However, the structural conditions were similar. In both cases, there erupted a civil war, in which the opponent sides were supported, openly or not, by external powers: by the United States, Russia, and the EU (in the case of Ukraine), and by the United States, Russia, Turkey, Iran, and Hezbollah (in the case of Syria). The official legal situation, in both cases, is similar: there is one legitimate, democratically elected, internationally recognized government, several self-proclaimed unrecognized governments, and extraterritorial issues of human rights violations and the struggle against terrorism. In both cases, but particularly in Syria, one could apply the "Responsibility to Protect" doctrine and claim that the state fails to protect its own citizens, as a ground for intervention. In both cases, there is an ongoing peace process, which is complicated by the plurality of the sides to the conflicts and the delicate question of their right to participate in peace conferences. Thus, in the Ukrainian case, the leaders of the pro-Russian separatists were not allowed to attend the Minsk peace talks but had to wait in a nearby hotel. In the Syrian case, the talks in Astana in 2017–2018 excluded the radical Islamists—belonging both to ISIS and to Jabhat al—Nusra (and its derivatives)—an arrangement that satisfied most of the sides but made a ceasefire agreement hard to implement.

This issue of legal personality and standing recalls Leibniz's time. Yet in Leibniz's time, there were legitimate international hierarchies which allowed the smaller sovereigns to take part in the discussions alongside their patrons, senior sovereigns such as the emperor. Today, this is made difficult by the fictions of the equal sovereignty of states, of their internal sovereignty against separatists, and of the official noninvolvement of great powers who only avow their status as peacemakers and not as parties to the conflict (which they actually are).

Now, I am obviously not able to resolve such conflicts in practical terms within this chapter. But we can try to envision a legal system that would at least make sense of them, since the present chaos is in many ways driven by a law based on fictions.

3. STATE OF THE FUTURE

3.1. International Law

1. There is a general respect of sovereignty. Sovereignty is endowed both with independence and the duty to help and support its subjects. However, sovereignty is qualified by the respect of other sovereignties, both *inside* its immediate scope of responsibility (like Syria or Ukraine for the United States) and *outside* it (like Russia and arguably Iran for the United States). This is true on all levels (Leibniz's principle of multiple sovereignties). Thus, Syrian sovereignty is qualified by a respect for its constituencies, too.
2. There is a hierarchy of sovereigns measured by their size and material power (let us call this the "Spinoza principle"). The United States and Russia are not equivalent to the Ukraine and Syria. All other assumptions are conducive to war. However, as long as the principle of hierarchy is observed, *all* sovereigns (including "nanosovereigns") have a standing, and this includes all stable groups and individuals, in their relative weight as measured by their size, time of existence, space of extension, and ideological hegemony. Russia, the United States, and other major powers can and should declare themselves to be parties to the conflicts, and not external arbiters who cannot descend to real negotiations with "dictators," "terrorists," and the like.
3. However, the hierarchy of sovereigns is ideally *reversible*. And the subjects, at each level, are plural. Hence the *democratic* principle, according to which any sovereign, usually having a provisional or stable personal leader, must rely on an assembly of its micro-sovereign subjects. However, this assembly should not limit itself to majoritarian or party representatives, but include representatives, selected by lot, of groupings *larger* than individuals (from the so-called civil and political societies). This naturally applies also to the United States and Russia who, if they wish to exercise international influence, must confer with the United Nations (UN), which has to be reformed to include organizations lower in status than nation-states. Moreover, a higher or "foreign" sovereign can have a representation, even if minimal, in the "lower" assembly. National assemblies must be convoked by the UN, lower assemblies within the country, by the government. At each new election, at least one new party or organization should present itself and present a new program.
4. Violence against combatants is authorized in the following cases: a sovereign defending itself from an imminent revolution, a popular movement taking arms against an oppressor (the right to resistance), and a sovereign forcing a subordinate sovereign to comply with democracy and "The

Responsibility to Protect." *However*, there should be a rule that forbids the destruction of an antagonistic subject as an entity. The moment you take the arms you recognize, paradoxically, that your opponent remains in force, even if punished, weakened, and so forth. Therefore, any hostilities must be immediately accompanied by peace talks under the auspices of a reformed UN. This would gradually produce a web of peace conferences, which would almost coincide with democratic assemblies and eventually, with the UN. This would be the moment of the formation of a world state out of the global civil war.

3.2. Domestic Law

1. The principles of domestic law are the same as those of the principles of international law, with some quantitative differences in the limits of intervention. This makes any polity into a democratic federation of institutions.
2. State institutions limit themselves in order to provide freedom to societal actors. They tax or fund them according to the sphere of their activity. However, they can intervene in order to assure that societal actors also limit their power with regard to lower levels of authority. Thus, the purpose of the democratic state is the reproduction of the same structure of discretional self-limitation at all levels. This is an infinite, regulative principle that will, in practice, run into contradictions when we arrive to the lower indivisible levels, such as individuals. However, at this level, political and social regulations become ethical ones. Unlike the liberal regime, ethics plays an indispensable role in this system, which requires self-limitation beyond any legal provisions.
3. This gives us a federal social-democratic state where the state and its law require a democratic constitution at each level, including business corporations, NGOs, and *ad hoc* social movements. As in the present democratic constitution, the democratic self-government is dual; it includes an executive leader and an assembly which elects her, decides on generalities, and engages in criticism. However, in this model, assemblies will include the heads or other representatives of lower-level institutions. In this case, the assembly either becomes two-chambered (where a reunion of all individual members is manageable) or consists only of the heads or representatives of lower institutions.
4. Each institution permits and cultivates factions. However, there is a limit beyond which the faction becomes violent or antagonistic toward the very existence of the institution, in which case it may be closed down.
5. There is a universal rotation of officials across society and the state. Thus, a university professor and chair must be sent, for a time, to work at a municipal administration or in a factory (of course, with a due period of

apprenticeship). The order and details of the rotation are decided by lottery, but a person should move between those institutions devoted to intellectual, and those to manual labor, and between for-profit and nonprofit institutions. This would approach us to Aristotle's great principle of the rotation between the rulers and the ruled in a democracy and would also allow us to bring the bureaucratic rationality of *understanding* together with the critical rationality of *reason*, as well as with the practical rationality of *prudence*.

6. Central authority consists of the executive leader appointed by lot (sovereign of sovereigns), and of the general assembly formed by the federal principle: social and political institutions send their representatives to regional or professional assemblies, which elect representatives to the central assembly.

7. Because this is an extremely democratic structure, it is potentially violent and threatens permanent revolution. Therefore, the leader has the prerogative to block a movement or an uprising when it turns violent and imperils the existence of the state. Much in this system, as we see, depends on the virtue of leaders and their balancing act between self-limitation and the use of prerogative.

8. The regulative idea of any state is to become a *world state*, because the order described earlier would be logical only if it is universal, inclusive of all subjects. The world state would gradually develop through alliances, peace conferences, and the work of international assemblies.

You can see that in many ways this is a system that already takes place, but because of its contradictory, dialectical character, people do not dare to hold its elements together in mind. Thus, the personalistic and authoritarian elements of this system follow from its ultra-democratic ones, but they are hard to conceive together. This sketch is not a utopia, but, on the contrary, a mode in which the current state of affairs can be codified, become conscious, and thus avert disaster.

Two obvious objections arise:

(1) This is another normative theory that no one is going to abide by.

I respond: this may be true; however, we currently do not have such a doctrine in common or partial agreement, but even the existing normative principles of international law (state sovereignty, a ban on chemical weapons) are, if not adhered to, then obviously respected by the actors in the field: As Filippov rightly argues in Chapter 2, they actually do restrain themselves with regard to these principles. Powerful actors do not just act arbitrarily on the world stage but claim to abide by international law. Currently, no one except for the EU continues to believe in international law as an objectively binding law, because it consists of two contradictory norms (sovereignty and the rights to revolution and intervention), and is often seen as a cover for cynical power games. This would change if the law were renewed on the basis of objective reality. Moreover, the suggested system is not a set of precepts but a constitutive structure of the relations between political subjects.

(2) Alain Badiou[82] has described an arrangement similar to my 'assembly' in his theory, as the "set of subsets" of a given set, or what he calls a "state of the situation." Badiou thinks that this is a bureaucratic, alienating system of power that suppresses genuine innovation. He describes an alternative—a revolutionary subject born by the breakthrough of a new grouping, one that had existed but not been counted among the existing groups of this society. Badiou describes the non-statist 'militant' trajectory of this subject. His colleague and opponent Jacques Rancière speaks, in similar terms, of the need to recognize newly emergent political subjects.[83]

I respond: Yes, my model may appear to be too statist and to contradict these anarchic/revolutionary pleas for truth. However, I do recognize the need for the state and other sovereigns to foster opposition and even revolt, as long as it does not threaten the state's existence directly. Hence, the rule of one new party at each election. At the same time, I do not see anything subversive in the emergence of new political subjects *per se*: a 1970s theme in both Badiou and Rancière that has been formed by the emergence of new social movements. It depends on who these subjects are. And, it is important that they have a political agenda beyond an identity or the promise of a revolution. It is no less important to remember that in most cases, the state plays a crucial role, negative or positive, in the crystallization of new political subjects; it either enters into dialogue with them, or starts an unsuccessful armed struggle; then a new movement emerges—yet there are cases where such movements remain ignored and passed over in silence. A centralized media sphere is needed for a new political subject to "emerge," and who can organize such a public space if not the state?

Thus, this sketch of a normative theory makes sense as an extrapolation from actual political processes as well as from the actual life of political norms, as they are applied in an inconsistent and contradictory way, lacking a systematic logic, which I have attempted to provide. Following Hegel's nineteenth-century model, I use dialectics in both a descriptive and normative sense, and like him I see the state as a name for a comprehensive totality of top-down and bottom-up logics of political constitution. Yet, unlike Hegel, I refuse to subdivide the state into autonomous spheres (such as civil society and family) and see it as a homogeneous, continuous, and monotonously structured space governed by one main principle: the law of the subject. The same norms, deriving from this principle, apply at each level, and at each level they run into contradictions, which can be resolved or at least negotiated at a higher or lower level of this multilayered federation.

NOTES

1. Michael Mann, "The Autonomous Power of the State: Its Origins, Mechanisms and Results." *European Journal of Sociology* 25.2 (1984): pp. 185–213; on dialectic, see pp. 206–207; Evans, Rueschemeyer and Skocpol, *Bringing the State Back In*, p. 25; Bishwapriya Sanyal, *Cooperative Autonomy: The Dialectic of State-NGOs Relationship in Developing Countries* (International Labor Organization. International Institute for Labor Studies, 1994); Andreas Novy and Bernhard Leubolt, "Participatory Budgeting in Porto Alegre: Social Innovation and the Dialectical Relationship of State and Civil Society." *Urban Studies* 42.11 (October 2005): pp. 2023–2036.

2. Benjamin Barber, *Strong Democracy: Participatory Politics for a New Age* (Berkeley: University of California Press, 2003), p. IX.

3. Richard Sakwa, *The Crisis of Russian Democracy* (Cambridge: Cambridge University Press, 2010), p. 36.

4. Plato, *Parmenides* in *Plato, vol. IV, Loeb Classical Library 167* (Cambridge, MA: Harvard University Press, 1926).

5. G. W. F. Hegel, *The Science of Logic*, trans. George di Giovanni (Cambridge: Cambridge University Press, 2010), pp. 371–374.

6. Plato, *The Republic*, trans. Allan Bloom (New York: Basic Books, 1968), 372e, p. 49.

7. Aristotle, *Politics*, trans. H. Rackham (Cambridge, MA: Harvard University Press, 1959), 1252b28, p. 9.

8. John Locke and Peter Laslett, *Two Treatises of Government: A Critical Edition with an Introduction and Apparatus Criticus* (Cambridge: Cambridge University Press, 1988).

9. Georg Hegel, *Elements of the Philosophy of Right*, trans. H. B. Nisbet (Cambridge: Cambridge University Press, 1991).

10. Alain Badiou, *Being and Event*, trans. O. Feltham (New York: Continuum 2005), pp. 93–111.

11. Plato, *The Republic*, 556a-563d, pp. 234–239.

12. Thomas Hobbes, *Leviathan* (Oxford: Oxford University Press, 1998).

13. Jasper Hopkins, *Nicholas of Cusa on God as Not-Other* (Minneapolis: University of Minnesota Press, 1979).

14. Nicholas of Cusa, *The Catholic Concordance*, trans. P. Sigmund (Cambridge: Cambridge University Press, 1996).

15. Benedict Spinoza, "Political Treatise," in: Samuel Shirley (trans.), *Complete Works* (Indianapolis/Cambridge: Hackett, 2002), pp. 676–754. Quot. p. 690.

16. Gottfried Wilhelm Leibniz, *Die philosophischen Schriften von Leibniz*, ed. C. I. Gerhardt, 7 vols (Berlin and Halle: Weidmann, 1875), vol. VII. 147–149.

17. Christian Mercer, *Leibniz' Universal Metaphysics, Its Origins and Development* (Cambridge: Cambridge University Press, 2004). Patrick Riley, *Leibniz' Universal Jurisprudence. Justice as the Charity of the Wise* (Cambridge, MA: Harvard University Press, 1996).

18. Kyle McGee, "Demonomics. Leibniz and the Antinomy of Modern Power," *Radical Philosophy*, 168 (2011): pp. 33–45.

19. Jack Donnelly, *Universal Human Rights in Theory and Practice* (Ithaca, NY: Cornell University Press, 2003), p. 251, quotes Kofi Annan in saying that "individual sovereignty, rooted in human rights, is taking its place in international relations alongside state sovereignty." Cf. Jacques Derrida, *Rogues, Two Essays on Reason*, trans. Pascale-Anne Brault and Michael Naas (Palo Alto, CA: Stanford University Press, 2005).

20. Paul J. DiMaggio and Walter W. Powell, "The Iron Cage Revisited: Institutional Isomorphism and Collective Rationality in Organizational Fields." *American Sociological Review* 48.2 (1983): pp. 147–160.

21. This is the proximity of my theory to that of pluralists: see Harold Laski, "Law and the State," in: Paul Q. Hirst (ed.), *The Pluralist Theory of the State: Selected Writings of G.D.H. Cole, J.N. Figgis and H.J. Laski* (London: Routledge, 1989), pp. 199–228, cit. p. 221.

22. J. W. von Goethe, *From My Life: Poetry and Truth* (Princeton, NJ: Princeton University Press, 1994), p. 598. See also Carl Schmitt, *Political Theology II*, trans. M. Hoelzel and Graham Ward (Cambridge: Polity Press, 2008), p. 130.

23. Christian Wolff, *Ius Gentium Methode Scientifico Pertractatum*, English translation by Francis Hemelt (Oxford: Clarendon Press, 1934).

24. Nicholas Onuf emphasizes the importance of this argument by Wolff, which goes back not just to Leibniz but also to Althusius. See Nicholas Onuf "Civitas Maxima: Wolff, Vattel and the Fate of Republicanism Source." *The American Journal of International Law* 88.2 (April, 1994): pp. 280–303.

25. Karl Marx, "The Eighteenth Brumaire of Louis Bonaparte," in: *Karl Marx, Later Political Writings* (Cambridge: Cambridge University Press, 1996): pp. 31–127.

26. Friedrich Engels, *The Origins of Family, Private Property, and State* (London: Pathfinder Press, 1972), p. 229.

27. Vladimir Lenin, "State and Revolution," in: *Collected Works* (Moscow: Progress, 1974), p. 406.

28. Ibid., 402.

29. On this in detail, see my article: Artemy Magun, "Lenin on Democratic Theory." *Studies in East European Thought* 70 (2018), pp. 141–152.

30. Georg Jellinek, *Die Rechtliche Natur der Staatsverträge* (Wien: Georg Hölder, 1880), S. 18, my translation.

31. Ibid., S. 20.

32. Ibid., S. 21.

33. Ibid., 23.

34. Andrew Arato, *The Adventures of the Constituent Power* (Cambridge: Cambridge University Press, 2017).

35. Carl Schmitt, *The Concept of the Political*, trans. George Schwab (Chicago, IL: University of Chicago Press, 1996).

36. Stefan Weser, *Souveränitätsbegriff bei Georg Jellinek und Carl Schmitt* (Leipzig: GRIN Verlag, 2008), but this is only an examination essay by a student; a short treatment of the question is also available in Martin Loughlin, *Foundations of Public Law* (Oxford: Oxford University Press, 2012), p. 219.

37. Carl Schmitt, *Constitutional Theory*, trans. Ellen Kennedy (Durham, NC: Duke University Press 2008), pp. 60, 89.

38. Michael Hebeisen, *Souveranitat in Frage gestellt* (Baden-Baden: Nomos, 1995).

39. David Dyzenhaus, "Kelsen, Heller and Schmitt: Paradigms of Sovereignty Thought." *Theoretical Inquiries in Law* 16.2 (2015): pp. 337–366. Dyzenhaus further says that Schmitt developed Jellinek in a realistic way, and Kelsen, in a legalistic way. As seen here, I am not sure about the former claim.

40. Sandrine Baume, "On Political Theology: A Controversy between Hans Kelsen and Carl Schmitt." *History of European Ideas* 35.3 (2009): pp. 369–381.

41. Léon Duguit, *Traité de droit constitutionnel: La règle du droit; le problème de l'État* (Paris: De Boccard, 1911), p. 645.

42. Giorgio Agamben, *State of Exception* (Chicago, IL: University of Chicago, 2005).

43. Chantal Mouffe, "Deliberative Democracy or Agonistic Democracy." *Social Research* 66.3 (Fall 1999): pp. 745–758.

44. See Herfried Münkler, "Die Staat," for a notion of the "complementaries" of the state. Münkler lists church, empire, nation, and civil society. My list is somewhat different, but the idea is the same, except that Münkler stops without developing a dialectical argument.

45. Karl Marx, *Critique of Hegel's Philosophy of Right* (Cambridge: Cambridge University Press, 1977); cf. Miguel Abensour, *Democracy against the State: Marx and the Machiavellian Movement* (London: Polity, 2011).

46. Robert Roswell Palmer, "Notes on the Use of the Word 'Democracy' 1789–1799." *Political Science Quarterly* 68.2 (June 1953): pp. 203–226.

47. Alexis de Tocqueville, *Democracy in America*, trans. James Schleifer (New York: Liberty Fund, 2000).

48. John Dewey, *Democracy and Education: An Introduction to the Philosophy of Education* (London: Macmillan, 1916); T. G. Masaryk, *Nesndze demokracie* (Prague: Publisher unknown, 1913); Thomas Masaryk, *The Spirit of Russia*, trans. Eden and Cedar Paul (London: Allen & Unwin & McMillan, 1955 [1913]).

49. Karl Kautsky, *Der Parlamentarismus, die Volksgesetzgebung und die Sozialdemokratie* (Stuttgart: J. H. W. Dietz 1893); Karl Kautsky, *The Road to Power: Political Reflections on Growing into the Revolution* (Atlantic Highlands: Humanities Press, 1996 [1909]). Vladimir Lenin, "What Is to Be Done?" in: Joe Fineberg and George Hanna (trans.), *Lenin's Collected Works, Volume 5* (Moscow: Foreign Languages Publishing House, 1962 [1902]). See Lars Lih, *Lenin Rediscovered* (Leiden: Brill, 2005).

50. For example, Juan Linz and Alfred Stepan, *Problems of Democratic Transition and Consolidation* (Baltimore, MD: Johns Hopkins University Press, 1996); Larry Diamond, *Developing Democracy. Towards Consolidation* (Baltimore, MD: Johns Hopkins University Press, 1999); David Held, *Political Theory and the Modern State* (Cambridge: Polity Press, 1999); E. D. Mansfield, and J. L. Snyder, "The Sequencing

'Fallacy'," *Journal of Democracy* 18.3 (2007): pp. 5–10. Charles Tilly, *Democracy* (Cambridge: Cambridge University Press, 2007).

51. Ralph Miliband, *The State in Capitalist Society* (New York: Basic Books, 1969); Nicos Poulantzas, *State, Power, Socialism* (New York; London: Verso, 1978). Alain Badiou, "The Democratic Emblem," in: *Democracy: In What State?* (New York: Columbia University Press, 2011), 6–16; Giorgio Agamben, *Introductory Note on the Concept of Democracy*, ibid., 1–5.

52. Francis Fukuyama, "States and Democracy," in *Democratization* (2014), 1–15. Jason Brennan, *Against Democracy* (Princeton, NJ: Princeton University Press, 2016).

53. Pierre Clastres, *Society against the State* (Cambridge, MA: MIT Press, 1989). Abensour, *Democracy against the State*.

54. Antonio Negri, *Insurgencies. Constituent Power and the Modern State* (Minneapolis: Minnesota University Press, 1999); Andreas Kalyvas, "Popular Sovereignty, Democracy, and the Constituent Power." *Constellations* 12.2 (June 2005): pp. 223–244. Jason Frank, *Constituent Moments* (Durham, NC: Duke University Press, 2010).

55. See for instance, Hank Johnston, *States and Social Movements* (Cambridge: Polity Press, 2011), ch.1.

56. Giorgio Agamben, "What Is Destituent Power?" *Society and Space* 32 (2014): pp. 65–74. Yet Agamben Uses "Destituent Power" Pejoratively, Which Is Not Justified.

57. Diamond, *Developing Democracy*; Michael McFaul, *Russia's Unfinished Revolution: Political Change from Gorbachev to Putin* (Ithaca, NY: Cornell University Press, 2001).

58. Richard Sakwa. *Putin Redux* (London: Routledge 2014).

59. Hanna Bäck and Axel Hadenius, "Democracy and State Capacity: Exploring a J-Shaped Relationship." *Governance* 21.1 (2008): pp. 1–24.

60. Andrey Melville and Dmitry Yefimov, "Democratic Leviathan?" State Capacity and Regime Change, Talk at the ISA International Conference 2017, Hong Kong, June 15–18, 2017; Carl Henrik Knutsen and Håvard Mokleiv Nygård, "Institutional Characteristics and Regime Survival: Why Are Semi-Democracies Less Durable than Autocracies and Democracies?" *American Journal of Political Science* 59.3 (2015): pp. 656–670. Sergey Guriev, and Daniel Treisman, *How Modern Dictators Survive: An Informational Theory of the New Authoritarianism* (No. w21136) (Washington, DC: National Bureau of Economic Research, 2015).

61. Michel Foucault, *The Birth of Biopolitics: Lectures at the Collège de France 1978–1979*, trans. G. Burchell (London: Palgrave, 2008), David Harvey, *A Brief History of Neoliberalism* (Oxford: Oxford University Press, 2005).

62. Mariana Mazzucato, *The Entrepreneurial State: Debunking Public vs. Private Sector Myths* (New York: Anthem Press, 2013).

63. Harvey, *A Brief History of Neoliberalism*.

64. Jason Lindsey, *The Concealment of the State* (New York, London: Bloomsbury Press, 2013). See more on Lindsey in Maria Kochkina's chapter of this book.

65. Jason Lindsey, *The Concealment of the State, 19*. See an extended reading of Lindsey's book in the present volume, in chapter 5 of this book.

66. Ibid., 76.

67. Giorgio Agamben, *The Kingdom and the Glory*, trans. Lorenzo Chiesa (Stanford, CA: Stanford University Press, 2011).

68. Michel Foucault, *Security, Territory, Population*, trans. G. Burchell (New York; London: Palgrave Macmillan, 2009).

69. Paul J. DiMaggio and Walter W. Powell, "The Iron Cage Revisited: Institutional Isomorphism and Collective Rationality in Organizational Fields." *American Sociological Review* 48. 2 (1983): pp. 147–160.

70. Kyle McGee, "Demonomics. Leibniz and the Antinomy of Modern Power," *Radical Philosophy*, 168 (2011): pp. 33–45.

71. Harvey Mansfield, "On the Impersonality of Modern State." *The American Political Science Review* 77.4 (December 1983): pp. 849–857.

72. Claude Lefort, *Democracy and Political Theory*, trans. D. Macey (Oxford: Polity, 1988).

73. Georg Lukács, *History and Class Consciousness* (London: Merlin Press, 1975); Alfred Sohn-Rethel, *Intellectual and Manual Labour: A Critique of Epistemology* (London: Macmillan, 1978).

74. Ian McAllister, "The Personalization of Politics," in: Russell Dalton and Hans-Dietrich Klingemann (eds.), *Oxford Handbook of Political Behavior* (Oxford: Oxford University Press, 2007), 571–588.

75. See for instance Frank Hoffman, *Conflict in the 21st Century: The Rise of Hybrid Wars* (Washington, DC: Potomac Institute for Policy Studies, 2007).

76. See my detailed argument on this mimicry in Artemy Magun, "Hysterical Machiavellianism: Russian Foreign Policy and the International Non-Relations." *Theory & Event* 19, 3 (July 2016).

77. Martin Hewson and Timothy J. Sinclair (eds.), *Approaches to Global Governance Theory* (Albany: State University of New York, 1999); David Held, *Global Covenant* (Cambridge: Polity Press, 2004); Margaret P. Karns and Karen A. Mingst, *International Organizations: The Politics and Processes of Global Governance*, 2nd ed. (Boulder, CO: Lynne Rienner Publishers, 2009).

78. Antonio Negri and Michael Hardt, *Empire* (Cambridge, MA: Harvard University Press, 2000); Wendy Brown, *Walled Sovereignties, Waning States* (Cambridge, MA: MIT Press, 2010).

79. Pierre Rosanvallon, "Decentring Democracies," *Redescriptions* (2009), pp. 17–33, cit. p. 28.

80. *Michael* Marder, "The Categories of State," present volume, chapter 1.

81. Theodor Adorno, Max Horkheimer, *The Dialectic of Enlightenment* (Stanford, CA: Stanford University Press, 2002).

82. Badiou, *Being and Event*, 93–111.

83. Jacques Rancière, *On the Shores of Politics*, trans. Liz Heron (London; New York: Verso, 2007).

Index

Agamben, Giorgio, 51, 68, 82, 208, 252, 259
Althusser, Louis, 17, 97, 124, 193
Amin, Samir, 126, 144, 146
Anghie, Antony, 49
Aristotle, 12, 16, 25, 26, 29, 31, 34, 57, 77, 241–42, 273
Arrighi, Giovanni, 10
Avineri, Shlomo, 194

Bäck, Hanna, 256
Badiou, Alain, 6, 7, 8, 14, 163, 209, 221, 225, 242, 274
Balibar, Étienne, 94–95, 191
Baume, Sandrine, 251
Benton, Lauren, 50–51, 55, 60
Bluntschli, Johann Caspar, 46–48, 60
Brierly, James Leslie, 47–48
Budraitskis, Ilya, 219
Bull, Hedley, 59
Bumochir, Dulam, 215
Bunce, Valery, 209

capitalism, 1–2, 10, 101, 104, 123–54, 170–71, 187–93, 201, 208–21, 238, 240, 259, 265–66; competitive, 128–29, 131, 135, 138–39; and democracy, 101, 132–33, 144, 210, 215, 218–19, 238, 266; late, 140, 193; monopoly, 131, 135, 139, 145

communism, 6, 18, 29, 101–3, 106, 163–80, 188, 189–92, 198–99, 202–3, 209, 219–21, 224
constituent power, 5, 14, 16, 65–72, 76, 79–82, 255, 269
Cusanus, Nicolaus, 243, 246

Dean, Jodi, 116, 119, 228
Deleuze, Gilles, 58, 152
democracy, 2–5, 13–14, 17–18, 65–86, 98, 101–3, 115–19, 129–33, 137–44, 165, 167–69, 181–82, 205–24, 235, 238, 240, 243, 246, 252–58, 266–70, 273; democratization, 14, 132–34, 205–24, 254–56, 267; liberal, 9, 14, 101, 141, 165, 205–24; social, 96, 130–31, 142, 144, 147
Derrida, Jacques, 84, 220, 276
dialectics, 238–41
Diamond, Larry, 20, 224, 255
Duguit, Leon, 251, 269
Dupuit, Jean-Pierre, 191
Dyzenhaus, David, 251, 277

Empson, Rebecca, 218, 229
Engels, Friedrich, 7, 94–95, 124, 164, 165, 168, 170–73, 175, 177–78, 183, 190, 220, 248–49
Erasmus of Rotterdam, 33

Fanon, Frantz, 154
Foucault, Michel, 2, 6, 8, 188, 260

Gentile, Giovanni, 12
global value chains (GVC), 149–53
Gramsci, Antonio, 6, 92, 96, 105, 106, 124–25, 127–34, 143, 158
Green, Jeffrey Edwards, 118
Guattari, Felix, 58
GVC. *See* global value chains

Habermas, Jürgen, 78
Hadenius, Axel, 256
Hall, Stuart, 125
Harney, Stefano, 120
Harvey, David, 13, 214
Hauriou, Maurice, 16, 71–3, 76–80, 85, 251, 269
Hebeisen, Michael, 277
Hegel, Georg Wolf Friedrich, 8–9, 11, 12–14, 16, 18–19, 25, 29, 33, 37, 58, 70, 187–202, 204, 236–52, 260, 268, 274
hegemony, 11, 90, 92, 97, 98–106, 125, 131, 134, 143, 257, 271
Heidegger, Martin, 26–27, 34, 36
Hobbes, Thomas, 10, 12, 36, 67, 242, 243, 261
Honneth, Alex, 189–90

ideology, 28, 33, 63, 91–92, 98, 111, 115–20, 140, 154, 158, 188–89, 213, 215, 217, 240, 245, 257, 259, 266
imperialism, 16, 49, 99–100, 106, 131, 134, 139–40, 143–46, 148–49, 236, 264–65
international law, 5, 16, 39–64, 146, 246, 269, 271–74

Jackson, Robert, 60–62
Jay, Martin, 140
Jellinek, Georg, 70, 73, 76, 249–51
Jessop, Robert, 6, 16, 201

Kalyvas, Andreas, 143, 206
Kant, Immanuel, 6, 15, 29, 31, 34–36, 43, 57, 199, 238, 246, 249

Kelsen, Hans, 59, 69, 75, 141, 277
Klabbers, Jan, 52–53

Lacan, Jacques, 9, 18, 230
Lefort, Claude, 81, 116, 261
Leibniz, Gottfried, 191, 243–46, 252
Lenin (Ulyanov), Vladimir, 7, 14, 18–19, 28, 98, 106, 124, 163–86, 210, 221–23, 231, 249
Levitsky, Stephen, 206–7
Lindsey, Jason, 17, 111–20, 259–60, 264
Locke, John, 10, 242, 267
Loughlin, Martin, 67–69, 81, 85, 277
Luxemburg, Rosa, 124, 140, 144

Malberg, Carré de, 16, 71–82, 257
Mann, Michael, 236
Marx, Karl, 6, 11, 14, 30, 33, 94–97, 101, 116, 124, 128, 130, 132, 134, 140, 164, 166, 168, 170–80, 189–94, 201–2, 220, 236, 241, 248–49, 251, 253
Mazzucato, Marianna, 113, 278
McFaul, Michael, 255
Mieville, China, 144, 224
Milanovic, Branko, 144, 150
Miliband, Ralph, 21, 124, 128, 133, 278
Mirowski, Philip, 144–45, 158
Mongolia, 205–32
Moten, Fred, 120
Mouffe, Chantal, 14, 141, 277

nation/nation-state, 3, 11–12, 16, 52, 71–80, 111, 134, 149, 187, 196–201, 209–10, 236, 253, 257–58, 265, 269, 271
nationalism, 12–13, 154, 200, 212–13, 257–58
Negri, Antonio, 69, 112, 144–45, 183, 265
neoliberalism, 2–3, 6, 11–17, 93, 96–99, 113, 126, 133, 143–49, 153, 201, 213–14, 248–60, 266
Neoplatonism, 242–45
Neumann, Frantz, 17–18, 123–60
non-statal state/semi-state, 8, 14, 18, 176–78, 197, 199, 201, 249

Pedersen, Morton Axel, 214
people, the, 5, 12, 16, 33, 68, 50, 65–82, 119–20, 141, 167–70, 197, 207, 210, 212–15, 218, 222–23, 236, 252–55, 257; *demos*, 212, 255; *populus*, 33, 68
Plato, 12, 238, 241–44
Plueckhahn, Rebekah, 215
Poulantzas, Nikos, 5, 6, 8, 16–17, 99, 124, 128, 130, 201, 278
Przeworski, Adam, 133, 156, 206

Rancière, Jacques, 14, 274
Rawls, John, 60–61
Roitman, Janet, 206–7
Rosanvallon, Pierre, 21, 82, 267
Ross, Kristin, 117
Rossabi, Morris, 214
Russia, 1, 12–14, 18, 63, 96, 164, 205, 230, 255–59, 263–65, 270–71

Saramago, Jose, 218
Scheuerman, William, 138
Schmitt, Carl, 11, 12, 28, 36, 39, 42, 43, 49–51, 68–69, 78, 134–35, 140–41, 143, 146, 156–57, 246, 249–52, 267, 277
Sieyès, Emmanuel, 71–72, 74, 76, 84
Slobidian, Quinn, 146
socialism, 17, 94, 96, 101, 103, 136, 146, 167–80, 183, 185, 189–92, 200–203, 212–14, 219, 221; post-socialism, 210–14

sovereignty, 4–5, 10–12, 18, 29, 34, 39–63, 65–82, 100, 112–13, 127, 134, 140–42, 143, 153, 187, 245–52, 257, 263–74
Spinoza, 10, 193, 242–44, 253, 265, 271
standing, legal and political, 15, 26–36, 245, 266, 270, 276
subject, 2, 6, 11, 16, 36, 74–75, 116, 119, 188, 190, 215, 230, 241, 247, 252, 268, 272, 274–75
Sweezy, Paul, 126, 139–40, 144
Syria, 255–56, 270–71

territory, 4–5, 10, 34, 45–51, 57, 61–62, 139, 245
Teubner, Gunther, 52, 54, 56
Tooze, Adam, 149, 151, 153
Triepel, Heinrich, 48–49, 61
Tumurtogoo, Anand, 211

Vattel, Emmerich, 10–11, 46, 276
Verdery, Katherine, 210, 216

Weber, Max, 5–6, 8, 40, 45, 125, 129, 130, 155
Williams, Michelle, 125–26, 144
Wolff, Christian, 246, 276

Ziblatt, William, 206–7
Žižek, Slavoj, 6–9, 15, 18, 164, 181, 183, 187–202, 218, 221

Biographies

Olga Bashkina is a PhD student and PhD fellow at the Institute of Philosophy, KU Leuven, Belgium.

Ajay Singh Chaudhary is a political theorist and an executive director of the Brooklyn Institute for Social Research. He is working on a book devoted to the politics of Anthropocene.

Lorenzo Chiesa is lecturer in philosophy at Newcastle University (UK). He was professor of modern European thought at the University of Kent, where he founded and directed the Centre for Critical Thought. His most recent books are *The Not-Two* (2016) and *The Virtual Point of Freedom* (2016).

Alexander Filippov is professor and head of the Center for Fundamental Sociology at the Higher School of Economics, Moscow, Russia. He is the editor of the journal *Russian Sociological Review*. He is the author of several books on social theory in Russian (*Sociology of Space*; *Sociologia*, in two volumes) and of many articles in different languages.

Agon Hamza, PhD in philosophy, is the author of *Reading Marx* (2018; with Frank Ruda and Slavoj Žižek), *Althusser and Pasolini: Philosophy, Marxism, and Film* (2016), and *From Myth to Symptom: The Case of Kosovo* (2013; with Slavoj Žižek). In addition, he is the editor of *Althusser and Theology: Religion, Politics and Philosophy* (2016) and *Repeating Žižek* (2015), as well as coeditor, with Frank Ruda, of *Slavoj Žižek and Dialectical Materialism* (2016). He is founder and coeditor (with Frank Ruda) of the international philosophy journal *Crisis and Critique*.

Maria Kochkina is a PhD student at the European University at Saint-Petersburg, Russia.

Artemy Magun is professor of democratic theory at the European University at Saint-Petersburg, Russia; and the editor of the international journal of social and political theory *Stasis*. In English, he has published the books *Negative Revolution* and *Politics of the One* (edited volume), as well as numerous articles on various topics in political philosophy.

Michael Marder is an IKERBASQUE research professor in the Department of Philosophy at the University of the Basque Country (UPV-EHU). His most recent book is *Political Categories: Thinking beyond Concepts* (2019).

Christian Sorace is assistant professor of political science at Colorado College. He is the author of *Shaken Authority: China's Communist Party and the 2008 Sichuan Earthquake* (2017). He is also the coeditor of *Afterlives of Chinese Communism: Political Concepts from Mao to Xi* (2019).

Panagiotis Sotiris has a PhD from Panteion University and has taught social and political philosophy at various Greek universities. He is the author of *A Philosophy for Communism: Rethinking Althusser* (2020) and has edited the collective volume *Crisis, Movement, Strategy: The Greek Experience* (2018).

www.ingramcontent.com/pod-product-compliance
Lightning Source LLC
Chambersburg PA
CBHW022010300426
44117CB00005B/114